Predictive Analytics in Smart Agriculture

Predictive Analytics in Smart Agriculture explores computational engineering techniques and applications in agriculture development. Recent technologies, such as cloud computing, IoT, big data, and machine learning, are focused on for smart agricultural engineering. This book also provides a case-oriented approach for IoT-based agricultural systems.

This book deals with all aspects of smart agriculture with state-of-the-art predictive analysis in the complete 360-degree view spectrum. The book includes the concepts of urban and vertical farming using Agro IoT systems and renewable energy sources for modern agriculture trends. It discusses the real-world challenges, complexities in Agro IoT, and advantages of incorporating smart technology. It also presents the rapid advancement of the technologies in the existing Agri model by applying the various techniques. Novel architectural solutions in smart agricultural engineering are the core aspects of this book. Several predictive analysis tools and smart agriculture are also incorporated.

This book can be used as a textbook for students in predictive analysis, agriculture engineering, precision farming, and smart agriculture. It can also be a reference book for practicing professionals in cloud computing, IoT, big data, machine learning, and deep learning working on smart agriculture applications.

Predictive Analytics in Smart Agriculture

Edited by
Saravanan Krishnan, A. Jose Anand, Narayanan Prasanth, Sam Goundar, and Christo Ananth

CRC Press
Taylor & Francis Group
Boca Raton London New York

CRC Press is an imprint of the
Taylor & Francis Group, an **informa** business

Designed cover image: Shutterstock

MATLAB® is a trademark of The MathWorks, Inc. and is used with permission. The MathWorks does not warrant the accuracy of the text or exercises in this book. This book's use or discussion of MATLAB® software or related products does not constitute endorsement or sponsorship by The MathWorks of a particular pedagogical approach or particular use of the MATLAB® software.

First edition published 2024
by CRC Press
2385 NW Executive Center Drive, Suite 320, Boca Raton FL 33431

and by CRC Press
4 Park Square, Milton Park, Abingdon, Oxon, OX14 4RN

CRC Press is an imprint of Taylor & Francis Group, LLC

© 2024 selection and editorial matter, Saravanan Krishnan, A. Jose Anand, Narayanan Prasanth, Sam Goundar, and Christo Ananth; individual chapters, the contributors

ISBN: 978-1-032-47950-7 (hbk)
ISBN: 978-1-032-48898-1 (pbk)
ISBN: 978-1-003-39130-2 (ebk)

DOI: 10.1201/9781003391302

Typeset in Times
by KnowledgeWorks Global Ltd.

Contents

Contributors

Jayakrishnan A.
College of Engineering Karunagappally
Kollam, India

Sawant Swara Anant
Vellore Institute of Technology
Vellore, India

S. Anita
R.M.K. Engineering College
Kavaraipettai, India

R. Arunbharathi
Sri Krishna College of Engineering
and Technology
Coimbatore, India

R. Bharathi
University College of Engineering
Nagercoil, India

Raghav Biyani
Vellore Institute of Technology
Vellore, India

E. Brindha
Cheran College of Arts and Science
Tiruppur, India

R. Deepalakshmi
The Tamilnadu Dr. Ambedkar Law
University
Chennai, India

J. Dhakshayani
National Institute of Technology
Puducherry, India

C. Justin Dhanaraj
University College of Engineering
Nagercoil, India

Yogesh Gangurde
NMICPS TiHAN Foundation Indian
Institute of Technology
Hyderabad, India

J. Nandha Gopal
Velammal Institute of Technology
Tiruvallur, India

Manav Goyal
Vellore Institute of Technology
Vellore, India

Parveen Sultana H.
Vellore Institute of Technology
Vellore, India

Sneha Leela Jacob
Vellore Institute of Technology
Vellore, India

Shubham Jagtap
Vellore Institute of Technology
Vellore, India

J. Jyothsna
Jawaharlal Nehru Krishi
Vishwavidyalaya
Jabalpur, India

Karthikeyan Kaliyaperumal
Ambo University
Ethiopia

Dhiraj Kapila
Lovely Professional University
Phagwara, India

Priti Kandewar
St. Martin's Engineering College
Secunderabad, India

Beulah J. Karthikeyan
J.B. Institute of Engineering
  and Technology
Hyderabad, India

S. Sathish Kumar
J.B. Institute of Engineering
  and Technology
Hyderabad, India

V. Mahalakshmi
Panimalar Engineering College
Chennai, India

S. Mahenthiran
Vellore Institute of Technology
Vellore, India

Naga Praveen Babu Mannam
NMICPS TiHAN Foundation
  Indian Institute of Technology
Hyderabad, India

Rakesh Kumar Maurya
MJP Rohilkhand University
Bareilly, India

S. Mayakannan
Vidyaa Vikas College of Engineering
  and Technology
Namakkal, India

Alkha Mohan
Indian Institute of Information
  Technology
Trichy, India

S. Muthukaruppasamy
Velammal Institute of Technology
Tiruvallur, India

B. Lakshmi Narayana
St. Martin's Engineering College
Secunderabad, India

Kauser Ahmed P.
Vellore Institute of Technology
Vellore, India

Rajalakshmi P.
NMICPS TiHAN Foundation
  Indian Institute of Technology
Hyderabad, India

Nandasai Penumuchu
Vellore Institute of Technology
Vellore, India

S. Venkatesa Prabhu
Addis Ababa Science and Technology
  University
Addis Ababa, Ethiopia

T. Pradeep
Kongu Engineering College
Erode, India

T. Priya
NPR College of Engineering
  & Technology
Dindigul, India

Perepi Rajarajeswari
Vellore Institute of Technology
Vellore, India

Sujatha Rajkumar
Vellore Institute of Technology
Vellore, India

S. Ravindra
Vasireddy Venkatadri Institute
  of Technology
Guntur, India

Deraj RM
Vellore Institute of Technology
Vellore, India

Anchana B. S.
Marthandam College of Engineering
  and Technology
Marthandam, India

Vinila Jinny S.
Vellore Institute of Technology
Vellore, India

Syam Narayanan S.
NMICPS TiHAN Foundation Indian
   Institute of Technology
Hyderabad, India

Shriram S. S.
Vellore Institute of Technology
Vellore, India

V. Santhi
Vellore Institute of Technology
Vellore, India

R. Saraswathi
Sreenivasa Institute of Technology
   and Management Studies
Chittoor, India

K. Saravanan
College of Engineering
Guindy
Anna University
Chennai, India

M. Saravanan
Annamalai University
Chidambaram, India

P. M. Sithar Selvam
RVS School of Engineering
   & Technology
Dindigul, India

Nishant Sharma
Vellore Institute of Technology
Vellore, India

R. Sharmila
Dhanalakshmi Srinivasan
   Engineering College
Perambalur, India

V. Prasanna Srinivasan
RMD Engineering College
Kavaraipettai, India

V. Srishti
Vellore Institute of Technology
Vellore, India

R. Siva Subramanian
Sri Krishna College of Engineering
   and Technology
Coimbatore, India

P. Sujatha
Vels Institute of Science
Technology & Advanced Studies
Pallavaram, India

B. Surendiran
National Institute of Technology
Puducherry, India

Y. P. Arul Teen
University College of
   Engineering
Nagercoil, India

G. Arun Sampaul Thomas
J.B. Institute of Engineering
   and Technology
Hyderabad, India

Nestor Ulloa
Escuela Superior Politecnica
   de Chimborazo
Riobamba, Ecuador

K. Divya Vani
St. Martin's Engineering
   College
Secunderabad, India

1 Farming Assistance Using Machine Learning and Internet of Things

Kauser Ahmed P. and V. Srishti

1.1 INTRODUCTION

1.1.1 BACKGROUND OF THE PROBLEM

The cornerstone of many nations, agriculture, serves as the backbone of the global economy for developing countries. The proper crop must be planted in a certain location for the optimum outcome. The majority of farmers and other agricultural activists recommend crops using poor, tested scientific methods, which is an issue [1] In order to boost productivity and profit from the suggested technique, our suggested effort will assist farmers in choosing the ideal crop based on elements like cost of cultivation, cost of production, and yield.

1.1.2 MOTIVATION OF THE PROPOSED WORK

In India, agriculture is important to the country's economy. In recent years, industrialization and excessive pesticide use have led to a decrease in soil strength. Many agricultural practices now in use are insufficient to increase yield. The biggest problem that Indian farmers are facing is their ignorance about the optimum crop to plant based on the needs of their land, which reduces production [2–4]. Indian farmers face a variety of challenges while determining which farming technique to employ and which crop to select for which environment. When choosing crops for maximum yield, which are influenced by topographic conditions and economic concerns, Indian farmers frequently make mistakes. In the agriculture sector, achieving maximum crop yield at minimum cost is the goal of production [5]. In order to boost productivity and profit from the suggested technique, our suggested effort will assist farmers in choosing the ideal crop based on elements like cost of cultivation, cost of production, and yield.

1.1.3 FOCUS OF THE PROPOSED WORK

India uses conventional farming techniques. To automate and monitor farm operations, we can use wireless sensor networks and Internet of Things (IoT) devices. Farmers can get the most recent agricultural conditions using a smartphone using the IoT system's mobile app. The selection of a crop that is suitable for the provided field will be the main objective of this exercise.

DOI: 10.1201/9781003391302-1

1.1.4 Proposed Work Contribution

The suggested strategy improves the existing system by introducing cutting-edge methods into the work plan that was previously in place. A soil moisture sensor, temperature and humidity sensors, a pH sensor, a current amplifier, and Mail make up the hardware. To gather data, the sensors are placed in various field areas. The soil's alkalinity, temperature, relative humidity, and moisture content are a few of the many factors analyzed. Using sensor data that is first kept in a database and then delivered to a web interface, the crop is predicted using the K-Nearest Neighbor (KNN) algorithm [6]. The predicted crop or outcome is then mailed to the farmer.

1.2 RELATED WORK

Reshma et al. [7] use existing statistics and data mining techniques to categorize soil into high, medium, and low in order to estimate crop production. These factors were used in an analysis to determine which crops could be grown in the specific soil type.

Limitations of the existing work: Fuzzy or intelligent methods, which are not used in the current study, could increase this effort by predicting the soil that will be used to grow future crops.

Result and inference: The study's objective is to identify the type of soil and the optimum crop to produce there using classification algorithms. The accuracy score is used to choose between the Support Vector Machine and Decision Tree techniques that employ the most effective classification method.

Katarya et al. proposes a framework applicable to crop recommendation systems, a subset of precision agriculture that uses various machine learning algorithms to propose crops in accordance with predetermined rules and data. The type and quantity of data used determine the quality of the recommendations. These algorithms' statistical properties enable increase in yield. The need for a precision measure is driven by the negative consequences of not having one, which include substantial productivity losses, time and seed waste, among other things. The parameters that can be considered while making suggestions include things like temperature, soil properties, humidity, and others.

Limitations of the existing work: Soil qualities and nutrients are the most important factors in crop recommendation; thus, they deserve special attention. It is hoped that a user-friendly web/mobile application will result in an increase in yield.

Result and inference: Machine learning models and other techniques are covered in this study. These algorithms furnish the best recommendations.

In order to assist farmers in choosing crops for their agricultural area, Rajeswari et al. [8] suggest a rough set method based on fuzzy data. The suggested strategy has been tested on 24 different types of plants. The pH, soil type, and location are the most important factors to consider while selecting the crop for the area. The proposed approach splits numerical properties and applies fuzzy reasoning to handle border situations. With the use of crude set-based rule induction, the fuzzy rules are developed. The membership function (MF) with three and five linguistic terms uses the suggested method.

Limitations of the existing work: There was no deployment of an Android application to Support Vector Machine (SVM) assist new and inexperienced farmers in learning more about suitable crops, soil types, and soil health.

Result and inference: The experimental findings show that the Learning from Examples Module (LEM2) algorithm's fuzzy rules beat rival algorithms in terms of prediction accuracy for both discretized and fuzzified datasets.

Oswal et al. (2021) [9] propose a technique for saving the optimal values of given properties for various plants. For this paper, they chose five variables: minimum and maximum temperatures, minimum and maximum rainfall, types of soil, minimum and maximum soil pH, and previous crop. The algorithm scans through the entire dataset and then recommends the plant with the highest score and overall ranking of a plant.

Limitations of the existing work: Weather forecasts must be integrated into the system using external weather Application Programming Interfaces (APIs). When compared to Machine Learning (ML) models, the recommendation's correctness was not tested.

Result and inference: The system uses a mathematical approach based on membership functions for fuzzy logic instead of a machine learning-based approach.

Farmers will be helped by the hardware and software parts of the system described in this paper by Nair [10] in selecting the best crop for their soil and type of land. The agricultural industry has a lot to gain from IoT and machine learning. By using sensors like the DHT11 and soil pH sensor, it is possible to determine the temperature, humidity, and pH levels of the soil. Using a Wi-Fi module, we can send data that has been fetched to a machine learning model. Using the values, the machine learning model will find a few crops suitable for the agricultural region and distribute them to the farmers via a web application. To monitor the farm environment, we placed IoT sensors; the sensor equipment may help measure temperature, humidity, and soil pH. Data is sent to the server from our IoT sensors. The database can be used to extract all sensor data, which can then be put through data analysis. Our technology does analyze the farm's environmental factors before selecting the best crops. Before analyzing any data, such as appropriate months and soil types, our system performs feature extraction to guarantee that the analyzed data and the analysis result of preset targets are accurate. Our recommended plan of action and goals can increase crop productivity while supporting research on farmers' agricultural practices.

Result and inference: Because the plant that was advised grew enormously and the other plant that was not recommended did not, we could conclude that our method was successful in recommending the right crop for the suitable climatic conditions. Thus, our method might be used on a bigger farm, which might result in good harvests and let the farmer get more out of his or her field. Agriculture is gradually being replaced and improved by more precise and advanced digital and electrical technology.

Adithya et al. [11] suggested an IoT-based sensor network for smart agriculture. Since standard development is more serious, risky, and silly in light of low yield or an exhibit of God, little ranchers, who don't know anything about the sharp agribusiness framework, geniuses and corporate regions are getting the awards for skillful agriculture advancement. Because of pandemic Covid-19, which returned homeless people to their solitary towns with next to no kind of income, they are restless to return to their fascinating horticulture.

Limitations of the existing work: With the new time of development come more frustrated techniques for a humble farmer. The deficiency of a solid association is the beginning stage for the underpinning of such critical level interconnectivity. There has been no discussion of unequivocal or standard simple-to-use interfaces.

Result and inference: IoT-based sensors can be used for green cutoff points. Sensor networks' correspondence and ranchers' difficulties can similarly be lessened, and a predominant corresponding way for the exchange of significant information can be accomplished among various focuses. Ranchers can supervise different rural-related stuff and screen their yield on smartphones or Personal Computers (PCs) in that capacity.

Doshi et al. [12] design a device that screens the ranch or nursery and sends various messages to the rancher about the continuous situation considering the readings of various sensors, for instance, temperature, steadiness, soil-soaked quality, UV, IR, soil improvements, and soil supplements. The ranchers' quick exercises will help them in extending the efficiency of their creation and genuine utilization of ordinary assets, which will make our thing climate agreeable too. By means of carefully dissecting the different current circumstances, our thing will grow the sum and combination of harvests. It is an IoT device with "Fitting and Sense." On PCs and Personal Digital Assistants (PDAs), live information for various limits should be recognizable.

Limitations of the existing work: The design of this system is extremely convoluted, and no working model is proposed to screen the reap prosperity at standard ranges. Moreover, the cost of building such a model is prohibitively exorbitant and drawn out to a gigantic degree.

Result and inference: Expected benefits of this development are remote checking for farmers, resource protection, and water. Extraordinary organization moreover allows additionally created tamed animal developing; the things which are not apparent to the unaided eye ought to be noticeable, bringing about exact farmland and reap appraisal, incredible quality, and further entertainment.

Chakraborty et al. [13] develop a crop decision to help farmers by using Artificial Intelligence (AI) and mind associations to think about all factors, for instance, establishing cropping season, soil, and land region.

Methodology: A few datasets from Kaggle and government sites were used to feed the model. The dataset incorporated a few boundaries, for example, crop development costs, yield, crop types developed, and precipitation and temperature information. These datasets were preprocessed prior to being prepared using AI calculations, like straight relapse, and taken care of by a brain organization.

Result and inference: Using the KNN classifier, the model suggested which harvest was the best coordinate and anticipated supportability with up to 89% precision using brain organizations. In any case, there was no genuine equipment execution or even reenactment for computerized water system for a totally changed horticulture framework.

Talaviva et al. (2020) [14] talk about including AI in the field of agriculture region and the looming propels that can help with conveying disturbance to the specific field. Different new concentrated contemplations, including image affirmation and wisdom, chatbots for farmers, and electrically related water framework strategies, including dielectric and neutron control, are referred to in the paper. Also, there has been notice of substance-based techniques to deal with weeding. The use of Unmanned Aerial Vehicles (UAVs) like robots can moreover be a strong plan from this perspective. Advance-based crop checking and data examination can moreover go probably as the cherry on the most noteworthy place of the splendid cultivation structure.

Limitations of the existing work: This paper needs practical presentation of any of the contemplations discussed previously. There is a notice of various headways disregarding the way that there has not been any hardware or establishment done in the improvement time of any of these contemplations.

Khandelwal et al. [15] suggest ML- and AI-based agriculture information. In farming, there is a catalyst change to AI in its different creating methods. The chance of mental enrollment is the one which mirrors human viewpoint as a model in PC. This outcome as angry headway in AI-fueled development conveys its association in unwinding, gaining, and noting various circumstances (taking into account the learning acquired) to additionally foster ampleness. Besides, a part of the captivating considerations that are inspected in the paper consolidates image-related understanding of age, disease disclosure in crops, fielding the board, recognizing confirmation of ideal mix for agronomic things, automation methods that are used in water framework, and the use of robots and other UAVs. Moreover, one huge and exceptional thought analyzed in the paper included precision development that was associated with working on significant standard pictures and using ML and AI to expect delegate information. Yield management is also discussed in this paper where satellites are used for crop planning and affiliation.

Limitations of the existing work: The thoughts examined here are brilliant, no matter how costly they are to finish and require enormous capital speculations. The examinations talked about here are also not related to the ground or the root level; thusly, the contemplations dissected in this paper are not reasonable for little ranchers.

Result and inference: With everything considered, the fate of making in the times to come is all about changing mental and certifiable strategies. Regardless, a colossal appraisal is still on, and different applications are in the end open, but the making business is right now not having satisfying help, which stays to be underserved. While it drops in directing steady inconveniences and requests looked at by the ranchers, recalling AI dynamic frameworks and farsighted designs for managing them, making with AI is essential in an early phase. To take advantage of the gigantic level of AI being created, applications ought to be all the more really hot.

Chong et al. [16] suggest a plan to create tasks, for example, a fish holding tank or a rack for making harvests. The attributes that are known to be sincere to the yield of improvement are being surveyed and followed by sensors. PC vision is used, for example, with a camera mounted over the subjects, to screen and track the produce of improvement. The responsibilities for information openness using AI may likewise unite extra information that might be connected with the yield subject to earlier information. A food creation affiliation could set up the information disclosure framework proposed in the paper for the situation when it wishes to learn or find a ton of ideal natural parts for a particular fish or vegetable sort that it could use to assist the yield with rating. He will unequivocally keep on cultivating the particular fish or veggie while getting together sensor and vision information for a long time. The creating affiliation could change the cutoff values during the information-gathering period with an extreme goal to expand yield. After the given out time has elapsed, the collected information might be passed on in bunches for information disclosure. Regardless, using the reasonable learning calculations, for example, a phony safe learning structure, on the web or dynamic learning is possible.

Limitations of the existing work: Singapore needs to help its food security by expanding food creation. Over the course of the following decade, significantly increasing its ability for food production is presently planned. The city-state intends to meet 30% of its wholesome requests by 2030, frequently known as the "30-by-30 vision." Overall, 10% is made right now. This undertaking is meant to expand the neighborhood food creation's yield in this present circumstance.

Result and inference: Ranchers could hence have the option to set up a comparative framework to computationally comprehend the developing qualities of explicit yields corresponding to various natural boundaries in view of the outcomes. This will be particularly useful for cultivating organizations that are simply beginning or for laid-out organizations working with novel yields.

Revathi et al. (2019) [17] propose a framework that thoroughly chips away at three sections right off the bat to identify temperature, dampness level, and human location by associating all temperature, soil dampness, PIR sensor, water siphon, and GSM module to Arduino microcontroller, then, at that point, transferring programs to computerize the water system framework, and sending information to ranchers versatile as often as possible and also sending information to cloud [18]. Second, sending data to ranchers at different temperatures is high, SavvySystem ships off ranchers at high temperatures, LD demonstrates Land Dry, HD shows Human Detection regularly through GSM module by embedding SIM card; lastly, sending information to cloud through GPRS by making an account in AWS; IP address will be given and through that IP address, information will be transferred and a page will open where all the information will be put away.

Limitations of the existing work: There are a few restrictions inside the task executed, like a cost-major issue in horticulture is the expense of equipment gadgets which are exorbitant to manage for ranchers, then, at that point, battery life wireless sensors used here run on a battery which gets released soon and there is a need to change the batteries of the relative multitude of sensors, then there is an issue with band range – were we know the greater part of the farming is being finished in rustic distant regions where there is less accessibility of the organization, and efficiency of the remote innovations is likewise the main thing at long last, there is likewise more power utilization that ought to be productive.

Result and inference: The developed smart framework assists with checking crop fields and robotizes the water system framework in view of dampness level, so wastage of water is diminished. All the data is shipped off to various ranchers through instant messages, and information is put away in Amazon Cloud administrations for additional examination. This brilliant framework decreases the wastage of water, diminishes rancher time and their actual work at less expense, and increments their harvest yield.

Swetha et al. [19] develop regular AI procedures, which were applied involving IoT for continuous checking of harvests and gave improved yield. By using machine learning procedures, the yields were delegated a sound and unfortunate class to show up at a choice regardless of whether to water them, which can help ranchers in crop the board by getting the information connected with crop the executives, viz., temperature, soil dampness, and mugginess.

Methodology: Here, an exploratory arrangement was planned that comprised sensors like soil dampness and moistness and temperature sensors for information assortment for the model as well with respect to continuous observing for the yields. Two harvests – fenugreek and coriander – were picked and tried in different natural circumstances all through their development period, and these information were shipped off the cloud by means of Arduino for additional handling. At long last, a water siphon was likewise impelled in view of the framework that was proposed regardless of whether the plant would require it.

Result and inference: Hence, a programmed water system framework was laid out as well as the framework anticipated whether a harvest was sound with 94% precision in the event of coriander and 87% precision in the event of fenugreek. The model in any case had no arrangement that would suggest a yield or a stage where the rancher could really get to know these new advances.

Prabavathi et al. [20] use an absurd AI estimation; the proposed model in this paper predicts crop yield. The soil properties were gotten from the public power site. On the dataset, this model purposes an 80:20 split for planning and testing. Ridiculous learning machines will outmaneuver standard learning computations. This estimation is genuinely skilled at learning cerebrum associations. To achieve the most negligible readiness screw-up, Gaussian Extreme Learning Machine (ELM) is used to set up a singular mystery layer feedforward network (SLFN) with different commencement capacities.

Limitations of the existing work: The experts are endeavoring to find advancement deals with serious consequences regarding the cultivating dataset, and they are facing three key obstructions. In any case, making conjecture estimations that work across each geographic circumstance and wide soil data is trying. Second, because the dataset is jumbled, decision and isolation are critical parts that could provoke an underfit or overfit gauge plan. Third, the deficit of a general model makes it difficult to design an estimation that will produce crops with incredible yield.

Result and inference: A soil supplement examination is finished using different AI estimations, for instance, SVM, neural net, Decision Tree, Naive Bayes, and ELM, with the Gaussian preposterous AI computation beating the others.

1.3 PROPOSED METHODOLOGY

1.3.1 Method and Approaches

The work focuses on the following methods and approaches:

1. Data for a set of crops is collected using sensors.
2. The DHT11 sensor is placed in the soil and left to detect the values of temperature and humidity.
3. The sensors are connected to the Arduino to give the output values of the sensors attached to it.
4. Then we interface Arduino with NodeMCU and send the values to it.
5. Then using the API keys of the chosen cloud platform, we send the temperature and humidity values to the cloud for NodeMCU.
6. The data is then analyzed using machine learning algorithms.
7. The best crop is suggested for the type of soil input into the model.
8. A website is then built around this crop recommendation system so as to make it easy for farmers to use it.

1.3.2 Metrics and Measurements

The yield would be recommended based on the following features of the environment:

1. Nitrogen content
2. Potassium content
3. Phosphorus content
4. Temperature
5. Humid
6. pH
7. Rainfall

1.3.3 Data Analysis Methods

One of the best accuracy-producing ML algorithms will be trained on the dataset generated from the sensors which will be then used to generate crop recommendations for the type of soil the farmer inputs into the model.

1.4 SYSTEM ARCHITECTURE

The Architecture diagram for best crop prediction is shown in Figure 1.1.

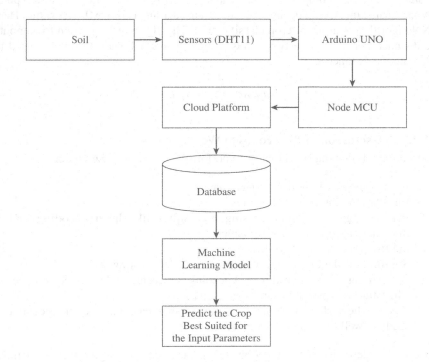

FIGURE 1.1 Architecture diagram for best crop prediction.

1.4.1 Architecture Diagram Explanation

Data for a set of crops is collected using sensors:

1. The DHT11 sensor is placed in the soil and left to detect the values of temperature and humidity.
2. The sensors are connected to the Arduino to give the output values of the sensors attached to it.
3. Then we interface Arduino with NodeMCU and send the values to it.
4. Then utilizing the API keys of the picked cloud stage, we send the temperature and dampness values to the cloud for NodeMCU.
5. The data is then analyzed using machine learning algorithms.
6. The best crop is suggested for the type of soil input into the model.
7. A website is then built around this crop recommendation system so as to make it easy for farmers to use it.

1.4.2 Proposed Algorithm for Crop Prediction

To recommend the best crop, the user had to input parameters to get the details.

A dataset comprising six different parameters such as nitrogen, phosphorus, potassium, and other mineral content, temperature, and humid conditions required to grow certain crops. It includes the details of 20+ different crops with suitable conditions.

Since the dataset comprises input parameters along with their output (the type of crop), it turned into a classifying problem that used a supervised ML algorithm. Here KNN algorithm is used for crop classification. The algorithm is chosen to compute the distance between these two points using KNN. Euclidean distance is used to calculate the distance.

$$d(\mathrm{p}, \mathrm{q}) = \sqrt{\sum_{i=1}^{n}(q_i - p_i)^2}$$

1.4.2.1 Description of the Proposed Work

These are the following steps that were performed in our proposed model:

1. Data mining and finding the right dataset.
2. Importing the necessary libraries.
3. Performing some preprocessing techniques like label encoding and interchanging/filling missing numbers.
4. Splitting into X and Y data.
5. Splitting the data into 70% training set and 30% testing set.
6. Performing KNN algorithm by choosing the correct values of K variable. The value of K variable here was taken as 3.
7. Finding the performance metric of the model to calculate the accuracy and see how well the model performed.

Once the model was built using Figure 1.2, the user had to give the seven input parameters.

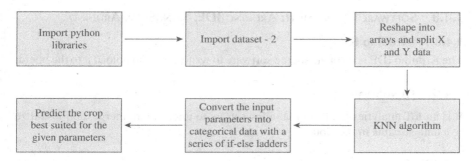

FIGURE 1.2 Crop prediction model using KNN algorithm.

The model calculates the three closest neighbors for the given parameters and recommended the best crop suited.

1.4.3 APPLICATION INTERFACE AND EXPERIMENTAL SETUP

The temperature and humidity values from the soil are measured using DHT11 sensors which are sent to the Arduino UNO microprocessor. After that, these values are sent to the Node MCU board through which we can upload these values to a cloud platform for further usage of the values.

1.4.4 COMPONENTS REQUIRED

1. DHT 11
2. Arduino UNO
3. Node MCU
4. Connecting wires
5. Bread board

1.4.5 DHT11

The DHT11 sensor is an efficient and cost-effective sensor which helps in sensing temperature and humidity. The sensor has a temperature range of 0–50°C with chances of error of ±1°C and humidity range of 20%–90% with error rate of ±1%. It also wants a power supply of 3.5–5.5 V.

1.4.6 ARDUINO UNO

Arduino UNO is a microcontroller board. It has 14 digital input and output pins, 6 analog inputs, a USB connection, a power jack, 16-MHz quartz crystal, and ICSP header and a reset button. It is useful to interface it to a PC with a USB link or power it with an AC-to-DC connector or battery to begin.

1.4.7 NODE MCU

It is an open-source LUA-based firmware delivered for the ESP8266 Wi-Fi chip.

1.4.8   Software Requirement: Arduino IDE, ThingSpeak Arduino

1.4.8.1   Arduino IDE

The Arduino IDE is an open-source software to write code and upload it to the board.

1.4.9   ThingSpeak

It is an IoT analytics platform that allows users to understand, merge, and visualize live data streams in the cloud.

1.4.10   Hardware Implementation

To monitor our crops, Arduino with NodeMCU are used as hardware.

1.4.10.1   Procedure

- The DHT11 sensor is placed in the soil and left to detect the values of temperature and humidity.
- The sensors are connected to the Arduino to give the output values of the sensors attached to it.
- Then we interface Arduino with NodeMCU and send the values to it.
- Then using the API keys of the chosen cloud platform, we send the temperature and humidity values to the cloud for NodeMCU.

1.4.10.2   Arduino

1. Import required libraries.
2. Set up or initialize ports used.
3. Convert the temperature and humidity values to JSON format.
4. Begin serial communication and transfer values.

1.4.10.3   NodeMCU

1. Import required libraries.
2. Set up or initialize port used.
3. Begin serial communication and receive values from Arduino.
4. Convert the values to de-JSON format.
5. Initialize the cloud platform to be used.
6. Input Wi-Fi SSID and password.
7. Import values to the cloud.

1.4.11   Algorithm Improvement and Justification
of the Proposed Methodology

In KNN algorithm, the distance measurement is the only factor that influences the algorithm's prediction. For applications with more to sufficient area information, this KNN algorithm makes a good sense. The KNN algorithm is also referred to as lazy-learner algorithm. Despite the fact that this strategy raises processing costs, KNN is as yet the better decision for applications where exactness is significant yet conjectures are not much of the time examined.

KNN is suitable for information with fewer aspects. It is truly easy to comprehend and set in motion. Because of its incredibly close to results, KNN estimation can rival the most solid models. You can likewise involve the KNN computation for applications that need high accuracy yet don't need a characterized model. The idea of the assumptions is affected by the aspects and distance.

It is to be noticed that the strategy is dimensionality-reviled and is particularly powerless against uproarious information sources, exceptions, missing information, and anomaly ID. To streamline the KNN strategy, a pre-handling layer should be added before the last information is grouped.

1.5 EXPERIMENTAL RESULT ANALYSIS

1.5.1 EVALUATION CRITERIA

The crop would be suggested based on the following characteristics of the soil:

1. Nitrogen content
2. Potassium content
3. Phosphorus content
4. Temperature
5. Humid
6. pH
7. Rainfall

1.5.1.1 Performance Metrics Used
- Accuracy
- Precision
- Recall
- F1 score

Experimental setup for crop prediction is explained in Figure 1.5. Figure 1.3 and Figure 1.4 represent the sample dataset and different categories of crops.

	Nitrogen	Phosphorus	Potassium	Temperature	Humidity	pH	Rainfall	Crop
0	90	42	43	20.879744	82.002744	6.502985	202.935536	rice
1	85	58	41	21.770462	80.319644	7.038096	226.655537	rice
2	60	55	44	23.004459	82.320763	7.840207	263.964248	rice
3	74	35	40	26.491096	80.158363	6.980401	242.864034	rice
4	78	42	42	20.130175	81.604873	7.628473	262.717340	rice
...	...	...	...	...	...	...	...	...
2195	107	34	32	26.774637	66.413269	6.780064	177.774507	coffee
2196	99	15	27	27.417112	56.636362	6.086922	127.924610	coffee
2197	118	33	30	24.131797	67.225123	6.362608	173.322839	coffee

FIGURE 1.3 Sample dataset.

```
In [15]: print(excel['CROP'].unique())

['rice' 'maize' 'chickpea' 'kidneybeans' 'pigeonpeas' 'mothbeans'
 'mungbean' 'blackgram' 'lentil' 'pomegranate' 'banana' 'mango' 'grapes'
 'watermelon' 'muskmelon' 'apple' 'orange' 'papaya' 'coconut' 'cotton'
 'jute' 'coffee']
```

FIGURE 1.4   Different categories of crops.

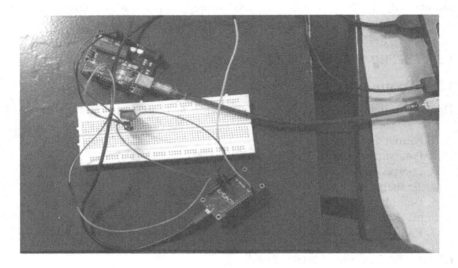

FIGURE 1.5   Experimental setup for crop prediction.

1.6   RESULTS OBTAINED THROUGH PROPOSED APPROACH

The results obtained through proposed approach are given in Figures 1.6 and 1.7.

1.7   APPLICATION INTERFACE

The User interface Figure 1.8 that we've designed takes inputs from the user and returns with the best crop suited for the soil. Our interface supports text to speech as well.

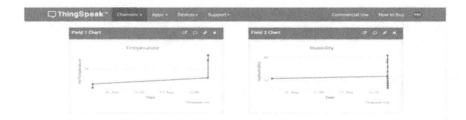

FIGURE 1.6   ThingSpeak (cloud platform).

FIGURE 1.7   Predicted crop based on proposed model.

1.8   DESCRIPTION OF THE RESULTS OBTAINED THROUGH PROPOSED APPROACH

Performance metrics: Precision, Recall, Accuracy, and F are calculated for proposed model from [21–24]. Our model gave 98.4% accuracy (Figure 1.9).

$$Precision = \frac{|TP|}{|TP + FP|}$$

$$Recall = \frac{|TP|}{|TP + FN|}$$

$$Accuracy = \frac{|TP + TN|}{|TP + FP + TN + FN|}$$

$$F = 2 \times \left(\frac{Precision \times Recall}{Precision + Recall} \right)$$

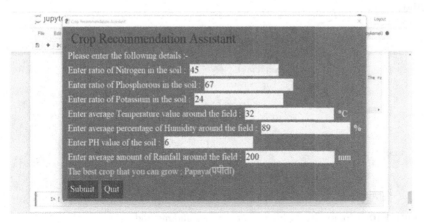

FIGURE 1.8   Crop recommendation assistant.

	precision	recall	f1-score	support
0	1.00	1.00	1.00	30
1	1.00	1.00	1.00	30
2	0.97	0.97	0.97	30
3	1.00	1.00	1.00	30
4	1.00	1.00	1.00	30
5	0.97	1.00	0.98	30
6	0.97	1.00	0.98	30
7	1.00	1.00	1.00	30
8	0.85	0.97	0.91	30
9	1.00	1.00	1.00	30
10	0.97	0.97	0.97	30
11	1.00	0.97	0.98	30
12	1.00	1.00	1.00	30
13	1.00	1.00	1.00	30
14	1.00	1.00	1.00	30
15	1.00	1.00	1.00	30
16	1.00	0.97	0.98	30
17	1.00	1.00	1.00	30
18	1.00	1.00	1.00	30
19	0.97	1.00	0.98	30
20	1.00	0.83	0.91	30
21	1.00	1.00	1.00	30
accuracy			0.98	660
macro avg	0.99	0.98	0.98	660
weighted avg	0.99	0.98	0.98	660

FIGURE 1.9 Performance analysis.

1.8.1 PERFORMANCE ANALYSIS

Figure 1.10 is from paper [25], showing the results of the proposed methodology of that paper which is a crop recommendation system with cloud computing. Our proposed methodology has more precision, recall, and f-1 score than the existing method used widely.

Classification report:				
	precision	recall	f1-score	support
1	0.88	1.00	0.93	7
0	1.00	0.88	0.93	8
accuracy			0.93	15
macro avg	0.94	0.94	0.93	15
weighted avg	0.94	0.93	0.93	15

FIGURE 1.10 Comparison with existing studies and methods.

1.9 CONCLUSION, LIMITATION AND FUTURE SCOPE OF WORK

This framework overcomes any barrier between uninformed farmers and current rural advances. We have effectively executed our thoughts and made a straightforward yet easy-to-use interface for suggesting the best harvest. It additionally upholds text to discourse transformation. We have carried out a KNN-based calculation to find the pattern of the great yields filled in that soil and suggest the harvest likewise. We have gotten the information from IoT sensors and transferred it to a cloud stage.

The farmers might foster more, procure more, and live longer as they have a more noteworthy consciousness of their property and grounds, as well as the potential dangers to their territory and efficiency. Regardless of the way that ranchers know nothing about it, the nation will confront significant emergencies for a long time to come. Little landowners ought to be designated by the public authority, which ought to be taught and urged to moderate the plant's hereditary assets for a more promising time to come. FAO's unification of assets and data can without a doubt help with bettering state-funded instruction.

REFERENCES

1. Katarya, Rahul, Raturi, Ashutosh, Mehndiratta, Abhinav, and Thapper, Abhinav, "Impact of Machine Learning Techniques in Precision Agriculture," 2020 3rd International Conference on Emerging Technologies in Computer Engineering: Machine Learning and Internet of Things (ICETCE), Jaipur, India, 2020, pp. 1–6, doi: 10.1109/ICETCE48199.2020.9091741
2. Rawal, Srishti. (2017). IoT-based smart irrigation system. International Journal of Computer Applications, 159(8), pp. 7–11.
3. Togneri, Rodrigo, Kamienski, Carlos, Dantas, Ramide, Prati, Ronaldo, Toscano, Attilio, Soininen, Juha-Pekka, and Cinotti, Tullio Salmon. (2019). Advancing IoT-based smart irrigation. IEEE Internet of Things Magazine, 2(4), pp. 20–25.
4. Anand, Jose, and Raja Paul Perinbam, J., "Automatic Irrigation System using Fuzzy Logic", AE International Journal of Multidisciplinary Research, 2 (8), pp. 1–9, August 2014.
5. Ojha, M., Mohite, S., Kathole, S., and Tarware, D. (2016). Microcontroller based automatic plant watering system. International Journal of Computer Science and Engineering, 5(3), pp. 25–36.
6. Priyadharshini, A., Chakraborty, Swapneel, Kumar, Aayush, and Pooniwala, Omen Rajendra. "Intelligent Crop Recommendation System Using Machine Learning," 2021 5th International Conference on Computing Methodologies and Communication (ICCMC), IEEE, 2021, pp. 843–848.
7. Reshma, R., Sathiyavathi, V., Sindhu, T., Selvakumar, K., and SaiRamesh, L., "IoT Based Classification Techniques for Soil Content Analysis and Crop Yield Prediction," 2020 Fourth International Conference on I-SMAC (IoT in Social, Mobile, Analytics and Cloud) (I-SMAC), Palladam, India, 2020, pp. 156–160, doi: 10.1109/I-SMAC49090.2020.9243600
8. Rajeswari, A. M., Selva Anushiya, A., Seyad Ali Fathima, K., Shanmuga Priya, S., and Mathumithaa, N., "Fuzzy Decision Support System for Recommendation of Crop Cultivation Based on Soil Type," 2020 4th International Conference on Trends in Electronics and Informatics (ICOEI)(48184), Tirunelveli, India, 2020, pp. 768–773, doi: 10.1109/ICOEI48184.2020.9142899
9. Oswal, Manas, Mahajan, Karan, Pagare, Shubham, Kasa,Vishal, Malhotra, Jyoti, and Sarode, Sambhaji, "Feature-Based Analytical Crop Recommendation System," 2021 IEEE Pune Section International Conference (PuneCon), Pune, India, 2021, pp. 1–6, doi: 10.1109/PuneCon52575.2021.9686530

10. Nair, Sujaya. (2020). Crop selection using IoT and machinelearning.International Journal for Research in Applied Science and Engineering Technology,8, pp.1241–1244, doi:10.22214/ijraset.2020.30462

11. Vadapalli, Adithya, Peravali, Swapna, and Rao Dadi, Venkata (2020). Smart agriculture-system using IoT technology. International Journal of Advance Research in Science and Engineering, 9(9), pp. 58–65.

12. Doshi, Jash, Patel, Tirthkumar, and Bharti, Santosh Kumar. "Smart Farming Using IoT, a Solution for Optimally Monitoring Farming Conditions," The 3rd International Workshop on Recent Advances on Internet of Things: Technology and Application Approaches(IoT-T&A 2019), Coimbra, Portugal, November 4–7, 2019.

13. Priyadharshini, A., Chakraborty, Swapneel, Kumar, Aayush, and Pooniwala, Omen Rajendra, "Intelligent Crop Recommendation System Using Machine Learning," 2021 5th International Conference on Computing Methodologies and Communication (ICCMC), 2021, pp. 843–848, doi: 10.1109/ICCMC51019.2021.9418375

14. Talaviva, Tanha, Shah, Dhara, Patel, Nivedita, Yagnik, Hiteshri, and Shah, Manan, (2020). Implementation of artificial intelligence in agriculture for optimisation of irrigation and application of pesticides and herbicides. Artificial Intelligence in Agriculture, 4, pp.58–73. https://doi.org/10.1016/j.aiia.2020.04.002

15. Khandelwal, Paras M., and Chavhan, Himanshu. "Artificial Intelligence in Agriculture: An Emerging Era of Research", 2019.

16. Chong, Y. T., Loo, P. K., and Ding, Z. Q., "Knowledge Discovery Through the Machine Learning of Farming Parameters and Yield Performance," 2019 IEEE International Conference on Industrial Engineering and Engineering Management (IEEM), 2019, pp. 1550–1552, doi: 10.1109/IEEM44572.2019.8978814

17. Revathi, G. P., and Vanishree, K. (2019). Development of smartagriculturalmonitoring and automaticirrigationsystem. International Journal of Innovative Research in Computer Science & Technology (IJIRCST), ISSN: 2347-5552, 7(3), doi: 10.21276/ijircst.2019.7.3.5

18. Dhanalakshmi, R., Anand, Jose., Kumar Sivaraman, Arun, and Rani, Sita, "IoT-based Water Quality Monitoring System using Cloud for Agriculture Use", Cloud and Fog Computing Platforms for Internet of Things, Edited by Pankaj Bhambri, Sita Rani, Gaurav Gupta and Alex Khang, Taylor & Francis, Hersey, PA, pages 14, 2022, ISBN: 9781003213888.

19. Swetha, Tiramareddy Manasa, Yogitha, Tekkali, Kuruba Sai Hitha, Manche, Syamanthika, Puppala, Poorna, S. S., and Anuraj, K., "IOT Based Water Management System For Crops Using Conventional Machine Learning Techniques," 2021 12th International Conference on Computing Communication and Networking Technologies (ICCCNT), 2021, pp. 1–4, doi: 10.1109/ICCCNT51525.2021.9579651

20. Prabavathi, R., and Chelliah, Balika J., "An Optimized Gaussian Extreme Learning Machine (GELM) for Predicting the Crop Yield using Soil Factors," 2022 International Conference on Electronic Systems and Intelligent Computing (ICESIC), 2022, pp. 219–222, doi: 10.1109/ICESIC53714.2022.9783578

21. Acharjya, Debi. Prasanna., and Kauser Ahmed, P. (2022). A hybridized rough set and bat-inspired algorithm for knowledge inferencing in the diagnosis of chronic liver disease. Multimedia Tools and Applications, 81, pp. 13489–13512. https://doi.org/10.1007/s11042-021-11495-7

22. Kauser, Ahmed P., and Acharjya, Debi. Prasanna. (2021). Knowledge inferencing using artificialbeecolony and roughset for diagnosis of hepatitisdisease. International Journal of Healthcare Information Systems and Informatics (IJHISI), 16(2), pp. 49–72.

23. Kauser, Ahmed P., and Rishabh, Agrawal, "Cluster Analysis of Health Care Data Using Hybrid Nature-Inspired Algorithms", Recent Advances in Hybrid Metaheuristics for Data Clustering, First Edition, Edited by Sourav De, Sandip Dey, and Siddhartha Bhattacharyya, John Wiley & Sons Ltd, 2020. https://doi.org/10.1002/9781119551621.ch6

24. Kauser, Ahmed P., and Senthil Kumar, Narayanswamy.,"A Comprehensive Review of Nature Inspired Algorithms for Feature Selection (Chapter)",Handbook of Research on Modeling, Analysis, and Application of Nature-Inspired Metaheuristic Algorithms, Edited by Sujata Dash, B.K. Tripathy, and Attaur Rahman, IGI Global Publishers, Pennsylvania, pp. 331–345, 2017. ISBN13: 9781522528579, (ACM).
25. Dhabal, G., Lachure, J., and Doriya, R., "Crop Recommendation System with Cloud Computing," 2021 Third International Conference on Inventive Research in Computing Applications (ICIRCA), 2021, pp. 1404–1411, doi: 10.1109/ICIRCA51532.2021.9544524

2 Automated Seasonal Crop Mapping and Acreage Estimation Framework Using Machine Learning Algorithms
A Survey

V. Santhi[1] *and S. Mahenthiran*[2]
[1] School of Computer science and Engineering,
Vellore Institute of Technology, Vellore – India
[2] School of Civil Engineering, Vellore Institute
of Technology, Vellore – India

2.1 INTRODUCTION

In recent years, the agricultural system has been adversely impacted and degraded due to natural disasters such as floods and drought. It greatly influences the food supply and economic development of a country. The large population in India depends on agriculture, and there are numerous challenges in agricultural activities due to diverse patterns in topography and climate. There will be an increase in demand for food production in future due to the increase in population (Singh et al., 2021). The urbanization, degradation of land, and climate change impose a serious threat to agricultural production (Behera et al., 2018). Thus, it is necessary to develop a strategy for the sustainable development and management of agricultural resources. Effective crop mapping is a great challenge to stakeholders in farming due to diverse crop patterns and a lack of clearly defined field boundaries (Liu et al., 2010; Rogan and Chen, 2004). However, crop mapping is essential for monitoring agricultural land and calculating the spatial distribution of crop acreage (Hudait and Patel, 2018; Kuemmerle et al., 2013). Crop insurance is necessary for agricultural planning, and crop insurance estimation requires information such as crop acreage and its yield at a micro level. The crop surveying in the field using standard procedures such as the interpolation method is inefficient and uneconomic and provides inconsistent results. Thus, it is essential to develop an effective method for accurately mapping different

DOI: 10.1201/9781003391302-2

types of seasonal crops in less time with low manpower. The automated seasonal crop mapping is essential for water resources and agriculture managers in policy- and decision-making processes. Numerous researchers (Adrian et al., 2021; Devadas et al., 2012; Ibrahim et al., 2021; Li et al., 2022; Mulyono, 2016) use satellite data for automated seasonal crop mapping and acreage estimation with the aid of machine learning algorithms. Prins and Van Niekerk (2021) integrated LiDAR, Sentinel-2, and aerial imagery with machine learning algorithms for crop mapping. Saad El Imanni et al. (2022) used high-resolution Sentinel images for crop mapping in highly heterogeneous regions. Liu et al. (2022) used Sentinel-1, Sentinel-2, and planet images to identify the tillage activities in small field farms. Kasimati et al. (2022) estimated the quality of grapes by combining Normalized Difference Vegetation Index (NDVI) data and machine learning algorithm. The crop mapping (in-season and dynamic) is done by Gallo et al. (2023) through the integration of 3D convolutional neural networks (CNN) and Sentinel-2 time series data. Integrating satellite data and machine learning is an emerging technology to map the crop pattern and acreage estimation with high accuracy.

Remote sensing (RS) is the technical process of locating features on the earth's surface and determining the physical characteristics of those features by employing electromagnetic radiation as the medium of contact (Xavier et al., 2006). The major properties of the sensor that help with target identification include spectral, spatial, temporal, and polarization signatures (Navalgund et al., 2007). Before extraction of spectral information, the data collected from the earth's surface by the sensors at various wavelengths (reflected, dispersed, and/or emitted) should undergo radiometric and geometric correction (Vicente and De Souza Filho, 2011). RS is categorized as optical and microwave (Rahman and Di, 2020). In optical RS, the sensors detect the energy radiated from the sun in the visible, near-middle, and thermal infrared ranges (Roy et al., 2017). This radiation is either reflected/scattered or emitted from the earth, creating images that are similar to photographs taken by a camera or sensor located in space at a great distance (Kumar and Singh, 2013). The wavelength is longer than visible, infrared rays are microwaves, and sensors detect them. The observation of microwave RS is not affected by day/night and climate conditions. RS is widely used in applications such as monitoring the ocean, agricultural land mapping, crop inventory, yield forecasting, assessing the damage caused by flood/drought, and land use management. Because of India's varied and scattered land holdings, complex crop sowing patterns, and limited ground data, automated satellite-based crop mapping is still difficult in the country (Ibrahim et al., 2021). The growing geographical and temporal resolution of satellite data time series in various wavelength ranges, such as Sentinel-2 and Sentinel-1 images, presents new opportunities for generating crop-type maps on a local or regional scale (Kpienbaareh et al., 2021).

Because of the significance of crop mapping and land monitoring, extensive literature studies using machine learning techniques and image processing is the need of the hour (Whyte et al., 2018). The automated seasonal crop mapping is essential for water resources and agriculture managers in policy- and decision-making processes. It is also vital for planning in the zones of multiple cropping patterns (Behera et al., 2019). In the event of a disaster, this would serve as guidelines for carrying out evaluation procedures for crop insurance (Munawar et al., 2021). Thus, automated seasonal crop mapping is essential for enhanced food security. In this context, a comprehensive review of existing automated seasonal crop mapping by machine learning techniques is discussed in greater depth in this chapter. This chapter also aims to determine the best machine learning model type for regional crop mapping and its performance evaluation under varying conditions.

The accurate crop mapping and acreage estimation is very important, because it helps to calculate yields of a particular crop/acre, loss of particular crop/acre, helps to take decision on farmer's crop insurance if crops are getting affected by heavy flood or water scarcity, and also helps the agricultural managers to design a policy in decision-making process. It is also required to plan water and other resource management in agricultural fields. It is necessary to automate the seasonal crop mapping to ease the process of estimation due to the various reasons mentioned earlier. Hence, in this chapter, various machine learning methodologies employed for automatic mapping of different types of seasonal crops in less time with low manpower are discussed in detail.

2.2 MATERIALS AND METHODS

In this section, the methods adopted to collect data, various pre-processing techniques, and machine learning methodologies employed to perform automatic crop mapping are discussed in detail.

2.2.1 Synthetic Aperture Radar (SAR)

The data which covers the targeted land area exactly is required to build an automated seasonal crop mapping model. Acquiring more data is important before the prediction of any type of class. Numerous research studies use Sentinel 1, Sentinel 2, Landsat, and GaoFen-1 (GF-1). The Wide-field View (WFV) imageries for automated seasonal crop mapping (Moumni and Lahrouni, 2021; Prins and Van Niekerk, 2021; Zhou et al., 2019). After dataset acquisition, image pre-processing is mandatory for accurate perdition of crop types before feeding input images into the model. In this section, various pre-processing techniques are discussed in detail.

2.2.1.1 Resampling

Dataset resampling is creating or producing a new dataset by changing the existing dataset. The resampling method is very useful for an unbalanced dataset. If the dataset is unbalanced and feeding the unbalanced dataset into the model results in inaccurate class prediction, the model will also result in overfitting. Thus, dataset should be balanced by data augmentation techniques prior to introducing the dataset into a model (Waldner et al., 2019). The researchers use various methods such as oversampling (Zhang et al., 2022), undersampling (Valdar et al., 2009), and hybrid (Susan and Kumar, 2021) for dataset resampling.

Oversampling is increasing the sample numbers in a class to balance the classes. The methods such as augmentation (Yan et al., 2021) and Generative Adversarial Network (GAN) (Zhao et al., 2021) are used to increase the samples. Both techniques multiply the current dataset sample count. The undersampling reduces the samples present in a class to balance the classes. Hybrid sampling combines both undersampling and oversampling to provide a balanced dataset for creating decision tree classification models.

2.2.1.1.1   Oversampling Methods

i. **Random oversampling (ROS)** randomly selects the data from the minority class and replaces them in the training dataset (Chawla, 2009). The main disadvantage of ROS is overfitting when creating more duplicate data.

ii. **Synthetic minority oversampling technique (SMOTE)** generates fresh occurrences of the minority class by combining nearby occurrences in convex ways (Chawla et al., 2002). When k is a configurable hyperparameter, SMOTE generates synthetic occurrences by random along a line connecting a minority occurrence to its k-nearest neighbors. Here, overfitting is uncommon because SMOTE generates fresh instances. Conversely, synthetic cases are developed close to the majority of occurrences, and the surroundings of the artificial instances are disregarded, which increases the possibility of misclassification.

iii. **Safe-level SMOTE (SLS)** creates minority occurrences in "secure" places to get around SMOTE's flaws (Bunkhumpornpat et al., 2009). Depending on the percentage of nearby minority instances, a secure ratio is allocated to every minority instance. When the secure proportion is closer to 0, an instance is regarded as noise, whereas when it is higher, it is seen as secure. Then, synthetic instances are put close to minority occurrences with a high secure ratio.

iv. **Adaptive neighbor SMOTE (ANS)** creates virtual instances by adjusting the number of neighbors required for sampling around some marginal regions in a dynamic manner (Siriseriwan and Sinapiromsaran, 2017). ANS also describes outcasts as minority occurrences, the close neighbors of which belong to a different class.

v. The **adaptive synthetic (ADASYN)** sampling strategy for unbalanced learning (ADASYN) weights minority cases based on their learning difficulty. It creates additional synthetic data for occurrences that are more difficult to learn (He et al., 2008). In contrast to SMOTE, the number of neighbors synthesizing minority occurrences is not defined.

2.2.1.1.2   Undersampling Methods

Random undersampling (RUS) is a non-heuristic approach to balance the class distribution by randomly eliminating instances belonging to the majority class. One disadvantage of this strategy is that essential instances for the learning process are eliminated.

The **Tomek link (Tk)** detects pairings of instances that are nearest neighbors and pertain to separate classes (Tomek, 1976). It is performed either in undersampling (removing the majority of instances) or cleaning (removing both instances) mode.

Edited nearest neighbor **(ENN)** eliminates most instances in which the class label varies from most of its k-nearest neighbors (Wilson, 1972).

2.2.1.2   Mosaics

The mosaic technique merges multiple images into a single image, which is carried out after acquiring the data. The image with high resolution is generated using an image mosaic approach. It merges multiple images with overlapped portions, like the images taken at various times, from various observation points, or with various sensors (Schmale Iii et al., 2008). There are some existing image mosaicking ways, and the steps vary, but the overall procedure is the same. There are five different ways present that are described next (Moravec, 1981):

1. **Image pre-processing**. It involves de-noising the digital image, processing of histogram, and picture-matching template creation.
2. **Image matching**. The significance of picture mosaic technology is image matching. It applies a specific matching approach to determine the relevant location of the template in the reference image to be stitched. As a result, the two images' transformation relationship is also determined.
3. **Establish a transformation model**. The parameter value in the mathematical model is determined based on the corresponding relationship between templates or image features. As a result, a mathematical transformation model of the two images is established.
4. **Uniform coordinate transformation**. On the basis of mathematical transformation model, the image to be stitched is transformed to reference image coordinate system. Thus, transformation of unified coordinate is performed.
5. **Fusion reconstruction**. The overlapping section of the image to be stitched is merged together to create a continuous panoramic image which is spliced and rebuilt. Based on the requirements of various purposes of stitching, its speed and accuracy, the low-altitude RS image splicing of Unmanned Aerial Vehicle (UAV) is divided into four categories. It includes uncontrolled ortho-photo mosaic, quick mosaic with seam, panoramic image mosaic and controlled ortho-photo mosaic (Harris and Stephens, 1988).

2.2.1.3 Atmospheric Correction

It eliminates the atmospheric effect on the reflectance values of images obtained by satellite or airborne sensors (Hadjimitsis et al., 2010). Any sensor that records electromagnetic radiations from the earth's surface by visible or near-visible light, records a combination of two forms of energy (Fraser et al., 1992). While taking a picture from a satellite, the location of that particular pixel will not be the ground truth or original object because of some illumination. Illumination means the sunlight falls on that object or atmospheric disturbance like shadows. While extracting the information from the image leads to the loss of original information (Jothiaruna et al., 2019). Because the separation of contributions is uncertain at the outset, atmospheric correction seeks to quantify those elements. In this case, the analysis is based on modified target reflectance or radiance values.

2.2.1.4 Radiometric Correction

The purpose of radiometric correction is to eliminate radiometric inaccuracies induced by sensitivity of sensor, angle of sun, and topography (Chen et al., 2005; Pons et al., 2014). The two types of radiometric correction are relative correction and absolute correction. The calibration data of sensor, angle of sun, its view angle, atmospheric models, and ground truth data are used to determine the correct radiance or reflectance. Radiometric correction is used to correct the incident energy input to sensors. The atmospheric model is so complex and accurate measurement of atmospheric conditions is problematic that relative correction is used in most applications

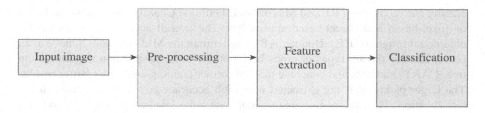

FIGURE 2.1   General architecture.

(Johansen et al., 2022). The relative correction normalizes multi-temporal data collected on various dates to a particular reference data at a particular time.

2.2.2 Feature Extraction and Classification

Feature extraction extracts features from satellite images for accurate crop detection. Before extracting the features, pre-processing is done, which is described in Section 4.2.1. The classification is carried out by training the model after extracting the features. Later some of the feature extraction and classification techniques are described. The classification process is shown in Figure 2.1.

2.2.2.1 Random Forest Classification

Random Forest (RF) is a supervised machine learning method that is commonly used for classification and regression applications (Akbari et al., 2020; Rodriguez-Galiano et al., 2012). It comprises more decision trees, and the classes are predicted or classified by the average of all the decision trees (Figure 2.2). It is similar to an ensemble learning model and helps avoid overfitting issues while training the model (Cheng et al., 2022; Vuolo et al., 2018). If the number of trees increases, the model's accuracy also increases (Cheng et al., 2022). As a result, there is a positive correlation between the number of trees and the model's accuracy. RF is the cost-effective and accurate method for estimating crop acreage (Hudait and Patel, 2022). Ok et al. (2012)

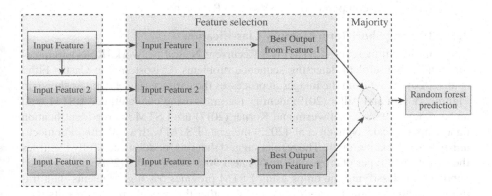

FIGURE 2.2   Random Forest prediction process.

classify the crops using RF and Maximum Likelihood Classification methods, based on pixel-based and parcel-based approaches. The overall accuracy (OA) of results obtained through the RF technique is 8% higher than the MLC method. Sonobe et al. (2014) classify the six types of crops based on RF and classification and regression tree (CART) methods and conclude that the former technique provides better results. The larger paddy plots are extracted with high accuracy based on RF-based image classification. The obtained accuracy values are quite low in high LULC (land use/ land cover) heterogeneity zones and small field areas (Hudait and Patel, 2022). The crop identification in the monsoon season with a combination of SAR and optical data gives a better result. Useya and Chen (2019) state that single-date SAR image provides OA of only 46%, which is not satisfactory.

2.2.2.2 Support Vector Machine Classification

Support Vector Machine (SVM) is a type of supervised learning used for classification and regression. It is a statistical technique that categorizes diverse data accurately by non-consideration of the input data distribution. Support vectors are used to maximize the classifier's margin. Support vectors are data points nearer to the margin and help match the hyper-plane. The other datasets are deleted since they do not contribute to hyper-plane location or orientation. Dhumal et al. (2019) suggest that the classification of crops using SVM and Gray Level Co-occurrence Matrix (GLCM) techniques provides good results with an OA of 90.29% and kappa coefficient of 0.88. Khobragade and Raghuwanshi (2015) state that using a genetic algorithm with SVM for optimization provides better results. Camps-Valls et al. (2003) describe that SVM results are better than neural networks and efficiently work, even if pre-processing is impossible. SVM also spots the noisy bands effectively. Devadas et al. (2012) define object-based SVM functioned more effectively than pixel-based maximum likelihood classifier (MLC). Mazarire et al. (2020) classify nine types of crops using SVM and RF algorithms. They conclude that the SVM technique (OA – 95%) provided better results than RF technique (OA – 85%) in a heterogeneous environment. To overcome the class imbalance problem and attain high accuracy in crop classification, Zhang et al. (2022) couple Gray Wolf Optimizer (GWO) with SVM. The results are enhanced in the GWO-SVM method by 0.8% and 1.2% compared to the SVM and RF methods, respectively.

2.2.2.3 Long Short-Term Memory Classification

Long short-term memory (LSTM) is a Recurrent Neural Network (RNN) architecture, and it is useful in detecting sequence problems (Crisóstomo de Castro Filho et al., 2020). Apart from the images, it processes the entire series of data, as shown in Figure 2.3. Xin and Adler (2019) identify the grass using convolutional LSTM with an accuracy of 98.8%. Rußwurm and Korner (2017) use LSTM in crop identification on a temporal scale. Nguyen et al. (2022) integrate LSTM with a self-attention mechanism to track plant growth. The results suggest that this model successfully identifies the six different types of crops with an OA near 90%. Zhou et al.'s (2019) parcel-based approach to classifying the crops using LSTM provides 5% higher results than traditional methods. This research also describes that this model provides results with high accuracy in rainy and cloudy areas. Chang et al. (2022) used a convolutional

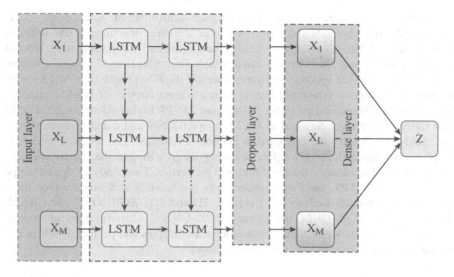

FIGURE 2.3   LSTM architecture.

LSTM rice field classifier (ConvLSTM-RFC) to classify the crops. The convolutional block attention module (CBAM) is integrated with convolutional LSTM to detect rice at different periods. The accuracy of this model is 98.08%. Bi-LSTM models are generally more effective in dealing with contextual data than unidirectional LSTM models (Zhou et al., 2019). The Bi-LSTM architecture has LSTM units that can detect past and future data in both the forward and backward layers.

2.2.2.4   U-Net

U-Net is a feature extraction technique. For crop mapping, it uses de-noised back-scatter/texture and spectral information from multi-temporal Sentinel-1 SAR data and multi-temporal Sentinel-2 data, respectively. Zhao et al. (2019) state that RGB images provide better results than multi-spectral images in the recognition of rice lodging. Adrian et al. (2021) integrated multi-temporal Sentinel-1 data with multi-temporal optical Sentinel-2 data to increase the classification accuracy for crop categories. The obtained outcomes from this study are compared with RF and deep learning networks, which include SegNet and 2D U-Net. Adrian et al. (2021) conclude that 3D CNN provides results with high accuracy than 2D CNN for crop mapping. Wei et al. (2019) added Batch Normalization (BN) algorithm to the U-Net model to enhance the network training efficiency. Liu et al. (2022) expanded the U-Net structure by introducing atrous spatial pyramid pooling (ASPP) structure to enhance the model ability, and dropout layer is hosted to avoid overfitting.

2.2.2.5   Convolutional Neural Networks (CNN)

The CNN is a network architecture for the identification of patterns in images to recognize objects and classes. Wang et al. (2021) integrate CNN and Geo-CBAM to handle more features. The Geo-CBAM-CNN approach reduces the impact due to geographic heterogeneity and filters the excess information. Kwak et al. (2021) combine the models CNN and RF to overcome the error encountered due to minimum data availability. This model is best suited in the early crop stage when limited training samples and fewer images are available for input. Li et al. (2022) combine the geodesic distance spectral similarity method (GDSSM) and 1D CNN to overcome the problems encountered due to an inadequate number of labeled samples. The GDSSM-CN method provides 19.94% and 23.91% higher results than GDSSM and CNN, respectively. Seydi et al. (2022) coupled CNN and a dual attention module (DAM) to classify the crops using Sentinel-2 datasets. The spectral module is employed to detect the crop's behavior during its growth, and the spatial attention module is used to identify the neighborhood properties. This study's OA and kappa coefficient are 98.54%, and 0.981, respectively. It efficiently classifies the crop more than the other models such as RF, CNN (R, 2D and 3D), XGBOOST, and CBAM. Moreno-Revelo et al. (2021) use enhanced 2D-CNN to classify crops in tropical regions. This model is developed for smaller scale settings and performs well in low spatial-resolution images and imbalanced classes.

2.3   PERFORMANCE MEASURES

Performance measure depicts the model accuracy in class prediction using machine learning and deep learning methods. There are different performance measures, including Cohen's kappa coefficient (CKC), OA, producer accuracy (PA), and user accuracy. Table 2.1 compares different crop classifications using machine learning and deep learning techniques.

2.3.1   COHEN'S KAPPA COEFFICIENT

CKC determines the correlation between two rates that categorize a certain number of items (N) into mutually exclusive categories. It is a more reliable measure than a simple percent estimation (Vieira et al., 2010). Cohen's kappa coefficient is defined in Equation (2.1):

$$\textbf{Cohen's Kappa coefficient} = \frac{C_a - C_c}{1 - C_c} = 1 - \frac{1 - C_a}{1 - C_c} \qquad (2.1)$$

where C_a is the level of perceived agreement between raters and C_c is the hypothetical possibility of chance agreement using the acquired data for calculating the probability of observing randomly for each category. If CKC value is zero, it represents no relation between classification data and referenced data. If CKC value is one, it means the classified image is equal to the original image (Xu et al., 2020).

2.3.2   OVERALL ACCURACY

A confusion matrix is a quantitative way to describe the accuracy of image classification. A table illustrates how reference and classified data correspond (Sun et al., 2020). The percentage of correctly mapped reference data out of all the reference data is known as OA (You et al., 2021). Typically, the OA is given as a percentage,

TABLE 2.1
Comparison of Different Crop Mapping Classification Using Machine Learning and Deep Learning

Authors	ML/DL Classifier	Accuracy (%)	Advantages
Zhang et al. (2022)	GWO-SVM	96.26	Slow convergence.
Yan et al. (2021)	Random Forest	88.0	It is applicable to all other crop types.
Akbari et al. (2020)	RF+PSO	92.85	Similar biophysical characteristics lead to misclassification issues.
Rodriguez-Galiano et al. (2012)	Random Forest	92.00	It is robust when training data reduction and also in noise.
Vuolo et al. (2018)	Random Forest	96.00	Multi-temporal crop-type classification efficiently mitigates negative effects.
Dhumal et al. (2019)	SVM	86.04 90.29	Combining GLCM and SVM obtained better accuracy in crop-type classification.
Mulyono (2016)	SVM	90.78	It can be applied to all other crop-growing areas.
Devadas et al. (2012)	Object-based SVM	95	The object-based approach is superior to the pixel-based approach.
	Pixel-based classification (Maximum Likelihood Classification)	89	
Xin and Adler (2019)	Convolutional LSTM	98.8	Both models perform well and give better accuracy.
	3-layer fully connected neural network	92	
Mazarire et al. (2020)	Random Forest	85	Sentinel-2 data performs better in SVM classifier in comparison with the RF classifier.
	SVM	95	
Crisóstomo de Castro Filho et al. (2020)	Bi-LSTM	99.14	Analyze non-periodic time series data.
	LSTM	98.86	
Xu et al. (2020)	LSTM	95	Exploiting NDVI and Enhanced Vegetation Index (EVI) profiles is necessary.
Belgiu and Csillik (2018)	TWDTW	96.2	Misclassification in all test classes.
	RF	97.6	
Verma et al. (2017)	DT	87.93	ISODATA and MLC algorithms are unable to classify accurately.
Zhao et al. (2019)	U-Net	96.26	Without extracting the features from RGB images, the outcome is better when compared with the multi-spectral image in recognizing the rice lodging.
Adrian et al. (2021)	3D U-Net	99.20	3D CNN provides results with high accuracy than 2D CNN for crop mapping.
	2D U-Net	94.30	
	SegNet	87.10	
Liu et al. (2022)	U-Net	92.14	The model has a better ability for crop classification and crop recognition.

(Continued)

TABLE 2.1 (*Continued*)

Comparison of Different Crop Mapping Classification Using Machine Learning and Deep Learning

Authors	ML/DL Classifier	Accuracy (%)	Advantages
Wang et al. (2021)	RF	95.04	Geo CBAM-CNN model spontaneously distributed different weights to features and attained better accuracy compared to another model.
	CNN	96.43	
	CBAM-CNN	97.13	
	Geo CBAM-CNN	97.82	
Li et al. (2022)	1D CNN	67.29	It improves classification accuracy quickly, which is a new motivation for crop classification.
	GDSSM	71.26	
	GDSSM-CNN	91.20	
Moreno-Revelo et al. (2021)	2D-CNN	81.00	It is capable of dealing with imbalanced classes and low-spatial-resolution images.

with 100% accuracy denoting an accurate classification in which all references are correctly categorized, which is shown in Equation (2.2):

$$Overall\ accuracy = \frac{Correctly\ classified\ samples}{overall\ data} \qquad (2.2)$$

2.3.3 PRODUCER'S ACCURACY

PA is fully based on the classification. PA is the map's correctness as seen by the map maker (the producer) (De Wit and Clevers, 2004, Foody, 2005). This is the frequency with which real features on the ground are appropriately depicted on the classified map (Enderle and Weih, 2005). PA is well-defined in Equation (2.3):

$$Producer\ accuracy = \frac{No.\ of\ pixels\ are\ correct\ classification\ in\ each\ category}{Total\ no.\ of\ pixel\ classified\ in\ that\ category\ (row)} * 100$$
$$(2.3)$$

The correctness from the perspective of a map user, rather than the map developer, is known as the user's accuracy (Virnodkar et al., 2020). The user's accuracy basically conveys to us how frequently the class on the map will be existing on the ground (Liu et al., 2007), which is well defined in Equation (2.4).

$$User\ accuracy = \frac{No.\ of\ pixels\ are\ correct\ classification\ in\ each\ category}{Total\ no.\ of\ pixel\ classified\ in\ that\ category\ (column)} * 100$$
$$(2.4)$$

2.4 CONCLUSION AND FUTURE WORK

This chapter concludes that the crop mapping accuracy level attained for regions of variability and small field area is reasonably low. The dependability of results obtained at agricultural field boundaries is also relatively low. It is significantly more difficult to predict the categorization of crop mapping using these methods than to get a general judgment. Fewer characteristics were extracted and examined for crop mapping, resulting in a decline in precision. During the growth season, the phenological stages of a crop have a significant impact on the amount of accuracy acquired using present methodologies. For greater precision, the crop's phenological stages must be considered. For all types of crop mapping, a new and universal method must be proposed rather than one for a specific crop. Thus, the shortcomings of the research work augment the need for creating an approach to perform crop-type mapping systems. The observation showed that integrated CNN and DAM got higher classification accuracy than other classification techniques. Thus, integrated models provide higher accuracy results than individual crop mapping models. In addition, appropriate steps should be carefully carried out in the image pre-processing process to eliminate the accumulation of errors, and it is important to come up with a new automated way to map crop types in a certain area with high accuracy and less processing time.

REFERENCES

Adrian, J., Sagan, V., & Maimaitijiang, M. (2021). Sentinel SAR-optical fusion for crop type mapping using deep learning and Google Earth Engine. *ISPRS Journal of Photogrammetry and Remote Sensing, 175*, 215–235.

Akbari, E., Darvishi Boloorani, A., Neysani Samany, N., Hamzeh, S., Soufizadeh, S., & Pignatti, S. (2020). Crop mapping using random forest and particle swarm optimization based on multi-temporal Sentinel-2. *Remote Sensing, 12*(9), 1449.

Behera, M. D., Biradar, C., Das, P., & Chowdary, V. M. (2019). Developing quantifiable approaches for delineating suitable options for irrigating fallow areas during dry season—A case study from Eastern India. *Environmental Monitoring and Assessment, 191*(Suppl 3), 805.

Behera, M. D., Tripathi, P., Das, P., Srivastava, S. K., Roy, P. S., Joshi, C., Behera, P. R., Deka, J., Kumar, P., Khan, M. L., Tripathi, O. P., Dash, T., & Krishnamurthy, Y. V. N. (2018). Remote sensing based deforestation analysis in Mahanadi and Brahmaputra river basin in India since 1985. *Journal of Environmental Management, 206*, 1192–1203.

Belgiu, M., & Csillik, O. (2018). Sentinel-2 cropland mapping using pixel-based and object-based time-weighted dynamic time warping analysis. *Remote Sensing of Environment, 204*, 509–523.

Bunkhumpornpat, C., Sinapiromsaran, K., & Lursinsap, C. (2009). Safe-level-smote: Safe-level-synthetic minority over-sampling technique for handling the class imbalanced problem. In *Pacific-Asia Conference on Knowledge Discovery and Data Mining* (pp. 475–482). Springer, Berlin, Heidelberg.

Camps-Valls, G., Gómez-Chova, L., Calpe-Maravilla, J., Soria-Olivas, E., Martín-Guerrero, J. D., & Moreno, J. (2003). Support vector machines for crop classification using hyperspectral data. In *Iberian Conference on Pattern Recognition and Image Analysis* (pp. 134–141). Springer, Berlin, Heidelberg.

Chang, Y. L., Tan, T. H., Chen, T. H., Chuah, J. H., Chang, L., Wu, M. C., Tatini, N. B., Ma, S. C., & Alkhaleefah, M. (2022). Spatial-temporal neural network for rice field classification from SAR images. *Remote Sensing, 14*(8), 1929.

Chawla, N. V. (2009). Data mining for imbalanced datasets: An overview. *Data Mining and Knowledge Discovery Handbook*. Springer, Boston, MA. (875–886).

Chawla, N. V., Bowyer, K. W., Hall, L. O., & Kegelmeyer, W. P. (2002). SMOTE: Synthetic minority over-sampling technique. *Journal of Artificial Intelligence Research, 16*, 321–357.

Chen, X., Vierling, L., & Deering, D. (2005). A simple and effective radiometric correction method to improve landscape change detection across sensors and across time. *Remote Sensing of Environment*, *98*(1), 63–79.

Cheng, M., Jiao, X., Shi, L., Penuelas, J., Kumar, L., Nie, C., Wu, T., Liu, K., Wu, W., & Jin, X. (2022). High-resolution crop yield and water productivity dataset generated using random forest and remote sensing. *Scientific Data*, *9*(1), 1–13.

Crisóstomo de Castro Filho, H., Abílio de Carvalho Júnior, O., Ferreira de Carvalho, O. L., Pozzobon de Bem, P., dos Santos de Moura, R., Olino de Albuquerque, A., Rosa Silva, C., Guimaraes Ferreira, P. H., Fontes Guimarães, R., & Trancoso Gomes, R. A. (2020). Rice crop detection using LSTM, bi-LSTM, and machine learning models from sentinel-1 time series. *Remote Sensing*, *12*(16), 2655.

De Wit, A. J. W., & Clevers, J. G. P. W. (2004). Efficiency and accuracy of per-field classification for operational crop mapping. *International Journal of Remote Sensing*, *25*(20), 4091–4112.

Devadas, R., Denham, R. J., & Pringle, M. (2012). Support vector machine classification of object-based data for crop mapping, using multi-temporal landsat imagery. *International Archives of the Photogrammetry, Remote Sensing and Spatial Information Sciences*, *39*(1), 185–190.

Dhumal, R. K., Vibhute, A. D., Nagne, A. D., Solankar, M. M., Gaikwad, S. V., Kale, K. V., & Mehrotra, S. C. (2019). A spatial and spectral feature based approach for classification of crops using techniques based on GLCM and SVM. In *Microelectronics, Electromagnetics and Telecommunications* (pp. 45–53). Springer, Singapore.

Enderle, D. I., & Weih, R. C., Jr. (2005). Integrating supervised and unsupervised classification methods to develop a more accurate land cover classification. *Journal of the Arkansas Academy of Science*, *59*(1), 65–73.

Foody, G. M. (2005). Local characterization of thematic classification accuracy through spatially constrained confusion matrices. *International Journal of Remote Sensing*, *26*(6), 1217–1228.

Fraser, R. S., Ferrare, R. A., Kaufman, Y. J., Markham, B. L., & Mattoo, S. (1992). Algorithm for atmospheric corrections of aircraft and satellite imagery. *International Journal of Remote Sensing*, *13*(3), 541–557.

Gallo, I., Ranghetti, L., Landro, N., La Grassa, R., & Boschetti, M. (2023). In-season and dynamic crop mapping using 3D convolution neural networks and sentinel-2 time series. *ISPRS Journal of Photogrammetry and Remote Sensing*, *195*, 335–352.

Hadjimitsis, D. G., Papadavid, G., Agapiou, A., Themistocleous, K., Hadjimitsis, M. G., Retalis, A., … & Clayton, C. R. I. (2010). Atmospheric correction for satellite remotely sensed data intended for agricultural applications: Impact on vegetation indices. *Natural Hazards and Earth System Sciences*, *10*(1), 89–95.

Harris, C., & Stephens, M. (1988). A combined corner and edge detector. *Alvey Vision Conference*, *15*(50), 10.5244.

He, H., Bai, Y., Garcia, E. A., & Li, S. (2008). ADASYN: Adaptive synthetic sampling approach for imbalanced learning. In *2008 IEEE International Joint Conference on Neural Networks (IEEE World Congress on Computational Intelligence)* (pp. 1322–1328). IEEE.

Hudait, M., & Patel, P. P. (2018). Acreage analysis of Betel vine crop through Boroj detection from high resolution imagery and internal architectural layout in Moyna Block of Tamluk Subdivision, Purba Medinipur. *Geoinformatics for Sustainable Environment Management*, *1*, 69–82.

Hudait, M., & Patel, P. P. (2022). Crop-type mapping and acreage estimation in smallholding plots using Sentinel-2 images and machine learning algorithms: Some comparisons. *The Egyptian Journal of Remote Sensing and Space Science*, *25*(1), 147–156.

Ibrahim, E. S., Rufin, P., Nill, L., Kamali, B., Nendel, C., & Hostert, P. (2021). Mapping crop types and cropping systems in nigeria with sentinel-2 imagery. *Remote Sensing*, *13*(17), 3523.

Johansen, K., Dunne, A. F., Tu, Y. H., Almashharawi, S., Jones, B. H., & McCabe, M. F. (2022). Dye tracing and concentration mapping in coastal waters using unmanned aerial vehicles. *Scientific Reports, 12*(1), 1–11.

Jothiaruna, N., Sundar, K. J. A., & Karthikeyan, B. (2019). A segmentation method for disease spot images incorporating chrominance in comprehensive color feature and region growing. *Computers and Electronics in Agriculture, 165*, 104934.

Kasimati, A., Espejo-García, B., Darra, N., & Fountas, S. (2022). Predicting grape sugar content under quality attributes using normalized difference vegetation index data and automated machine learning. *Sensors, 22*(9), 3249.

Khobragade, A. N., & Raghuwanshi, M. M. (2015). Contextual soft classification approaches for crops identification using multi-sensory remote sensing data: Machine learning perspective for satellite images. In *Artificial Intelligence Perspectives and Applications* (pp. 333–346). Springer, Cham.

Kpienbaareh, D., Sun, X., Wang, J., Luginaah, I., Bezner Kerr, R., Lupafya, E., & Dakishoni, L. (2021). Crop type and land cover mapping in northern Malawi using the integration of sentinel-1, sentinel-2, and planetscope satellite data. *Remote Sensing, 13*(4), 700.

Kuemmerle, T., Erb, K., Meyfroidt, P., Müller, D., Verburg, P. H., Estel, S., Haberl, H., Hostert, P., Jepsen, M. R., Kastner, T., & Levers, C. (2013). Challenges and opportunities in mapping land use intensity globally. *Current Opinion in Environmental Sustainability, 5*(5), 484–493.

Kumar, M., & Singh, R. K. (2013). Digital image processing of remotely sensed satellite images for information extraction. In *Conference on Advances in Communication and Control Systems (CAC2S 2013)* (pp. 406–410). Atlantis Press.

Kwak, G. H., Park, C. W., Lee, K. D., Na, S. I., Ahn, H. Y., & Park, N. W. (2021). Potential of hybrid CNN-RF model for early crop mapping with limited input data. *Remote Sensing, 13*(9), 1629.

Li, H., Lu, J., Tian, G., Yang, H., Zhao, J., & Li, N. (2022). Crop classification based on GDSSM-CNN using multi-temporal RADARSAT-2 SAR with limited labeled data. *Remote Sensing, 14*(16), 3889.

Liu, C., Frazier, P., & Kumar, L. (2007). Comparative assessment of the measures of thematic classification accuracy. *Remote Sensing of Environment, 107*(4), 606–616.

Liu, Y., Rao, P., Zhou, W., Singh, B., Srivastava, A. K., Poonia, S., Berkel, P., & Jain, D. V. (2022). Using Sentinel-1, Sentinel-2, and Planet satellite data to map field-level tillage practices in smallholder systems. *PLoS One, 17*(11), e0277425.

Liu, Z., Su, B., & Lv, F. (2022). Intelligent identification method of crop species using improved U-Net network in UAV remote sensing image. *Scientific Programming*, Article ID 9717843, 1–9.

Liu, Y., Wang, E., Yang, X., & Wang, J. (2010). Contributions of climatic and crop varietal changes to crop production in the North China Plain, since 1980s. *Global Change Biology, 16*(8), 2287–2299.

Mazarire, T. T., Ratshiedana, P. E., Nyamugama, A., Adam, E., & Chirima, G. (2020). Exploring machine learning algorithms for mapping crop types in a heterogeneous agriculture landscape using Sentinel-2 data. A case study of Free State Province, South Africa. *South African Journal of Geomatics, 9*(2), 333–347.

Moravec, H. P. (1981). Rover Visual Obstacle Avoidance. In *IJCAI* (Vol. 81, pp. 785–790).

Moreno-Revelo, M. Y., Guachi-Guachi, L., Gómez-Mendoza, J. B., Revelo-Fuelagán, J., & Peluffo-Ordóñez, D. H. (2021). Enhanced convolutional-neural-network architecture for crop classification. *Applied Sciences, 11*(9), 4292.

Moumni, A., & Lahrouni, A. (2021). Machine learning-based classification for crop-type mapping using the fusion of high-resolution satellite imagery in a semiarid area. *Scientifica*, Article ID 8810279, 1–20.

Mulyono, S. (2016). Identifying sugarcane plantation using LANDSAT-8 images with support vector machines. In *IOP Conference Series: Earth and Environmental Science* (Vol. 47, No. 1, p. 012008). IOP Publishing.

Munawar, H. S., Hammad, A. W., Waller, S. T., Thaheem, M. J., & Shrestha, A. (2021). An integrated approach for post-disaster flood management via the use of cutting-edge technologies and UAVs: A review. *Sustainability*, *13*(14), 7925.

Navalgund, R. R., Jayaraman, V., & Roy, P. S. (2007). Remote sensing applications: An overview. *Current Science*, *93*(12), 1747–1766.

Nguyen, D., Zhao, Y., Zhang, Y., Huynh, A. N. L., Roosta, F., Hammer, G., Chapman, S., & Potgieter, A. (2022). Crop type prediction utilising a long short-term memory with a self-attention for winter crops in Australia. In *IGARSS 2022-2022 IEEE International Geoscience and Remote Sensing Symposium* (pp. 2742–2745). IEEE.

Ok, A. O., Akar, O., & Gungor, O. (2012). Evaluation of random forest method for agricultural crop classification. *European Journal of Remote Sensing*, *45*(1), 421–432.

Pons, X., Pesquer, L., Cristóbal, J., & González-Guerrero, O. (2014). Automatic and improved radiometric correction of Landsat imagery using reference values from MODIS surface reflectance images. *International Journal of Applied Earth Observation and Geoinformation*, *33*, 243–254.

Prins, A. J., & Van Niekerk, A. (2021). Crop type mapping using LiDAR, Sentinel-2 and aerial imagery with machine learning algorithms. *Geo-Spatial Information Science*, *24*(2), 215–227.

Rahman, M. S., & Di, L. (2020). A systematic review on case studies of remote-sensing-based flood crop loss assessment. *Agriculture*, *10*(4), 131.

Rodriguez-Galiano, V. F., Ghimire, B., Rogan, J., Chica-Olmo, M., & Rigol-Sanchez, J. P. (2012). An assessment of the effectiveness of a random forest classifier for land-cover classification. *ISPRS Journal of Photogrammetry and Remote Sensing*, *67*, 93–104.

Rogan, J., & Chen, D. (2004). Remote sensing technology for mapping and monitoring land-cover and land-use change. *Progress in Planning*, *61*(4), 301–325.

Roy, P. S., Behera, M. D., & Srivastav, S. K. (2017). Satellite remote sensing: Sensors, applications and techniques. *Proceedings of the National Academy of Sciences, India Section A: Physical Sciences*, *87*(4), 465–472.

Rußwurm, M., & Korner, M. (2017). Temporal vegetation modelling using long short-term memory networks for crop identification from medium-resolution multi-spectral satellite images. In *Proceedings of the IEEE Conference on Computer Vision and Pattern Recognition Workshops* (pp. 11–19).

Saad El Imanni, H., El Harti, A., Hssaisoune, M., Velastegui-Montoya, A., Elbouzidi, A., Addi, M., EI Iysaouy, L., & El Hachimi, J. (2022). Rapid and automated approach for early crop mapping using Sentinel-1 and Sentinel-2 on Google Earth Engine; A case of a highly heterogeneous and fragmented agricultural region. *Journal of Imaging*, *8*(12), 316.

Schmale Iii, D. G., Dingus, B. R., & Reinholtz, C. (2008). Development and application of an autonomous unmanned aerial vehicle for precise aerobiological sampling above agricultural fields. *Journal of Field Robotics*, *25*(3), 133–147.

Seydi, S. T., Amani, M., & Ghorbanian, A. (2022). A dual attention convolutional neural network for crop classification using time-series Sentinel-2 imagery. *Remote Sensing*, *14*(3), 498.

Singh, R. K., Rizvi, J., Behera, M. D., & Biradar, C. (2021). Automated crop type mapping using time-weighted dynamic time warping-a basis to derive inputs for enhanced food and nutritional security. *Current Research in Environmental Sustainability*, *3*, 100032.

Siriseriwan, W., & Sinapiromsaran, K. (2017). Adaptive neighbor synthetic minority oversampling technique under 1NN outcast handling. *Songklanakarin Journal of Science & Technology*, *39*(5), 565–576.

Sonobe, R., Tani, H., Wang, X., Kobayashi, N., & Shimamura, H. (2014). Random forest classification of crop type using multi-temporal TerraSAR-X dual-polarimetric data. *Remote Sensing Letters, 5*(2), 157–164.

Sun, Z., Di, L., Fang, H., & Burgess, A. (2020). Deep learning classification for crop types in north dakota. *IEEE Journal of Selected Topics in Applied Earth Observations and Remote Sensing, 13*, 2200–2213.

Susan, S., & Kumar, A. (2021). The balancing trick: Optimized sampling of imbalanced data-sets—A brief survey of the recent State of the Art. *Engineering Reports, 3*(4), e12298.

Tomek, I. (1976). A generalization of the k-NN rule. *IEEE Transactions on Systems, Man, and Cybernetics, SMC -6*(2), 121–126.

Useya, J., & Chen, S. (2019). Exploring the potential of mapping cropping patterns on small-holder scale croplands using sentinel-1 SAR data. *Chinese Geographical Science, 29*(4), 626–639.

Valdar, W., Holmes, C. C., Mott, R., & Flint, J. (2009). Mapping in structured populations by resample model averaging. *Genetics, 182*(4), 1263–1277.

Verma, A. K., Garg, P. K., & Hari Prasad, K. S. (2017). Sugarcane crop identification from LISS IV data using ISODATA, MLC, and indices based decision tree approach. *Arabian Journal of Geosciences, 10*(1), 1–17.

Vicente, L. E., & De Souza Filho, C. R. (2011). Identification of mineral components in tropical soils using reflectance spectroscopy and advanced spaceborne thermal emission and reflection radiometer (ASTER) data. *Remote Sensing of Environment, 115*(8), 1824–1836.

Vieira, S. M., Kaymak, U., & Sousa, J. M. (2010). Cohen's kappa coefficient as a performance measure for feature selection. In *International Conference on Fuzzy Systems* (pp. 1–8). IEEE.

Virnodkar, S. S., Pachghare, V. K., Patil, V. C., & Jha, S. K. (2020). Application of machine learning on remote sensing data for sugarcane crop classification: A review. *ICT Analysis and Applications, 93*, 539–555.

Vuolo, F., Neuwirth, M., Immitzer, M., Atzberger, C., & Ng, W. T. (2018). How much does multi-temporal Sentinel-2 data improve crop type classification? *International Journal of Applied Earth Observation and Geoinformation, 72*, 122–130.

Waldner, F., Chen, Y., Lawes, R., & Hochman, Z. (2019). Needle in a haystack: Mapping rare and infrequent crops using satellite imagery and data balancing methods. *Remote Sensing of Environment, 233*, 111375.

Wang, Y., Zhang, Z., Feng, L., Ma, Y., & Du, Q. (2021). A new attention-based CNN approach for crop mapping using time series Sentinel-2 images. *Computers and Electronics in Agriculture, 184*, 106090.

Wei, S., Zhang, H., Wang, C., Wang, Y., & Xu, L. (2019). Multi-temporal SAR data large-scale crop mapping based on U-Net model. *Remote Sensing, 11*(1), 68.

Whyte, A., Ferentinos, K. P., & Petropoulos, G. P. (2018). A new synergistic approach for monitoring wetlands using Sentinels-1 and 2 data with object-based machine learning algorithms. *Environmental Modelling & Software, 104*, 40–54.

Wilson, D. L. (1972). Asymptotic properties of nearest neighbor rules using edited data. *IEEE Transactions on Systems, Man, and Cybernetics, 3*, 408–421.

Xavier, A. C., Rudorff, B. F., Shimabukuro, Y. E., Berka, L. M. S., & Moreira, M. A. (2006). Multi-temporal analysis of MODIS data to classify sugarcane crop. *International Journal of Remote Sensing, 27*(4), 755–768.

Xin, Y., & Adler, P. R. (2019). Mapping miscanthus using multi-temporal convolutional neural network and google earth engine. In *Proceedings of the 3rd ACM SIGSPATIAL International Workshop on AI for Geographic Knowledge Discovery* (pp. 81–84).

Xu, J., Zhu, Y., Zhong, R., Lin, Z., Xu, J., Jiang, H., Huang, J., Li, H., & Lin, T. (2020). DeepCropMapping: A multi-temporal deep learning approach with improved spatial generalizability for dynamic corn and soybean mapping. *Remote Sensing of Environment, 247*, 111946.

Yan, S., Yao, X., Zhu, D., Liu, D., Zhang, L., Yu, G., Gao, B., Yang, J., & Yun, W. (2021). Large-scale crop mapping from multi-source optical satellite imageries using machine learning with discrete grids. *International Journal of Applied Earth Observation and Geoinformation, 103*, 102485.

You, N., Dong, J., Huang, J., Du, G., Zhang, G., He, Y., Yang, T., Di, Y., & Xiao, X. (2021). The 10-m crop type maps in Northeast China during 2017–2019. *Scientific Data, 8*(1), 1–11.

Zhang, H., Gao, M., & Ren, C. (2022). Feature-ensemble-based crop mapping for multi-temporal Sentinel-2 data using oversampling algorithms and gray wolf optimizer support vector machine. *Remote Sensing, 14*(20), 5259.

Zhao, X., Yuan, Y., Song, M., Ding, Y., Lin, F., Liang, D., & Zhang, D. (2019). Use of unmanned aerial vehicle imagery and deep learning unet to extract rice lodging. *Sensors, 19*(18), 3859.

Zhao, H., Zhang, M., & Chen, F. (2021). GAN-GL: Generative adversarial networks for glacial lake mapping. *Remote Sensing, 13*(22), 4728.

Zhou, Y. N., Luo, J., Feng, L., Yang, Y., Chen, Y., & Wu, W. (2019). Long-short-term-memory-based crop classification using high-resolution optical images and multi-temporal SAR data. *GIScience & Remote Sensing, 56*(8), 1170–1191.

3 Artificial Intelligence in Precision Agriculture

A Systematic Review on Tools, Techniques, and Applications

J. Dhakshayani, B. Surendiran, and J. Jyothsna

3.1 PRECISION AGRICULTURE – AN INTRODUCTION

Precision agriculture (PA) is a comprehensive data and yields production framework. The goal of PA is to increase long-term, site-specific production efficiency, economic output, and profit growth while reducing unpredictable consequences on wildlife and the environment [1]. Although production has increased thanks to genetic advancement, pesticide techniques, irrigation, and farm equipment, this hasn't been enough to keep up with population growth's constant need. Global food security and the environment are both threatened by rising demand. Numerous cutting-edge initiatives have been attempted to enable sustainable agricultural production. One of the initiatives made during the early 1990s was the Precision Farming System (PFS). Based on the information and technology, this manifested itself in many ways.

Due to the inputs in the current situation being of the ideal quantity and having enhanced yield in comparison, PA in India differs from classic models. Data, innovation, and control from a collaborative system are the fundamental components of PA, which increase crop output, production quality, and energy efficiency while preserving the environment. While implementing PA, the general public should be environmentally conscious. In order to enable the sustainability of natural resources (such as water, air, and soil quality), conventional agricultural management must be changed. The basic steps followed in PA are illustrated in Figure 3.1.

Further explanation of the five "Rs" in the PA [2] is as follows:

- Right time
- Right input
- Right place
- Right amount
- Right manner

Site-specific management is the term for this. The primary threat to conventional agricultural systems is market-based international competition in agricultural goods. Hence PA's focus is on this issue. As we map the factors of soil, crop, and field

DOI: 10.1201/9781003391302-3

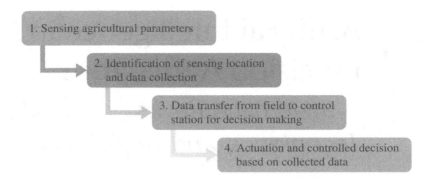

FIGURE 3.1   Fundamental process of PA.

environment in PA, we must gather enormous amounts of data from various sources. PA is referred to as being "information intense" as a result [3]. Figure 3.2 represents the overall study of this proposed work.

The structure of this chapter is organized as follows. Section 3.2 presents the tools and techniques in PA. In Section 3.3, we present applications of artificial intelligence (AI). In Section 3.4, we described the machine learning (ML) and role of ML in PA. Sections 3.5 and 3.6 explain the role of big data and cloud computing in PA. We deliberated the present status and hurdles of PA in India in Section 3.7.

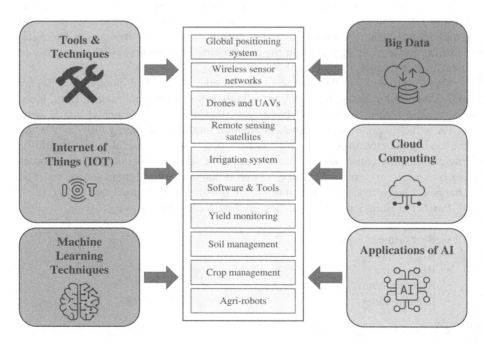

FIGURE 3.2   Graphical representation of the overall workflow in PA.

3.2 TOOLS AND TECHNIQUES IN PRECISION AGRICULTURE

The PA involves various tools and techniques, which are briefed later.

3.2.1 GLOBAL POSITIONING SYSTEM (GPS)

PA's key tool is the Global Positioning System (GPS). It is defined as a satellite-based navigation system that permits the detection of region (100–0.01 m) [3]. This includes details about that particular area of the field, including its latitude, longitude, and elevation, to identify information on the crops, water, soil, impediments, pest activity, weed invasion, and other pertinent items there. PA is possible for a user with an advanced and precise location positioning system. GPS has several advantages, including the ability to map soil and crop measurements, apply inputs to specific regions, monitor yields, and manage farms. Some of the key ways that GPS is used in PA include as follows:

Crop Monitoring: GPS can be used to track the location and growth of crops, providing valuable information about crop health and yields. This information can be used to optimize planting and harvesting schedules and to identify areas of the field that may need additional resources or attention [4].

Vehicle Guidance: GPS-based vehicle guidance systems can be used to help farmers navigate their fields, reducing the need for manual labor and improving the accuracy and efficiency of planting, harvesting, and other operations [5].

Livestock Tracking: GPS-based tracking systems can be used to monitor the location and movements of livestock, helping farmers to manage their herds more effectively and to improve the overall health and welfare of their animals [6].

Yield Monitoring: GPS-based yield monitoring systems can be used to track crop yields in real time, providing valuable information about crop health and productivity. This information can be used to make informed decisions about fertilizer application, irrigation, and other important aspects of crop management [7].

Soil Sampling: GPS-based soil sampling systems can be used to identify areas of a field that have different soil properties, such as pH levels, nutrient content, and water retention. This information can then be used to optimize fertilization and irrigation practices and to improve crop health and yields [8].

Variable Rate Technology: GPS-based variable rate technology (VRT) systems can be used to apply inputs, such as fertilizer or pesticides, at different rates depending on the specific needs of different areas of a field. This helps farmers to reduce waste, lower costs, and improve the overall efficiency and sustainability of their operations.

Automated Irrigation: GPS-based irrigation systems can be used to automate the application of water to crops, reducing the need for manual labor and improving the accuracy and efficiency of irrigation practices.

3.2.2 GEOGRAPHIC INFORMATION SYSTEM (GIS)

A rebellious piece of technology that makes it possible to deal with data connected to a spatially mapped area of the globe is the geographic information system (GIS). It is a repository designed especially to manage map data. Geographical data from several sources may be more easily stored and organized in various layers owing to GIS software. Each GIS coverage is made up of topologically related geographic elements. It possesses computation and analysis power that produces complicated field views and creates sound agrotechnological judgments. GIS cannot be confused with the actual decision-making systems, though. For data synthesis and decision-support systems across a range of fields, GIS systems are essential [9]. Many commercial agriculture information management tools are available, including ADAPT, SST software, SpiderWeb GIS, AGERmetrix, AgVerdict Inc., WinGIS, Trimble, FieldView, and others.

In particular, software-based agricultural management tools [10] promote automation in gathering and processing of data, monitoring, planning, maintaining records, making decisions, and managing agricultural operations. In addition, these systems assist with fundamental tracking activities, namely crop production and management, field work scheduling, monitoring soil nutrient levels, weather forecasting, field mapping, and other intricate activities for automating field management. For various precision agricultural applications, a specialized GIS was built called the farm management information system (FMIS) [11].

Geographic information system (GIS) technology is widely adopted in PA for a variety of purposes, including:

Field Mapping: GIS can be used to create accurate, detailed maps of agricultural fields, including information about crop types, soil properties, topography, and other relevant features. These maps can be used to plan planting and harvesting operations, to monitor crop growth, and to track the movement of machinery.

Crop Monitoring: GIS can be used to track the location and growth of crops in real time, providing valuable information about crop health and yields. This information can be used to make informed decisions about planting and harvesting schedules and to identify areas of the field that may need additional resources or attention.

Climate Monitoring: GIS can be used to collect and analyze data on temperature, precipitation, and other climatic factors, helping farmers to understand the impact of weather conditions on crop growth and to make informed decisions about planting, harvesting, and other operations.

Soil Sampling: GIS can be used to collect and analyze soil sample data, providing valuable information about soil properties and fertility, which can then be used to optimize fertilization and irrigation practices.

Yield Monitoring: GIS-based yield monitoring systems can be used to track crop yields in real time, providing valuable information about crop health and productivity. This information can be used to make informed decisions about fertilizer application, irrigation, and other important aspects of crop management.

Data Management: GIS provides a powerful platform for managing and analyzing large amounts of data from various sources, including yield monitors, soil sensors, weather stations, and more. This data can be used to make informed decisions about crop management, resource allocation, and other important aspects of PA.

3.2.3 WIRELESS SENSOR NETWORKS (WSN)

The efficient implementation of smart farming is hampered by the gathering and analysis of vast data generated by IoT networks and wireless sensor networks (WSN), including images and other data from Unmanned Aerial Vehicles (UAVs), satellites. Emerging technologies in AI and data mining offer prospective ways to form opinions from this information [12–14]. These methods can help analyze wider and more unexpected amounts of data and accurately identify correlations. For various reasons examined later, farming has not placed enough value on these methods' capacity to analyze enormous amounts of data.

It possesses computation and analysis power that produces complicated field views and creates sound agrotechnological judgments. As a result of advancements in sensor development, sensors are now substantially more accurate. In Pennsylvania, sensors are mostly used to determine things like humidity, vegetation, temperature, texture, structure, physical character, humidity, nutrition profile, water vapor, and air. These data are processed and analyzed to produce useful information that supports PA's goals [3].

3.2.3.1 Adoption of WSNs in PA

WSN technology has been widely adopted in PA for a variety of purposes, including crop monitoring, environmental monitoring, livestock monitoring, yield monitoring, machine monitoring, data management, and more. For example, WSNs can be used to monitor the health and growth of crops and to make informed decisions about irrigation, fertilization, and other important aspects of crop management. WSNs can also be used to monitor the environment in agricultural fields and to optimize planting and harvesting schedules. Additionally, WSNs can be used to monitor the health and behavior of livestock, providing valuable information about animal welfare and productivity.

3.2.3.2 Benefits of WSNs in PA

WSN technology provides a wide range of benefits to farmers, researchers, and other stakeholders in PA. For example, WSNs provide real-time information about the location and status of crops, livestock, and other resources, allowing farmers to respond quickly to changing conditions and to make informed decisions in real time. Additionally, WSNs provide a powerful platform for collecting and managing large amounts of data from various sources, including sensors in the field, yield monitors, and weather stations. This data can be used to make informed decisions about crop management, resource allocation, and other important aspects of PA.

3.2.4 DRONES AND ROBOTS

Drones are adaptable and have been used across many industries, including agriculture. Drones' use in PA has considerably expanded since AI was integrated into them since it is practical for farmers. Drones are useful for several tasks, including data collecting, disease diagnosis, crop and field monitoring, and many PA procedures, such as input spraying and surveillance. The goal of AI has always been to reduce the amount of work that humans must do to use this innovative technology. This PA sector is the crucial industries that require automation and smart gadgets that can carry out tasks that require human intervention [15].

As part of an efficient approach to precision agricultural method, the use of UAVs (drones and remote aircraft) in agricultural production is growing steadily. This technology enables agri-engineers, farmers, and geologists to help their processes while using powerful information analytics to gain insightful knowledge about the crops. UAVs have made meticulous plant monitoring over vast agricultural land areas feasible, allowing for the identification of optimal crop suggestions and the ability to estimate production using more accurate data [16].

Overall, the adoption of drones and robots in PA provides farmers with new ways to improve crop yields, reduce waste, and enhance the sustainability of their operations. As technology continues to evolve, it is likely that drones and robots will play an increasingly important role in PA, helping farmers to stay ahead of the curve and to take advantage of new opportunities for improvement and innovation.

3.2.5 SATELLITES

Compared to conventional approaches, satellite data offers various benefits for PA, especially in terms of fast decision-making processes, portrayal, and coverage. Many crucial issues are addressed with the help of space data, including estimating crop area, production, crop stages, obtaining fundamental soil data, crop management research, and more [17]. Because satellite photos are used to characterize a grower's fields precisely and are frequently combined with GISs, satellites are also good in the form of management tools in PA. With this information, farmers can create comprehensive maps of their fields, assess crop health and growth, and identify areas that may need extra attention or resources [18]. For instance, satellites can gauge the chlorophyll content of crops to determine their health and productivity. This enables more intensive and effective cultivation operations [19].

3.2.6 PRECISION IRRIGATION SYSTEM

Precision irrigation systems are an essential component of PA. These systems aim to provide the right amount of water to crops at the right time, based on their needs and environmental conditions. The system uses advanced sensors and software to monitor soil moisture levels, weather conditions, and plant growth and then adjusts the amount of water provided to the crops accordingly. This helps to conserve water resources, improve crop yields, and reduce the risk of crop damage from over- or under-watering. Precision irrigation systems also help to minimize water waste and reduce runoff, which can have significant environmental and economic benefits. They can be integrated with other PA technologies, such as GPS and remote sensing, to provide a comprehensive approach to managing crop production. In summary, precision irrigation systems are a critical component of modern agriculture that helps to increase crop productivity while reducing the impact on the environment.

A crucial technology in PA is a sprinkler irrigation system with GPS-based controllers. These irrigation systems use WSNs to monitor the soil and surrounding conditions as well as the operating parameters, such as flow and pressure levels, of the irrigation system [9].

Several DSS (decision support systems) proposed in the literature take into account various use cases with various goals. Using data on soil moisture and climate [13] built a DSS to predict the periodic irrigation needs for citrus. This uses a soil management system to reduce inaccuracies. The effectiveness of the employment of DSS technologies is influenced by their simplicity, efficiency, financial sustainability, significance among farmers.

3.2.7   SOFTWARE, OPEN-SOURCE FRAMEWORKS, AND TOOLKITS

There are software developed for various purposes, *viz.*, mapping, map generators, variable-rate applications, overlay of maps, advanced geostatistical features, and statistical tools. IoT enables new agricultural management systems, namely remotely controlling a safe-driving vehicle, which enhances software maintenance. The modern-day IoT and PA's ability permit concurrent control of numerous equipment components [20]. The use of software decision-making tools in PA is considered to be important since such technologies improve management effectiveness. However, research remains to be performed to make innovation-based tools sufficiently desirable, easy to use, and environmentally friendly. However, manufacturers must have the proper training for managing such tools.

The PA makes extensive use of contemporary technology, like as information and communication technologies, to boost and enhance the effectiveness and productivity of agro-ecosystems. For data storage, analysis, and decision-making, there are various open-source frameworks and toolkits available for PA. Some of the popular toolkits are listed in the following:

TensorFlow: It is a free open-source ML framework that can be used to assess and forecast outcomes in PA. It, for instance, may be used to determine the best season for planting and harvesting based on climatic data or to estimate agricultural yields based on statistics and current climatic conditions. Because of its adaptable design, it allows programmers to develop and build machine-learning models for a diverse range of agricultural applications.

QGIS: A free, open-source GIS called QGIS is used in precision farming to organize and analyze spatial data, including soil, weather, and crop data. For representing, analyzing, and transforming geographical data, it offers a variety of capabilities. It can be used to make maps, design unique projections, and do geospatial research. In PA, it can be employed to map and track crop development across temporal as well as assess soil type and quality.

Agro-Know: An open-source platform called Agro-Know offers various precision agricultural technologies and services, such as data management, processing, and mapping. With capabilities for data discovery, access, and recovery, it offers a single repository for agricultural data. With the help of it, producers, researchers, and others may access and evaluate data to make accurate decisions regarding crop management, fertilizer use, and other challenges.

OpenCV: In order to analyze images and videos for applications including crop yield prediction and crop monitoring, PA can utilize the open-source computer vision library known as OpenCV. A variety of tools for interpreting images and videos are provided by it, such as image segmentation, object classification, and feature detection. It can be employed in PA to analyze aerial photographs of crops to spot regions of disease or damage or to calculate crop yields based on the specific plant development patterns.

DIVA-GIS: It is another open-source software package for managing, analyzing, and visualizing geographical data. Data processing, visualization of data, and data analysis capabilities are all included in DIVA-GIS, which offers a user-friendly platform for working with geographical data. With the use of DIVA-GIS, precision farmers can create maps of the soil's fertility and quality, track crop growth over time, and spot disease or stress points on the crops.

R: It is a statistical computing environment and open-source programming language that can be used to analyze and interpret enormous volumes of data in PA. It provides an extensive set of statistical tools and functions, along with a substantial user and development community that contributes tools and packages for several applications. This can be used in PA to analyze vast volumes of data, including meteorological, soil, and crop data, to help farmers decide how best to manage their crops, apply fertilizer, and more.

Each of these tools provides unique capabilities and can be used in different ways to support PA and improve the productivity and efficiency of agricultural systems. In addition, open-source tools provide the flexibility and accessibility necessary for the development of customized and innovative solutions for specific needs and challenges.

3.2.8 YIELD MONITORING

The yield monitoring method comprises several parts, including sensors, storage devices, user interfaces, computers, and control systems for integrating and coordinating these parts. Yield monitors are mounted to machinery, as tractors or combined harvesters, to collect diversified data, including grain yield, soil parameters, moisture content, and much more. In order to offer rich, important data for management information and the analysis of regional and temporal patterns, this data has been gathered over the course of more than 10 years. A GPS and yield monitoring system can be used for yield mapping [21]. The agricultural yield prediction aims to assess aspects that affect and impact production, such as irrigation, natural soil content, physical characteristics of the soil, climate and metrological conditions, crop diseases, stress, and pests. It enables effective resource management; early and accurate product estimation may provide decision-makers with a trustworthy platform from which one can determine whether there will be a shortage or surplus and then to react suitably in the context of the situation.

3.2.9 REMOTE SENSING

Remote sensing is advantageous in soil mapping, determination of climate and land characteristics, detection of crop nutrients, vegetative analysis, production forecast, pest control, evaluation of the viability of the land for agriculture, satellite-based agrometeorology services, and flood monitoring. Applications for agricultural remote sensing have increasingly used DL and CNNs [22, 23]. In order to produce structural features for semantic data, CNN requires a vast amount of data [24]. Artificial satellite-based remote sensing has played a significant role in the PA by enabling remote access to field data. The major satellites producing agriculture data [25], such as multispectral, hyperspectral data, and NIR and RGB data, are the RapidEye constellation satellite system, GeoEye-1 system, WorldView-3 system, American Landsat satellites, etc. Another main application of remote sensing with deep learning in PA is crop classification and prediction. Deep learning models can process satellite and aerial imagery to identify different crops and estimate their yield, allowing farmers to make informed decisions about crop management practices. The use of deep learning algorithms in combination with remote sensing can improve the accuracy and efficiency of crop classification and yield prediction, compared to traditional methods [18].

3.3 APPLICATIONS OF ARTIFICIAL INTELLIGENCE IN PA

The bigger goal of digital farming is to automate all PF processes by employing all of the knowledge and experience that is now accessible [26]. To gain some useful insights and advance precision farming, it primarily focuses on the "value of the data." Some experts say digital farming combines precision farming with smart farming [27]. In some places, digital farming is now a reality: For instance, GPS guidance networks for site-specific fertilization, organized traffic farming, or plant protection measures are available by means of a whole production cycle through unique cloud-based connectivity. Despite this computerized data processing that is fully linked, coordinated networks are still in agriculture and agricultural equipment's near future.

3.3.1 CROP MANAGEMENT

Regarding boosting crop output and quality, crop management is a crucial duty. Historical information is essential in crop management for this reason. For each step to be as effective as possible, PA needs vision gained from an augmented examination of data. Examples include the amount of water needed, when to water, how much fertilizer to use, and when to apply pesticides. If appropriate, real-time information is provided to the farmer using a sophisticated IoT-based management technique via email or SMS. Agriculture, in general, has benefited greatly from the use of AI and ML in PA for crop management because many parts of the industry have been improved. Predictive analytics are basically used in crop sowing to determine the ideal timing and manner for sowing. Additionally, crops can be sown using AI-assisted machinery at appropriate depths and at equal intervals. A key factor in influencing yield is choosing the right crop, and this decision is manipulated by many components, including the topography of the area, climate, kind of soil, its composition, and market trends. AI and ML aid in identifying new opportunities for all the action in agriculture should be improved [15].

3.3.2 SOIL MANAGEMENT

A thorough understanding of soil is required to increase agricultural productivity; as a result, correct soil information should be provided to achieve satisfactory soil management. Agricultural soil characteristics data, including estimates of soil moisture, dryness, temperature, and other things, are fed into a ML model that acts as a trustworthy way to deliver insightful information. As a result, it is easier to use soil management to its fullest potential for agricultural purposes [28]. Trace Genomics, situated in California, offers services for soil analysis to farmers. Illumina, the company's principal investor, contributed to the development of the system that employs ML to advise clients about the advantages and disadvantages of their soil. Users supposedly obtain an intensive description of their soil components from Trace Genomics after sending in a soil sample [9].

3.3.3 IRRIGATION AND WATER QUALITY MANAGEMENT

Sensors frequently measure the temperature and soil moisture content and transmit their findings to a processing unit or, in some cases, the sensor itself for interpretation. Real-time monitoring of water quality is also possible through the aid of the same IoT system. All of these considerations basically make irrigation and water quality management simpler. Additionally, AI-driven intelligent automated irrigation systems can continuously deliver the exact and ideal irrigation required to sustain specified soil conditions. This boosts overall yield while lowering labor expenses, manufacturing costs, and water waste. Many scientists think that wise water management in such irrigation systems will tend to have a good global water effect [15]. A smart irrigation system must be designed and managed using the estimation of evapotranspiration; however, this calculation proves challenging. AI and ML algorithms that can accurately estimate evapotranspiration can solve this problem [28].

3.3.4 AGRICULTURAL ROBOTS

Precision farming tools like agricultural robots are getting more crucial, helping farmers to improve crop yields and reduce production costs. These robots can perform a variety of tasks, including planting, harvesting, pruning, and soil analysis, allowing farmers to be more efficient and effective in their operations. One of the key advantages of agricultural robots is their ability to perform repetitive tasks with high accuracy and speed, reducing the need for manual labor and increasing the efficiency of agricultural operations.

The agriculture industry is among the most major industries around the world that has profited from automation and intelligent devices that can do activities that previously required human involvement. Companies are creating and programming autonomous robots that can perform crucial agricultural jobs, such as harvesting more crops more quickly than human laborer's, thanks to this game-changing technology. An illustration of this is the robot RIPPA, which eliminates weeds and pests [29].

3.3.5 PLANT DISEASE PREDICTION, DETECTION, AND CONTROL

Based on computer analysis, predictions are made. The forecasting of illnesses and insect assaults makes use of both deep learning and ML techniques. For training the system, convolutional neural networks are also used. IoT can alert the farmer using his or her phone and a cellular network so they can take the appropriate action [30]. A breakthrough in smart, precise agriculture is accurate disease prediction. Better quality yields have been encouraged by early disease diagnosis and even disease prediction. AI and ML algorithms allow for accurate detection. AI and ML models can effectively evaluate noisy and heterogeneous data more effectively [31].

3.3.6 MITIGATION OF LABOR AND HUMAN RESOURCE

According to reports, significant farming regions have lost millions of dollars in revenue as a result of manpower scarcity. The decline in available labor for agricultural activities has been made up for by machines that are used in intelligent PA. Harvest CROO Robotics, particularly useful for harvesting crops, is an example of such attempts [9].

3.3.7 GREENHOUSE MANAGEMENT

The greenhouses' WSN can track the climate and transfer the data to a facility, where it is analyzed using a variety of cutting-edge tools and diagnostic models. Numerous aspects, such as the drip irrigation, luminance system, and climate control system, can be monitored remotely [32]. In a greenhouse, using AI to examine operations is essential. The AI-based technology is made for monitoring, maintaining greenhouse's climate, focusing on meticulous data analysis to reach a high degree of precision. The greenhouse's climate must be adjusted while taking into account a number of factors, making it difficult to complete using conventional methods. Fuzzy logic controllers (FLCs) and artificial neural networks (ANNs) are two techniques used in this procedure to achieve great precision in managing temperature and humidity [15].

3.4 IoT AND APPLICATIONS OF IoT IN PA

Kevin Ashton mentioned the term "Internet of Things" (IoT) for the first time in 1999 to explain the process of gathering data from "things," processing it at the individual or collective level and then using AI (usually ML) to make decisions based on massive amounts of data and the location of the source (data). Farming became intelligent farming. As a result, formerly, PA just considered the data's position when making decisions [33]. IoT allows for real-time data transfer to storage databases, where a pre-installed application uses the knowledge it has already been taught to make accurate decisions and provide the appropriate information to the user. Traditional farming has evolved into a cyber-physical system (CPS, which combines software and hardware components). It is now possible to monitor practically all the factors, and IoT has enabled farming practices to be automated to a higher degree. IoT has therefore strengthened smart farming [34].

3.4.1 IoT PLATFORMS FOR PA

FarmBeats: An end-to-end IoT platform for agriculture called FarmBeats makes it easy to collect data from numerous sensors, cameras, and drones. A cheap and accessible IoT arena for agriculture is called FarmBeats. It assists TVWS, a cost-effective, long-range technology supporting high bandwidth sensors. It combines an intelligent gateway and a weather-aware IoT base station to make sure that services are accessible both online and off. Novel path-planning algorithms, which increase drone battery life, are also included. An IoT platform called FarmBeats achieves the goals in a highly changeable and resource-limited setting [35].

SmartFarmNet: A multidisciplinary Australian team called "SmartFarmNet" comprised growers, farmers, computer scientists, and crop biologists. In terms of the number of users, it is the biggest system in the globe. It offers agricultural performance analysis and suggestions. It has sensors attached, crops are appraised, and it aids people. It offers solutions for quick and scalable data that can handle the huge volume of data (big data) produced by millions of IoT sensors.

Infiswift: The revolutionary edge-to-cloud connection, analytics software engine, and reliable Intel architecture make up the Infiswift IoT platform.

thethings.iO: It is an IoT application enablement platform that provides several protocols, stunning dashboards, and robust APIs to enable quick and scalable connectivity of things to the internet (thethings.iO).

Raspberry Pi: Recently, it has become the preferred IoT platform. The Linux-powered Raspberry Pi also comes with a set of GPIO (general purpose input/output) pins that let users explore the IoT with a variety of connecting choices and control electronic components for physical computing. Memory storage of up to 8GB (Raspberry Pi). It functions in an open-source environment because it is closed-source hardware (the board itself is not open hardware), which is affordable, adaptable and has received a lot of community support because so many IoT projects have already been ported to it.

Arduino: Agriculture and Arduino have a very long history together. An assortment of electronic boards with microcontrollers makes up the open-source hardware platform known as Arduino. An adequate combination of IoT hardware and software can be found on the user-friendly IoT platform

Arduino. It functions using a variety of hardware requirements that are familiar to users of interactive electronics. The Arduino software is included in the Integrated Development Environment (IDE) design and the Arduino programming language for programming microcontrollers. The recently released Pro IDE is far more practical and speeds up coding (Geekflare).

3.5 MACHINE LEARNING (ML) AND THE ROLE OF MACHINE LEARNING IN PA

Agriculture must adapt to changes that are taking place globally in order to survive and get the full benefits of the newest technology. The benefit of the knowledge imparted to farmers by professionals who apply ML techniques to the data gathered from agriculture and numerous other sources has substantially increased PA. Additionally, they infer useful information, and ML models' implicit prediction capability could be integrated into automatic procedures like expert systems. Smart farming, backed by high-precision AI/ML algorithms, keeps farmers up to speed with technology and has significantly improved the agricultural sector [36]. The following are some examples of specific AI and ML applications in PA.

3.5.1 SOIL MANAGEMENT

A better understanding of soil is required to increase agricultural productivity since the soil is a heterogeneous natural resource that is most important in agriculture. In soil, there are intricate processes at work and systems that call for an arduous investigation. In order to achieve good soil management, information on the available soil should be correct. Data on agricultural soil attributes, including estimations of soil dryness, quality, temperature, and humidity levels, is loaded into a ML model to provide a reliable result and provide insightful information [37]. Trace Genomics, a technique that uses ML to detect soil flaws and is akin to the Plantix app, is one example of this technology (Plantix). Farmers can get soil analysis services from the California-based company Trace Genomics. The system, which employs ML to give clients a sense of their soil's strengths and limitations, was developed with assistance from its major investor, Illumina. Users supposedly obtain a comprehensive description of the soil components from Trace Genomics after sending in a sample of their soil (Home).

3.5.2 IRRIGATION MANAGEMENT

Intelligent automated irrigation systems powered by AI can deliver the optimal and consistent irrigation required to sustain targeted soil conditions. This lowers labor expenses, raises production costs, and decreases water waste. Many scientists think that the wise use of water in such irrigation systems tends to affect water supplies worldwide. It's vital to estimate evapotranspiration to construct and such system; however, precisely calculating it is a difficult procedure. AI and ML algorithms that accurately estimate evapotranspiration are used to overcome this problem. Cultyvate and DIGITEUM are examples of this technology (NEWA).

3.5.3 WEATHER FORECASTING SYSTEM

Models for seasonal forecasting aid in boosting agricultural output and accuracy. To help farmers make decisions, these models are able to forecast forthcoming weather patterns months in advance. For tiny farms that depend on the weather, such as those in developing nations like India, seasonal forecasting is very useful. These technologies include IMD, ViSeed, and NEWA (VineView). Due to its impact on mankind worldwide, weather forecasting has attracted the attention of several researchers from various research communities. Many studies have been motivated to explore hidden hierarchical patterns in the large volume of weather datasets for weather forecasting as a result of the recent advancement of deep learning techniques. This is due to the widespread availability of tremendous weather data and the emergence of information and communication technology.

3.5.4 AGRICULTURAL ROBOTS

Autonomous robots that can do crucial agricultural jobs, such as harvesting crops at a faster rate and bigger volume than human employees, are being developed and programmed by businesses [15]. The "See & Spray" robot was created by Blue River Technology (John Deere), and it is said to use computer vision and ML to spray herbicide just where it is needed accurately. Many models, including framework, transfer function, and black-box simulation, have been used to assist farmers in maintaining appropriate greenhouse conditions. Many models, including framework, transfer function, and black-box simulation, have been used to assist farmers in maintaining appropriate greenhouse conditions. The mechanism model, like the early static or dynamic model described by Bot [38] and the enhanced models proposed by van Henten [39] and de Zwart [40], gives a clear scientific interpretation of the greenhouse environment. In accordance with the metrological circumstances and the greenhouse component values, static and dynamic models are used for this purpose [41, 42]. The transfer function model [43] has a straightforward structure, which can only be applied to linear systems. While with the black-box model, both linear and nonlinear modeling may be done based on input data [44–46]. Therefore, numerous studies work to create these models and implement them in greenhouses to appease farmers and lower overall costs [47–49]. To simulate the greenhouse temperature in China, He and Ma [50] used a neural network with PCA. The findings demonstrated that the BPNN based on PCA was more accurate than the stepwise regression technique.

3.5.5 GREENHOUSE MANAGEMENT

The use of AI in greenhouse operations is crucial. The AI-backed greenhouse temperature control and management system place a strong emphasis on data analysis in order to attain high precision. It becomes a laborious process to regulate a greenhouse's climate manually due to the different components that must be considered. Some of the techniques used in this process include FLCs and ANNs, achieving high accuracy in temperature and humidity regulation [15].

3.6 BIG DATA AND ITS ROLE IN PA

The amount of data produced by the globe today is immense, and it is continually being recorded and captured. Numerous sources of data result in the generation of structured, unstructured, and semi-structured data. Although most of the data generated is unstructured, some is still structured and kept in conventional relational databases or data warehouses. Due to big data, the traditional methods of organizing, processing, and interpreting data have undergone a significant transformation. The existing methods did not effectively manage the data collected from many sources. Deep analysis has the wonderful skills to uncover trends, identify hidden patterns, detect hidden connections, disclose new information, extract insight, and improve decision-making and automatic processes, among other things. Big data has been shown to be crucial for smart agriculture [51].

3.7 CLOUD COMPUTING IN AGRICULTURE

Cropland and biodiversity both continue to be lost on a global scale. If we assume that cloud computing technology can be used in real time to create entire ecosystems, then using the appropriate sensors and monitoring software to collect data from the field, such as pictures of farmer's terrains and annotations of human actors in the field, feed data repositories with their GPS that coordinates with accuracy. For instance, sensors are now capable of locating hay bales in a field and determining how much moisture they contain. In order to access the data from predictive analytics institutions and obtain precise predictions of the products that will be in demand across marketplaces, farmers can be enabled to use cloud computing techniques [52]. A knowledge-based archive with a plethora of data on agricultural techniques, crop inputs, agricultural innovations, insecticides, seeds, composts, nutrition, and weed resistance is also urged to be used by farmers. All of this is supported by professional assistance from a variety of sources, such as agriculture and the processing of agricultural products. The mechanism of cloud computing in PA is illustrated in Figure 3.3.

The advantages of cloud computing are listed in the following [53]:

- Enhancement of the GDP of the nation
- Ensured food security and food quality
- Developed economy and financial conditions
- Build-up of worldwide communication
- Accessibility of data at any time, at any location
- Increased market price
- Availability of the data at a faster rate
- Inspiration to scientists and scholars

Furthermore, some of the recent research carried out with the aid of above-mentioned techniques in the domain of PA are elaborately tabulated, as shown in Table 3.1.

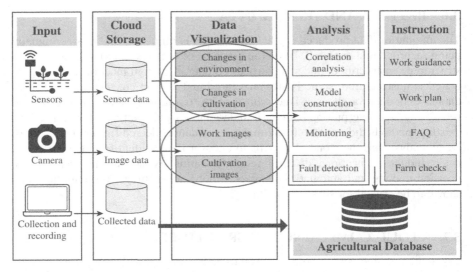

FIGURE 3.3   Mechanism of cloud computing in PA.

3.8   PRESENT STATUS AND HURDLES OF PA IN INDIA

The implementation and progress of PA in India would be influenced by the design of the adoption strategies. Planning is essential before providing PA to Indian agriculture, which entails carrying out a significant number of experiments and assessments. Using multimedia, seminars, and workshops, the public is made aware of the PA idea at this early phase. This entails the creation of adequately expertized and specialized personnel, appropriate PA institutions, and consistent crop and soil management. To validate computer models with zone-specific data, this is done after a stratified random sample within the region that accurately depicts the management zone across the entire nation. Agricultural parameters, specialized monitoring and control, involving regular grid sampling and monitoring, are duplicated in this stage using zone-specific computer models.

The National Agricultural Innovation Project (NAIP) has a US$285 million budget that is solely allocated to PA research [65]. The Tamil Nadu government launched the "Tamil Nadu Precision Farming Project." It is currently in use in two districts, with plans to expand to six more in the future. It primarily focuses on high-value crops such as hybrid tomatoes, capsicum, baby corn, white onions, cabbage, and cauliflower. With the support of the Central Institute of Agricultural Engineering and the Project Directorate for Cropping Systems Research (PDCSR UP), Bhopal also began applying variable rate inputs to various cropping systems (CIAE). Ahmedabad has approved testing with the Space Application Center (ISRO) at the Central Potato Research Station farm in Punjab, in order to carry out thorough research on remote sensing in assessing the diversity in consideration to both time and space. There are 17 PFDCs (Precision Farming Development Centers); to fulfill PA, different locations around the nation must satisfy the respective regional standards. Therefore, it is crucial for PA to build specialized institutions and a scientific data bank.

TABLE 3.1
Recent Work Carried Out on Precision Agriculture Using AI

S. No.	Reference	Application of AI in PA	Techniques Involved	Contribution of the Study
1	Karydas et al. [54]	Crop management	GIS and machine learning	A precision fertilization service for crop management, namely "PreFer" as an additional module in a cloud-based farm management system.
2	Thilakarathne et al. [55]	Crop recommendation	Machine learning	Proposed a cloud computing-based crop recommendation system for assisting farmers in decision-making.
3	Afzaal et al. [56]	Irrigation and water quality management	Deep learning	Evapotranspiration estimation using LSTM and bi-LSTM and selection of contributing input through regression analysis.
4	Berger et al. [57]	Agricultural robots	Unmanned aerial systems (UAS) and deep learning	A multiple-cooperative robot system for UAS and UGV with that collaboratively examines the traps in an olive grove.
5	Murugamani et al. [58]	Plant disease prediction, detection and control	Machine learning and IoT	Proposed a machine learning model for detection and classification of cotton leaf disease by monitoring soil quality.
6	Singh et al. [59]	Mitigation of loss and quality management	Deep learning	Analysis of the U-Net, DeepLab, and Mask R-CNN models based on CNN to identify and forecast apple postharvest degradation zones.
7	Sakthi and DafniRose [60]	Intelligent decision support system	Cloud computing	A hyperledger-based knowledge discovery system for the secure and private exchange and storing of sensor data.
8	Bakthavatchalam et al. [61]	Yield prediction	IoT and machine learning	Machine learning model with IoT data for predicting the high-yield crop
9	Ngo et al. [62]	Fertilizer recommendation	Big data	With the proposed EAR and a hive-based warehouse, a fertilizer recommendation system is proposed with the help of statistical models.
10	Cama-Pinto et al. [63]	Greenhouse management	wireless sensor networks	Developed a modeling approach of radio wave attenuation for the purpose of managing the foliage in greenhouses.
11	Qamar and Bawany [64]	Crop management	Big data	Developed a big data-based framework "Agri-PAD" for effective crop management and decision-making system such as precision, recommendation, and enterprise.

REFERENCES

1. Pierce, F. J., & Nowak, P. (1999). Aspects of precision agriculture. Advances in Agronomy, 67, 1–85.
2. Zimmerman, C. "The Five 'R's' of Precision | Precision," 11-Nov-2008. [Online]. Available: http://precision.agwired.com/2008/11/11/the-five-rs-of-precision/
3. Hakkim, V. A., Joseph, E. A., Gokul, A. A., & Mufeedha, K. (2016). Precision farming: The future of Indian agriculture. Journal of Applied Biology and Biotechnology, 4(6), 0–7.
4. Garcia-Sanchez, A. J., Garcia-Sanchez, F., & Garcia-Haro, J. (2011). Wireless sensor network deployment for integrating video-surveillance and data-monitoring in precision agriculture over distributed crops. Computers and Electronics in Agriculture, 75(2), 288–303.
5. Benson, E. R., Stombaugh, T. S., Noguchi, N., Will, J. D., & Reid, J. F. (1998). An evaluation of a geomagnetic direction sensor for vehicle guidance in precision agriculture applications. ASAE paper, 983203.
6. Berger, R., & Hovav, A. (2013). Using a dairy management information system to facilitate precision agriculture: The case of the AfiMilk® system. Information Systems Management, 30(1), 21–34.
7. Jensen, T., Baillie, C., Bramley, R., Di Bella, L., Whiteing, C., & Davis, R.. (2010, January). Assessment of sugarcane yield monitoring technology for precision agriculture. In Proceedings of the 32nd Annual Conference of the Australian Society of Sugar Cane Technologists (ASSCT 2010) (Vol. 32, pp. 410–423). University of Southern Queensland.
8. Rossel, R. V., & McBratney, A. B. (1998). Soil chemical analytical accuracy and costs: Implications from precision agriculture. Australian Journal of Experimental Agriculture, 38(7), 765–775.
9. Ahmad, L., & Nabi, F. (2021). Introduction to precision agriculture. In Agriculture 5.0: Artificial Intelligence, IoT, and Machine Learning (pp. 1–23). CRC Press. Boca Raton DOI: https://doi.org/10.1201/9781003125433.
10. Tummers, J., Kassahun, A., & Tekinerdogan, B. (2021). Reference architecture design for farm management information systems: A multi-case study approach. Precision Agriculture, 22(1), 22–50.
11. Liu, S., Zhu, Y., & Guo, X. (2020). Key technology and application platform of agricultural economic spatial information service—Chinese agricultural economic electronic map. In China's e-Science Blue Book 2018 (pp. 269–289). Springer, Singapore.
12. Kamilaris, A., Kartakoullis, A., & Prenafeta-Boldú, F. X. (2017). A review on the practice of big data analysis in agriculture. Computers and Electronics in Agriculture, 143, 23–37.
13. Navarro-Hellín, H., Martinez-del-Rincon, J., Domingo-Miguel, R., Soto-Vallés, F., & Torres-Sánchez, R. (2016). A decision support system for managing irrigation in agriculture. Computers and Electronics in Agriculture, 124, 121–131.
14. Ip, R. H., Ang, L. M., Seng, K. P., Broster, J. C., & Pratley, J. E. (2018). Big data and machine learning for crop protection. Computers and Electronics in Agriculture, 151, 376–383.
15. Kharkovyna, O. (7). "Reasons Why Machine Learning Is a Game Changer for Agriculture," Towards Data Science, 04-July-2019.
16. Kim, J., Kim, S., Ju, C., & Son, H. I. (2019). Unmanned aerial vehicles in agriculture: A review of perspective of platform, control, and applications. IEEE Access, 7, 105100–105115.
17. "Agriculture and Soils – ISRO," Government of India. [Online]. Available: https://www.isro.gov.in/AgricultureandSoil.html
18. Lobell, D. B., & Asner, G. P. (2003). Climate and management contributions to recent trends in US agricultural yields. Science, 299(5609), 1032–1032.
19. "Agriculture - Earth Online – ESA." [Online]. Available: https://www.esa.int/Applications/Observing_the_Earth/Agriculture
20. "Precision Agriculture Technology: The Future of Precision Farming with IoT – Digiteum," 2019. [Online]. Available: https://www.digiteum.com/precision-agriculture-technology/

21. Bakhtiari, A. A., & Hematian, A. (2013). Precision farming technology, opportunities and difficulty. International Journal for Science and Emerging Technologies with Latest Trends, 5(1), 1–14.
22. Kussul, N., Lavreniuk, M., Skakun, S., & Shelestov, A. (2017). Deep learning classification of land cover and crop types using remote sensing data. IEEE Geoscience and Remote Sensing Letters, 14(5), 778–782.
23. Ampatzidis, Y., & Partel, V. (2019). UAV-based high throughput phenotyping in citrus utilizing multispectral imaging and artificial intelligence. Remote Sensing, 11(4), 410.
24. Krizhevsky, A., Sutskever, I., & Hinton, G. E. (2017). Imagenet classification with deep convolutional neural networks. Communications of the ACM, 60(6), 84–90.
25. Brown, M. E. (2015). Satellite remote sensing in agriculture and food security assessment. Procedia Environmental Sciences, 29, 307.
26. Shchutskaya, A. V., Afanaseva, E. P., & Kapustina, L. V. (2020). Digital farming development in Russia: Regional aspect. In Digital Transformation of the Economy: Challenges, Trends and New Opportunities (pp. 269–279). Springer, Cham.
27. "What Is the Difference between Precision, Digital and Smart Farming? – AgroCares." [Online]. Available: https://agrocares.com/what-is-the-difference-between-precision-digital-and-smart-farming/.
28. Liakos, K. G., Busato, P., Moshou, D., Pearson, S., & Bochtis, D. (2018). Machine learning in agriculture: A review. Sensors, 18(8), 2674.
29. "See & Spray Agricultural Machines – Blue River Technology." [Online]. Available: http://www.bluerivertechnology.com/
30. Gutierrez, D. D. (2015). Machine Learning and Data Science: an Introduction to Statistical Learning Methods With R. Technics Publications, LLC, Mumbai.
31. Mehra, L. K., Cowger, C., Gross, K., & Ojiambo, P. S. (2016). Predicting pre-planting risk of *Stagonospora nodorum* blotch in winter wheat using machine learning models. Frontiers in Plant Science, 7, 390.
32. Wolfert, S., Goense, D., & Sørensen, C. A. G. (2014). A future internet collaboration platform for safe and healthy food from farm to fork. In 2014 Annual SRII Global Conference (pp. 266–273). IEEE.
33. Zhiyu, L. (2012). An overview of internet of things. Computer Measurement & Control, 6.
34. Pradeep, B., Balasubramani, R., Martis, J. E., & Sannidhan, M. S. (2020). Generic IoT platform for analytics in agriculture. In Internet of Things and Analytics for Agriculture, Volume 2 (pp. 225–248). Springer, Singapore.
35. Vasisht, D., Kapetanovic, Z., Won, J., Jin, X., Chandra, R., Sinha, S., … & Stratman, S. (2017). {FarmBeats}: An {IoT} Platform for {Data-Driven} Agriculture. In 14th USENIX Symposium on Networked Systems Design and Implementation (NSDI 17) (pp. 515–529).
36. Bagchi, A. "Artificial Intelligence in Agriculture-White Paper," Mindtree-Larsen Toubro Group Company. [Online]. Available: https://www.mindtree.com/sites/default/files/2018-04/ArtificialIntelligenceinAgriculture.pdf.
37. Dakshayini, M., & Balaji Prabhu, B. V. (2020). An effective big data and blockchain (BD-BC) based decision support model for sustainable agriculture system. In EAI International Conference on Big Data Innovation for Sustainable Cognitive Computing (pp. 77–86). Springer, Cham.
38. Mark, R. (2019). Ethics of using AI and big data in agriculture: The case of a large agriculture multinational. The ORBIT Journal, 2(2), 1–27.
39. Torky, M., & Hassanein, A. E. (2020). Integrating blockchain and the internet of things in precision agriculture: Analysis, opportunities, and challenges. Computers and Electronics in Agriculture, 178, 105476.
40. Kim, H. M., & Laskowski, M. (2018). Agriculture on the blockchain: Sustainable solutions for food, farmers, and financing. In: D. Tapscott (Ed.), Supply Chain Revolution. Barrow Books http://dx.doi.org/10.2139/ssrn.3028164.

41. Demestichas, K., Peppes, N., Alexakis, T., & Adamopoulou, E. (2020). Blockchain in agriculture traceability systems: A review. Applied Sciences, 10(12), 4113.

42. Patil, A. S., Tama, B. A., Park, Y., & Rhee, K. H. (2018). A framework for blockchain based secure smart green house farming. In International Conference on Ubiquitous Information Technologies and Applications, International Conference on Computer Science and its Applications (pp. 1162–1167). Springer, Singapore.

43. Di Vaio, A., Boccia, F., Landriani, L., & Palladino, R. (2020). Artificial intelligence in the agri-food system: Rethinking sustainable business models in the COVID-19 scenario. Sustainability, 12(12), 4851.

44. López, E. M., García, M., Schuhmacher, M., & Domingo, J. L. (2008). A fuzzy expert system for soil characterization. Environment International, 34(7), 950–958.

45. Li, M., & Yost, R. S. (2000). Management-oriented modeling: Optimizing nitrogen management with artificial intelligence. Agricultural Systems, 65(1), 1–27.

46. Tajik, S., Ayoubi, S., & Nourbakhsh, F. (2012). Prediction of soil enzymes activity by digital terrain analysis: Comparing artificial neural network and multiple linear regression models. Environmental Engineering Science, 29(8), 798–806.

47. Lal, H., Jones, J. W., Peart, R. M., & Shoup, W. D. (1992). FARMSYS—a whole-farm machinery management decision support system. Agricultural Systems, 38(3), 257–273.

48. Song, H., & He, Y. (2005, July). Crop nutrition diagnosis expert system based on artificial neural networks. In Third International Conference on Information Technology and Applications (ICITA'05) (Vol. 1, pp. 357–362). IEEE.

49. Ji, B., Sun, Y., Yang, S., & Wan, J. (2007). Artificial neural networks for rice yield prediction in mountainous regions. The Journal of Agricultural Science, 145(3), 249–261.

50. Balleda, K., Satyanvesh, D., Sampath, N. V. S. S. P., Varma, K. T. N., & Baruah, P. K. (2014, January). Agpest: An efficient rule-based expert system to prevent pest diseases of rice & wheat crops. In 2014 IEEE 8th International Conference on Intelligent Systems and Control (ISCO) (pp. 262–268). IEEE.

51. Balac, N. (2020). Big data. In Intelligent Internet of Things (pp. 315–356). Springer International Publishing, Cham.

52. Kamath, S., & Chetan, A. A. (2011). Affordable, interactive crowd sourcing platform for sustainable agriculture: Enabling public private partnerships. Cloud Computing Journal, 9(2), 46–54.

53. Kapse, A. S., Kapse, A. S., & Thakare, V. M. (2022). Importance of cloud computing technique in agriculture field using different methodologies. In: Cloud Computing Technologies for Smart Agriculture and Healthcare. (Eds. Shrawankar U, Malik L and Arora, S). CRC Press, Boca Raton. https://doi.org/10.1201/9781003203926-7.

54. Karydas, C., Chatziantoniou, M., Stamkopoulos, K., Iatrou, M., Vassiliadis, V., & Mourelatos, S. (2023). Embedding a precision agriculture service into a farm management information system – ifarma/PreFer. Smart Agricultural Technology, 4, 100175. https://doi.org/10.1016/j.atech.2023.100175.

55. Thilakarathne, N. N., Bakar, M. S. A., Abas, P. E., & Yassin, H. (2022). A cloud enabled crop recommendation platform for machine learning-driven precision farming. Sensors, 22(16):6299. https://doi.org/10.3390/s22166299

56. Afzaal, H., Farooque, A. A., Abbas, F., Acharya, B., & Esau, T. (2020). Computation of evapotranspiration with artificial intelligence for precision water resource management. Applied Sciences, 10(5), 1621. https://doi.org/10.3390/app10051621

57. Berger, G. S., Teixeira, M., Cantieri, A., Lima, J., Pereira, A. I., Valente, A., de Castro, G. G. R., & Pinto, M. F. (2023). Cooperative heterogeneous robots for autonomous insects trap monitoring system in a precision agriculture scenario. Agriculture, 13(2), 239. https://doi.org/10.3390/agriculture13020239

58. Murugamani, C., Shitharth, S., Hemalatha, S., Kshirsagar, P. R., Riyazuddin, K., Naveed, Q. N., ... & Batu, A. (2022). Machine learning technique for precision agriculture applications in 5G-based internet of things. Wireless Communications and Mobile Computing, 2022, 11.
59. Singh, A., Vaidya, G., Jagota, V., Darko, D. A., Agarwal, R. K., Debnath, S., & Potrich, E. (2022). Recent advancement in postharvest loss mitigation and quality management of fruits and vegetables using machine learning frameworks, Journal of Food Quality, 2022, Article ID 6447282, 9. https://doi.org/10.1155/2022/6447282
60. Sakthi, U., & DafniRose, J. (2022). Blockchain-enabled smart agricultural knowledge discovery system using edge computing. Procedia Computer Science, 202, 73–82.
61. Bakthavatchalam, K., Karthik, B., Thiruvengadam, V., Muthal, S., Jose, D., Kotecha, K., & Varadarajan, V. (2022). IoT framework for measurement and precision agriculture: Predicting the crop using machine learning algorithms. Technologies, 10, 13. https://doi.org/10.3390/technologies10010013
62. Ngo, V. M., Duong, T. V. T., & Nguyen, T. B. T. et al. (2023). A big data smart agricultural system: Recommending optimum fertilisers for crops. International Journal of Information Technology, 15, 249–265. https://doi.org/10.1007/s41870-022-01150-1
63. Cama-Pinto, D., Damas, M., Holgado-Terriza, J. A., Arrabal-Campos, F. M., Martínez-Lao, J. A., Cama-Pinto, A., & Manzano-Agugliaro, F. (2023). A deep learning model of radio wave propagation for precision agriculture and sensor system in greenhouses. Agronomy, 13(1), 244. https://doi.org/10.3390/agronomy13010244
64. Qamar, T., & Bawany, N. Z. (2023). Agri-PAD: A scalable framework for smart agriculture. Indonesian Journal of Electrical Engineering and Computer Science, 29(3), 1597–1605.
65. Ahmad, L., & Nabi, F. (2021). Agriculture 5.0: Artificial intelligence, IoT and Machine Learning (1st ed.). CRC Press. https://doi.org/10.1201/9781003125433

4 Chatbot for Smart Farming Using AI and NLP Techniques

Parveen Sultana H., Nishant Sharma, and Sneha Leela Jacob

4.1 INTRODUCTION

Internet connectivity is commonplace in the modern world. As a result, services deployed on the internet find great relevance today. An area where web services can be essential is the area of smart farming. As the internet becomes more affordable, low-income farmers should be able to afford it and benefit from services deployed on the Cloud. Web services, in general, can offer reliable and timely assistance to end users. One use case for such a service is a chatbot process that answers queries by farmers in a timely manner and/or provides timely assistance from domain experts. General purpose search engines do not provide specialized help to the farmers in need. There has been an incremental advancement in chatbots to address this problem. However, chatbots today lack in providing reliable and intelligent help. In earlier times, it was a common conception that a knowledgeable computer system would be the one that had enough facts stored in its memory. However, the advancement and research in the field of artificial intelligence (AI) has reliably shown us that learning from experience is a better paradigm than reiterating stored facts.

Chatbots are programs that simulate a conversation with an end user and can assist them with a particular enquiry. They can attend to queries tirelessly and in a timely manner. In principle, chatbots analyse user input and generate appropriate response. They can engage in conversation or act as a classification and routing agent. As a classification or routing agent, they discern the intent behind the user input and route the enquiry to the designated responder. There has been a shift in chatbot process that used to respond from stored database of facts to an agent that uses methods from AI to generate responses based on experience. Chatbots can be general purpose (like Google Assistant) or special purpose (meant for a single application domain). An example of a chatbot that uses static responses is shown in Figure 4.1.

Some of the key terminologies when discussing conversational chatbots are as follows:

- **User input:** Typically, an end user could give their query as a text input, or through voice, or through a series of feed-forward questions.
- **Training:** Based on the training process that has happened for the chatbot, the chatbot discerns from the user input the intent behind the query.

DOI: 10.1201/9781003391302-4

- **Intent:** This is the core intention in the user input.
- **Entity:** A key aspect of user input other than its intent.
- **Dialogue:** This is the entire to and fro between the end user and the chatbot until the query is resolved. To maintain a conversation, the chatbot may need to store context.

We see from Figure 4.1 that the chatbot process employed is not very intelligent. The process tries to force an enquiry on the end user. This takes away from the natural way in which humans interact, making it well known that we are indeed conversing with a limited bot. Asking well-formed queries that should have been answered actually breaks the chatbot process. As a result, these processes fail to create a sense of reliability on them. The end user is left unsatisfied and wanting to get assistance from a real human being.

A good training process can be critical to giving satisfactory responses to the end user. A well-trained chatbot could reduce the need for human intervention. Industrial sector also recognizes the importance of an automated AI assistant. Therefore, sectors like banking, food, agriculture, and airlines have incorporated these types of agents in their web services.

An AI technique that helps chatbots is natural language processing. Since one of the major components of natural language processing (NLP) is to understand the dynamics of language and its usage, it has gained much traction to develop the backend of the chatbot process. The challenges involved in using NLP for automated processes are discussed through a variety of theories and methods in the domain of NLP. Some of these challenges include managing massive amounts of text data and structuring highly unstructured data. NLP is proving to be instrumental in changing processes from a data-driven approach to an intelligence-driven approach.

A typical chatbot process flow is as follows. A user inputs their query into the chatbot's dialogue management engine. The query is then processed through the usage of NLP. This processed query is then converted into an appropriate intent. The intent and entity (if any) are either used to generate or retrieve a response, or in

FIGURE 4.1 An example of an online chatbot process.

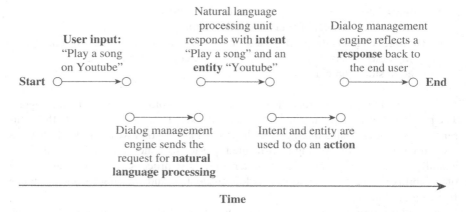

FIGURE 4.2   An activity diagram for the chatbot process in an AI assistant.

case of an AI assistant, the intent and entity may be used to perform an action. An appropriate response is given to the end user by the dialogue management engine in both these cases. An activity diagram for the chatbot process in an AI assistant is shown in Figure 4.2. The user inputs a query into the chatbot's front end, "Play a song on YouTube". The dialogue management system sends this query to the NLP unit that determines the intent of the user input that is to play a song, and the entity that is YouTube. Finally, as part of the chatbot process in an AI assistant, the intent and the entity are used to play a random song on the YouTube application. The dialogue management engine then provides an appropriate response back to the end user. One of the key things that must be noted here is that in an effective chatbot process, the user only sees the input that they entered and the final response from the dialogue management engine. The reliability of the process then rests on the effective delivery of the user's intent.

A chatbot process must include a component for NLP and understanding. This component usually consists of a classifier process and an entity detection process. In case of an AI assistant, the output from the classifier and entity detection process can be used to perform an action, and in the case of a routing chatbot, the output from the classifier process can be used to route the query to the designated responder.

The NLP and understanding component of the chatbot process uses an internal classifier to find the intent of the user input. A block diagram showing this process flow is shown in Figure 4.3.

User input: User input can be text based where the end user inputs the question as a text. However, in some cases, it may be desirable to have a front end where the end

FIGURE 4.3   The block diagram for the internal classifier process of the chatbot.

```
PowerShell 7.3.2
Loading personal and system profiles took 2587ms.
(base) PS C:\Users\nishant18973\Documents\AppRootFirebase\FrontEnd\Audio> python3 .\audio.py
Please be careful! Your audio is being recorded.
(base) PS C:\Users\nishant18973\Documents\AppRootFirebase\FrontEnd\Audio> python3 .\SpeechToText.py
result2:
{    'alternative': [   {    'confidence': 0.88687527,
                             'transcript': 'which weather is most suitable for '
                                           'harvesting crops'}],
     'final': True}
(base) PS C:\Users\nishant18973\Documents\AppRootFirebase\FrontEnd\Audio>
```

FIGURE 4.4 An example instance of speech-to-text conversion.

user is allowed to ask their query through a microphone and then that audio query be converted into the corresponding text. This text can then be fed to the classifier process. An example use case is *smart farming*. Farmers in developing countries may have a weak formal education background, thereby making typing not an appealing user interface to them. A speech recognizer in the front end that can identify the native language can be very appealing to the farmers of a particular place. Support for classification through native languages is the right future direction. Two methods can be explored to provide speech-to-text conversion at the front end of the chatbot application. One method is that of a web service such as Google's Web Speech API Demonstration. The other method is through a Python application. For this task, the two libraries of Python: pyAudio and Wave come in handy. A .wav file can be recorded through the microphone on a smart device. By using the speech-to-text recognition library provided by Google, we can convert the audio file to text. An example instance of speech-to-text conversion using a Python program on Windows 11 host machine is shown in Figure 4.4. We ask one of the questions from the test dataset shown in Table 5.6, and we can see that it is correctly transcribed with a confidence of 88.7%.

Speech front ends are way of the future for the chatbots. However, the way of speaking for different people may vary even for a popular language such as English. The speech-to-text conversion may not be able to properly transcribe the user's speech input. For example, on reading the same test case again but with an absurd slang, the transcribed output is shown in Figure 4.5.

To measure the accuracy of the speech-to-text transcription, we can use the measure of word error rate (WER). The WER measure is calculated by dividing the number of incorrect words in the transcribed output to the total number of correct words in the original expected outcome. For example, our test case was as follows: "Which weather

```
PowerShell                                                                      —   □   ×
(base) PS C:\Users\nishant18973\Documents\AppRootFirebase\FrontEnd\Audio> python3 .\SpeechToText.py
result2:
{    'alternative': [   {    'confidence': 0.85579228,
                             'transcript': 'which weather is more suitable for '
                                           'harvesting cops'},
                         {    'transcript': 'which weather is most suitable for '
                                            'harvesting cops'},
                         {    'transcript': 'weather is more suitable for '
                                            'harvesting cops'}],
     'final': True}
(base) PS C:\Users\nishant18973\Documents\AppRootFirebase\FrontEnd\Audio>
```

FIGURE 4.5 A mis-transcribed output given by speech-to-text convertor.

TABLE 4.1

Use an Existing Classifier or Build Your Own Classifier; General Recommendations Are Made Specific to This Chapter

Requirement	Preference	Fits Our Requirement
Building a conversational AI	Use an existing classifier	✗
Building a classification and routing assistant	Build your own classifier	✓
Not skilled at data science	Use an existing classifier	✗
Skilled at data science	Build your own classifier	✓
If you require complete control over the coding of the individual components	Build your own classifier	✓
Low on free time	Use an existing classifier	✗
Learning for the sake of it	Build your own classifier	✓

is most suitable for harvesting crops?". The first option given by the speech-to-text convertor is as follows: 'which weather is more suitable for harvesting cops'. If we ignore the punctuation and the case of the words, we can observe WER in the transcribed output. The words that correctly match are as follows: 'which', 'weather', 'is', 'suitable', 'for', and 'harvesting'. The words that are mismatched are as follows: 'more' for 'most' in the original query, and 'cops' for 'crops' in the original query. Therefore, the WER is 2 incorrect words in the transcribed output out of the total 8 correct words in the original query. This gives the WER as 0.25 or 25%.

Classifier process: Since a classifier is a central process in the chatbot process, it is indispensable that this process be as efficient and effective as possible. This process is ultimately responsible for how reliable the chatbot will be in either maintaining a dialogue or performing a task.

Now, arises another central question. Should we use an existing classifier or should we build our own custom classifier. In this regard [1], gives a general recommendation for building your own classifier if we satisfactorily answer yes to most, if not all, of the recommendations against building our own classifier as shown in Table 4.1. In this book chapter, we wish to classify a user input as either belonging to the category of 'farming' or belonging to the category of 'not farming'. In essence, we wish to train a binary classifier on our training dataset. In this regard, we add tick marks to all those conditions that apply to us or to our use case in this chapter.

While the general recommendations given by [1] are to be taken as a guideline, it is still obvious that we may build our own classifier to obtain the objective being pursued in this chapter. Our responses to the general recommendations also loosely validate that we shall build our own classifier for this task.

User's intent: Once the user intent is identified using the classifier process of the chatbot, the identified user intent can be used to either answer the question in case of a conversational chatbot, perform an action in case of an AI assistant, or route the request to the designated responder in case of a classification and routing chatbot.

4.2 LITERATURE REVIEW

In this section, we discuss the state-of-the-art in the field of chatbot and its application to smart farming. We also discuss the key issues presented by the researchers in the domain of chatbot and smart farming.

Unspecialized general purpose virtual assistants cannot be effective in providing expert help to the farmers. A chatbot powered by specialized domain knowledge is a great solution for this problem. In this regard, there is an incremental progress going on in advancing the chatbot technology. The authors of [2] present the history, technology, and applications of chatbots. The authors differentiate between pattern-matching-based response generation and generating responses through AI. Even though learning from experience and generative models are essential to create the chatbots of the future, popularly today, a lot of chatbots use pattern-matching-based responses. This reduces the overhead related to processing and understanding the user input and generating complex responses. For pattern-matching-based chatbots, the authors compare three popular languages for the representation of the fundamental knowledge unit of the chatbot. These languages are Artificial Intelligence Markup Language (AIML), RiveScript, and Chatscript. The most popular among them is AIML which is like XML. AIML represents the fundamental knowledge unit of the chatbot as a category. This category has two subparts: pattern and template. The pattern tag clubs together query of the similar type and which can be responded to in a similar manner. The template tag provides a response. The response can be static, a random choice from a set of choices, or a background generative process.

There is a lack of reliable chatbot applications in the market. In the farming sector, this has consequences in that it increases the request load on some popular information centre like the Kisan Call Centre (KCC) in India. If more reliable applications enter the market, then it will help balance the load of requests and those requests can be addressed in a distributed and timely manner. In this regard, the authors of [3] developed a conversational AI bot for smart agriculture to answer farmer queries related to farming and market analysis. The authors of [4] presented a framework using chatbots to allow farmers to get 24/7 service on issues such as fertilizers, diseases, and soil conditions. The authors used machine learning and NLP for automatic response generation for its users in a language familiar to the end users. The authors of [5] presented a system that uses NLP to help the farmers in improving their farming techniques. A chatbot process is implemented that generates new responses based on previously collected sets of questions and answers. The system is presented as a virtual assistant to guide the farmers. The authors of [6] presented an agricultural chatbot application built on artificial intelligence that answers queries related to weather, plant protection and usage of fertilizers, animal husbandry, market analysis, soil condition, and schemes of government.

There is another set of chatbot processes that are inclined towards helping farmers in maintaining plant health and doing disease detection. The authors of [7] presented a smartphone application to detect diseases in paddy leaves and to suggest pesticides to these farmers. The authors of [8] developed a method using CNN and images of tomato leaves for the automatic identification of eight different tomato diseases. It also identifies pest categories. The authors also developed a chatbot controller to receive enquiries and send responses using an Instant Messaging Service.

The authors of [9] used deep learning and neural networks to detect rice diseases from paddy field images. The authors of [10] used IoT and Fuzzy Logic to help the farmers in better understanding plant health. The authors of [11] also presented an AI technique using CNN to detect diseases in plants. They used the dataset from Kisan Call Centre which contained logs of calls by farmers. The authors of [12] developed a chat room and chatbot using Cloud to help the farmers discuss issues with their peers or experts to improve their decision-making. The implementation on the Cloud ensures that the client does not need heavy computational resources.

Many research papers, including those presented in this section, have highlighted two major points. The first is the inability of the physical centres in providing timely and accurate help to the farmers, thereby generating a need for chatbot processes. The second is the current inability of the chatbots in providing reliable and comprehensive help to the farmers. To make chatbots intelligent, their classification process should be reliable, and their response generation should be comprehensive. In this chapter, we study the application of two popular classification techniques and present their ability to correctly classify the user intent. The first technique is logistic regression that is traditional machine learning, and the second technique uses sequential model from the domain of deep learning.

4.3 TRAINING DATASET

To train our chatbot as a classification and routing agent, we need data. We consider two types of tags: 'farming' and 'not farming'. Under the tag of 'farming', we put questions that adhere to the pattern commonly identified with farming. Similarly, under the tag of 'not farming', we put questions that do not adhere to the patterns commonly identified with farming. We create two custom sets of these question patterns. By putting specific keywords into Google, we picked questions that were posed publicly under that theme on the knowledge sharing platform called Quora. For the farming tag, we included questions related to themes such as future of farming, smart farming, smart irrigation, cattle farming, bee farming, pest control, seed quality and acquisition, cultivation of potatoes, and mixed farming. A few questions that are present under the farming tag are shown in Table 4.2. There are a total of

---

TABLE 4.2

Questions under the Farming Tag

"What is the future of farming?"

"What should we do to get the maximum yield in agriculture?"

"How do fertilizers increase crop yield?"

"In what ways can technology improve crop yields on a farm?"

"How to control pests and diseases in organic gardening?"

"What are the advantages of a smart irrigation system?"

:

.

"How to design precision irrigation system?"

TABLE 4.3

Questions under the 'Not Farming' Tag

"How to Use Quora for Marketing"

"What is your philosophy of life and why?"

"What are your thoughts regarding religion?"

"What does music mean to you?"

"What exactly is open source software?"

"Why is a good university so important?"

$\vdots$

"What languages do you know, and why did you learn them?"

---

150 questions related to the tag of farming in the training dataset. These questions describe the patterns for questions that are related to farming.

Similarly, the questions under the 'not farming' tag include questions from a variety of interesting themes such as using an online social platform for marketing products, philosophy, religion, God, science and mathematics, sports, television, movies, computer games, human languages, and education. Some questions that show the pattern for questions related to 'not farming' are shown in Table 4.3. Similar to the 'farming' tag, there are a total of 150 questions in the 'not farming' tag.

4.4 TRAINING PROCESS FOR OUR CHATBOT

In this section, we train our chatbot process to correctly distinguish the end-user intent, whether it belongs to the 'farming' tag or to the 'not farming' tag.

Representation of a knowledge unit: Essentially, we are aiming to create many fundamental knowledge units for chatbot. This fundamental knowledge unit can follow a structure of a category having as its subfields: pattern and template. The category names the fundamental knowledge unit. The subfield pattern provides different queries with the same underlying pattern to train the chatbot to respond in the same way when a different query similar to this pattern is posed to the chatbot process. In this book chapter, we create a classification agent that distinguishes between two categories: 'farming' and 'not farming'. We represent the class of 'farming' patterns as 0 and that of the 'not farming' patterns as 1. Each category contains questions similar in pattern to the category under which they are considered. Based on the classification, the response by the chatbot is another important aspect. One possible implementation of the response is to have a fixed set of responses for a specific category and then choose a response randomly to give to the end user. Another possible implementation of the response can be to run a subprocess that generates an appropriate outcome. While creating a classification and routing agent, the response by the chatbot may be to forward the query to the designated responder.

Training data *file*: Our training data file consists of two types of tags. The first tag is named 'farming' signifying that it contains all the questions that are related to farming. The second tag is called 'not farming' to signify that it contains questions that are not related to farming. Under each of these tags are patterns of questions related to that tag. In machine learning terminology, we may envision this as follows: each question that has a pattern related to farming has 'farming' as its class label. The same is true for the 'not farming' tag. Each question that has a pattern unrelated to farming has 'not farming' as its class label [13].

Tokenization: In the process of tokenization, we break up a sentence into its constituent parts. These constituent parts can be either words or punctuation marks.

Lemmatization: In the process of lemmatization, we classify a group of words by their lemma (or root) so that they may be analysed under the same lemma form.

The natural language toolkit library of Python (nltk) provides an API for tokenizing a sentence. Once the sentence is decomposed into individual tokens, the process of lemmatization can be carried out. To lemmatize the tokens into their respective lemmas, we can ignore the punctuation marks such as "?", "!", and ".". WordNetLemmatizer function of the nltk library returns the lemma of the word. For example, the words "break", "broke", "broken", or "breaking", they all come from the same root "break". An example of converting a string to its root is to convert its plural form into its singular form. The lemmatize method by default takes care of removing the suffix *s*. For example, if we use the lemmatize method of the WordNetLemmatizer class on the string "samples", we are returned the string "sample" without the suffix *s*. However, in many cases, the WordNetLemmatizer does not give us the correct root for the given word. In some cases, however, we may assist the lemmatizer method by doing parts of speech tagging. The lemmatizer method recognizes the following parts of speech tags: *n* for nouns, *a* for adjectives, *r* for adverbs, and *v* for verbs. For example, if we use the lemmatize method of the WordNetLemmatizer class on the string "doing", we are returned "doing" back without any changes. However, if we associate the string "doing" with the part of speech tag for nouns, i.e., *n,* then we are effectively returned the string "do" which is the correct lemma for the given string "doing".

4.5   BAG OF WORDS IMPLEMENTATION

All lemmatized keywords from the training data file are considered in the bag of words implementation. Consider Table 4.4. It lists some of the words belonging to both 'farming' and 'not farming' tag. As is apparent from this table, a good variety of themes have been discussed under both 'farming' and 'not farming' tags. These themes appear in a sorted manner in Table 4.4.

For the training of the chatbot, the bag of words implementation is as follows. Let a list *T* store all lemmatized words from the entire training data file. We convert each pattern under a tag into its constituent tokens and then extract the lemma from those words. We create a list *B* for each pattern, the length of which is the same as the length of T. *B*[index] is set to 1 if the lemmatized word T[index] occurs in our pattern. If the lemmatized word T[index] does not occur in our pattern, then we set B[index] = 0. Against this list B, we create a class label to identify this pattern with its respective class label. We do this for each pattern in both the 'farming' and 'not farming' tags.

TABLE 4.4

Some of the Lemmatized Words (in Alphabetic Order) Belonging to Either 'Farming' or 'Not Farming' Tags for the Entire Training File

Agriculture	Automatic	Beekeeping	Cattle
Chemical	Code	Computer	Crop
Cultivate	Dairy	Disease	Education
Engineering	Farm	Fertilizer	Game
Gardening	God	Herbicide	Honey
Irrigation	Language	Marketing	Mathematics
Movie	Music	Organic	Philosophy
Plant	Potato	Precision	Purpose
Series	Sowing	Soybean	Sustainable
Technology	Truth	Understanding	University
Vegetable	Virus	Water	Wheat
Yield			

4.6 CLASSIFICATION MODEL

We use two types of training models and compare their results. The first model that we use is the logistic regression model and the second is a sequential model with an input layer, two hidden dense layers and an output layer.

4.6.1 BINARY LOGISTIC REGRESSION

In Binary Logistic Regression (BLR), we assign a probability measure to a categorical event based on the value of one or more independent variables. For instance, if we have data that states whether a student passed or failed an examination based on the number of hours that the student studied. Consider that, in Figure 4.6, there is a student that studied for 3.25 hours and passed. Yet, another student that studied for 3.5 hours failed. From the data, the logistic regression classifier creates the best fit curve. At some number of hours of study, for the logistic regression curve that is fit to this data, there will be a 50% chance for a student passing or failing the examination. This happens when the number of hours is 2.654. On the right of this measure for the number of hours spent studying before examination, the student's chance of passing the examination is higher. On the left side of this measure, the student's chance of failure is higher. Although all students that studied for more than 4 hours passed the examination, the logistic regression curve is a smooth curve from 4 hours until 5 hours 50 minutes.

4.6.2 SEQUENTIAL MODEL

Deep learning is a technique to teach computers to learn by example. Deep learning methods have proved to be useful for classification tasks. Deep learning achieves impressive results because it uses a large amount of labelled data and heavy computational power. Due to the advancement in GPU technology, which is efficient for

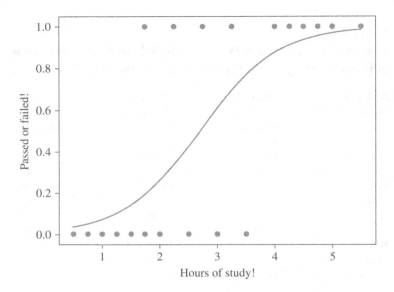

FIGURE 4.6   An example of a logistic curve.

deep learning, deep learning models have gained traction in the modern world. Deep learning models use neural network architectures that learn features directly from data without the need for manual feature extraction. One such neural network architecture in deep learning is a sequential model. In a sequential model, the training information is passed from one layer to the other in a sequential way. In the sequential model considered in this chapter, there is one input layer, two dense hidden layers and one output layer. A diagrammatic representation of the sequential model used in this chapter is shown in Figure 4.7, and the key characteristics of the sequential model are given in Table 4.5.

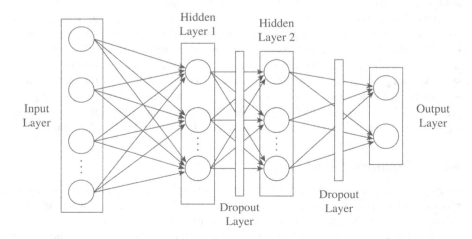

FIGURE 4.7   Sequential model used in the classification process of the chatbot in this chapter.

TABLE 4.5

Characteristics of the Sequential Model used in the Book Chapter

Hidden layer 1: Input shape	431
Hidden layer 1: Type	Dense
Hidden layer 1: Nodes	128
Hidden layer 1: Activation	"relu"
Dropout layer 1: Percentage dropout	50%
Hidden layer 2: Type	Dense
Hidden layer 2: Nodes	64
Hidden layer 2: Activation	"relu"
Dropout layer 2: Percentage dropout	50%
Output layer: Type	Dense
Output layer: Nodes	2
Output layer: Activation	"softmax"
Learning method	Stochastic Gradient Descent
Learning rate	0.01
Loss	Categorical cross entropy
Total number of epochs	200
Batch size	5

4.6.2.1 Dense Layer

A node in a neural network can create one single decision boundary. Hence, logical operations like 'AND' and 'OR' can be classified using a single node. However, a more sophisticated operation such as exclusive or (XOR) cannot be classified using a single node in the neural network. It can however be classified using a dense layer with two nodes and a separate singular node. Let the two nodes in the dense layer be named x and y and the separate singular node be named z. To create a decision boundary for an XOR, we need to classify through z in the x-y plane. In this way, the dense layer helps shift the perspective of data. Dense layer also has the property that assignment of input to many nodes and providing multi-node output to the next layer can happen simultaneously. Another aspect of dense layer is the ability to assign probability values to each class label and then choose the one with the highest probability as our resultant class label. To normalize the resultant values in the output layer, the output layer usually is activated using the 'softmax' function.

4.6.2.2 Dropout Layer

While attempting to improve the accuracy of the model with many features, there remains an active chance that overfitting of the model may occur [14]. To reduce the chances of overfitting, a strategy may be employed wherein we drop out a given percentage of features while training the model in a hidden layer. This ensures that we are training our model to classify a class label with a reduced set of features. Dropping a given percentage of features has an added benefit that it may reduce the variance between the remaining features, thus making the classification process timely.

TABLE 4.6

Patterns for Testing the Efficiency of the Classification Models Wherein We Intrinsically Know Their Actual Ground Truth Values

"What do you do for a living?"

"How much do you weigh?"

"Are you a working professional or a student?"

"How many hours do you work in a day?"

"Do your crops demand extra care?"

"Which weather is most suitable for harvesting crops?"

"How much do pesticides cost?"

"What is the core philosophy behind garbage collection?"

"Where should I buy my seeds from?"

"How to make friends and influence people?"

4.7   TEST DATA

For the testing of the two classification models used in this chapter based on the training data file containing 'farming' and 'not farming' tags, we used the ten sentences shown in Table 4.6 as test patterns wherein we know their actual pattern class. It is hereby noted that this test dataset consists of questions that are custom made by the authors to challenge the classifier process, sometimes with the explicit intention that they may be a little absurd.

4.8   PERFORMANCE EVALUATION

To perform the evaluation for the considered classification models, we consider the parameter misclassification count. We compare the predicted value of the classifier with the ground truth values for the test patterns. While iterating over the test patterns, if the classifier incorrectly predicts the class of the pattern, we increment the misclassification count by 1. The higher the misclassification count, the weaker the classification by the considered training model.

4.8.1   Results from Classification

We use the logistic regression classifier of the scikit-learn library in Python. For the given test cases, the classifier can successfully classify all test cases with 0 misclassification. To set up the sequential model, we must set up the TensorFlow in the host machine. After that, we can run the Python program that uses the Keras library. Even the sequential model can successfully classify all test cases with 0 misclassification. The sequential model is more elaborate than the logistic regression model. It takes a longer time to train. After creating the sequential classification model, we can save the fitted model as a .h5 extension file. We can use the saved model for any chatbot application.

4.8.2 Effects of Mis-Transcribed Words on The Classification Process

If the speech-to-text conversion API is not robust, it may lead to higher WER. Some words even if they are substituted, inserted, or deleted do not have an impact on the classifier process. However, there are certain words that are indispensable to a correct classification by the classifier process. When we run the logistic regression classifier on the mis-transcribed query as given in Figure 4.5, it misclassifies our tag/category to 'not farming', when the query is related to the 'farming' tag. The substitution of the word 'more' in the mis-transcribed query in place of the word 'most' in the correct original query has no effect on the classification process. However, the keyword 'crops' is essential to correctly classify the tag of the query as 'farming'. As is the case with Figure 4.5, this word 'crops' has been substituted for the word 'cops' and thus even if we re-substitute the other mis-transcribed word 'more' with 'most', the overall query is still misclassified as 'not farming'.

4.9 PACKAGING OUR SOLUTION AS A SERVICE

When our solution is ready to be deployed, we may wish to provide our solution as a service. A common way today is to deploy that service on the Cloud and let the clients access the service from all over the globe. One platform that can assist in that is Docker.

4.9.1 Docker

Docker provides us with a virtual environment on which we can run our software. It implements the separation between various virtualized environments by means of a container. A container is a self-contained unit that has all that you need to run your software image. While performing the experiments for this chapter, the host machine that we used is Windows 11 and Docker Desktop version 4.16.3. There are three parts that are needed to run an image on a Docker container. The first is the image itself that we wish to build. The contents of the image are what form the business logic. This could be a Python script, for instance, that achieves a particular task. The second part is the container on which the image gets deployed and run. The third most essential part is the Dockerfile. The Dockerfile sets up the container unit with all the required dependencies before the software image can be successfully deployed and run on the container.

4.9.1.1 Case 1: Running and Packaging Classification Task Using Logistic Regression inside Docker

Image: Our image is the same as the one that is used in the previous section. It uses logistic regression classification model from the scikit-learn library for Python to predict the class of 'farming' or 'not farming' on the set of ten test patterns. The classification model was trained on a dataset with 150 patterns each for 'farming' and 'not farming' tags.

Dockerfile: The Dockerfile sets up the Docker container with all prerequisites for running our classification model for our chatbot process. The contents of the Dockerfile are given in Table 4.7.

TABLE 4.7

Contents of the Dockerfile for Running the Classification Process for Our Chatbot inside the Docker Container

FROM python:3.9
ADD classification_logistic_regression.py.
ADD classes.pkl.
ADD words.pkl.
ADD intents.json.
RUN pip install –upgrade pip
RUN pip install nltk
RUN pip install numpy
RUN pip install scikit-learn
COPY ./tokenizers /root/nltk_data/tokenizers
COPY ./corpora /root/nltk_data/corpora
CMD ["python","./classification_logistic_regression.py"]

There are these following commands with the following intentions in the Dockerfile. The FROM command sets up the container to use the Python environment to run the image file. Following that, we have a bunch of ADD commands. First, we add our main image file classification_logistic_regres sion.py to the current working directory in Docker container. Then, we add the pickle files. Following that, we add the intents.json file that contains the training data of 150 question patterns each, both for the 'farming' and 'not farming' tag. After the ADD processes, we have the RUN processes that get executed on the Docker container during the build process. We ask the Dockerfile to install and set up nltk, numpy, and scikit-learn libraries on the container. This setup should have been sufficient to finally run the script file using *python ./classification_ logistic_regression.py* under the CMD tag. The Python script file had instructions to download nltk libraries punkt, wordnet, and omw-1.4 using the nltk downloader. However, due to special circumstances involved around installing nltk library in the correct place, the authors used the following strategy. By downloading punkt, wordnet, and omw-1.4 to the working directory on the host machine, two folders by the name of tokenizers and corpora were created. Then, these folders were copied as is and in full to the/root/nltk_data/directory insider the Docker container. Applying this fix, all setup was completed successfully. An image instance of the build is shown in Figure 4.8.

Running the Build Image on the Container: The built image can be run using the command *Docker run python-classification-lr:latest*, and it gives the correct output for our test cases. This image is a packaged image and can be deployed as a service on the Cloud, which we shall do in the following section.

4.9.1.2   Case 2: Running Classification Task Using Sequential Model inside Docker

In this case, we wish only to demonstrate that the same answer is replicated while running the classification task using a sequential model inside the Docker container powered by TensorFlow as it is when running the program on the host machine with

FIGURE 4.8   Build log for the image file python-classification-lr (logistic regression classification).

TensorFlow installed. Using the command *"docker run -it –rm -v ${PWD}:/tmp -w/ tmp tensorflow/tensorflow"*, we can mount the current working directory in the host onto the Docker container that contains the TensorFlow setup. Once the working directory is mounted, we have access to the training file that uses the sequential model and dense layers. The NLP component of the training file requires three modules installed. They are punkt, wordnet, and omw-1.4. To install these modules, we enter the Python interpreter inside the Docker container. We use the nltk.download() provided by the nltk library to install these three modules. The successful installation of each module is characterized by the printing of True on the Docker terminal. We can then run our training file inside Docker. The output is correctly replicated on the Docker container as shown in Figure 4.9. The output is verbose. However, it gives the taste of the bag of words implementation adopted for representing training and testing data in this chapter.

4.10   DEPLOYING OUR CLASSIFICATION SERVICE TO THE CLOUD

The Cloud computing paradigm is an essential component for modern-day applications. Users can access services hosted on Cloud from anywhere via proper authentication. Business can store data on the Cloud that can help them in predicting trends and optimizing workflows. Cloud service providers like Google, Amazon, and Microsoft provide APIs and frameworks to interact with their services. With Cloud computing, the central idea is to do away with buying our own hardware and instead use the infrastructure, or platform, or service provided by any of these Cloud service providers. Businesses can rent or give up the resources as per their needs and pay for only what they use. In this way, Cloud computing provides ubiquitous and on-demand access to configurable resources such as storage and servers. The resources are swiftly assigned based on their availability and terminated with minimum effort from the end user. There are several benefits to using Cloud solutions. For low- and medium-scale industries, this paradigm of low-cost setup of infrastructure, or of a platform, or of a service is very attractive. The responsibility of upgrading resources to the latest state-of-the-art is also shifted from these low- to medium-scale industries

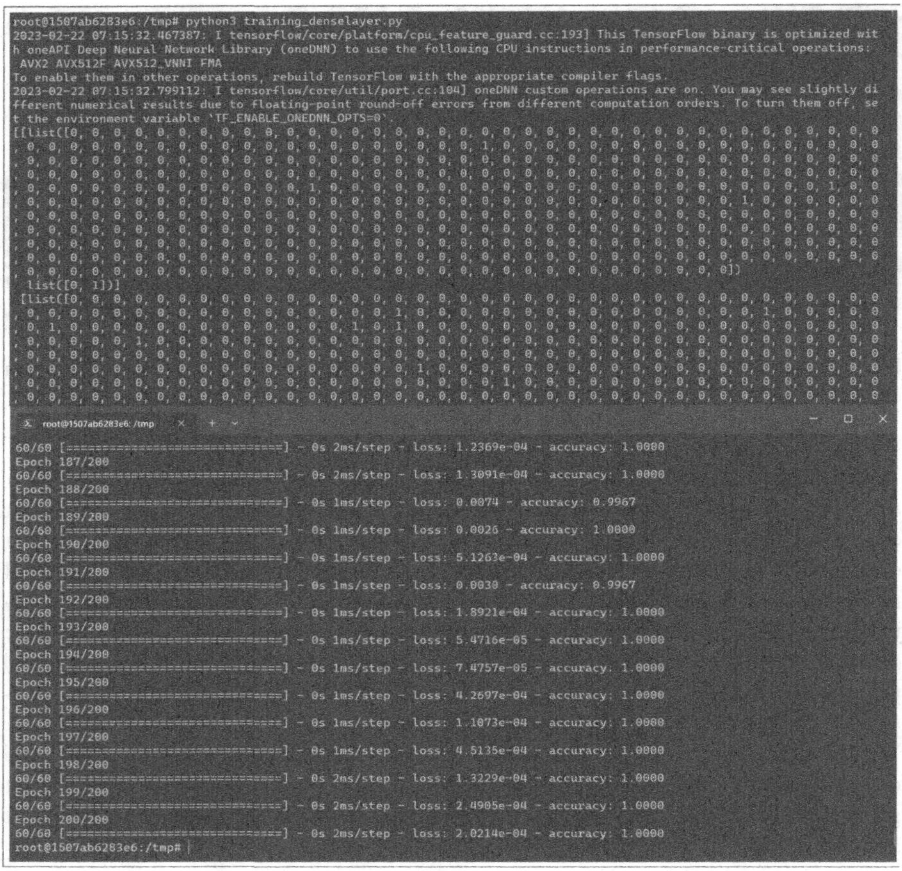

FIGURE 4.9   Replication of training process for sequential model inside the Docker container.

to the Cloud service providers. Other maintenance and growth parameters like scalability of resources and providing security to hardware infrastructure are also responsibilities of the Cloud service providers.

In this section, we wish to deploy our classification service onto the cloud. Due to the simplicity of the logistic regression classification model and its ability to successfully classify all ten of the test case, we decide to deploy this image as a service on the cloud. In this regard, we packaged and built our image using the Dockerfile in the previous section.

An image built locally in Docker can be deployed to the cloud as a service. Amazon Web Services (AWS) provides a framework to deploy and run the image on the Cloud. AWS achieves its objective using the three Es: The Elastic Container Registry (ECR), the Elastic Container Service (ECS), and the virtual servers on the Cloud (EC2). The interconnection between these three Es is diagrammatically shown in Figure 4.10.

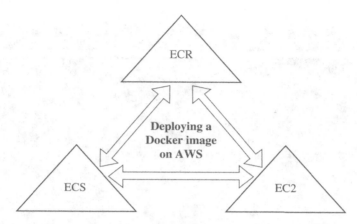

FIGURE 4.10 The three Es of the AWS platform.

Following is a brief overview of the processes involved in uploading and running the locally built Docker image on virtual servers on the Cloud:

- **Elastic Container Registry (ECR):** Before pushing the Docker image on the cloud, it is good practice to build and run the Docker image locally to be sure that there are no errors. After creating a new repository, ECR provides us with the commands to push the prebuilt Docker image onto this repository. This repository then hosts our image.
- **EC2:** On EC2, we launch a new instance with the settings for application and OS image, the instance type, and the key pair for SSH login. We can make changes to the network setting such as adding the inbound rules for SSH traffic. We must make sure that auto assignment of public IP is enabled. After we launch the instance, we can make use of an SSH client on the Windows 11 host machine such as putty to connect to the newly launched instance. On clicking the instance, we are given the way to connect through SSH. We shall have the key pair downloaded. Through putty, we can enter the hostname, and under the SSH, we have an Auth tab, and under credentials, we can browse for our key pair under the private key file for authentication tab. On clicking open, putty connects us to the EC2 instance, and we may log in as an EC2 user.
- **Elastic Container Service (ECS):** Under ECS, we set up an EC2 Linux+Networking Cluster. Similar to EC2 setup, in ECS setup, we can choose the appropriate EC2 instance type and key pair, make changes to the networking field, and so on. Once we create the cluster, we must register an external ECS instance with the cluster. In order to do this, ECS provides a command that we may run as root from inside the EC2 instance using putty. Once we execute the provided command as a root from inside the EC2 instance, it does two things. One, it registers this instance with the cluster. The other is that it sets up the EC2 instance with the prerequisites like the required setup and the installation of Docker inside the EC2 instance. Then, we must create the task definition which we wish to deploy

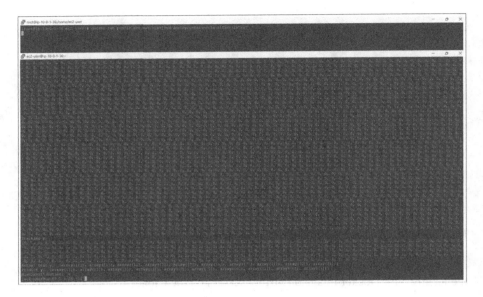

FIGURE 4.11   Running the Docker image on the AWS Cloud.

on our EC2 cluster. The task definition is also of the EC2 type. We choose the networking mode to be bridge. Choose a task execution IAM role. Set the task memory and task Vcpu. In this task definition, we are asked to add a container. The mandatory requirement in the container definition is its name and the image that would run on this container. It is in this image tab that we enter the image URL from the ECR. Once this setup is done, we can finalize the task definition. In our cluster, the EC2 instance is registered, our EC2 task is defined, and the container has been loaded with the image from the ECR. Now, we run the task. If the task is successfully executed on the cluster, then we may proceed to run this task and view results from inside the EC2 instance. For this, we log in to our EC2 instance using putty. We start the Docker service using the command *sudo service docker start.* Finally, we can run the image hosted on the ECR by running the command *docker run* and using the image URL from the ECR. After running the commands, we get the results from our classification program executed as a service on the Cloud as shown in Figure 4.11.

4.11   FURTHER EXTENSION TO DOCKER LOGISTIC CLASSIFICATION IMAGE USING CLOUD DATABASE

One further extension that can be achieved in the Docker Image for logistic regression classification is to have an integrated interaction with the Cloud database. In this section, we present the re-packaging of the logistic regression classification image that provides the classification between 'farming' and 'not farming' tags for an input query inside the Docker environment by having its training dataset drawn from a

FIGURE 4.12 Patterns under 'farming' and 'not farming' tags kept in Google Firestore.

Cloud database. The Cloud database considered here is the Google Cloud Firestore. Earlier the training dataset was in the form of the intents.json file which was added to our Dockerfile to build the logistic regression classification image. Figure 4.12 shows the dataset stored as collections in the Cloud Firestore.

Now, the Dockerfile gets updated from Tables 4.7 to 4.8. The coding changes to reflect the integration of Cloud Firestore are as follows. Earlier the intents.json file is loaded using the json library in Python and its load method. The intents.json file is no longer needed because we get all our patterns and their tags form the Cloud Firestore. Here, we first set up the firebase admin app and create two objects named farming and not_farming that store all the fields for the document named 'farming' and 'not farming', respectively, from the collection named tag. Now, in a manner like the previous process, we tag each pattern with its corresponding label. The rest

---

TABLE 4.8
Dockerfile Updated to Include the Integration with Cloud Firestore

FROM python:3.9
ADD fir-cloudupload-xxxxx-firebase-adminsdk-xxxxx-xxxxxxxxxx.json.
ADD classification_logistic_regression.py.
ADD classes.pkl.
ADD words.pkl.
RUN pip install --upgrade pip
RUN pip install nltk
RUN pip install numpy
RUN pip install scikit-learn
RUN pip install firebase_admin
COPY ./tokenizers /root/nltk_data/tokenizers
COPY ./corpora /root/nltk_data/corpora
CMD ["python","./classification_logistic_regression.py"]

of the process is like the logistic regression process presented before. In order for the Python script to be able to access the collections in Cloud Firestore, it needs the credentials file which has been added in row 2 of Table 5.8 to the current build process. Another command that has been added to the Dockerfile is the command *pip install firebase_admin* in row 10 of Table 5.8. This is the prerequisite to access Cloud Firestore from the Python app. The revised classification model using logistic regression that has integration with Cloud Firestore can be re-built using the command *docker build -t python-classification-lr*. The program can be run using the command *docker run python-classification-lr:latest*. On running the command, the correct output is displayed. This exercise is useful because if this image is deployed on the Cloud, for instance on AWS, and since, this image makes use of a Cloud database, we have an all-in-all Cloud solution for our classification process in the chatbot. New training data can be added to the Cloud Firestore and that can continuously refine the training process for classification process in the chatbot.

4.12 CONCLUSION

The chatbot process finds the user intent in the query by the client and uses this intent to either maintain a dialogue with the end user or to take an action based on that intent. The core process that helps in generating this user intent is the classification process. In this chapter, we create a dataset for two tags: 'farming' and 'not farming' from questions that are publicly posted to a popular knowledge sharing service on the internet. Questions under the 'farming' tag are meant to train the chatbot in the query patterns related to farming. Questions under the 'not farming' tag are meant to train the chatbot in the query patterns unrelated to farming. We train the classification model using a logistic regression technique from the traditional machine learning domain and a sequential model from the state-of-the-art deep learning domain. For our test dataset, both models give a zero-misclassification error. However, the sequential model takes longer to train because of the training epoch size of 200. Since the logistic regression model is simpler to train and set up, we present a way to deploy logistic regression classifier as a service on the Cloud. To achieve this, we build the logistic regression classifier image inside the Docker container. After checking the image locally for errors and bug-fixes, we present the framework of three Es provided by Amazon Web Services that allows the Docker image to be deployed on virtual servers on the Cloud. The packaged solution is deployed successfully on the AWS EC2 clusters, and they replicate the output like the host machine. We provide a heterogeneous integration of the Google Cloud Firestore as a training database in the Python script running logistic regression classifier. We package this enhanced setup inside the Docker, build and run it successfully. All in all, a blanket framework for Cloud-based classification service is presented in this book chapter.

REFERENCES

1. Conversational AI. *Freed, Andrew. Simon and Schuster*, 2021.
2. *Chatbots: History, technology, and applications.* Adamopoulou, Eleni and Moussiades, Lefteris. s.l.: Elsevier, 2020, Machine Learning with Applications, Vol. 2, p. 100006.

3. *Farmer's Friend: Conversational AI BoT for Smart Agriculture.* Venkata Reddy, P. S., Nandini Prasad, K. S. and Puttamadappa, C. 2022, Journal of Positive School Psychology, Vol. 6, pp. 2541–2549.

4. *Agrobot: An Agricultural Advancement to Enable Smart Farm Services Using NLP.* Gounder, Susheel, et al. 2021, Journal of Emerging Technologies and Innovative Research. https://ssrn.com/abstract=3890591

5. *Agroxpert-Farmer assistant.* Nayak, Vandana, Sowmya, N. H. and others. s.l.: Elsevier, 2021, Global Transitions Proceedings, Vol. 2, pp. 506–512.

6. *Krushi–The Farmer Chatbot.* Momaya, Mihir, et al. 2021. 2021 International Conference on Communication information and Computing Technology (ICCICT). pp. 1–6.

7. *Automatic Rice Disease Detection and Assistance Framework Using Deep Learning and a Chatbot.* Jain, Siddhi, et al. s.l.: MDPI, 2022, Electronics, Vol. 11, p. 2110.

8. *Identifying tomato leaf diseases under real field conditions using convolutional neural networks and a chatbot.* Cheng, Hsueh-Hung, et al. s.l.: Elsevier, 2022, Computers and Electronics in Agriculture, Vol. 202, p. 107365.

9. *A system for automatic rice disease detection from rice paddy images serviced via a Chatbot.* Temniranrat, Pitchayagan, et al. s.l.: Elsevier, 2021, Computers and Electronics in Agriculture, Vol. 185, p. 106156.

10. *Chatting with Plants (Orchids) in Automated Smart Farming using IoT, Fuzzy Logic and Chatbot.* Wiangsamut, Samruan, Chomphuwiset, Phatthanaphong and Khummanee, Suchart. 2019, Advances in Science, Technology and Engineering Systems Journal, Vol. 4, pp. 163–173.

11. *Agribot: a natural language generative neural networks engine for agricultural applications.* Arora, Bhavika, et al. 2020. 2020 International Conference on Contemporary Computing and Applications (IC3A). pp. 28–33.

12. *E-AGRO: Intelligent Chat-Bot. IoT and Artificial Intelligence to Enhance Farming Industry.* Ekanayake, Jayalath and Saputhanthri, Luckshitha. 2020, AGRIS on-line Papers in Economics and Informatics, Vol. 12, pp. 15–21.

13. NeuralNine. Intelligent AI Chatbot in Python. *Intelligent AI Chatbot in Python.* [Online] 2020. https://www.youtube.com/watch?v=1lwddP0KUEg.

14. Heo, Minsuk. [TensorFlow 2 Deep Learning] Dense Layer. *[TensorFlow 2 Deep Learning] Dense Layer.* [Online] 2020. https://www.youtube.com/watch?v=lor2LnEVn8M&list=PLVNY1HnUlO25XeZstpj7m-2RTtyOhv6hO&index=4.

5 Soil Analysis and Nutrient Recommendation System Using IoT and Multilayer Perceptron (MLP) Model

Y.P. Arul Teen, R. Bharathi, C. Justin Dhanaraj, and Anchana B.S.

5.1 INTRODUCTION

Agriculture is the backbone of many societies, providing food and nutrition to millions around the world [1, 2]. As the world's population continues to grow, it is essential that we develop better methods of producing food to ensure that all people have access to adequate nutrition. To achieve this, we must invest in research to improve agricultural methods and increase food production. Advances in technology and scientific understanding have led to a greater understanding of soil, crop growth, and pest management, which has enabled farmers to more effectively produce the food we need [3]. Further investment in research, development, and infrastructure is essential to ensuring that the agricultural industry can meet the needs of a growing global population [4]. Low productivity is the fundamental challenge facing the agriculture industry; hence, it is necessary to maximise agriculture production per unit of land. Typically, Indian farmers do not determine the nutrient composition of the soil. To address this issue, investing in soil testing technologies would enable farmers to assess the nutrient content in their soil and make more informed decisions about which crop to grow and what fertiliser to use. The solution to this problem is to adopt smart IoT technology, which will help Indian farmers collect soil data quickly, accurately, and efficiently [5]. In addition, using the data collected from the soil testing technology, farmers can take proactive measures to enhance their crop productivity [6]. This technology not only provides farmers with accurate soil data, but it also enables them to make better decisions about their crops, fertilisers, and other agronomic practices [7]. This technology also helps farmers save time, money, and labour, as well as reduce the environmental impact of their farming activities [8].

If the assessment techniques are not properly used to identify and analyse the correct nutrient composition of the land, it can lead to land degradation and decreased crop productivity, leading to losses in both the agricultural sector and economy [9]. The growth and the production yield of crops depend significantly on the nutrient composition of the land [10]. With technological advancements, more precise and accurate assessment techniques that can accurately determine the

DOI: 10.1201/9781003391302-5

nutrient composition of the soil and, based on this, suggest suitable fertilisers to use in order to maximise crop yields have been developed. This has enabled farmers to know more accurately what fertilisers and nutrients their land needs so that they can use the correct ones for optimal crop yields. As a result, crop cultivation has been significantly improved by the development of these precise and accurate assessment techniques, helping farmers use the most appropriate fertilisers for optimal yields.

The IoT is an exciting set of technologies that could be leveraged to deliver a wide range of agricultural modernisation solutions [11]. IoT offers farmers the opportunity to connect various sensors, actuators, and other devices to the internet, enabling them to capture real-time data about soil composition, nutrient levels, and weather conditions. This data-driven approach to farming allows farmers to make informed decisions and take corrective action in a timely manner, potentially resulting in increased yields and improved crop quality. Scientific institutions, research centres, and universities are playing a key role in the development of IoT-enabled solutions for farmers [12]. Moreover, AI can be used to analyse large amounts of data and identify patterns that lead to more effective decision-making. This data-driven approach to farming also reduces the risk of human error, resulting in higher yields and improved crop quality. Current soil management systems are highly limited in their ability to predict soil conditions accurately and effectively due to human error and poor sensor performance. IoT is commonly used for soil monitoring and is capable of collecting precise and real-time data that can be used to monitor soil conditions. However, IoT alone is not enough to ensure accurate predictions; it requires the use of advanced algorithms to analyse the collected data and make reliable forecasts [13]. To successfully solve this problem, advanced algorithms, such as artificial intelligence (AI) and machine learning, must be used in conjunction with the data collected by IoT sensors.

In this chapter, we used the IoT and a multilayer perceptron (MLP) model to develop soil monitoring and nutrition recommendations for different crop varieties. The proposed system uses a soil NPK (Nitrogen (N), Phosphorus (P), and Potassium (K)) sensor to measure the soil water content. The MLP model is then used to recommend the optimal fertiliser doses for different crop varieties. The MLP neural network is composed of an input layer, hidden layers, and an output layer, and it uses back propagation to adjust the weights between neurons. The input layer consists of the features extracted from the data collected by IoT sensors, while the hidden layers use activation functions such as sigmoid and tanh to process the input data. Finally, the output layer produces the predictions, which can be used to make decisions about irrigation and other soil-related operations. The proposed system is highly efficient, as the MLP model is trained to recognise different soil and fertiliser characteristics that are suitable for different crop varieties. The proposed system is both cost-effective and dependable because it allows farmers to precisely monitor soil nutrient levels in real time and recommend the optimal fertiliser dose while using minimal resources. Additionally, the proposed system is energy-efficient and eco-friendly, as it does not require any additional energy source for its operation. This makes it a great asset for sustainable agriculture and helps farmers maximise their yield while using fewer resources and reducing their environmental footprint.

5.1.1 RESEARCH BACKGROUND

Soil is a crucial component of the ecosystem that provides essential nutrients for plant growth and serves as a foundation for the food chain. However, soil quality is under threat from various factors, including climate change, land use, and human activities. Monitoring soil nutrient levels and recommending appropriate nutrient management strategies can help maintain soil fertility and enhance crop productivity. Recent advances in IoT technology enable the collection of real-time data on soil properties such as pH, temperature, moisture content, and nutrient levels. These data can be used to develop models that predict soil quality and nutrient requirements. MLP is a type of Artificial Neural Network (ANN) that has been widely used in soil science research to model soil properties. By integrating IoT and MLP, an efficient and accurate soil analysis and nutrient recommendation system can be developed to assist farmers in making informed decisions about crop management. Although previous studies have investigated soil analysis and nutrient recommendation systems using various technologies, there is still a significant research gap in integrating IoT and MLP models. Existing systems rely primarily on laboratory analysis, which is time-consuming and costly. Moreover, they may not provide real-time feedback on soil nutrient levels, leading to suboptimal nutrient management decisions. While MLP models have been used to predict soil properties and nutrient requirements, most studies have used laboratory data, which may not reflect soil properties in the field. Hence, there is a need for a soil analysis and nutrient recommendation system that combines the benefits of IoT technology and MLP models to provide real-time feedback on soil nutrient levels and accurate nutrient management recommendations. This system can help farmers make informed decisions about crop management, reduce the use of fertilisers and pesticides, and improve soil health while protecting the environment.

5.1.2 RESEARCH MOTIVATION

The motivation behind the proposed research on developing a soil analysis and nutrient recommendation system using IoT and MLP models is to address the challenges faced by farmers in managing soil fertility and improving crop productivity. Soil degradation and nutrient depletion have become major concerns due to factors. Traditional methods of soil analysis and nutrient management are time-consuming, costly, and may not provide real-time feedback on soil nutrient levels. The integration of IoT technology and MLP models offers a promising solution to these challenges. IoT sensors can provide real-time data on soil properties, and MLP models can process this data to predict soil nutrient levels and provide accurate recommendations on nutrient management strategies. The proposed system can help farmers make informed decisions about crop management, reduce the use of fertilisers and pesticides, and improve soil health while protecting the environment. Additionally, the system can be easily scaled and customised to meet the specific needs of different regions and crops. Overall, the research aims to provide a practical and efficient solution to the challenges of soil management and crop production, which can have significant implications for food security, environmental sustainability, and economic growth.

The following section discussed the recently developed IoT-based smart farming systems that use AI algorithms to make precise decisions about irrigation and other farming operations. The next chapter will explain the proposed system in more detail, discussing the architecture of the system and how it uses AI algorithms to make decisions. Section 5.4 presents a comparison of the system with other existing technologies. Section 5.5 concludes the chapter by discussing the potential of the system and some potential areas for future work.

5.2 LITERATURE REVIEW

This section provides a detailed analysis of the recently published soil analysis and nutrient recommendation systems. The analysis includes an overview of the existing soil testing methods, their strengths and limitations, as well as their recommendations for nutrient application.

M. Pyingkodi et al. [14] created a soil nutrient analysis and monitoring system using IoT. The system consists of various sensing components, such as soil moisture and temperature sensors, an electronic pH metre, and an automatic nutrient delivery system. The system also features an automated data collection and processing module that collates and stores the data from the sensing components. This data is then transmitted wirelessly to the cloud, where it can be accessed by farmers in order to analyse the soil conditions and decide on the best course of action for their crops.

Rab Nawaz Bashir et al. [15] proposed IoT-based soil salinity mapping. In their proposal, they discussed how to use a remote sensing system coupled with an IoT-enabled wireless mesh network in order to gather data from various sensors that are embedded in the soil. This method employed three types of soil sensors, including an electrical conductivity (EC) sensor, a pH sensor, and a total dissolved solids (TDSs) sensor. An EC sensor was used to measure the EC of the soil and served as an indicator of salinity; a pH sensor measured the acidity or alkalinity of the soil, and a TDS sensor measured the TDS in the soil. This solution characterises the soil salinity, moisture, and nutrient levels of the environment.

Blesslin Sheeba et al. [16] evaluated the soil samples with respect to a range of fertility parameters, including organic carbon (OC), indices for boron (B), phosphorus (P), available boron (B), potassium (K), and soil reaction (pH). The extreme learning machine (ELM) is used to classify the soil samples into several categories based on the different fertility parameters. In order to optimise the ELM, the results of Blesslin Sheeba's soil evaluation showed that a wide range of fertility parameters are necessary to accurately classify the different soil samples.

Burton et al. [17] developed an IoT gardening soil sheet system for soil nutrient analysis. The Waspmote ZB Pro SMA 5dBi radio is responsible for transmitting data over a long-range wireless network. Additionally, the system is equipped with a 6600-mAh rechargeable battery and a 7.4-volt solar panel for continuous energy supply. All the components work together in harmony, allowing the sheet system to send data over a long-range wireless network while relying on solar power. However, these components are only able to perform properly with the appropriate settings, as incorrect settings can significantly reduce the performance of the Waspmote ZB Pro SMA 5dBi radio.

Zhang et al. [18] developed an Internet of Things (IoT)-based soil monitoring system for Chinese citrus. The system consisted of a mix of single-point, multilayer, sensor nodes for detecting citrus soil temperature and humidity, and a citrus precision fertilisation. The system also can collect data on soil nutrients and soil moisture in real time, analyse and process them using a model-based approach, and then provide decision support for citrus production. However, there are still some challenges to be addressed, such as the calibration of soil sensors, the reliability and accuracy of sensor data, and the implementation of a long-term system maintenance plan.

R. Raut et al. [19] developed an IoT-based soil monitoring system to measure soil moisture content. The system comprised three primary components: a web server, a processing unit (ARM 7), and sensors. The sensors, which included temperature and humidity sensors and a moisture sensor, were installed in the soil to detect moisture levels. The collected data was transmitted to the ARM 7 processing unit, where it was analysed and processed before being sent to the web server. The web server displayed the results in a user-friendly format, enabling users to view and analyse the data more effectively. Modifications were made to improve the system's usability and efficiency.

Xin Yi Lau et al. [20] developed an IoT-based intelligent agriculture soil monitoring system that employs a proposed photon counting system and additional sensors such as temperature, humidity, and conductivity sensors to measure soil conditions. Additionally, a low-cost visible range wavelength (630 nm, 550 nm, and 470 nm) photon counting system with an input signal varying from 0 to 200 kHz was used. The sensors gathered data from the soil, which was then transmitted to the IoT-based platform for processing. The results were sent back to the user's mobile device in real time, allowing them to make informed decisions regarding crop management. Despite the system's usefulness, power consumption and data security remain significant challenges.

Muthumanickam Dhanaraju et al. [21] created a sustainable agriculture system based on the IoT. They explored the various tools and technologies available to farmers that could help improve crop production. Specifically, they focused on how wireless sensor networks can be used to monitor the health of crops and provide insights into the best practices for harvesting, irrigation, and pest management. The authors emphasised the need for more research into the use of sensors and other technological advancements in order to provide farmers with the necessary tools to produce higher yields. The authors also noted that these tools can improve the efficiency of farming and reduce the overall environmental impact.

Amna Ikram et al. [22] created a crop production maximisation using an IoT Intelligent Decision System. This system uses a dataset of meteorological variables, soil condition, and crop productivity information from various fields. The crop production maximisation system was tested against the SCS model, which uses an average of 11 crops' production over a period of time to make predictions.

Zihuai Lin et al. [23] designed an analysis of soil and environmental variables in the IoT smart farming scenario. This study proposed an integrated smart farming solution with the capability of monitoring and controlling environmental parameters, as well as soil properties. Through their research, they demonstrated the reliability of the system by deploying it in a field test for four weeks. In this study, they used the low-cost volumetric water content (VWC) sensor to measure the (VWC) of soil. This data was used to optimise the irrigation system, thus increasing the efficiency of water utilisation. The team found that the VWC sensor was reliable for use in an agricultural setting and showed an accuracy of less than 0.5% when compared to manual readings.

5.3 MATERIALS AND METHODS

The proposed soil monitoring and nutrient recommendation system comprises three main modules, soil monitoring, soil data analysis, and recommendation, as shown in Figure 5.1. In the soil monitoring layer, key soil parameters, such as pH, EC, organic matter (OM), available phosphorus (P), and available potassium (K), are monitored in real time using IoT sensors. The collected soil data is then transmitted to a centralised cloud storage system via the Wi-Fi module for storage. The soil data analysis and prediction module uses the collected soil data to predict the current fertility level of the soil. This module takes the five key parameters mentioned earlier as input and generates predictions for the soil fertility level. With the predicted fertility level, farmers can determine the required amount of fertilisers and other nutrients necessary to maintain their soil's fertility level.

5.3.1 SOIL MONITORING

Through the implementation of this IoT soil monitoring layer, the effects of soil degradation can be monitored in real time, providing farmers and other agricultural professionals with valuable insight into current soil conditions. The soil monitoring layer consists of a broad IoT network architecture that is connected to a variety of IoT soil smart sensors (NPK sensor), microcontrollers (Arduino microcontroller), Wi-Fi modules (ESP8266), and other IoT devices. These soil smart sensors collect and store data

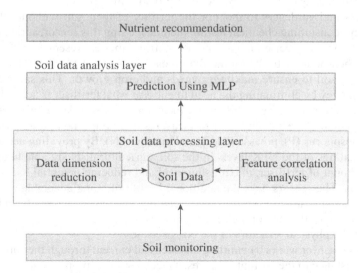

FIGURE 5.1 Overall architecture of proposed soil nutrient recommendation.

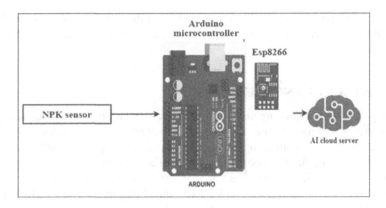

FIGURE 5.2 Soil monitoring layer's architecture.

related to the physical and chemical properties of the soil, such as temperature, moisture content, pH levels, and nutrient composition. The data collected from these sensors is then transmitted to a cloud-based data analytics platform, where it is processed and analysed. From the analysis of this data, predictive models can be developed to identify patterns and provide early warning signs of potential soil degradation. Figure 5.2 shows the architecture of soil monitoring layer.

5.3.2 NPK Sensor

The soil NPK sensor provides an accurate measure of the nutrient content in soil, allowing farmers to make well-informed decisions on what crops to plant and how much fertiliser is needed [24, 25]. Also, it provides an easy and cost-effective way for farmers and gardeners to monitor the fertility of their soil without relying on costly, time-consuming chemical testing methods. Using this sensor, agriculturalists can determine the precise amount of each nutrient that is present in the soil. This data can then be used to determine the precise amounts of nutrients that must be given to the soil to ensure maximum yields and crop growth. This saves farmers' time and money by eliminating the need to guess at what fertiliser is needed, as well as reducing the risk of over-fertilising, which can cause soil degradation and harm local ecosystems. The soil NPK sensor measures three important parameters of soil health: phosphorus (P), potassium (K), and nitrogen (N). By providing accurate and precise readings of the NPK levels in the soil, agriculturalists are able to apply the correct amount of fertiliser, maximising yield and reducing potential harm to local ecosystems. The sensors have the additional benefit of being adaptable to different soil types, and because it is non-invasive, readings may be taken quickly and simply. It is suitable for all kinds of soil, including sandy, clay, and loam soils. Figure 5.3 illustrates the physical structure of the NPK sensor.

The NPK sensor works by emitting an electrical current through the soil, measuring the resistance to the current. This resistance is directly proportional to the nutrient concentration of the soil, allowing for a precise reading of the soil NPK levels.

FIGURE 5.3 NPK sensor.

NPK sensor can be used with any microcontroller or computer system that has an analogue input port.

5.3.3 ARDUINO MICROCONTROLLER

Arduino microcontroller is a basic computer compared to other more powerful devices available today; it is an ideal tool for IoT applications such as soil monitoring. Some of the key advantages of the Arduino microcontroller are its ease of use, flexibility, and low cost, making it an ideal choice for IoT developers who want to quickly prototype and test their ideas. In the context of soil monitoring, the Arduino microcontroller is an ideal choice for interfacing with various sensors, such as NPK sensors and other environmental sensors, and collecting and processing data from these sensors. With the help of the Wi-Fi module, data collected by the sensors can be transmitted to the cloud-based data analytics platform for further processing and analysis. Moreover, Arduino is an open-source platform, which means that developers can use existing libraries and code snippets, which can save time and effort during the development process. Additionally, the large community of developers associated with Arduino ensures that a wide range of online resources, and troubleshooting guides are available, making it easier for developers to learn and work with the platform. [25].

Arduino's architecture includes an on-board processor and memory, an open-source development environment (IDE) for programming, a communication interface for wired and wireless connections, and an open-source I/O library for sensor integration. The on-board processor of the Arduino microcontroller helps process the raw data collected from the sensors in real time and provides advanced signal processing capabilities. Its on-board memory is used to store the data collected by the sensors, allowing for efficient data storage. The open-source IDE of the Arduino allows users to create their own programmes and upload them to the on-board processor. Finally, its open-source I/O library enables easy integration of external components such as cameras and GPS modules, allowing for a wide range of applications. The pins of the Arduino allow users to easily connect sensors, actuators, and other components. The architecture of this system allows for both efficient and effective data management, as well as the ability to create algorithms to detect subtle patterns of soil monitoring over time. The image in Figure 5.4 depicts the Arduino microcontroller's physical architecture.

FIGURE 5.4   Arduino microcontroller.

5.3.4 ESP8266 Wi-Fi Module

The ESP8266 Wi-Fi module is an important part of the Arduino system, as it allows for wireless communication with other devices. With this module, users are able to connect Arduino boards to the internet and send data from the physical world (sensors, actuators, etc.) over the web. Additionally, the ESP8266 Wi-Fi module can also be used to allow for remote control of the system. By combining these features with the architecture of the system, Arduino users are able to create powerful applications that allow for efficient and effective data management, while also being able to detect subtle patterns of soil monitoring over time. The architecture of the ESP8266 Wi-Fi module includes networking protocols such as TCP/IP, UDP, MQTT, and REST APIs. These protocols enable the device to communicate over the web, whether it be sending data to a remote server or receiving commands from an application. The ESP8266 Wi-Fi module has four pins that allow for a direct connection to other devices such as sensors, servos, and motors. The first pin is the power pin, which provides the necessary electricity to the module, while the remaining three pins are I/O pins that allow the ESP8266 Wi-Fi module to receive data from and send commands to other devices. Figure 5.5 depicts the physical architecture of the ESP8266 Wi-Fi module.

5.3.5 AI Cloud Server

The ESP8266 Wi-Fi module is compatible with the AI cloud server, making it possible to send data to and receive commands from the cloud server. By connecting the ESP8266 Wi-Fi module to the AI cloud server, users can control and monitor other devices from any location. This offers a huge advantage for IoT applications, as users can access their devices from anywhere with an internet connection. Additionally,

FIGURE 5.5 ESP8266 Wi-Fi module.

with the AI cloud server, users can store and share data collected from their devices with other users or applications. The fundamental principle of these AI cloud servers is to analyse the soil data collected from the IoT sensors. AI cloud servers are capable of processing massive amounts of soil data. AI cloud servers offer machine learning and AI capabilities to analyse the data collected from the IoT sensors. The adaptation of AI cloud servers in soil monitoring provides an efficient method of real-time monitoring and managing agricultural land, improving the quality and yield of crops.

5.4 PREDICTION MODEL USING MLP

5.4.1 DATASET DETAILS

The dataset used in this investigation was obtained from various regions in the Kanyakumari district, situated in the Tamil Nadu state of India. The dataset comprised soil nutrient samples gathered from diverse sources, including organic matter content, exchangeable cations, EC, TDSs, and pH. IoT soil sensors generate voluminous amounts of noisy data that traditional techniques may find challenging to process. This may result in a decline in the efficiency of prediction models. Therefore, it is critical to clean and pre-process the noisy data to derive useful insights. In this chapter, the principal component analysis (PCA) method was employed to decrease the dimensionality of the data, while the min-max normalisation technique was used to normalise the soil data.

5.4.2 DATASET NORMALISATION AND DIMENSION REDUCTION

Dataset normalisation was also performed in order to make the datasets more suitable for training and testing. In this study, dataset normalisation is accomplished using min-max normalisation, which transforms each feature in the dataset to a value between 0 and 1. This transformation allows for a more uniform representation of the data and prevents any single feature from having an outsized influence on the training and testing process. The min-max normalisation ensures that all features are on the same scale, which helps the algorithms more effectively train and test on the dataset. In addition, the min-max normalisation helps prevent large differences in range between features that can lead to bias in the training process. Ultimately, this is beneficial for the algorithm, as it can more effectively identify patterns in the data when all features are represented on the same scale:

$$X_{norm} = \frac{X - min(X)}{(max(X) - min(X))} \tag{5.1}$$

For min-max normalisation, use the following formula, where X_{norm} is the normalised value of the feature X and $min(X)$ and $max(X)$ are the minimum and maximum values of the feature X, respectively.

PCA was used to reduce the dimensionality of the soil dataset and enhance the accuracy of each algorithm. The principal components, which are the eigenvectors of the covariance matrix, form a new coordinate system where the variance in the data can be visualised more effectively. In the soil dataset, PCA was employed to merge similar features into a single feature that better explains the variation in the data, thereby reducing the number of features. The typical soil dataset includes undesired features that result from IoT sensor failures and other manual errors, which do not affect the classification algorithms. By implementing PCA, the dimensionality of the dataset was reduced, and only significant features were retained. The goal of using PCA on the soil dataset was to improve the accuracy of each machine learning algorithm by removing noise from unwanted features. The following formula was used to compute the principal components from the input data:

$$\bar{Y} = \sum_{i=1}^{n} DX, 1 \le i \le n, \tag{5.2}$$

where X represents the dataset. The data dimension is denoted by $D = (D1, D2....Dn)$. The actual number of data variables in the data collection is denoted by $X = (X_1, X_2...X_n)$ and $(\bar{Y} = \bar{Y}_1, \bar{Y}_2,...\bar{Y}_n)$ is the new data variable produced by the PCA. This formula seeks to extract the maximum amount of variance from the input data by projecting it onto a new set of orthogonal components that are derived from the eigenvectors of the covariance matrix.

5.4.3   FEATURE EXTRACTION

The efficiency of machine learning and deep learning algorithms is estimated using optimal feature selection approaches. The goal of feature selection is to decrease the problem's complexity and focus on a collection of critical variables capable of effectively capturing the correlation between soil characteristics and target variables. Incorporating erroneous data into the soil data analysis increases the risk of mistakes during the nutrient recommendation. It is necessary to consider which features have the most influence on the model's prediction performance. As a result, feature selection methods must be used to choose the most significant features from the soil dataset and remove the irrelevant ones. In this study, a multidimensional soil dataset is used to train the MLP-based prediction model. The dataset was constructed by creating a binary matrix of size nxn, where each entry in the matrix indicates whether two soil features are highly connected or not. The number of columns, n, includes the features obtained from soil samples such as phosphorus (P), nitrogen (N), and potassium (K). Each row of the dataset represents a sample collected from a specific soil region. The dataset also contains the corresponding label for each sample, which is the soil classification associated with it. Equation 5.3 is used to represent the class labels and features:

$$F = \begin{bmatrix} \vec{f1} \\ \vec{f2} \\ \vec{f3} \\ \cdot \\ \cdot \\ \vec{fn} \end{bmatrix}, \quad C = \begin{bmatrix} c1 \\ c2 \\ c3 \\ \cdot \\ \cdot \\ cm \end{bmatrix} \tag{5.3}$$

The features vectors (F) and class labels (C) each include n and m distinct class labels. n and m can vary depending on the nature of the soil parameters. The relationship between F and C is determined by Equation 5.4:

$$Cor_{fc} = \frac{\sum (F_i - \bar{F})(C_i - \bar{C})}{\sqrt{\sum (F_i - \bar{F})^2 \sum (C_i - \bar{C})^2}} \tag{5.4}$$

The observed mean value of the ith soil character is represented by $\bar{F}$, while the average value of the class label is represented by $(\bar{C})$. Using Equation 5.4, we can get values ranging from 0 to 1. The association between the soil parameters and the class labels impacts these numbers. It returns positive numbers between 1 and 0, or negative values, depending on how well the soil parameters correlate with the class label. Table 5.1 shows the correlations between the class values and the soil parameters.

TABLE 5.1

Correlation Coefficients between Soil Parameters and Prediction Values

Similarity Values	Similarity Range
1	The value 1 denotes very highly connected soil features means that the features in that soil sample are highly correlated.
1–0.8	A value between 1 and 0.8 denotes moderately connected soil features, meaning that some of the features are correlated, while others may be relatively independent.
0.6–0.8	A value between 0.6 and 0.8 denotes very small connectivity, which means that the features in that soil sample are not correlated to each other.
0	The value 0 denotes very low connectivity of soil features, which means that the features in that sample are not as strongly correlated.

Correlation coefficients between 1 and 0.5 are employed in this study to train MLP models to improve the accuracy of soil nutrient recommendation. By employing Equation 5.5, highly associated features are selected in this case:

$$H_{CF} = \begin{cases} 0.6 \le N \le 1; \\ 0.6 \le P \le 1; \\ 0.6 \le K \le 1 \end{cases} \tag{5.5}$$

5.4.4 PREDICTION MODEL

Deep learning algorithms have been increasingly used to develop predictive models for various agricultural applications, such as crop yield forecasting, soil management, and disease detection. This chapter incorporates this technology by using a pre-trained deep learning model to automatically analyse the soil composition and accurately predict the required fertiliser dose. In general, the MLP algorithm has been the most popular deep learning algorithm used in agricultural applications due to its ability to process complex data, identify hidden patterns, and perform automated feature selection. So this chapter uses MLP to predict the fertiliser dose according to the soil composition.

5.4.4.1 Multilayer Perceptron

The architecture of a MLP is designed to mimic the structure and function of the human brain, using neurons and layers of interconnected nodes to process complex data [26]. MLP architecture consists of several layers of neurons, or nodes that are interconnected with each other and can receive input from the environment or from previous layers in the network [27]. Each node performs simple operations on the input data, such as summation or multiplication, and then passes this information along to the next layer of nodes in the network [28]. The data that is passed through the network is weighted according to its relevance and importance, with more relevant and important data being given higher weights. Figure 5.6 represents the overall structure of the MLP model.

The output of each node is determined by a formula of the form f(w, x), where w is a vector of weights and x is the input vector. The primary functions of this MPL model are described as follows:

$$a_H = f1(W_H a_H + b_H) \tag{5.6}$$

where the activation function is denoted by the formula f1, where ReLU is used in the proposed soil nutrient recommendation system. The number of nodes in the input layer is represented by a, and H denotes the number of nodes in the hidden layer. The error function (E) employed in the system is cross-entropy, which measures the disparity between the output of the MLP algorithm and the optimal fertiliser dose. Subsequently, the optimal fertiliser dose recommendation is obtained through the use of the training feature and the output of the final hidden layer:

$$\hat{Y} = P^t a_H \tag{5.7}$$

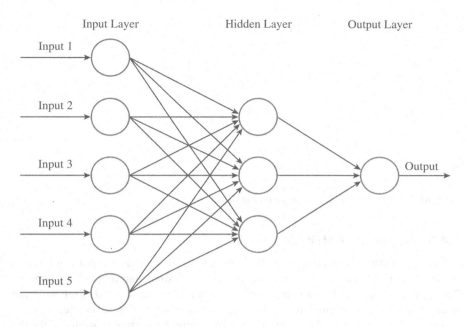

FIGURE 5.6 General architecture of MLP model.

where optimal fertiliser dose is represented by the variable $\hat{Y}$ and is determined by the output of the MLP algorithm. According to this study, the neural network's weights can be dynamically adjusted, allowing it to detect errors and improve prediction accuracy:

$$-W = W + L \times (\mathbb{E} - \mathbb{p}) \times X \tag{5.8}$$

where W is the weight vector of the MLP algorithm and represents a set of values associated with each neuron, indicating the strength of the connection between two neurons in an adjacent layer. L is the learning rate parameter, which indicates how quickly the weights are adjusted in order to reduce errors and improve prediction accuracy. E represents the expected result that the MLP is attempting to predict, and P represents the actual result. The difference between the expected and actual results (E − P) is known as the prediction error. Figure 5.7 depicts the suggested MLP-based soil nutrient recommendation model.

The soil nutrient recommendation model has three layers: the input layer, which is composed of the soil composition features; the hidden layers, where the features are processed and connected to each other; and finally, an output layer consisting of a single node for predicting the optimal. The MLP algorithm is able to learn the nonlinear relationships between the soil composition features and the optimal fertiliser dose through multiple iterations, each time updating the weights of its nodes. The MLP algorithm is trained using a training dataset, which consists of samples of soil composition and their corresponding optimal fertiliser dose. During the training process, the MLP algorithm iteratively updates its weights in order to minimise an error function.

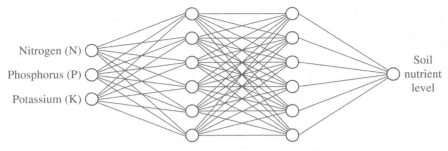

Input Layer $\in$ R^3 Hidden Layer $\in$ R^6 Hidden Layer $\in$ R^6 Output Layer $\in$ R^1

FIGURE 5.7   Soil nutrient recommendation model.

5.4.5   TRAINING THE MLP MODEL

Training is a critical component of MLP as it allows the model to adjust weights and biases associated with each neuron such that the desired output can be obtained. Through learning, MLP can assign weights to each feature in the dataset such that it can accurately determine the soil classification based on its associated characteristics. Using advanced learning algorithms can provide greater accuracy for the model, such as back propagation (BP) and stochastic gradient descent (SGD). BP, SGD, and the momentum coefficient (MC) are used in MLP in this study to adjust the weights associated with each feature of the dataset. The BP algorithm works by taking the error of a prediction and sending it back through the neural network in order to update the weights associated with each neuron. SGD works by adjusting the weights associated with each neuron after evaluating a single training example. By adjusting the weights after evaluating a single training example, SGD helps to reduce the amount of time necessary to evaluate the entire dataset. The MC is used to help the BP algorithm continue in the right direction when it reaches a local minimum, as well as to provide smoother convergence of the cost function. With this combination of algorithms, the MLP is able to adjust the weights associated with each feature in order to accurately predict a result given a set of inputs. The standard BP algorithm's pseudo-code is depicted in Algorithm 5.1.

Algorithm 5.1: Pseudo-code of the traditional BP algorithm

Initialize Weights:
While *not StopCriterion* **do**
    for *all i, j* **do**

$$\Delta w_{ij} = \left(\eta * \frac{\partial E}{\partial w_{ij}} \right)$$

    end **for;**
end **while;**

The formula used to adjust the weights in the BP algorithm is given by

$$w_{(t+1)} = w_t - \eta \frac{d(E)}{d(w_1)} \tag{5.9}$$

where w represents the weights, η is the learning rate, E is the error obtained from the output layer. By applying Equation 5.9, weights are adjusted to minimise the error of the output, but it takes time to reach the optimal weight values. To reduce the time taken to reach optimal SGD is used. SGD randomly selects training samples from the dataset, processes them, and updates the weights according to Equation 5.9. SGD allows us to quickly adjust the weights so that the error of the output is minimised in a much shorter amount of time than traditional weight updating techniques.

The MC, which is typically set to a value between 0 and 1, is used to modify the weight update in order to avoid getting stuck in local minima or increasing the oscillations of the cost function. The MC is denoted by α:

$$\Delta w_t = \alpha \Delta w_{(t-1)} + \eta \frac{d(E)}{d(w_1)} \tag{5.10}$$

This MC helps SGD by reducing the oscillations and allowing the model to converge faster to an optimal set of weights.

5.4.6 Soil Nutrition Recommendation

The recommendation layer of the proposed system displays the data in an easy-to-understand format, allowing farmers to make informed decisions about their farming practices. The system can provide actionable insights about soil nutrition levels and other farming metrics, which will help farmers optimise their yields and reduce their environmental footprint. Furthermore, the data is continuously monitored and updated on an ongoing basis, giving farmers real-time access to the most up-to-date information.

5.5 RESULTS AND DISCUSSION

5.5.1 System Setup and Software Tools

Matlab 2018 and Matlab machine learning packages were used in the development of this soil nutrient recommendation system. For accelerated training, the MLP model was implemented on a desktop computer with 8 GB of RAM, an Intel Core i7 processor, and an Nvidia Graphics Processing Unit (GPU).

5.5.2 Accuracy Analysis

The performance analysis of the proposed MLP model for soil nutrient recommendation systems is compared with the most popular machine learning algorithms, including support vector machine (SVM), decision tree (DT), k-nearest neighbour (KNN), and Naive Bayes (NB).

The most widely used supervised machine learning algorithm is the SVM, which is used for both classification and regression tasks [29]. It is used to map a set of given data points in an n-dimensional space into two or more classes. By mapping the data points onto the classes, SVM is able to draw a boundary line that best separates the two classes. With this line, it is then able to determine which data points belong to which class by measuring the distance of each point from the boundary line. In addition, SVM also takes into account any outliers that may be present in the data and assigns higher weights to them so that they don't get ignored while making the decision boundary. In this way, SVM is able to draw a hyperplane that accurately predicts the classes of a given set of data points.

DT unlike SVM creates a DT from the training data and uses the DT to make predictions [30]. The DT is composed of nodes, each representing a single attribute or value of an attribute, and edges that represent the relationships between different attributes. DT is able to draw a single, linear decision boundary that separates data points into their respective classes by using the hierarchical structure of the DT. This is particularly useful when there are a large number of classes in the dataset, as it allows for more efficient prediction. In addition, the structure of the DT makes it easy to interpret and explain how a model is making predictions. As such, DTs have become a popular choice for data scientists and machine learning engineers, especially in the fields of finance, healthcare, and marketing.

KNN is a machine learning algorithm that is commonly used for classification problems [31]. KNN is a supervised learning algorithm that works by looking at the k-nearest points to the data point being predicted and assigning it to whichever class those points belong to. KNN is advantageous for its ease of implementation and interpretability, as the user only needs to specify the number of neighbours to consider when making a prediction. KNN is particularly useful for datasets with small sample sizes, where it can provide more reliable predictions than DTs. KNN is also computationally efficient, as the algorithm only needs to look at the k-nearest points to make a prediction. Despite its advantages, KNN is not suitable for datasets with large numbers of features.

NB is another powerful algorithm that can be used in place of KNN when working with large datasets [32]. NB is a probabilistic algorithm that uses the Bayes theorem to calculate the probability of an event occurring based on prior knowledge. NB is known to be faster and more accurate than KNN when working with datasets containing a large number of features, making it an attractive option for many machine learning tasks. NB also has some advantages over KNN, such as not requiring any distance calculations. However, one of the biggest drawbacks of NB is that it is a supervised learning algorithm, meaning that it requires labelled data to work properly. Therefore, if the dataset is unlabelled, NB cannot be used, and KNN would be the more appropriate choice. Additionally, KNN can be used for regression as well as classification problems, whereas NB is primarily a classifier.

The pre-processed dataset was partitioned into distinct training and testing datasets. The training dataset was employed to train each of the five algorithms, while the testing dataset was reserved to evaluate their performances. Each algorithm was trained on the soil dataset using a 10-fold cross-validation technique with a partitioning of 70% training data and 30% testing data. To assess the efficacy of each algorithm, key performance indicators such as accuracy, precision, recall, and F1 score were employed. These metrics served to quantify the algorithms' abilities to correctly classify the soil data and to provide a comprehensive evaluation of their respective performances.

5.5.2.1 Accuracy

In soil nutrient recommendations, accuracy is the most important measure of performance as it shows how accurately the algorithms can recommend nutrient levels for a given soil sample. Thus, the performance of each algorithm was assessed based on its accuracy in recommending the correct soil nutrient levels for a given sample. The soil nutrient recommendation systems' accuracy is determined by the following equation:

$$Accuracy = \frac{TP + TN}{TP + TN + FP + FN} \tag{5.11}$$

In soil nutrient recommendations, a "true positive" (TP) means the system correctly identifies a soil sample as requiring specific nutrient, and those recommendations are indeed accurate, while a "false positive" (FP) refers to the system correctly identifies a soil sample as not requiring specific nutrient, and this is indeed accurate. On the other hand, FP means the system recommends adding certain nutrients to a soil sample, but it's found that those recommendations were not needed. This can occur when the system is not accurate in its assessment of the soil sample's nutrient needs, while false negative (FN) means the system fails to recommend certain nutrients for a soil sample, but those recommendations were actually needed. This can occur when the system is not sensitive enough to detect the soil sample's nutrient needs.

5.5.2.2 Precision

Precision is the other most important metric in soil nutrient recommendation systems, which is calculated by the ratio of TPs to the sum of TPs and FPs. Precision helps to measure how accurately the soil nutrient recommendation systems are able to identify what nutrients are actually present in the soil sample. The soil nutrient recommendation systems' precision is determined by the following equation:

$$Precision = \frac{TP}{TP + FP} \tag{5.12}$$

5.5.2.3 Recall

Recall is a measure of how effective the soil nutrient recommendation system is in identifying all nutrients that should be present in the soil sample, calculated by the ratio of TPs) to the sum of TPs and FNs. Thus, the combination of precision and recall provides a holistic overview of how effective soil nutrient recommendation systems are in accurately determining what nutrients should be present in the soil sample. The soil nutrient recommendation systems' recall value is determined by the following equation:

$$Recall = \frac{TP}{TP + FN} \tag{5.13}$$

5.5.2.4 F1 Score

The F1 score is a metric that combines precision and recall, providing a measure of the balance between them. In soil nutrient recommendation system evaluation, the F1 score is important as it takes into account both precision and recall, providing a single metric that reflects the effectiveness of the system. A higher F1 score indicates better performance of the soil nutrient recommendation system, as it shows that both precision and recall are good. This means that the system is accurate not just in identifying which nutrients are present but also in predicting what other nutrients should be present in the soil sample:

$$F1 - score = \frac{2(Recall \times Precision)}{Recall + Precision} \tag{5.14}$$

The confusion matrices presented in Figure 5.8 provide insights into the performance of each machine learning model. The matrices show the TP, TP, true negative, and FN rates of each model, as well as the areas of focus for improvement. From the confusion matrices, it is evident that the machine learning models achieved varying levels of success on the soil dataset. A total of 1500 soil samples are used to evaluate the MLP model and other machine learning methods. The confusion matrices show that the MLP model had a higher TP rate and a higher true negative rate. This means that it correctly identified both positive and negative samples with a high level of accuracy.

On the basis of the confusion matrices, the above mentioned precision metrics are calculated.

Figures 5.9–5.12 show the accuracy analysis of proposed model with the existing machine learning models. After testing and validating the algorithms on the soil dataset, it was found that the proposed MLP outperformed the other algorithms in terms of accuracy, recall, precision, and F1 score, suggesting that it is a viable option for analysing soil datasets. The MLP model's accuracy was significantly higher than the other machine learning models, and it achieved an overall precision of 0.76, which is a considerable improvement over the existing machine learning models. These findings suggest that MLP models can be used to effectively analyse soil datasets and produce accurate results, making them a valuable tool for scientists and engineers working with soil data. This was supported by the confusion matrices, which showed that the MLP model had a higher TP rate than all other models, indicating that it was able to accurately identify positive samples more reliably. This shows that the MLP model was able to identify both positive and negative samples with a high degree of accuracy, outperforming the other algorithms.

5.5.3 TRAINING EFFICIENCY ANALYSIS

A dataset of 1500 samples was used for training the model, with 1000 samples allocated for training and 500 samples for validation purposes. The implementation of the model required careful tuning of various hyperparameters. The training process employed a combination of BP, SGD, and MC algorithms, with a learning rate of 0.001 and a batch size of 32. The model was trained for 200 epochs and monitored to prevent over-fitting or under-fitting. Following the training phase, the performance of

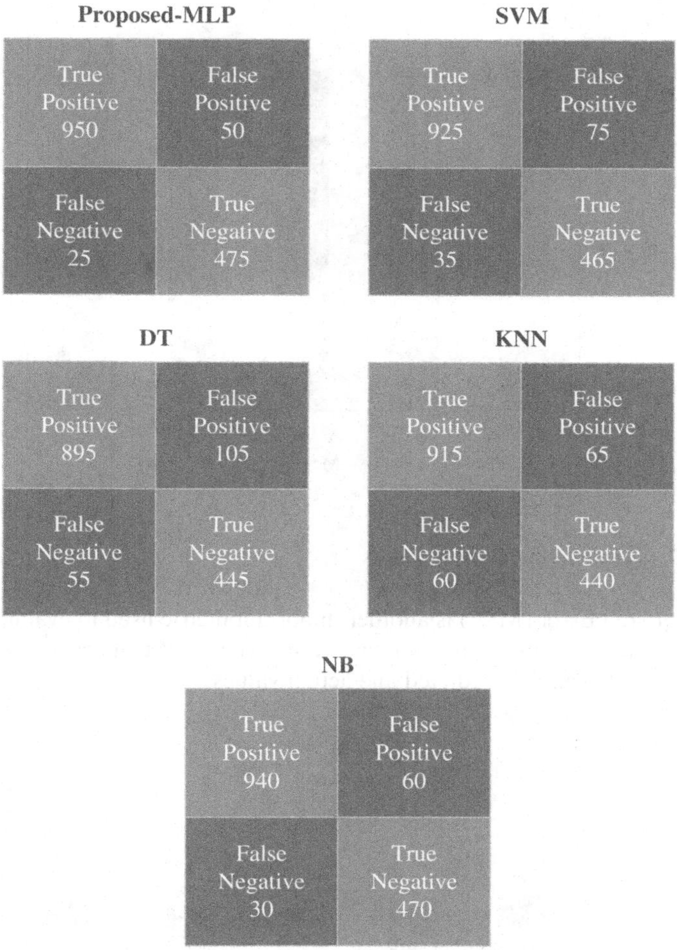

Proposed-MLP

True Positive 950	False Positive 50
False Negative 25	True Negative 475

SVM

True Positive 925	False Positive 75
False Negative 35	True Negative 465

DT

True Positive 895	False Positive 105
False Negative 55	True Negative 445

KNN

True Positive 915	False Positive 65
False Negative 60	True Negative 440

NB

True Positive 940	False Positive 60
False Negative 30	True Negative 470

FIGURE 5.8 TP, TN, FP, and FN proportions of proposed MLP and existing machine learning models.

the MLP model was evaluated using popular error analysis metrics, including mean absolute error (MAE), mean square error, and root mean square error (RMSE). These metrics are effective in determining the discrepancy between the predicted values and the expected values of the soil nutrient recommendation system, with lower error values indicating a higher level of accuracy.

MAE is the most important error metric, as it measures the average magnitude of errors in a set of predictions, without considering their direction. The following formula is used to determine the MAE values:

$$MAE = \frac{1}{n} \sum_{i=1}^{n} |yi - \widehat{yi}| \tag{5.15}$$

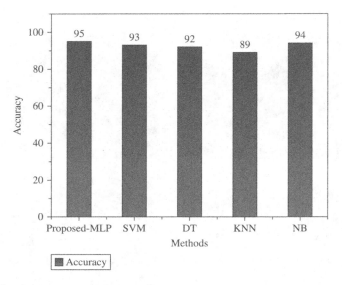

FIGURE 5.9 Accuracy comparison results.

Mean Squared Error (MSE) is another important metric used to evaluate the performance of the soil nutrient recommendation system. MSE measures the average squared error between the predicted and actual values.

$$MSE = \frac{1}{N} \sum_{i=1}^{N} \left| yi - \widehat{yi} \right|^2 \qquad (5.16)$$

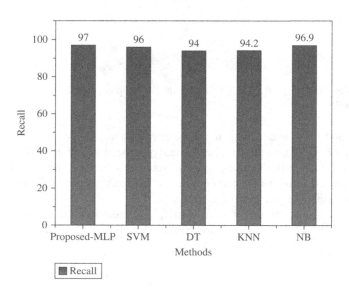

FIGURE 5.10 Recall comparison results.

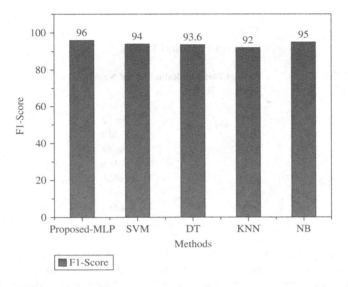

FIGURE 5.11 F1 score comparison results.

In the earlier-mentioned formulas, X is a vector of predictions, and Y is the vector of true values.

The more training data there is, the more it influences the AI model's accuracy and the more computer resources it requires (memory and processing power). With an increased amount of training data, the MLP proposed in this chapter can become more efficient and provide more accurate predictions. This was seen in the

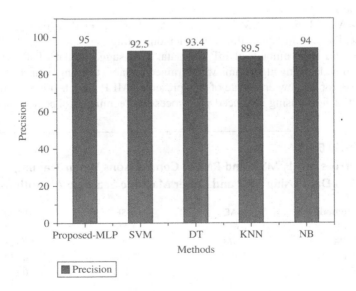

FIGURE 5.12 Precision comparison results.

TABLE 5.2
DataSet Partition Ratios

Dataset Partition Ratio (Training, Testing)	Fold Name
60:40	Fold 1
65:35	Fold 2
70:30	Fold 3
75:25	Fold 4
80:20	Fold 5
85:15	Fold 6
90:10	Fold 7
95:5	Fold 8

experimental results, with more data resulting in a decrease in MAE, MSE, and RMSE. In order to determine the effectiveness of the soil nutrient recommendation model, the dataset has been separated linearly, and training and testing have been completed. The partitioning of the dataset is described in detail in Table 5.2.

In order to obtain trustworthy comparison results, as shown in Table 5.2, MLP and other machine learning algorithms are trained and evaluated, and their average values are used for comparative analysis.

According to Table 5.3, the MAE, MSE, and RMSE values of the presented MLP model are relatively low compared to other machine learning algorithms. The results of the training showed that the model had an MAE of 0.661, an MSE of 2.924, and an RMSE of 0.103, indicating that it had an excellent generalisation ability and was able to learn.

The MAE, MSE, and RMSE errors of MLP are lower than those obtained by other machine learning algorithms, thus demonstrating the superiority of MLP when trained with a large amount of IoT soil data. This suggests that MLP outperforms other machine learning algorithms when trained on large training data. There are two key reasons for the low error rate of this presented MLP model. Initially, the dataset is cleaned of noise using advanced pre-processing techniques. The second essential

TABLE 5.3
Errors (MAE, MSE, and RMSE) Comparisons When Training Soil Data Using MLP and Other Machine Learning Algorithms

Methods	MAE	MSE	RMSE
MLP	0.661	2.924	0.103
SVM	0.673	2.297	0.123
DT	0.728	2.078	0.112
KNN	0.653	2.110	0.109
NP	0.741	2.081	0.117

aspect is that the combination of SGD and MC improves the training efficiency of the BP algorithm. By using a combination of SGD and MC, the MLP model can reach an optimal error rate in much less time than would be possible by using BP alone. Both of these methods and algorithms efficiently train the critical soil parameters to MLP in less time. Furthermore, SGD and MC can be combined to increase the accuracy of the model as well.

5.5.4 The Following Are Significant Advantages of the Proposed System

- The proposed architecture allows soil nutrients to be mapped quickly, accurately, and portably.
- This new system can provide farmers with a detailed understanding of soil fertility levels, allowing them to make more informed decisions when applying fertilisers and other soil amendments.
- This system provides an innovative way for modern farmers to save time and money by quickly and easily moving their systems to meet different needs.
- The portability of the proposed system has major implications for modern farmers, as they can now move their systems to different areas as their needs change.
- Anyone can access this data with the help of the internet, and it is beneficial for regulatory authorities, researchers, and farmers. It is important to note that the data stored in the database can be used to inform decisions and plans for improving soil salinity in different parts of the world.

5.6 CONCLUSION

In recent years, the emergence of IoT and AI has brought significant advancements in various fields, and agriculture is no exception. IoT technology has enabled farmers to monitor soil conditions and water levels, providing them with insights on the best time for planting, irrigation, and harvesting. Soil monitoring is a crucial application of IoT technology in farming as it enables farmers to keep track of soil nutrient levels and moisture content, thereby improving crop yield. This chapter has successfully presented a soil nutrition recommendation system using IoT and MLP models, which can be applied to a wide range of agricultural applications. Specifically, the NPK sensor was employed to collect essential soil nutrition parameters, which were processed using the MLP model to develop the soil nutrition recommendation system. The accuracy of the system was evaluated with real-time soil testing results, enabling an accurate assessment of the effectiveness of the proposed system. The proposed soil nutrition recommendation system was tested with experimental data, and the results demonstrated a high degree of accuracy achieved by the MLP model. The monitoring system's collected data can be used to guide farmers' decision-making processes, such as determining when to apply fertilisers or pesticides, or when to plant specific crops. With the system's assistance, farmers can accurately measure soil nutrition levels with minimal effort and cost, making it a cost-effective, reliable, and user-friendly system for farmers.

REFERENCES

1. Devaux, A. et al. (2020). Global Food Security, Contributions from Sustainable Potato Agri-Food Systems. In: Campos, H., Ortiz, O. (eds) The Potato Crop. Springer, Cham. https://doi.org/10.1007/978-3-030-28683-5_1
2. Singh, R., Singh, G.S., "Traditional Agriculture: A Climate-Smart Approach for Sustainable Food Production," Energy, Ecology and Environment, vol. 2, pp. 296–316, 2017. https://doi.org/10.1007/s40974-017-0074-7
3. Popp, J., Pető, K., Nagy, J., "Pesticide Productivity and Food Security. A Review," Agronomy for Sustainable Development, vol. 33, pp. 243–255, 2013. https://doi.org/10.1007/s13593-012-0105-x
4. Jacquet, F., Jeuffroy, M.H., Jouan, J. et al., "Pesticide-Free Agriculture as a New Paradigm for Research," Agronomy for Sustainable Development, vol. 42, p. 8, 2022. https://doi.org/10.1007/s13593-021-00742-8
5. Ayyasamy, S., Eswaran, S., Manikandan, B., Mithun Solomon, S.P., Nirmal Kumar, S., "IoT based Agri Soil Maintenance through Micro-Nutrients and Protection of Crops from Excess Water," 2020 Fourth International Conference on Computing Methodologies and Communication (ICCMC), Erode, India, 2020, pp. 404–409. doi: 10.1109/ICCMC48092.2020.ICCMC-00076
6. Srivastava, A., Das, D.K., Kumar, R., "Monitoring of Soil Parameters and Controlling of Soil Moisture through IoT Based Smart Agriculture," 2020 IEEE Students Conference on Engineering & Systems (SCES), Prayagraj, India, 2020, pp. 1–6. doi: 10.1109/SCES50439.2020.9236764
7. Athani, S., Tejeshwar, C.H., Patil, M.M., Patil, P., Kulkarni, R., "Soil Moisture Monitoring Using IoT Enabled Arduino Sensors with Neural Networks for Improving Soil Management for Farmers and Predict Seasonal Rainfall for Planning Future Harvest in North Karnataka—India," 2017 International Conference on I-SMAC (IoT in Social, Mobile, Analytics and Cloud) (I-SMAC), Palladam, India, 2017, pp. 43–48. doi: 10.1109/I-SMAC.2017.8058385
8. Ramson, R.J. et al., "A Self-Powered, Real-Time, LoRaWAN IoT-Based Soil Health Monitoring System," IEEE Internet of Things Journal, vol. 8, no. 11, pp. 9278–9293, 2021. doi: 10.1109/JIOT.2021.3056586
9. Chen, D., Chen, N., Zhang, X., Ma, H., Chen, Z., "Next-Generation Soil Moisture Sensor Web: High-Density In Situ Observation Over NB-IoT," IEEE Internet of Things Journal, vol. 8, no. 17, pp. 13367–13383, 2021. doi: 10.1109/JIOT.2021.3065077.
10. Hossain, F.F. et al., "Soil Moisture Monitoring through UAS-Assisted Internet of Things LoRaWAN Wireless Underground Sensors," IEEE Access, vol. 10, pp. 102107–102118, 2022
11. Pal, P., Tripathi, S., Kumar, C., "Single Probe Imitation of Multi-Depth Capacitive Soil Moisture Sensor Using Bidirectional Recurrent Neural Network," IEEE Transactions on Instrumentation and Measurement, vol. 71, pp. 1–11, 2022, Article ID 9504311. doi: 10.1109/TIM.2022.3156179
12. Quy, V. K., et al., "IoT-Enabled Smart agriculture: architecture, applications, and challenges," Applied Sciences, vol. 12, pp. 3396–3415, 2022. doi: 10.3390/app12073396
13. Kumar, A.A., Kumar, N., Fernandez, R.E., "Real Time Sensing of Soil Potassium Levels Using Zinc Oxide-Multiwall Carbon Nanotube-Based Sensors," IEEE Transactions on NanoBioscience, vol. 20, no. 1, pp. 50–56, 2021. doi: 10.1109/TNB.2020.3027863
14. Pyingkodi, M., Thenmozhi, K., Karthikeyan, M., Kalpana, T., Palarimath, S., Kumar, G.B.A., "IoT Based Soil Nutrients Analysis and Monitoring System for Smart Agriculture," 2022 3rd International Conference on Electronics and Sustainable Communication Systems (ICESC), Coimbatore, India, 2022, pp. 489–494. doi: 10.1109/ICESC54411.2022.9885371

15. Bashir, R.N., Bajwa, I.S., Abbas, M.Z. et al., "Internet of Things (IoT) Assisted Soil Salinity Mapping at Irrigation Schema Level," Applied Water Science, vol. 12, p. 105, 2022. https://doi.org/10.1007/s13201-022-01619-1

16. Blesslin Sheeba, T., Vijay Anand, L.D., Manohar, G., Selvan, S., Bazil Wilfred, C., Muthukumar, K., Padmavathy, S., Ramesh Kumar, P., Asfaw, B.T., "Machine Learning Algorithm for Soil Analysis and Classification of Micronutrients in IoT-Enabled Automated Farms," Journal of Nanomaterials, vol. 2022, p. 7, 2022, Article ID 5343965. https://doi.org/10.1155/2022/5343965

17. Burton, L. et al., "Smart Gardening IoT Soil Sheets for Real-Time Nutrient Analysis," Journal of The Electrochemical Society, vol. 165, no. 8. pp B3157–B3162, 2018. doi: 10.1149/2.0201808jes.

18. Zhang, X., Zhang, J., Li, L., Zhang, Y., Yang, G., "Monitoring Citrus Soil Moisture and Nutrients Using an IoT Based System," Sensors (Basel), vol. 17, no. 3, p. 447, 2017. doi: 10.3390/s17030447. PMID: 28241488; PMCID: PMC5375733.

19. Raut, R., Varma, H., Mulla, C., Pawar, V.R. (2018). Soil Monitoring, Fertigation, and Irrigation System Using IoT for Agricultural Application. In: Hu, Y.C., Tiwari, S., Mishra, K., Trivedi, M. (eds) Intelligent Communication and Computational Technologies. Lecture Notes in Networks and Systems, vol. 19. Springer, Singapore. https://doi.org/10.1007/978-981-10-5523-2_7

20. Lau, X.Y., Soo, C.H., Yusof, Y., Isaak, S. (2021). Integrated Soil Monitoring System for Internet of Thing (IOT) Applications. In: Proceedings of the 11th National Technical Seminar on Unmanned System Technology 2019, NUSYS 2019, Lecture Notes in Electrical Engineering, vol. 666. Springer, Singapore. https://doi.org/10.1007/978-981-15-5281-6_50.

21. Dhanaraju, M., Chenniappan, P., Ramalingam, K., Pazhanivelan, S., Kaliaperumal, R., "Smart Farming: Internet of Things (IoT)-Based Sustainable Agriculture," Agriculture, vol. 12, p. 1745, 2022. https://doi.org/10.3390/agriculture12101745

22. Ikram, A., Aslam, W., Aziz, R.H.H., Noor, F., Mallah, G.A., Ikram, S., Ahmad, M.S., Abdullah, A.M., Ullah, I., "Crop Yield Maximization Using an IoT-Based Smart Decision," Journal of Sensors, vol. 2022, p. 15, 2022, Article ID 2022923. https://doi.org/10.1155/2022/2022923

23. Placidi, P., Morbidelli, R., Fortunati, D., Papini, N., Gobbi, F., Scorzoni, A., "Monitoring Soil and Ambient Parameters in the IoT Precision Agriculture Scenario: An Original Modeling Approach Dedicated to Low-Cost Soil Water Content Sensors," Sensors, vol. 21, p. 5110, 2021. https://doi.org/10.3390/s21155110.

24. Liu, R.-T., Tao, L.-Q., Liu, B., Tian, X.-G., Mohammad, M.A., Yang, Y., Ren, T.-L., "A Miniaturized On-Chip Colorimeter for Detecting NPK Elements," Sensors, vol. 16, p. 1234, 2016. https://doi.org/10.3390/s16081234

25. Mumtaz, Z., Ullah, S., Ilyas, Z., Aslam, N., Iqbal, S., Liu, S., Meo, J.A., Madni, H.A., "An Automation System for Controlling Streetlights and Monitoring Objects Using Arduino," Sensors, vol. 18, p. 3178, 2018. https://doi.org/10.3390/s18103178

26. Taud, H., Mas, J. (2018). Multilayer Perceptron (MLP). In: Camacho Olmedo, M., Paegelow, M., Mas, J.F., Escobar, F. (eds) Geomatic Approaches for Modeling Land Change Scenarios. Lecture Notes in Geoinformation and Cartography. Springer, Cham. https://doi.org/10.1007/978-3-319-60801-3_27

27. Bourlard, H.A., Morgan, N. (1994). Multilayer Perceptrons. In: Connectionist Speech Recognition. The Springer International Series in Engineering and Computer Science, vol. 247. Springer, Boston, MA. https://doi.org/10.1007/978-1-4615-3210-1_4

28. Sarker, I.H., "Machine Learning: Algorithms, Real-World Applications and Research Directions," SN Computer Science, vol. 2, p. 160, 2021. https://doi.org/10.1007/s42979-021-00592-x

29. Awad, M., Khanna, R. (2015). Support Vector Machines for Classification. In: Efficient Learning Machines. Apress, Berkeley, CA. https://doi.org/10.1007/978-1-4302-5990-9_3

30. Fürnkranz, J. (2011). Decision Tree. In: Sammut, C., Webb, G.I. (eds) Encyclopedia of Machine Learning. Springer, Boston, MA. https://doi.org/10.1007/978-0-387-30164-8_204

31. Taunk, K., De, S., Verma, S., Swetapadma, A., "A Brief Review of Nearest Neighbor Algorithm for Learning and Classification," 2019 International Conference on Intelligent Computing and Control Systems (ICCS), Madurai, India, 2019, pp. 1255–1260. doi: 10.1109/ICCS45141.2019.9065747

32. Yang, F.-J., "An Implementation of Naive Bayes Classifier," 2018 International Conference on Computational Science and Computational Intelligence (CSCI), Las Vegas, NV, USA, 2018, pp. 301–306. doi: 10.1109/CSCI46756.2018.00065

6 IoT-Enabled Smart Irrigation with Machine Learning Models for Precision Farming

Sujatha Rajkumar[1], Raghav Biyani[2],
Shubham Jagtap[2], Nandasai Penumuchu[2],
and Shriram S. S.[2]
[1] Associate Professor, School of Electronics Engineering,
 Vellore Institute of Technology, Vellore, India
[2] Student, School of Electronics Engineering,
 Vellore Institute of Technology, Vellore, India

6.1 INTRODUCTION

Kevin Ashton introduced the idea of the Internet of Things (IoT) in 1999, when he was working in an RFID community. IoT has outgrown itself after the rapid growth of mobile devices, data analytics, cloud computing, and other new technologies. The IoT is a new revolution in computing and communication in which everyday things are outfitted with sensors, microcontrollers, and transceivers to sense external parameters. Various scientists, engineers, and IT professionals are working to use cutting-edge technology to improve life on Earth in the recent Fourth Industrial Revolution (IR). One of these four IR pillars is the IoT, also known as the fuel of the IR, because it effectively connects billions of things and sensors, which collectively produce real-time data that helps humans to some extent in improvising their work. A continuous manual effort was required to monitor the field environmental variables and take appropriate action, which is quite impractical and impossible. IoT technology has already started improving the lives of individuals in the fields of home appliances, transportation, natural calamities, the health sector, etc. In the world, many countries, including India, are heavily dependent on agriculture, as it contributes a lot to the GDP of the nation. The workforce engaged in agricultural development is diminishing as a result of professionals relocating to urban areas and large cities in search of employment opportunities. Also, the use of land for agricultural cultivation is rapidly being used up by the development of industrial economies in the region. In response, the government has decided to develop a national agricultural policy with three objectives: increasing domestic production, adjusting the balance of supply and demand for agricultural products, and ensuring food security. As a result, most agricultural activities must be automated to meet the demand for food. The earlier-mentioned problems

DOI: 10.1201/9781003391302-6

in the agriculture and food industries may be resolved by the IoT and similar technologies. IoT can assist in increasing farming's effectiveness and quality, increasing agriculture's competitiveness in the long run. Although the IoT revolution is already underway, it will take some time before its benefits become evident.

Precision farming is defined as the implementation of various edge devices and software technologies like the internet, cloud, and IoT devices together. IoT technologies can completely revamp the way agriculture is carried out to make it faster, better, and cheaper. By using IoT technologies and edge devices, data can be sensed, collected, and transmitted to an application. The application will then store and process the data to identify the optimal ways to enhance agricultural output. The proposed IoT solution will help the farmers to remotely observe their crops and make decisions accordingly for the future. For example, the farmer can observe the need for irrigation or fertilizer for the crops and take appropriate action based on the information. Agriculture meets people's food needs while also providing raw materials for other industries. Traditional farming uses old techniques and methods and is mostly done without any assessment of rates in the market, weather reports, market demand, etc. However, comprehensive knowledge should be acquired by the farmers regarding the usage of smart farming techniques before the proposed system is implemented on a wide scale. IoT technology will allow farmers to view and manage their farms remotely, while large agricultural farms can be easily implemented and accurately monitored. Whenever the moisture in the soil is less than a predetermined value, the model will send a signal to start the water pump to maintain the moisture and keep the crops healthy. The data can be used by the farmers to determine how many trees should be planted to provide a certain amount of oxygen. Based on the information collected by the sensors, a farmer might monitor the weather and decide what steps to take for the crop. By raising the temperature, the farmer may take measures to shield the crop from rain and keep it from freezing. Climate change is the main difficulty conventional farming faces. The consequences of climate change include very heavy rain, the fiercest storms, heat waves, and less rain, which have led to a significant decrease in the production of crops. Crop production prediction is the most difficult problem in precision agriculture, and various models have been proposed and successfully tested so far. This problem requires the use of many datasets since agricultural productivity depends on a wide range of factors, including climate, weather, soil, the usage of fertilizers, and seed variety. It can be observed that predicting agricultural output is a challenging task that involves several intricate stages. Although greater yield prediction accuracy is still needed, today's crop yield prediction methods can fairly anticipate the actual yield. Machine learning (ML) can identify patterns, correlate data, and find information. The model is trained in such a way that the output is dependent on past results. There are two types of models in ML: the first is descriptive, which tells about the results that occurred in the past, and the other is predictive, which predicts future outcomes. For quick decision-making, it is crucial for decision-makers at the national and regional levels to predict crop yields. Farmers can decide what to plant and when by using a reliable agricultural production forecast model [1].

Sensors and actuators such as the Arduino, PIR sensor, DHT11, relay, motor driver, and moisture sensor were used in the proposed method to solve this problem. Since soil moisture is essential for effective photosynthesis, respiration, transpiration, and transfer of minerals and other nutrients throughout the plant, soil PH and moisture content are regularly checked. Since soil nutrients like nitrogen (N), potassium (K), and phosphorus (P) are lost due to soil erosion but are necessary for plants to thrive, the pH level of the soil is also very significant. Knowing about the increasing demand for food as the world's population grows, IoT involvement in agriculture is critical to meeting future demands. Therefore, it becomes especially important to protect the fields from getting damaged. Another major issue discussed in this chapter is animal intrusion. Various wild animals, such as tigers, leopards, and elephants, come to the fields near the forest in search of food and then destroy the crops, which eventually leads to huge financial losses for farmers. This model was developed to protect the farmland from animals using PIR sensors connected to the ESP32, which also sends the notification to the farmer's device. It aims to reduce the burden on the farmer's end, who earlier had to check his or her field many times a day. This model will help in gathering field conditions throughout the day. It will also protect the cattle in and around the field from wild animals. Water is a limited resource for the whole world, but farmers generally switch on the water pumps and leave them in the ON position for a long time, which supplies extra water to the crops, which can damage them and lead to the wastage of water. Lots of water can be saved if there is a system that sends an alert to the farmer when there is a requirement for water in the fields, and the water pump can be turned on or off accordingly.

6.2   RELATED WORK

The work proposed by Prathibha et al. [2] involves the use of smart farming solutions, which include employing various sensors and a single CC3200 chip to monitor temperature and humidity in agricultural fields. In this article, the camera is connected to the CC3200 so that images can be taken and sent via MMS over Wi-Fi to farmers' mobile phones. This proposed system's main component, the CC3200, is made up of a microcontroller, a network processor, and a Wi-Fi module on one chip. It ensures a lightweight, quick, safe, and secure connection that runs on batteries. The overall crop output will be influenced by environmental factors and variations.

An IoT-based technique for keeping track of the atmosphere and soil conditions for productive crop growth is given by Abhiram et al. [3]. With the help of NodeMCU and a collection of sensors attached to it, the built system can monitor changes in temperature, humidity, and soil moisture levels. Also, a notification regarding the field's state will be transmitted through Wi-Fi as an MMS to the farmer's cell phone.

Because of the high cost of electricity, the authors, Gutierrez et al. [4], devised an irrigation system powered by photovoltaic solar panels. Here, a microcontroller gateway was equipped with an algorithm for efficient and optimal water use, along with temperature and soil moisture threshold values. This not only makes it energy efficient, but the algorithm also conserves water by only pumping the required amount of water.

The work proposed by Sushanth and Sujatha [5] includes the development of a system that uses sensors on an Arduino board to monitor various environmental factors such as temperature, humidity, and moisture in agricultural fields. The system is also capable of detecting the movement of animals that may pose a threat to crops. In case of any irregularities, the system is designed to notify the farmer through multiple channels, such as SMS and a smartphone application. The notifications are sent using available wireless communication technologies such as Wi-Fi, 3G, or 4G. The system is equipped with a duplex communication link that uses a cellular internet interface. By means of an Android application, this link enables data analysis and programming of irrigation schedules.

The idea of using a wireless smart sensor network based on Zigbee for environmental monitoring was initially introduced by Chavan and Karnade [6]. In their model, individual nodes have the ability to transmit data to a central server, which will then store, process, and present the collected data. One limitation of their proposed system, however, is the absence of features for determining nutritional content and weather forecasting.

In the research work, a collaborative approach that involved using both wired and wireless communication technologies, the Remote Monitoring System (RMS), was proposed by the authors Patil and Kale [7]. The main goal is to collect up-to-the-minute data on environmental conditions relevant to agricultural production so that agricultural facilities can easily access it. For example, alerts through Short Message Service (SMS) and guidance on weather patterns, crop management, etc. are two examples of how this information can be provided.

Here the authors Mat et al. [8] developed a smart farming system based on the IoT that is capable of automating irrigation and monitoring crop fields using various sensors, including those for light, humidity, temperature, and soil moisture. By implementing smart technology, farmers may remotely check the state of their fields. This makes IoT-based smart farming significantly more effective than the traditional method.

A wireless sensor network that uses ultra-wideband (UWB) technology was suggested by the authors Xu et al. [9]. The grouped signal is duplicated on the stage environment to show how analyzing ultra-wideband signals may aid in arranging interference identification. The system uses various characteristics that are fed into multiple classifiers to detect intrusions. This approach results in an accuracy improvement of nearly 16.5% compared to standard feature extraction methods.

To enable irrigation in a proper manner, this research project incorporates a variety of features like soil moisture, temperature, and a humidity sensor (HS) by the authors C. Mageshkumar and Sugunamuki [10]. Various sensor nodes are to be deployed throughout the farm to automate irrigation at any time and from any location via the application. This application will give the farmer an overview of all the different data measures of the farm at all times, which will be updated in real time as the data is being collected by the edge devices.

This work by Marcu et al. [11] proposes a promising strategy for building a reliable IoT-based system that leverages Libelium for smart agriculture to monitor the key variables that impact crop growth and development. The monitoring system also strives to handle irrigation-related agricultural difficulties and evaluates how the measured factors affect agriculture, assisting farmers in growing healthy crops.

An IoT-based method for detecting animal intrusion was proposed by the authors Divya et al. [12]. Once an animal is identified by the PIR (passive infrared sensor), the signal is sent to the camera via an Arduino Uno microcontroller. The camera then captures the animal's image. The image is classified using sample images that are kept in the database. A bright light is used to distract a wild animal that has been identified as an elephant, and a loud noise is used to distract a leopard. The system triggers an SMS to notify forest officials and farmers of any potential threats caused by wild animals. This SMS is sent through a GSM module.

In this research, the work proposed by the authors Dahane et al. [13] is built on wireless sensor network technology, and its implementation includes three main stages: (i) data gathering using sensors placed in an agricultural field, (ii) data cleaning and storage, and (iii) prediction processing using some AI techniques.

In the research work, an image processing and ML-based method for animal intrusion detection was suggested by the authors Radhakrishnan and Ramanathan [14]. A watershed algorithm is used to segment an animal's image to extract different objects from the scene and determine whether any possibly dangerous animals were discovered. The goal of this method is to only draw the contour of the barrier when the indicated region encounters other markers.

The report by authors Kim et al. [15] mentioned placing a GPS tracking device on the animal that is responsible for leading the group of animals. The protective zone is surrounded by an imaginary border. When the leader crosses the boundary, an alert message is created, and these signals must be continuously monitored at a base station. Keep in mind that in this situation, the group leader is assuming control of a group of animals, and that these creatures always approach populated areas in packs. With most animals, this is not the case. Finding the animals' "leader" can be difficult because the group may split up and the animals may not follow the animal that was designated as the leader.

According to the report by Pampapathi and Manjunath [16], a simple method involves installing PIR sensors in the location that must be watched. The sensor is positioned in a tower arrangement. This system only carries out the work in one direction. This system's primary goal is to keep an eye on the region and track down any unauthorized entrances. The system's output, which indicates whether an animal or a human entered the system, is another outcome. Because the entire system simply relies on a sensor tower that distinguishes between the two classes based on the IR rays emitted by the object, even an object with comparable kinds of characteristics cannot be classified.

A system was built by the author, AshifuddinMondal and Rehena [17], that uses sensors, and the irrigation system is automated based on the server's decision according to the sensed data. The sensed data is transmitted using a NodeMCU to a cloud on a web server. When moisture and temperature readings change due to environmental conditions, the irrigation is automated. Using an automated system, a smart agricultural management system (SAMS) was proposed, which would help farmers use natural resources to increase crop production. The system would make use of various sensors to gather crop growth-related data, which is then fed into the Firebase.

A cost-effective and time-dependent irrigation scheduler that employs a microcontroller with a variety of sensors for measuring moisture and temperature has been proposed by authors Bhosale and Dixit [18]. Depending on these parameters, this system determines the proper actuators (relay, solenoid valves, and motor). Through the GSM module, the user receives and stores the captured data in the form of an SMS. The use of PCBs in this paper is consistent with previous studies in agricultural technology, highlighting its crucial role in developing cost-effective solutions for weather monitoring and irrigation control.

The fundamental notion is to use the IoT and image processing techniques together to achieve the desired outcomes. A system proposed by the authors Lakshmi and Gayathri [19] comprises information on plant fertilizers, current weather conditions by city name, plant health information such as plant growth and illness, and farm status information such as sensor and motor status of the farm field. In this control system, the Raspberry Pi model is connected to three sensors: a soil moisture sensor, a temperature sensor, and a HS. The Raspberry Pi is connected to the relay and the motor in the appropriate ways. By comparing the most recent image acquired with the photographs saved in the database, the health of the plant is evaluated. The app displays the outcome, and regarding plants, fertilizers were also on display. Information about fertilizers is kept in a database. Take a picture of the diseased plant and store it in a database to help in disease detection.

For checking soil moisture, a soil moisture sensor-based automated irrigation system was proposed by the authors Hanswal et al. [20]. With the help of drip irrigation, it is a user-friendly, reliable, and automated water pumping system that enables efficient water use as needed. The method proposed by the other author combines a pH sensor interface with a PIC microcontroller to produce a sensing module that is 100% stable, a module that perfectly calibrates the pH sensor, and a module that can precisely read the pH of a nutrient-enriched solution. The system's central component is an Atmel microcontroller, a widely accessible semiconductor with excellent performance and low power consumption. It has 14 digital ports, enough to connect up to 18 sensors, 6 channels of 10-bit analog to digital converters, 1Kb of EEPROM, and 2Kb of RAM.

According to Bowlekar et al. [21], soil moisture is especially important for the growth of plants. Today, there are satellites that measure soil parameters and are linked to various agriculture stations where data from the region is sent. However, as can be seen, the satellite provides data for a large region that is not very precise, and all of the farms in the country are not properly connected to the agriculture stations, so most farmers do not benefit from the satellite's soil parameter monitoring. The check gate, which is powered by solar energy, controls the water flow to the agricultural field and communicates wirelessly with the soil moisture sensors placed in the basin. To operate an irrigation event in real time, the gate automatically opens and closes according to a predetermined threshold value of the soil moisture sensor readings.

The report by Sharma [22] discusses a low-cost method for automatic animal detection on roads that uses digital picture techniques to prevent animal-vehicle collisions. The distance of an animal from the road is also determined using technology that can warn the driver. The proposed strategy results in a detection accuracy of 83% on average.

The authors, Maheswari and Rajan [23], proposed a method for detecting bird intrusion in an agricultural area using wireless sensors and buzzers. When the sensors detect a bird, the system generates acoustic sounds to deter the birds. The birds are disturbed by this noise. Therefore, when these sounds are produced, birds will flee since they cannot adapt to the sound. Thus, it is possible to prevent the damage that birds inflict on agricultural fields. These generated acoustic sounds will only be made when birds are found, and they will continue for a time until the birds fly away.

This study is based on the Animal Detection System, where a camera will be placed further away from the field. When an animal comes into the field of view, the camera will detect it based on the output images of different animals along with their characteristics. If the device recognizes it as a dangerous wild animal, such as an elephant or boar, it will raise an alarm so that the farmers get informed about it. In this model, the operator has to upload the images and characteristics of all the possible animals that can come to that farm, as suggested by the authors Rakesh et al. [24]. The characteristics are important because animals such as dogs and cats are not harmful to the farmers and their farms, so an alarm does not need to be raised. It can also provide information about the animal's location to help prevent human deaths. It helps reduce panic among the public due to fake alarms. It can also inform the nearest Forest Department about trespassing.

An idea was proposed by the authors, Prajna et al. [25], for the animal intrusion system, where the main components used are a camera and a PIR sensor. These components will be placed at the boundary of the field. The camera is powered by a solar panel and battery. When an animal is detected, the sensor sends a signal to the camera through the microcontroller, and a picture of the area is then captured. The computer then verifies the received image with its database. The system contains three functions which are the index image function, the retrieve function, and the set image function. The set of all images contains databases of images of various animals. The first function, the image function, is used to create a search, and the retrieved image is a combination of the image that has been queried and this image is stored in the database. The result will vary from 0 to 1; if the value is 0, the image is not matched. If the value lies between 0.1 and 0.9, there is a high chance that the image matches the stored image. There will be two types of prevention techniques, creating an irritating sound or using a high-beam flashlight.

The work prepared by the authors Patil and Ansari [26] describes the animal intrusion system in which the area will be divided into many sub-areas where the chances of encountering wild animals are high. At each location, PIR sensors will be placed to detect the activity. If there is motion detected by the sensor, it will initiate the camera to record the live streaming, which will then be stored on the Raspberry Media. After the animal is detected, the buzzer will sound or the flashlight will be turned on.

In this work, the value of the soil and temperature sensor was calculated by the authors Archana and Priya [27], which is to be implanted in plant roots to manage when to supply water and when to stop the supply to save water. The drawback of their project is that they did not include any technique to send the status of the agriculture field to the user.

Crop yield prediction using intelligent agriculture and the IoT was monitored by Tseng et al. [28]. The currently existing prediction models use big data in smart agriculture to forecast crop production farms because weather damage to crops is a common occurrence. The created model made use of an IoT sensor device that sensed air pressure, atmospheric humidity, soil moisture content, atmospheric temperature, and salinity of the soil while monitoring the entire agricultural land. The goal of big data analysis in smart farming was to examine environmental variations as well as analyze and comprehend farmers' crop-growing practices. The 3D cluster evaluation of the relationship between environmental components and the subsequent examination of the recommendations from the farmers was a benefit of the proposed model.

Robust deep learning was used by Fuentes et al. [29] to identify tomato plant diseases and insect infestations in crops. Due to pests and illnesses in crops that significantly increased economic loss, the current model had trouble predicting crop yields. To predict plant pests, the model developed for this use case introduces a complex architecture known as a "meta-architecture." The developed model considers three important indicator characteristics: the single-shot multi-box detector, also known as the SSD; a region-based convolutional neural network; and a region-based full convolutional neural network. Growing data improves precision while lowering the number of errors during training. The created model's advantage was its success in identifying various pests and diseases by handling challenging local circumstances. The robust deep learning technique uses advanced pre-processing algorithms, which take more time and cost more money to compute.

The crop production and manure recommendations were predicted using ML approaches by Bondre and Mahagonkar [30]. The development of a machine learning system solved the significant problem of yield prediction in agriculture. For precisely predicting crop production in agriculture, the effectiveness of the constructed ML model was assessed. An advantage of the proposed model was that it made use of earlier data to predict crops by using various ML algorithms like the random forest model and others like SVM. The data also suggested the best fertilizer for each specific crop. However, the method of using a smart water irrigation system for farms to generate a greater harvest was not used.

The calculation of the mustard crop yield by Pandith et al. [31] from a review of the soil made use of ML techniques. The soil has a big role in calculating crop production in agriculture, but this was resolved by creating ML technology. To predict mustard crop output in advance from soil data collection, a number of ML techniques were used, including MLR or multinomial logistic regression, k-nearest neighbors, also known as KNN, an artificial neural network, or ANN, the random forest model, and the Naive Bayes model. The ML model created has the ability to estimate crop yield even when different fertilizers are used, which is also used to support soil analysis and allow farmers to make better informed decisions in cases of low crop prediction.

Table 6.1 highlights the significant conclusions and insights, providing a thorough overview of the key contributions in this field.

6.3 CHALLENGES IN THE EXISTING SYSTEM

Although the IoT is having a huge impact on agriculture, farmers still face many challenges every day, even today. Agricultural land has decreased due to the growing population. Integrating smart IoT technologies with traditional farming methods is what makes it viable. First, the cost is a big issue in this field. Farmers cannot spend much money on investing in smart technologies as they believe in traditional methods. So, to get them to use this smart technology, it has to be provided at a reasonable price that they can afford without losing much. Scalability is another problem. As the farm grows, a larger number of sensors need to be integrated, which is more challenging. This can affect the collection rate of real-time data as the number of sensors and data traffic increases.

TABLE 6.1

Related Works on Smart Agriculture

Ref No	Author	Title	Summary of Findings
[3]	Abhiram et al.	Smart farming system using IoT for efficient crop growth	This work focuses on an SMS-based notification model that uses IoT techniques for monitoring weather and soil parameters, such as temperature, humidity, and soil moisture, for successful crop development.
[10]	Mageshkumar and Sugunamuki	IoT-based smart farming	This research work includes many aspects like soil moisture, temperature, and a humidity sensor to automate irrigation at any time as well as from any location via the application.
[28]	Tseng et al.	Applying big data for intelligent agriculture-based crop selection analysis	In this work, different environmental parameters were monitored like air pressure, humidity, and moisture which were then analyzed by performing data normalization and 3D clustering to find the relationship between different factors.
[11]	Marcu et al.	IoT-based system for smart agriculture	The factors that directly affect crops are monitored and analyzed in this article, using Libelium for smart agriculture as a potential solution for a far more reliable IoT-based model for farmers.
[33]	Liakos et al.	Machine learning in agriculture: A review	In this work, an automated system as well as a smart agricultural management system (SAMS) was proposed, to help farmers use natural resources to increase crop production. When moisture and temperature readings change due to environmental conditions, the irrigation is automated.
[32]	Kalimuthu et al.	Crop prediction using machine learning	By using machine learning, one of the most cutting-edge technologies in crop prediction, this research provides the farmer with a method that directs them toward sowing reasonable crops. A supervised learning algorithm called Naive Bayes suggests how to do it.

In smart agriculture, interoperability is a challenge as there are numerous IoT devices and platforms on the market, each with its own protocols and standards. This makes communication between devices from different vendors difficult and leads to a lack of integration and compatibility between the different systems. The type of communication chosen is also crucial, as it is important for the security of the data. It is necessary to ensure that the network is reliable and that there is no evidence of data theft, hacking, or cyber-attacks. The collected data is stored on a cloud platform to perform big data analytics. As scalability increases, more data needs to be stored, which in effect requires running a larger number of servers. This increases the overall cost of maintaining the system, making it inefficient in the long run. IoT devices may therefore have difficulty storing and processing massive amounts of data, which calls for additional infrastructure and effective data management techniques.

Forecasting using ML algorithms is also a challenging task, as there can be many difficulties in accurately predicting crop yields, weather patterns, and other important aspects of agriculture. Without access to data and predictive models, it is difficult for farmers to make informed decisions about crop selection, planting dates, and other important agricultural issues. Therefore, farmers need to use predictive models and make the right decisions for their fields.

Environmental conditions are crucial for the operation of the different sensors. The selected sensors must ensure that they work in all extreme weather conditions and harsh environments without any failures. Another important issue these days is the feasibility of the current system. The proposed system will ensure a less complex system and a more user-friendly model for the farmer. The user interface should be simple enough for the farmer to access all functions with a single click and detailed enough to provide him with all the important information about his farm.

6.4   FIRMWARE DEVELOPMENT FOR PRECISION FARMING

In the next section, IoT-enabled edge sensors and the embedded software are discussed.

6.4.1   IoT-Enabled Edge Sensors For Smart Farming

Components used in this work are as follows: ESP32, PIR sensor, soil moisture sensor, DC motor with relay, DHT-11, Arduino, water pump, and rainfall sensor. To do predictive analysis, data needs to be recorded in the field. The primary data required is soil moisture, rainfall status (time and date), temperature, and humidity of the surrounding environment. Using the mentioned components, the readings can be recorded at regular intervals. Sensors such as PIR, soil moisture, rainfall sensor, and DHT-11 are connected to the ESP32 microcontroller. The motor is powered by an Arduino and controlled using a relay. Whenever the moisture level in the field falls below a certain fixed threshold value, the motor pump turns on and pumps water into the field. Also, if any motion is detected in the field, a notification is sent to the farmer on the website about the intrusion. To get correct data, sensors were calibrated by observing multiple readings, and the ESP32 microcontroller was used to record this data, which was then uploaded to the website using Firebase as the cloud layer. Multiple readings of data from all sensors were collected and fed to the Firebase platform for greater accuracy in predicting. A website was created using React.js, which was later deployed and can show the current status of different field parameters to the farmers and can also send an email or notification to the farmer.

6.4.2   Software Integration with Edge Sensors to Enable Intelligent Cropping

React.js is a JavaScript front-end library that is used to build front-end UI components. This makes it easier to build and reuse the code throughout the web application. React.js also includes a testing library called the React Testing Library, as well as Jest. It is used to test the performance of the website and the general workings of the website. React Router DOM can be used to route the website's different pages. Bootstrap is a CSS framework that makes it easier to style the basic components of the website and makes the website responsive, which means it looks good on both mobile and larger screens. It includes built-in components such as cards, buttons, and input fields that can be accessed directly from the website. Bootstrap classes, along with a few custom styles in CSS, make the UI more beautiful and easier to use. The services provided by EmailJS are used to send reports to the farmers through email. EmailJS helps in converting the collected variables of data into a proper format for the email to the farmer. If the parameters are passed, the email will be automatically sent. This type of auto-generated email can be useful for the farmers to look at the current data and make decisions.

6.4.2.1   Cloud-Based Remote Monitoring of the Agriculture Fields

The authors used both Firebase authentication and Firebase's real-time database. Firebase authentication was used to allow farmers to log in to their accounts and access their farm data. The real-time database stores the values received from the sensors via ESP32 in real time, which are updated frequently. This data is then captured on the front end and displayed in the form of maps so that the farmer can visualize the data. In this model, data from different sensors and devices is displayed on a website, and a report can be sent by email. First, all sensors are connected to an ESP32 module. This microcontroller is able to transmit data to the cloud. In this project, the data is uploaded to Google Firebase. The acquired data is continuously recorded in a real-time database in Firebase. Then the data is transferred to the website. On the website interface, all real-time data is displayed on a tab so that the user can monitor the data. The user can also receive a report by email if they wish. It contains all the details about the activities that have taken place on the farmland. With the help of sensors and other electronic components, IoT technology enables the collection of real-time data in the agricultural field. Wireless technologies such as Wi-Fi have been adopted by the peripheral component to communicate with the data center through an upgraded IoT gateway. The NPK sensor checks the availability of nutrients such as nitrogen, phosphorus, and potassium in the soil at any given time. This data can be used to provide the required nutrients at any time by simply tapping on it. The amount of soil moisture can be measured by a soil moisture sensor, allowing farmers to monitor and adjust irrigation on the farm as needed.

6.4.3   Smart Farming IoT System Architecture

Therefore, the authors have developed an IoT-based monitoring system for agriculture, which is needed for continuous monitoring of crops in the field (see Figure 6.1), where this IoT server is easily accessible and can be monitored from any location. Based on IoT servers and apps, the system can be easily monitored from anywhere using mobile phones.

It is not easy to regularly monitor farms for all aspects, such as soil moisture, required and actual rainfall, and disturbance from wildlife. A farmer has to spend a large part of his meager profit on third-party sensors and updates to find a long-term

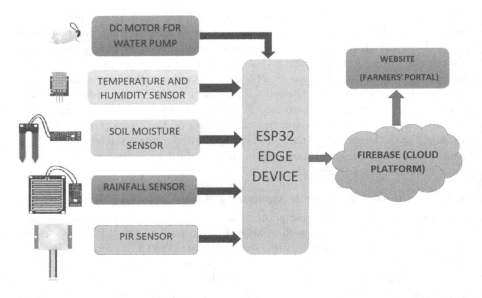

FIGURE 6.1 IoT-enabled smart farming architecture.

technical solution. Therefore, the chosen method is affordable, easy to use, and readily available via a self-use app that constantly informs about everything and can also provide immediate remedies. For example, water is automatically pumped in when needed if the humidity or the amount of precipitation is below the preset value. The movement of animals in the field also triggers alerts via motion, which can be linked to a buzzer in further development.

6.5   RESULTS AND DISCUSSIONS

The data from the sensors is sent to Firebase's real-time database, where a template is created in the real-time database for all sensor data. Figure 6.2 shows the sensor data, such as the HS, the proximity sensor (PIR), the precipitation sensor (RF) (both analog and digital values), and the soil moisture sensor (SM).

The data collected in real time is captured on the front-end website using the HTTP communication method. Figure 6.3 shows the data, which is presented in a simple and understandable format so that the farmer can quickly and easily view the data of his farm.

If the farmer wants to receive this data in a clear and readable format for future reference, he can email the data to himself using the Generate Report page, as shown in Figure 6.4. This feature can help the farmer if they want to keep a record of farm data at different points in the crop growth cycle.

A report can be generated and sent to the user as an email with the date and time when it was generated. This is done using Email.js' services.

In this email, as shown in Figure 6.5, all the details of the farmer's land will be given, along with the date and time during which the data was collected. This will help the

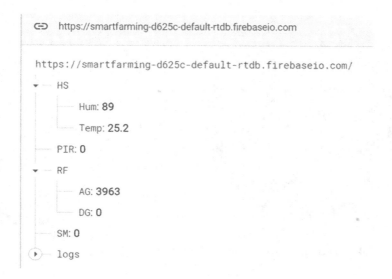

FIGURE 6.2 Real-time farm data in Firebase.

farmer keep a record of the data collected at different moments, which will help them better understand the farming conditions.

This website is fully secure as each farmer must create their own profile with their email and password. Each farmer can only see their data after logging into their account. Provisions for changing the password if they forget are also given.

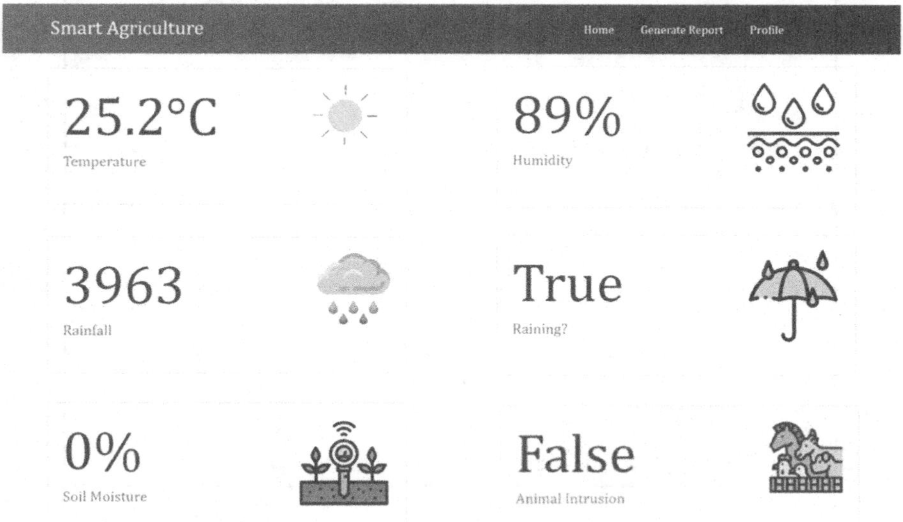

FIGURE 6.3 Real-time data displayed in the web interface.

FIGURE 6.4   Generating and emailing the farm data.

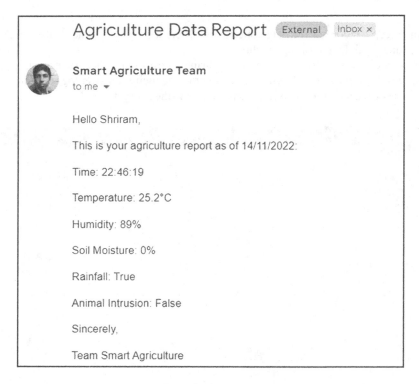

Email Content

FIGURE 6.5   Sample email of the real-time farm data.

6.6 MACHINE LEARNING MODELS FOR PREDICTIVE FARMING

ML can make farming more efficient and easier, which is a great help to farmers. Another major problem in traditional farming is pest and disease control. Most farmers spray pesticides and other chemicals evenly on their fields to minimize the chances of these pests and viruses affecting their crops and yields. This method is not very efficient as it requires a large amount of chemicals, which is not ideal as it incurs high financial costs and also has a negative impact on the environment. Excessive use of pesticides can also lead to contamination of groundwater, which can eventually affect animals and people who consume this water. By making accurate decisions about where and how much chemicals should be sprayed to prevent pests and infections, models from ML can reduce these unwanted side effects.

The most important area where ML is used in precision agriculture is predicting yields before harvest. By analyzing various factors such as weather patterns, soil moisture, and plant health, ML algorithms can make accurate predictions about crop yield. This information can help farmers make decisions about the best time to plant and harvest crops, as well as the best fertilizers and pesticides to use and how to use them. Another important application of ML in agriculture is soil analysis. By analyzing soil samples, ML's algorithms can determine soil properties such as nutrient content (nitrogen, phosphorus, and potassium), pH, and texture. This information can be used for precise planning of fertilization to optimize plant growth and increase yields.

ML also plays an important role in monitoring plant health and detecting various attacks. By analyzing images of crops, ML algorithms can detect negative signs such as diseases, pests, and nutrient deficiencies. This information can be used to take proactive measures to prevent crop losses, such as spraying pesticides or adjusting the composition of fertilizer before applying it to the field. In addition to improving crop yields and monitoring plant health, ML can also help optimize irrigation measures by analyzing data from weather stations. Algorithms from ML can predict future weather patterns and determine the optimal amount of water for crops. This can significantly improve water use efficiency and reduce unnecessary water waste.

Although ML is very useful in agriculture, one of the biggest challenges of smart farming is managing the data. Farmers need to collect huge amounts of data from various sources, such as weather stations, soil sensors, and aerial imagery, to make optimal decisions about their crops and farmland. To make farmers' work easier, models from ML can be used to automatically process and analyze this data, reducing farmers' workload.

One of the biggest challenges is ensuring the accuracy of the algorithms. To be effective, ML algorithms need to be trained on high-quality data, which is difficult to obtain in the agricultural sector. Farmers also need a certain level of technical expertise to use the algorithms effectively, which can be a barrier to large-scale deployment of ML. Data privacy and security are also additional challenges for any system. As more data is collected and analyzed in smart agriculture, there is growing concern about potential data breaches, hacking, and unauthorized use of sensitive information. To mitigate these risks, security measures must be put in place to prevent information leakage.

To create an ML model for precision farming, it is vital to collect a lot of data and create a model based on this existing data. The data fed into an ML model consists of examples, and each example has a set of characteristics by which it is classified by the ML model. Each of these features is considered a variable, and an ML model will consider as many of these variables as possible to classify the data. In the case of smart farming, some of the variables would be temperature, season, rainfall, sunlight, soil nutrients, and many others. The third stage of building the ML model is generalization. The proposed ML model can be used to predict data such as soil parameters, expected harvest times, and expected yields. This ML model can be improved through deep learning. This can be done by representing the data in a hierarchical flow.

ML models can be broadly split into two main categories which are unsupervised and supervised learning. In supervised learning techniques, test data is fed into the model along with the expected results. After receiving enough data, the ML model generates a generalization of the datasets that can classify all subsequent incoming data based on this generalization. In unsupervised learning, the training data is not mapped to a specific output before it is fed into the model. The ML model observes the data and discovers patterns in the data that can be used to predict the classification of future data.

Regression is a supervised ML technique that analyzes data based on a relationship model. This model establishes relationships based on how a dependent variable behaves in response to changes in an independent variable. There may be multiple independent variables affecting the dependent variable. A scatter plot can be created using this data, and a regression line can be found with respect to the plot.

$$Y = b0 + b1 * X1 + b2 * X2 + b3 * X3 + \ldots \ldots bn * Xn + err$$

where

Y is the output or the dependent variable like harvest yield;

$b0$ is the intercept of the regression line;

$b1, b2, b3, \ldots, bn$ are the regression coefficients of the input or independent variables like soil moisture, NPK levels in the soil, and rainfall;

err is the error coefficient.

Clustering is one of the unsupervised ML techniques that can be used to make better agricultural decisions. In this method, different clusters are formed based on certain parameters, starting with a data point. After collecting enough data, the algorithm formed many clusters based on the similarities in the data entries. Clustering can be used to analyze soil moisture and nutrient content in different regions of a farm. This information can be used to know exactly where to spray pesticides.

A decision tree is another ML algorithm that is one of the most commonly used predictive modeling techniques. In this technique, the training data is divided into nodes and leaves. The leaves represent the output, and the nodes represent the position of the data split between the two data entries. If there are several data entries, the model forms a tree, which can then be used for data classification. Classification is based on internal nodes and branches. The branches serve as the base rule, which is the first point of classification for the incoming data. Then each node in that branch classifies the data based on a specific feature. Nodes can be of two types: selection nodes and leaf nodes. The selection nodes make decisions based on the characteristics of the incoming data and classify it accordingly, and the leaf nodes are the result of where the data lies.

Decision trees are a popular ML technique that can be used in smart agriculture for various applications. A decision tree is a tree-like structure that uses a set of decision rules (branches) to predict an outcome based on input variables. In agriculture, decision trees can be used for crop yield prediction, irrigation management, and pest control, among other applications. For example, a decision tree model can be trained using data on crop yields, weather conditions, soil properties, and other factors to predict potential yield fairly accurately. The model can be used to make better decisions about planting, irrigation, and fertilization to achieve the best possible yield. Decision trees can also be used to optimize pest management strategies by predicting the likelihood of pest infestation based on weather conditions, crop stage, and other regional factors based on previously collected data. The model can help farmers decide when and how much pesticide to spray, reducing the amount of chemicals sprayed on crops, which in turn reduces costs for the farmer. Decision trees can also be used to predict crop prices based on past data and current market conditions, which helps farmers make decisions about when and where to sell their crops to maximize revenue. Overall, decision trees can be a valuable tool for the development of smart agriculture, helping to increase yields, reduce costs, and promote sustainability.

Some of the popular ML activation functions used in smart agriculture are as follows:

1. Sigmoid: Sigmoid activation function is used in binary classification in plants such as disease detection. This activation function returns a 0 or a 1 depending upon the result.

$$f(x) = 1/(1 + e^{-x})$$

2. Tanh hyperbolic sigmoid: Tanh activation function is used in cases where there can be a negative outcome or a positive outcome like harvest yield of net profit.

$$f(x) = (e^x - e^{-x})/(e^x + e^{-x})$$

3. Softmax: Softmax activation function is used in cases where there are multiple different classes for the classification or identification of a certain characteristic like plant diseases or types of weeds growing among the crops.

$$f(x) = e^x/sum(e^x)$$

In summary, ML is a critical technology for the future of smart agriculture. By analyzing big data, ML algorithms can help farmers make informed decisions about their crops and land, improve yields, and optimize water use. However, to fully realize the potential of ML in smart agriculture, challenges related to data accuracy and security must be overcome. With continued research and development, ML has the potential to revolutionize the agricultural sector and improve the lives of farmers around the world.

6.7 CONCLUSION

This chapter provides a detailed account of how agriculture can be made smart by collecting and analyzing real-time data and how ML can be used to better understand the data and make future decisions for better yields based on predictive analysis. Smart farming using the IoT can solve the problem of frequent field visits, and the farmer can get information about the condition of the field through a website or an application on his phone. The use of IoT in smart farming can help farmers minimize waste and increase production in various areas, such as optimizing fertilizer usage and making efficient use of resources such as water and energy. IoT in agriculture is promising and will be of great value for generations to come. The authors have developed a budget-friendly model for farmers that can be installed in fields and monitored from any location.

REFERENCES

1. Van Klompenburg, T., Kassahun, A., & Catal, C. (2020). Crop yield prediction using machine learning: A systematic literature review. *Computers and Electronics in Agriculture, 177*, 105709.
2. Prathibha, S. R., Hongal, A., & Jyothi, M. P. (2017, March). IoT based monitoring system in smart agriculture. In *2017 International Conference on Recent Advances in Electronics and Communication Technology (ICRAECT)* (pp. 81–84). IEEE.
3. Abhiram, M. S. D., Kuppili, J., & Manga, N. A. (2020). Smart farming system using IoT for efficient crop growth. In *2020 IEEE International Students' Conference on Electrical, Electronics and Computer Science (SCEECS)* (pp. 1–4). IEEE.
4. Gutiérrez, J., Villa-Medina, J. F., Nieto-Garibay, A., & Porta-Gándara, M. (2013). Automated irrigation system using a wireless sensor network and GPRS module. *IEEE Transactions on Instrumentation and Measurement, 63*(1), 166–176.
5. Sushanth, G., & Sujatha, S. (2018, March). IoT-based smart agriculture system. In *2018 International Conference on Wireless Communications, Signal Processing and Networking (WiSPNET)* (pp. 1–4). IEEE.
6. Chavan, C. H., & Karande, P. V. (2014). Wireless monitoring of soil moisture, temperature & humidity using Zigbee in agriculture. *International Journal of Engineering Trends and Technology (IJETT), 11*(10), 493–497.
7. Patil, K. A., & Kale, N. R. (2016, December). A model for smart agriculture using IoT. In *2016 International Conference on Global Trends in Signal Processing, Information Computing and Communication (ICGTSPICC)* (pp. 543–545). IEEE.
8. Mat, I., Kassim, M. R. M., Harun, A. N., & Yusoff, I. M. (2018, November). Smart agriculture using internet of things. In *2018 IEEE Conference on Open Systems (ICOS)* (pp. 54–59). IEEE.
9. Xue, W., Jiang, T., & Shi, J. (2017, September). Animal intrusion detection based on convolutional neural network. In *2017 17th International Symposium on Communications and Information Technologies (ISCIT)* (pp. 1–5). IEEE.
10. Mageshkumar, C., & Sugunamuki, K. R. (2020, January). IOT based smart farming. In *2020 International Conference on Computer Communication and Informatics (ICCCI)* (pp. 1–6). IEEE.

11. Marcu, I. M., Suciu, G., Balaceanu, C. M., & Banaru, A. (2019, June). IoT based system for smart agriculture. In *2019 11th International Conference on Electronics, Computers and Artificial Intelligence (ECAI)* (pp. 1–4). IEEE.

12. Divya, S., Kiran, U., & Praveen, M. (2018). IoT-based wild animal intrusion detection system. *International Journal on Recent and Innovation Trends in Computing and Communication*, 6(7), 06–08.

13. Dahane, A., Benameur, R., Kechar, B., & Benyamina, A. (2020, October). An IoT based smart farming system using machine learning. In *2020 International Symposium on Networks, Computers and Communications (ISNCC)* (pp. 1–6). IEEE.

14. Radhakrishnan, S., & Ramanathan, R. (2018). A support vector machine with Gabor features for animal intrusion detection in agriculture fields. *Procedia Computer Science*, 143, 493–501.

15. Kim, S. H., Kim, D. H., & Park, H. D. (2010, April). Animal situation tracking service using RFID, GPS, and sensors. In *2010 Second International Conference on Computer and Network Technology* (pp. 153–156). IEEE.

16. Pampapathi, B., & Manjunath, P. (2016). Intrusion detection using passive infrared sensor (PIR). *Asian Journal of Engineering and Technology Innovation*, 4, 134–139.

17. AshifuddinMondal, M., & Rehena, Z. (2018, January). IoT based intelligent agriculture field monitoring system. In *2018 8th International Conference on Cloud Computing, Data Science & Engineering (Confluence)* (pp. 625–629). IEEE.

18. Bhosale, P. A., & Dixit, V. V. (2012). Water saving-irrigation automatic agricultural controller. *International Journal of Scientific and Technology Research*, 1(11), 118–123.

19. Lakshmi, K., & Gayathri, S. (2017). Implementation of IoT with image processing in plant growth monitoring system. *Journal of Scientific and Innovative Research*, 6(2), 80–83.

20. Hanswal, P., Dale, O., Gupta, D., & Yadav, R. N. (2013, April). Designing a central control unit and soil moisture sensor based irrigation water pump system. In *2013 Texas Instruments India Educators' Conference* (pp. 306–310). IEEE.

21. Bowlekar, A. P., Patil, S. T., Kadam, U. S., Mane, M. S., Nandgude, S. B., & Palte, N. K. (2019). Performance evaluation of real time automatic irrigation system on the yield of cabbage (*Brassica oleracea* L.). *International Journal of Pure & Applied Bioscience*, 7, 160–165.

22. Sharma, S. U., & Shah, D. J. (2016). A practical animal detection and collision avoidance system using computer vision technique. *IEEE Access*, 5, 347–358.

23. Maheswari, P. U., & Rajan, A. R. (2016). Animal intrusion detection system using wireless sensor networks. *International Journal of Advanced Research in Biology Engineering Science and Technology (IJARBEST)*, 2, 10.

24. Rakesh, A., Vinod, A., Madhu, M., Daniel, R., Jose, J., & Joseph, R. (2022). Animal trespassing detection system. *International Journal of Engineering Research and Technology (IJERT)*, 2278-0181.

25. Prajna, P., Soujanya, B., & Divya, S. (2018). IoT-based wild animal intrusion detection system. *International Journal of Engineering Research and Technology (IJERT)*, 2278-0181.

26. Patil, H., & Ansari, N. (2021, May). Automated wild-animal intrusion detection and repellent system using artificial intelligence of things. In *Proceedings of the 4th International Conference on Advances in Science & Technology (ICAST2021)*.

27. Archana, P., & Priya, R. (2016). Design and implementation of automatic plant watering system. *International Journal of Advanced Engineering and Global Technology*, 4(1), 1567–1570.

28. Tseng, F. H., Cho, H. H., & Wu, H. T. (2019). Applying big data for intelligent agriculture-based crop selection analysis. *IEEE Access*, 7, 116965–116974.

29. Fuentes, A., Yoon, S., Kim, S. C., & Park, D. S. (2017). A robust deep-learning-based detector for real-time tomato plant diseases and pests recognition. *Sensors*, 17(9), 2022.

30. Bondre, D. A., & Mahagaonkar, S. (2019). Prediction of crop yield and fertilizer recommendation using machine learning algorithms. *International Journal of Engineering Applied Sciences and Technology, 4*(5), 371–376.

31. Pandith, V., Kour, H., Singh, S., Manhas, J., & Sharma, V. (2020). Performance evaluation of machine learning techniques for mustard crop yield prediction from soil analysis. *Journal of Scientific Research, 64*(2), 394–398.

32. Kalimuthu, M., Vaishnavi, P., & Kishore, M. (2020, August). Crop prediction using machine learning. In *2020 Third International Conference on Smart Systems and Inventive Technology (ICSSIT)* (pp. 926–932). IEEE.

33. Liakos, K. G., Busato, P., Moshou, D., Pearson, S., & Bochtis, D. (2018). Machine learning in agriculture: A review. *Sensors, 18*(8), 2674.

7 Leaf-CAP
A Capsule Network-Based Tea Leaf Disease Recognition and Detection

Alkha Mohan and Jayakrishnan A.

Tea is one of the principal cash crops for exporting and developing nations such as India, Sri Lanka, and Bangladesh. Tea production has its socio-economic impact as it is a primary source of income for many smallholder farmers and plantation workers. Numerous contagious tea diseases have an adverse impact on the quantity and quality of tea produced overall. Early detection and prevention of such communicable diseases are pivotal for ensuring increased yield and profit. This paper proposes a novel tea leaf classification model Leaf-CAP. Leaf-CAP introduces a capsule backbone neural structure combined with a pre-trained VGG-19 feature extractor, LP pooling, statistical pooling, and dynamic routing. The modifications in the dynamic routing module made the proposed model outperform the classical capsule networks. The model is evaluated using manually gathered data from the Nilgiris region of Tamil Nadu and publicly available "tea sickness dataset" from Mendeley data. The Leaf-CAP model is compared against various state-of-the-art techniques such as the Fuzzy Rough Set model, support vector machine (SVM), convolutional neural network (CNN), VGG-19, Efficient Net, and Conditional Deep Convolutional Generative Adversarial Networks (C-DCGAN). The results prove that the model demonstrates superior classification and generalisation ability compared to state-of-the-art classification methods.

7.1 INTRODUCTION

Worldwide, tea is a very significant beverage. Large-scale tea cultivation is practised in Assam and Darjeeling in the east, as well as districts of Nilgiris and Kerala in the south of India. One of the significant producers of tea worldwide is India. Ensuring the quality and amount of tea produced is crucial due to the considerable socio-economic impact of tea cultivation. Plant researchers and other public-private stakeholders are eager to increase tea cultivation. Tea leaves are harvested year-round and will grow through different seasons and climatic conditions. As a result, tea cultivation will be vulnerable to several illnesses that damage the leaves, stems, and roots. The primary leaf diseases affecting tea leaves and harming the entire plant are the focus of this study. Algal leaf spot, anthracnose, bird's eye spot, brown blight, grey blight, red leaf spot, white spot, blister blight, and scab are the main diseases that damage tea plants. Identification of these diseases at an early stage can reduce the overall plant damage and succeeding economic impacts. The advancements in science and technology enable researchers to introduce vision-based disease leaf classification techniques.

One of the ways to image classification is to consider it as an image retrieval problem. The image retrieval system receives the query as a diseased leaf and evaluates it with the query ranking system to map it with the most appropriate category. There are different methods to perform image retrieval pixel-based techniques, metadata-based techniques, morphology-based techniques, and hashing-based techniques. Among these, the pixel-based technique was introduced first. Pixel-level matching won't always guarantee the desired classification mapping, and it is error-prone. Metadata-based image retrieval technique was a transition, but the difficulties in manually tagging the image made this process complex. Hashing techniques are increasingly used to provide a distinctive signature for an image. Learning hash codes were a critical task in hash-based image retrieval tasks. Wu et al. [1] employed transfer learning to learn hashing functions for image retrieval; the network uses pre-trained weights from the AlexNet model. Autoencoder-based hashing techniques for image classification have also become popular [2]. Shrivastava et al. demonstrate an effective method for locating and classifying soybean diseases using texture feature detection and background subtraction [3]. Li et al. [4] proposed a similar model based on transfer learning. Using fewer layers than the actual base transfer model creates an effect of hashing with some layers that only recognise a limited number of yet valuable features. However, these models are unable to generalise; hence, there is a growing need for more precise models.

Classification using classical machine learning and neural networks has become popular, and plant researchers have conducted many studies [5–9]. One well-liked supervised learning method is support vector machine (SVM). The classification problem is solved by SVM by locating a marginal hyperplane that divides the classes. To classify tea leaf diseases, the SVM and its variants are used [6]. The detection of diseases is accomplished using a method that combines SVM with k-nearest neighbour (KNN) and Kernel Principal Component Analysis (KPCA) [10, 11]. Rumpf et al. combined SVM with Spectral Vegetation Indexes for detecting sugar beet disease [12]. Another supervised machine learning method that seeks out the best fit line is support vector regression (SVR). The possibility of SVR for categorising leaf disease in apple plants was investigated by [13]. The requirement of learning samples becomes a bottleneck here. With sufficient learning examples, the models become extremely fit. The major drawback of these models was the manual feature extraction and curse of dimensionality. The amount of learning samples was increased by applying various data augmentation techniques. However, the variability introduced by these augmentation techniques was minimal, and hence the model was suspected of overfitting [6, 8]. One way to cope with overfitting and underfitting is by learning more observations. Recent advances in deep learning make handling enormous amounts of data easier.

A convolutional neural network (CNN) is a deep learning algorithm that can learn a set of input images by extracting features automatically. A CNN assigns importance to various aspects or objects in the data and can differentiate one from the other. Many researchers used CNN for leaf image disease detection. CaffeNet, a variant of AlexNet, is used for classifying 13 different plant diseases [14]. Transfer learning based on AlexNet and GoogLeNet is applied for classifying 26 leaf diseases among 14 crop species [3, 15, 16]. A deconvolutional network (DN) approach is used to gain an understanding of selected features that are automatically learned by a CNN [17]. The pre-trained technique based on AlexNet and VGG16 is used to classify six classes of tomato leaf disease (A. K. Rangarajan 2018). Transfer learning models based on GoogLeNet and Cifar10 are suggested [18]. The model recognises nine different kinds of maize leaf diseases. The model is fine-tuned by adjusting parameters, pooling combinations and dropout. In 2018, Liu et al. exclusively employed AlexNet as a transfer learning base for apple leaf disease detection. This method learned 13,689 diseased apple leaves data for classifying them into 4 disease categories [19]. In a study involving 25 different plant families and 87,848 data, the CNN model was proposed to classify 58 disease classes [20]. An analysis of the critical factors that affect the design and efficiency of deep neural networks used for plant pathology is presented in [21]. This study analysed the learning outcome of 50,000 images on four different CNN. The deep CNN technique classified 39 different plant leaf disease classes [22]. This technique used six different data augmentation techniques to make the model overfit-free. In 2019, Ramcharan et al. put forward a CNN object detection model to identify foliar symptoms of diseases in cassava in the agricultural field in Tanzania [23]. A model for identifying tea leaf diseases based on CNN that requires the least amount of computational complexity and resources while producing accurate results is proposed in [24]. Automatic detection of grape leaf diseases based on image analysis and back-propagation neural network (BPNN) is introduced [25]. The technique worked on image samples of five disease categories denoised by wiener filtering and segmented by Otsu. The automatic detection and identification of tea leaf disease are proposed using an enhanced version of RetinaNet called AX-RetinaNet [26]. AX-RetinaNet uses multiscale feature fusion and attention mechanisms for classification.

Autoencoder networks vastly improved the classification performance and enabled feature reduction. The autoencoder transforms the data into code using only the essential features, then decodes the code to produce an output that is a more standardised version of the original data. The advantage of the autoencoder network was its non-linear encoder-decoder architecture compared to principal component analysis (PCA). Several research works have been conducted in classification using autoencoders [27, 28]. The introduction of skip connections further improved the accuracy of autoencoder-based image classification. Although CNN is the most used method for classifying diseased leaves, its computational complexity and generalisability raise some concerns. There is no guarantee that the model always performs with minimal overfit for all test cases.

The proposed Leaf-CAP, a capsule network-based disease leaf classification, considers these concerns and introduces a more effective and efficient disease classification. The rest of the paper is organised as follows: Section 7.2 details the materials and methods used for the proposed architecture. The proposed Leaf-CAP architecture, common tea leaf diseases, and dataset details are all covered in this section. The result and discussion part (Section 7.3) compares the suggested model against state-of-the-art techniques. Finally, Section 7.4 presents the conclusions of the study and future directions.

7.2   MATERIALS AND METHODS

Figure 7.1 illustrates the standard framework for the proposed classification of tea leaf diseases. Three main blocks make up the method. Dataset identification and loading come first, followed by pre-processing, which involves scaling, augmentation, and normalising the data. The final module is the capsule network architecture for disease prediction.

7.2.1   TEA LEAF DISEASE UNDER STUDY

Nine of the most widespread leaf diseases that afflict tea plants are attempted to be classified in the proposed research. The investigated disease includes algal leaf spot, anthracnose, bird's eye spot, brown blight, grey blight, red leaf spot, white spot, blister blight, and scab. This section summarises the disease's causes, symptoms, and treatments.

7.2.1.1   Algal Leaf Spot

The alga Cephaleuros virescens causes the algal leaf spot. The diseased leaf has an orange-brown rusty appearance and typically manifests itself in a circular pattern on the upper surface of the tea leaf. The spots are around 2 cm in diameter and don't have any clear geometric patterns. An algal leaf spot is also known as a green scarf because it can appear crusty, fuzzy, or flaky. The illness typically occurs in the summer and spreads during the rainy season. The tea plant is especially susceptible to this algal disease because of its dense leaf structure. The algal leaf spots reduce the photosynthetic surface area of plants by partially or entirely affecting the leave. Tea plants are more vulnerable to algal leaf spot infection due to poor soil drainage, unbalanced nutrition, and exposure to relatively high temperatures and humidity. The treatments

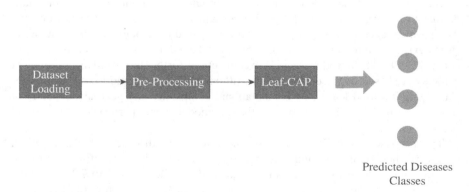

FIGURE 7.1   Overall architecture of the proposed tea leaf disease identification.

for preventing this algal illness include early discovery, the use of pesticides, adherence to appropriate cultivation techniques, and adequate fertilisation.

7.2.1.2 Anthracnose

Anthracnose is a prevalent foliar disease that first appeared in various tea-growing regions of China. The family of Colletotrichum fungus is responsible for this infection, which leads to a loss in the vigour of tea trees and may significantly lower the quality and yield of tea produced throughout the growing season. Once affected, the overall yield damage could be slashed to anywhere in the range of 30–75%. At first, diseased leaves typically have water-soaked sores, but as the disease progresses, the size of the lesions increases. If the condition is not swiftly diagnosed, it will spread uncontrollably throughout the tea estate. Fungi that cause anthracnose reside in plant waste. Pruning dead leaves and twigs at the appropriate time is one of the best ways to stop its spread. Sufficient availability of sunlight and air also helps to prevent anthracnose.

7.2.1.3 Bird's Eye Spot

Bird's eye spot disease in tea plants is caused by the fungus Cercospora theae's spread. This infection affects younger leaves initially, later confined to mature leaves and bare stalks, which in turn affects the yield potential. More sporadic cases of this disease were discovered in the plantations of India's southern states. The cell-degrading enzymes released by the phytopathogen cause necrotic spots of brown to black colour with a red border to appear on the damaged leaves. The illness spread is made worse by climate variations in the amount of sunlight, humidity, and rainfall. The disease can be controlled by providing the right amount of shade, drainage, soil aeration, and fertilisation, particularly with potassium for tea plants.

7.2.1.4 Brown Blight and Grey Blight

Brown and grey blight are caused by the pathogen Colletotrichum and Pestalotiopsis. Improper caring of plants is the root cause of this disease. These pathogens usually make entry through the wounds and cuts in the plant leaf and stem. These infections are also favoured by poor air circulation, high temperature, high humidity or prolonged periods of leaf wetness. Both brown and grey blight affect leaves at any stage of growth. Young, damaged leaves often have tiny, oval, light yellow-green dots with a short yellow border. Concentric rings with irregular, small black dots become visible as the disease progresses; the spots enlarge and turn dark or grey, and eventually, the dried tissue collapses, causing defoliation. The prevention method for this kind of disease is to space tea bushes apart sufficiently to allow for adequate sunlight and airflow.

7.2.1.5 Red Leaf Spot

The red leaf spot is caused by the pathogen Macrophoma theicola Petch. It damages foliage by producing large, cigar-shaped spores. Small red or reddish-brown leaf patches with a tan centre are the disease's visible signs. Several spots develop at random locations on the leaf, and all over it, they grow together and spread, leading to complete damage and yield loss. The early detection and application of correct pesticides is the one solution, whereas natural prevention can be done by providing sufficient sunlight and air circulation.

7.2.1.6 White Spot

Phyllosticta theifolia Hara fungi cause white spots in tea leaves. Several circular white-coloured spots are observed in random locations on the leaf surface, hence the name white spot. Older spots may get dark edges and lose their centres. Such lesions resemble bullet holes. Additionally, this illness impacts photosynthetic activity, yield, and leaf quality.

7.2.1.7 Blister Blight

The pathogen Exobasidium vexans is responsible for the most severe disease to harm tea leaves, blister blight. This pathogen will seriously reduce agricultural yields and degrade leaf quality. The disease spreads the most during the rainy seasons when there is little sunlight and constant leaf moisture. The pathogen directly penetrates the leaf surface, mainly through tender leaves. The sickness will first appear as tiny, pinhole-sized spots, which will grow into large, transparent brownish spots as the illness progresses. The lower surface of leaves exhibits formations like blisters; when the fungal spores continue to be secreted, the blisters eventually turn brown and ultimately destroy the leaf.

7.2.1.8 Scab

Leaf scab is caused by the pathogen Elsinoe theae. Scab is a serious disease that adversely affects tea production and quality. Tiny circular or elliptical spots of yellow or reddish-brown colour develop in the leaves during the early stage. The affected areas become scabby and merge. This disease affects tender leaves mostly. The leaves eventually shrivel into a cup-like shape.

7.2.2 DATASET DESCRIPTION

The Leaf-CAP model is evaluated using manually gathered data from the Nilgiris region of Tamil Nadu and publicly available "tea sickness dataset" from Mendeley data [29]. The benchmark "tea sickness dataset" is diverse and has eight categories: algal leaf spot, anthracnose, bird's eye spot, brown blight, grey blight, red leaf spot, white spot, and healthy. The proposed method takes 100 red, green, and blue (RGB) images from each class as input to the pre-processing stage. The input images for the training are resized to 300×300 sizes and passed to a data augmentation module that creates new learning samples from existing samples. This will improve the generalisation capability of the learning system. Six different augmentations, including four random rotations, one random Gaussian blur, and one random crop, are applied to each leaf sample. The augmented dataset is further standardised with a mean and standard deviation of 0.485 and 0.229 for each channel. Data normalisation enables the proposed Leaf-CAP module to learn faster with lesser computational overhead. The total sample size is increased to 4,800 samples by the six levels of augmentation (600 images per class).

The manually collected dataset from Nilgiris consists of samples for three major diseases: blister blight, scab, and spot. Twenty images for each foliage disease class are gathered, and the augmentation technique produces 480 images. The

FIGURE 7.2 Sample images from the tea sickness dataset and manually collected dataset. (a) Algal Leaf Spot, (b) Anthracnose, (c) Bird's eye spot, (d) Brown blight, (e) Gray blight, (f) Red leaf spot, (g) White spot, (h) Blister blight, (i) Scab and (j) Healthy.

normalisation procedure used on this dataset is similar to that used on the tea illness dataset. The disease samples from both datasets are depicted in Figure 7.2. The train-test-validation split used by the suggested Leaf-CAP model is 80:10:10. Table 7.1 tabulates the disease labels and train-test-validation number for both datasets after augmentation.

TABLE 7.1

Disease Classes with Train-Test-Validation Splits (After Augmentation)

Disease Class	Training Samples	Test Samples	Validation Samples	Total
	Tea Sickness Dataset			
Algal leaf spot	400	100	100	600
Anthracnose	400	100	100	600
Bird's eye spot	400	100	100	600
Brown blight	400	100	100	600
Grey blight	400	100	100	600
Red leaf spot	400	100	100	600
White spot	400	100	100	600
Healthy	400	100	100	600
	Manually Collected Dataset			
Blister blight	96	12	12	120
Scab	96	12	12	120
Spot	96	12	12	120

7.2.3   CAPSULE NETWORK

To address the shortcomings of traditional CNN, the capsule network is suggested as a superior alternative [30]. A capsule network consists of several autonomous computational structures called capsules. For an object detection task, the initial layers of CNN extract simple morphological features such as edges and structure, but the deeper layer extracts more complex information. These features are used in the test stage to recognise objects without considering the order or arrangement of features. This is one of the most severe flaws of conventional CNNs, and they do not consider spatial consistency during the prediction or classification process. A straightforward example is that if CNN is used for face detection, they will only look for the presence of eyes, nose, lips, etc., despite their global arrangement. These limitations in understanding and prioritising spatial feature relationships were solved by the introduction of capsule networks.

The capsules in the capsule network evaluate not only the features but also the parameters associated with them, such as order and orientation. The capsule neural network performs classification differently from the previous face detection example. The capsules in the neural network primarily look for the presence of peculiar facial traits.

They are not limited to just primary feature identification; they also evaluate the morphological arrangement characteristics of the face, such as the order of eyes, nose, and lips. Therefore, the network only recognises a face when the capsules determine that the components of that face are arranged correctly.

Max polling layers in CNN cause information delay, as they only choose to pass information from most active neurons. This polling operation causes considerable deprivation of spatial information. The introduction of "routing-by-agreement" marginalises this loss. This means that lower level features will only get sent to a higher level layer that matches its contents. If the features resemble an eye or a mouth, it will be classified as a "face"; if it contains fingers and a palm, it will be classified as a "hand". Spatial information is encoded into features via this comprehensive solution.

The need for more efficient algorithms and sufficient computational powers were the limiting factors in implementing capsule networks. Capsule network implementation became more resilient with the introduction of dynamic routing [31] and advanced expectation maximisation routing techniques. The dynamic routing iteratively transfers output vectors from lower level capsules to upper levels. The algorithm selects the most appropriate parent capsules, and the iterative operations introduce the sparse connection between routing layers. While comparing to CNN, two major technological innovations happened, one was the replacement of max-pooling layers by dynamic routing, and the other was the introduction squashing process that replaced the scalar output feature detectors of CNN with vector output capsules. These developments allowed capsule networks to perform better and outperform CNNs when it comes to certain object categorisation tasks. More sparse connections necessitate more iterations of routing, which further increases memory and computational costs.

7.3 LEAF-CAP ARCHITECTURE

Three crucial architectural layers make up the suggested Leaf-CAP model. A VGG-19 feature extractor first handles the normalised input data before feeding it to several primary capsules and, lastly, to the class-defining output capsules. VGG-19 is a pre-trained model trained on ImageNet [32]. This pre-trained CNN helps extract valuable features from the newly provided unseen samples of leaves. The number of classes of the multiclass problem defines the number of output capsules. This will change depending on the datasets being used. The input samples of 300×300 images are fed in 64 batches for the training process. First-level features are extracted using the VGG pre-trainer, which creates 256 feature maps. The first 2D convolution is designed with 64 kernels of size 3×3, with padding and stride set to 1. Batch normalisation is also incorporated in this layer. A 2D power average LP layer with a 3×3 mask and stride one is used for pooling. The downscaled output of this LP pooling layer is supplied to the following 2D convolution layer having 16 kernels of size 3×3 with padding and stride 1. All convolution operation uses Exponential Linear Unit (ELU) activation functions. The 2D features that were retrieved are sent into a statistical pooling layer and a series of 1D convolutions. For each 1D convolution, eight kernels of size 5×1 and one kernel of size 3×1 are used. Stride and padding are set to 2 for the initial 1D convolution and 1 for the subsequent 1D convolution. Dynamic routing is used to discover the key capsule, and the flattened features from each capsule are then combined and sent to a softmax for the final class label. The detailed architecture of the proposed leaf-CAP is shown in Figure 7.3.

7.3.1 PRIMARY CAPSULES

The outputs of the VGG-19 feature extractor are fed to several primary capsules. The number and initial weights of these primary capsules are one of the hyperparameters deciding the accuracy of the model. In this Leaf-CAP model, we choose ten primary capsules having random weight initialisation. Random initialisation assigns random weights that are too close to zero. This weight initialisation method introduces irregularity and ensures that different neurons are not performing the same weighted multiplications.

A series of 2D convolutions, statistical polling, and 1D convolutions constitute the primary capsules of the Leaf-CAP model. The primary capsules are connected to the class-defining output capsules via a dynamic routing algorithm. The activation on these output capsules passed through softmax activation for generating class probability. The convolution operation glides over the input data in a top-to-bottom left-to-right pattern to learn feature maps. A batch normalisation layer and ELU activation function are placed after each 2D convolutional layer [33]. The pooling procedure used to subsample the feature maps is LP pooling (learned-norm pooling) [34]. Batch normalisation standardises the inputs to a layer for each mini-batch. This helps to reduce training duration and allows faster learning rates.

The same effects of batch normalisation are introduced by ELU but at a reduced computational cost. ELUs have negative values in contrast to ReLUs, allowing them

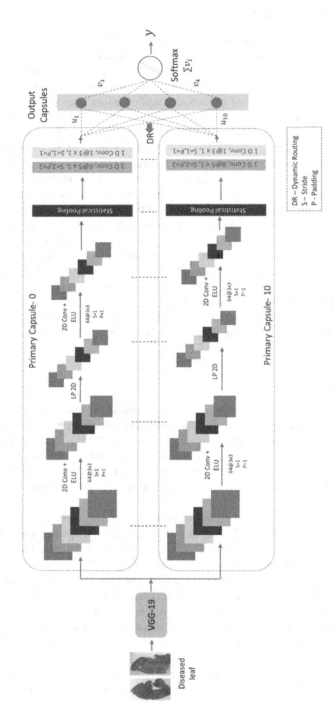

FIGURE 7.3   Proposed Leaf-CAP: A Capsule Network-Based Tea Leaf Disease Recognition and Detection.

to bring mean unit activations closer to zero. The Exponential Linear Unit activation function ELU(x) is defined by Equation (7.1) as follows:

$$ELU(x) = \begin{cases} x & x > 0 \\ \alpha.\left(e^x - 1\right) & x < 0 \end{cases} \tag{7.1}$$

where α is a hyperparameter that defines the levels of activation.

The LP pooling aggregated activations in the LP norm way, which can be seen as an adjustment between max and average pooling controlled by the parameter p. The p-value ranges between 1 and ∞, as the p-value is chosen as 1, it produces output equivalent to max pooling, and for ∞, it makes sub-scaling equivalent to sum polling. The performance of the diseased leaf classification is further enhanced by the LP pooling operation, which unifies max and average pooling. The mathematical representation of the LP pooling operation is shown in Equation (7.2).

$$LP(X) = \sqrt[p]{\sum_{x \in X} Z^p} \tag{7.2}$$

Pooling layers reduce the number of parameters to learn and the amount of computation performed in the network. The feature maps are downscaled to achieve this. Additionally, a small amount of information loss may result from this. The pooling layer summarises the features present in a region of the feature map generated by a convolution layer. Further convolution operations are performed on summarised features instead of precisely positioned features generated by the convolution layer. This makes the model more robust to variations in the position of the features in the input image. However, the choice of pooling operation affects the results.

Recognising the textural difference between diseased and healthy parts of the leaf is the key to an efficient classification. The morphological variations and colour patterns need to be distinguished statistically. Thus, rather than using standard pooling layers, mean and variance statistics can be used. The statistical pooling layer computes the means and variances of each filter and is shown in Equations (7.3) and (7.4)

$$Mean\left(\mu_k\right): \mu_k = \frac{1}{X \times Y} \sum_{i=1}^{X} \sum_{j=1}^{Y} T_{kij} \tag{7.3}$$

$$Variance\left(\sigma_k^2\right): \alpha_k^2 = \frac{1}{X \times Y - 1} \sum_{i=1}^{X} \sum_{j=1}^{Y} \left(T_{kij} - \sigma_k\right)^2 \tag{7.4}$$

In Equations (7.3) and (7.4), k denotes the layer index, T denotes the two-dimensional kernel, and Y and Z are the length and width of the filters.

7.3.2 DYNAMIC ROUTING ALGORITHM

Depending on the input, each primary capsule extracts a distinct feature. For example, one primary capsule might be highly effective at extracting "grey blight" features, while another may significantly extract "red leaf spot" features. This results from the random weight initialisation done at the individual capsules, which enables individual capsules to learn different features for the same input. The features from each capsule are combined by the dynamic routing method. The effectiveness of this feature fusion has an impact on classification accuracy as well. The "agreement" between all primary capsules is calculated and routed to the appropriate output capsule. This algorithm aims to reach a consensus because the primary capsules may have different opinions, and some may be incorrect. The activation of the output capsules further determines the output probability.

The length of the output vector of a capsule denotes the likelihood that the item it represents is present in the current input. A non-linear "squashing" function ensures that short vectors get shrunk to almost zero length, and long vectors get shrunk to a length slightly below 1. The squashing operation at the capsule is shown in Equation (7.5), where v_j and s_j denote the capsule's vector output and total input.

$$v_j = \frac{\|s_j\|^2}{1+\|s_j\|^2} \frac{s_j}{\|s_j\|} \tag{7.5}$$

The total input s_j for all the capsule except first layer capsules is the weighted sum of all "prediction vectors" $\hat{u}_{j|i}$ from precious layer and shown in Equation (7.6):

$$s_j = \sum_i c_{ij}\, \hat{u}_{j|i}, \; \hat{u}_{j|i} = W_{ij} u_i \tag{7.6}$$

where c_{ij} are coupling coefficients that are determined by the iterative dynamic routing process. The coupling coefficients c_{ij} are determined by a "routing softmax", the initial logits b_{ij} of which are the log prior probabilities that capsule i being coupled to capsule j, shown in Equation (7.7):

$$c_{ij} = \frac{\exp(b_{ij})}{\sum_k \exp(b_{ij})} \tag{7.7}$$

The implemented dynamic routing algorithm is shown next.

Procedure (dynamic routing)

1. for all capsule i in layer l and capsule j in layer $(l+1)$ set $b_{ij} = 0$
2. for n iterations do
3. for all capsule i in layer l find c_i (shown in Equation 7.7)
4. for all capsule j in layer $(l+1)$ find total input s_j (shown in Equation 7.6)
5. for all capsule j in layer $(l+1)$ find outpt v_j using squashing (shown in Equation 7.5)
6. for all capsule i in layer l and capsule j in layer $(l+1)$ find $b_{ij} = b_{ij} + \hat{u}_{j|i}.v_j$
7. return v_j

Softmax function is applied to each dimension of the output capsule vector, and the mean of all softmax output produces the prediction vector or output vector. The output vector is shown in Equation (7.8)

$$y = \frac{1}{n} \sum_{i=1}^{n} softmax\left(v_i^{(1)}, v_i^{(2)}, v_i^{(3)}, \ldots \ldots v_i^{(n)}\right) \qquad (7.8)$$

7.4 RESULTS AND DISCUSSION

The proposed Leaf-CAP: A capsule network-based tea leaf disease identification architecture is compared against six state-of-the-art classification techniques, including the Fuzzy Rough Set model, SVM, CNN, VGG-19, Efficient Net, and Conditional Deep Convolutional Generative Adversarial Networks (C-DCGAN). The cross-analysis of various evaluation parameters reveal that the suggested Leaf-CAP exhibit superior classification performance. The parameters Overall Accuracy (OA), Average Accuracy (AA), and Kappa statistics (K) are used to compare the classification performance of the proposed model to other cutting-edge approaches. The OA, which is equal to the sum of true positives and true negatives divided by the total number of individuals tested, is the percentage of correctly identified samples. AA denotes the mean of class-wise accuracy; this metric is desirable to analyse the classification performance of multiclass problems. The likelihood of agreement between the categorised result and the actual result is represented by the confusion matrix's row and column sum. K is the difference between these two values. OA, AA, and K are computed from the confusion matrix.

Tables 7.2 and 7.3 tabulate the training and testing values obtained for various evaluation parameters of a different disease classification technique and proposed Leaf-CAP. The statistics in the tables strongly suggest that, compared to current approaches, the Leaf-CAP model significantly improved overall performance. Leaf-CAP obtained training accuracies of 95.85% (OA) and 94.71% (AA) for the benchmark tea sickness

---

TABLE 7.2

Comparison of Training Evaluation Parameters for Tea Sickness Dataset and Manually Collected Dataset Using Different Methods

	Tea Sickness Dataset			Manually Collected Dataset		
Methods	**OA (%)**	**AA (%)**	**K (%)**	**OA (%)**	**AA (%)**	**K (%)**
Fuzzy Rough Set	71.30	79.03	73.14	67.33	73.45	71.11
SVM	75.48	81.14	77.96	70.15	77.18	73.48
CNN	81.10	84.58	79.98	74.45	78.19	74.66
VGG-19	84.41	86.23	84.11	79.68	80.65	77.93
Efficient Net	88.19	88.43	87.07	83.77	83.24	82.16
C-DCGAN	90.21	92.59	89.01	86.36	87.11	87.75
Proposed Leaf-CAP	95.85	94.71	93.76	92.74	89.79	90.05

TABLE 7.3

Comparison of Testing Evaluation Parameters for Tea Sickness Dataset and Manually Collected Dataset Using Different Methods

Methods	Tea Sickness Dataset			Manually Collected Dataset		
	OA (%)	AA (%)	K (%)	OA (%)	AA (%)	K (%)
Fuzzy Rough Set	69.13	73.13	70.37	65.72	71.42	69.04
SVM	71.45	77.27	72.92	68.48	74.65	70.83
CNN	75.67	79.65	76.85	72.11	73.18	73.32
VGG-19	79.48	79.37	81.75	77.36	78.57	75.66
Efficient Net	86.33	83.19	84.66	79.27	81.38	80.06
C-DCGAN	89.56	85.05	87.12	84.57	84.77	85.22
Proposed Leaf-CAP	93.32	92.20	91.19	89.08	88.49	89.31

dataset in the multiclass classification problem. Additionally, it displays a superior K value of 93.76% for this dataset. The number of samples in the manually collected dataset is relatively small, affecting the classification performance. However, the proposed method managed to produce superior performance while comparing other methods in the study. The manually gathered dataset yielded values of 92.74% (OA), 89.79% (AA), and 90.05 (K). The approach maintained quality performance even for the test set, demonstrating its robustness and effectiveness. Both datasets' testing results showed performance metrics of 93.32% (OA), 92.20% (AA), 91.19 (K) and 89.08% (OA), 88.49% (AA), 89.31 (K), respectively. The accuracy and loss curves for the train and test are shown in Figure 7.4 along with the number of epochs. Initial epochs of the test had lower test accuracy, but later epochs had an increase in accuracy that eventually caught up to training accuracy. (Epoch 33, Epoch 50).

7.5 CONCLUSION

This study proposes a new capsule network-based model, Leaf-CAP, for predicting tea leaf disease. The Leaf-CAP model is a multiclass classification solution that deals with various disease classes such as algal leaf spot, anthracnose, bird's eye spot, brown blight, grey blight, red leaf spot, white spot, blister blight, scab, and healthy. The six-way augmentation process increased the sample size and facilitated better learning. The Leaf-CAP model exhibit superior performance over state-of-the-art techniques. The model is trained on single leaves of the tea plant. Different diseases may affect the tea twig. The same leaf, for instance, may exhibit both brown and grey blight. Hence the study can be further extended by collecting disease tea twigs and training them to identify and classify diseases in a group. Another future direction of study is using a multi-spectral camera for leaf image capturing, enabling the model to extract 3D spectral features. The model can be further optimised to run on mobile devices and deployed in the fields to detect early-stage tea leaf diseases and initiate timely remedies.

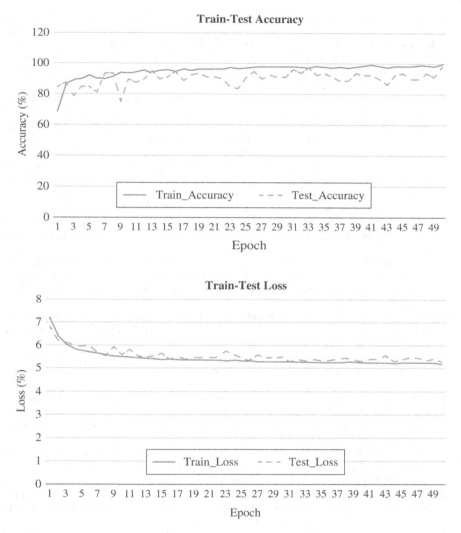

FIGURE 7.4   Train – Test accuracy and loss against epoch.

REFERENCES

1. W.J. Li, S. Wang, and W.C. Kang (2015). Feature learning based deep supervised hashing with pairwise labels. In: Twenty-Fifth International Joint Conference on Artificial Intelligence (IJCAI'16), AAAI Press, pp. 1711–1717.

2. M. Carreira-Perpiñán and R. Raziperchikolaei (2015). Hashing with binary autoencoders. In: 2015 IEEE Conference on Computer Vision and Pattern Recognition (CVPR), Boston, MA, pp. 557–566. doi: 10.1109/CVPR.2015.7298654

3. S. Shrivastava, S.K. Singh, and D.S. Hooda (2017). Soybean plant foliar disease detection using image retrieval approaches. Multimedia Tools and Applications, vol. 76, pp. 26647–26674. https://doi.org/10.1007/s11042-016-4191-7

4. Y. Li, Y. Zhang, X. Huang, H. Zhu, and J. Ma (Feb. 2018). Large-scale remote sensing image retrieval by deep hashing neural networks. IEEE Transactions on Geoscience and Remote Sensing, vol. 56, no. 2, pp. 950–965. doi: 10.1109/TGRS.2017.2756911

5. B. Karmokar, M. Ullah, Md. Siddiquee, and K. Alam (2015). Tea leaf diseases recognition using neural network ensemble. International Journal of Computer Applications, vol. 114, pp. 975–8887. doi:10.5120/20071-1993

6. S. Hossain, R. M. Mou, M. M. Hasan, S. Chakraborty and M. A. Razzak (2018). Recognition and detection of tea leaf's diseases using support vector machine. In: 2018 IEEE 14th International Colloquium on Signal Processing & Its Applications (CSPA), Penang, Malaysia, pp. 150–154. doi: 10.1109/CSPA.2018.8368703

7. R. Meena, G.P. Saraswathy, G. Ramalakshmi, K.H. Mangaleswari and T. Kaviya (2017). Detection of leaf diseases and classification using digital image processing. In: 2017 International Conference on Innovations in Information, Embedded and Communication Systems (ICIIECS), Coimbatore, pp. 1–4. doi: 10.1109/ICIIECS.2017.8275915

8. C. Dhaware and K. Wanjale (2017). A modern approach for plant leaf disease classification which depends on leaf image processing. In: 2017 International Conference on Computer Communication and Informatics (ICCCI), pp. 1–4. doi: 10.1109/ICCCI.2017.8117733

9. X. Sun, S. Mu, Y. Xu, Z. Cao and T. Su (2019). Image recognition of tea leaf diseases based on convolutional neural network. In: 2018 International Conference on Security, Pattern Analysis, and Cybernetics (SPAC), Jinan, China, 2018, pp. 304–309. doi: 10.1109/SPAC46244.2018.8965555

10. R. Muralidharan, and C. Chandrasekar (2011). Object recognition using SVM-KNN based on geometric moment invariant. International Journal of Computer Trends and Technology, vol. 1, no. 1, pp. 215–220.

11. R. Muralidharan, and C. Chandrasekar (2011). Object recognition using support vector machine augmented by RST invariants. International Journal of Computer Science Issues (IJCSI), vol. 8, no. 5, p. 280.

12. T. Rumpf, A.-K. Mahlein, and U. Steiner et al (2010). Early detection and classification of plant diseases with support vector machines based on hyperspectral reflectance. Computers and Electronics in Agriculture, vol. 74, pp. 91–99. https://doi.org/10.1016/j.compag.2010.06.009

13. E. Omrani, B. Khoshnevisan, and S. Shamshirband et al., (2014). Potential of radial basis function-based support vector regression for apple disease detection. Measurement, vol. 55, pp. 512–519. https://doi.org/10.1016/j.measurement.2014.05.033

14. S. Sladojevic, M. Arsenovic, A. Anderla, D. Culibrk, and D. Stefanovic (2016). Deep neural networks based recognition of plant diseases by leaf image classification. Computational Intelligence and Neuroscience, vol. 2016, pp. 1–11.

15. S. P. Mohanty, D. P. Hughes, and M. Salathé (2016). "Using deep learning for image-based plant disease detection. Frontiers in Plant Science, vol. 7, pp. 1–10.

16. A. K. Rangarajan, R. Purushothaman, and A. Ramesh (2018). Tomato crop disease classification using pre-trained deep learning algorithm. Procedia Computer Science, vol. 133, pp. 1040–1047.

17. S. H. Lee, C. S. Chan, S. J. Mayo, and P. Remagnino (2017). How deep learning extracts and learns leaf features for plant classification. Pattern Recognition, vol. 71, pp. 1–13.

18. X. Zhang, Y. Qiao, and F. Meng et al., (2018). Identification of maize leaf diseases using improved deep convolutional neural networks. IEEE Access, vol. 6, pp. 30370–30377. https://doi.org/10.1109/ACCESS.2018.2844405

19. B. Liu, Y. Zhang, D. He, and Y. Li (2018). Identification of apple leaf diseases based on deep convolutional neural networks. Symmetry, vol. 10, no. 1, p. 11.

20. K. P. Ferentinos (2018). Deep learning models for plant disease detection and diagnosis. Computers and Electronics in Agriculture, vol. 145, pp. 311–318.

21. J. G. Barbedo (2018). Factors influencing the use of deep learning for plant disease recognition. Biosystems Engineering, vol. 172, pp. 84–91.
22. G. Geetharamani, and A. Pandian (2019). Identification of plant leaf diseases using a nine-layer deep convolutional neural network. Computers & Electrical Engineering, vol. 76, pp. 323–338.
23. A. Ramcharan, P. McCloskey, K. Baranowski, N. Mbilinyi, L. Mrisho, M. Ndalahwa, J. Legg, and D. P. Hughes (2019). A mobile-based deep learning model for cassava disease diagnosis. Frontiers in Plant Science, vol. 10, pp. 1–8.
24. S. Bhowmik, A.K. Talukdar, and K Kumar Sarma (2020). Detection of disease in tea leaves using convolution neural network. In: 2020 advanced communication technologies and signal processing (ACTS), IEEE, Silchar, India, pp. 1–6.
25. J. Zhu, A. Wu, X. Wang, and H. Zhang (2020). Identification of grape diseases using image analysis and BP neural networks. Multimedia Tools and Applications, vol. 79, pp. 14539–14551. https://doi.org/10.1007/s11042-018-7092-0
26. W. Bao, T. Fan, and G. Hu et al., (2022). Detection and identification of tea leaf diseases based on AX-RetinaNet. Scientific Reports, vol. 12, p. 2183. https://doi.org/10.1038/s41598-022-06181-z
27. V. Zilvan et al., (Jun. 2022). Convolutional variational autoencoder-based feature learning for automatic tea clone recognition. Journal of King Saud University - Computer and Information Sciences, vol. 34, no. 6. Elsevier BV, pp. 3332–3342. doi: 10.1016/j.jksuci.2021.01.020
28. K. Trang, L. TonThat and N. G. Minh Thao (Jun.2020). Plant leaf disease identification by deep convolutional autoencoder as a feature extraction approach. In: 2020 17th International Conference on Electrical Engineering/Electronics, Computer, Telecommunications and Information Technology (ECTI-CON), IEEE. doi: 10.1109/ecti-con49241.2020.9158218
29. Gibson Kimutai and Anna Förster (2022). Tea sickness dataset. Mendeley Data, vol. V2. doi: 10.17632/j32xdt2ff5.2
30. G.E. Hinton, A. Krizhevsky, and S.D. Wang (2011). Transforming auto-encoders. In Honkela, T., Duch, W., Girolami, M., Kaski, S. (eds) *Artificial Neural Networks and Machine Learning – ICANN 2011*. Lecture Notes in Computer Science, vol. 6791. Springer, Berlin, Heidelberg, pp. 44–51. https://doi.org/10.1007/978-3-642-21735-7_6.
31. S. Sabour, N. Frosst, and G.E. Hinton (2017). Dynamic routing between capsules. In I. Guyon, U. V. Luxburg, S. Bengio, H. Wallach, R. Fergus, S. Vishwanathan, & R. Garnett (Eds.), *Advances in Neural Information Processing Systems*, vol. 30, https://proceedings.neurips.cc/paper_files/paper/2017/file/2cad8fa47bbef282badbb8de5374b894-Paper.pdf.
32. K. Simonyan and A. Zisserman (2014). "Very Deep Convolutional Networks for Large-Scale Image Recognition." arXiv, 2014. doi: 10.48550/ARXIV.1409.1556
33. D.-A. Clevert, T. Unterthiner, and S. Hochreiter (2015). "Fast and Accurate Deep Network Learning by Exponential Linear Units (ELUs)." arXiv, 2015. doi: 10.48550/ARXIV.1511.07289
34. Z. Gao, L. Wang, and G. Wu (2019). LIP: Local importance-based pooling. In: 2019 IEEE/CVF International Conference on Computer Vision (ICCV), Seoul, Korea (South), pp. 3354–3363. doi: 10.1109/ICCV.2019.00345

8 Agri Retail Product Management System

Perepi Rajarajeswari, Vinila Jinny S., R. Saraswathi,
Sawant Swara Anant, Manav Goyal, and Deraj RM

8.1 INTRODUCTION

In the agricultural sector, the farmers sell their production, i.e. vegetables and fruits, to third person who then sells those to other shop-keepers and takes a high margin of the farmer's profit due to which many Indian farmers are facing financial losses. This takes place because of loss of facts and for that reason middlemen input at every level from the manufacturers to the consumers, which no question aggregates the product however additionally will increase the stairs into the chain that will increase wastage and makes the machine much less transparent. An imaginative and prescient of a machine and intervention of generation can efficiently result in an exceptional alternate with inside the manner matters are currently going on. The venture pursuits to expand an interface. Previously crop models are used various essential tools to analyze the effects of climate changes on crop growth and development impact of adaptation strategies. We have described smart agri-food in other countries.

Malaga, Spain, for agri-food committee did work on digitalization and new technologies in agricultural food in 2019. Research works which have been done on agriculture were performed in 2019 at Florence. In Bilbao, active committee focused on smart platform with specialization in agri-food. In the year 2018, June 11th at Finland semi-annual working committee discussed S3P agri-food. Systematic review described the crop model with uncertainty decomposition. The gaps present in the systems of the survey were, while they have addressed the issue of how the agriculture products can be collected and sold, they don't address the issue of how each of the products can be made easily accessible to be bought by a public user. To overcome these issues, the proposed system is described in this system.

There are three types of users who interact with the system:

1. Mobile users' application and web portal.
2. Managing the administrators portal.
3. Farmers are considered primary owners.

This system provides validation of the experiments conducted and based on that innovative practices are followed to improve both cultivation and production. Farmers are provided with consultancy support to monitor and innovate the production.

This chapter consists of four sections. Section 8.2 describes the related work. Proposed methodology is presented in Section 8.3. Section 8.4 gives the results and discussion. Section 8.5 concluded this chapter.

                                           DOI: 10.1201/9781003391302-8

8.2   RELATED WORK

Gomathy et al, focused on e-commerce agriculture system. They have focused on technologies to help the farmers by selling their products on digital platforms. It can be more useful for making their business more efficiently and to speed up their marketing process.

As discussed in [8] describe the design and implementation of e-commerce web application. This chapter introduced data mining-oriented features and system structure of e-commerce system in online mode. It will help the development of the enterprises depending on such type of business [12]. Grubs and medicine details are stored in database. Cryptography principles were used for encrypting and decrypting the submitted data.

Harmani et al [1] focused on applying artificial intelligence in precision agriculture which supports farmers to increase agriculture land and increases the plant growth. The optimization expected by the farmers can be achieved with a correct model.

Patil et al [2] presented a smart agriculture work by using cloud-based IOT. This technique supports the farmer in monitoring and controlling the land from any location and at any time. The use of smart phones makes the effort easier and possible. But the farmer affording the supporting device and its installation and maintenance are not considered.

Moutsinas et al [3] suggested an AgroNIT which considers all aspects in agriculture. It monitors the management of pesticide and fertilizer use. But automated alert will help take immediate action which is missing.

Rahmouni et al. suggested the use of two mega-digital concepts leading to a highly affected agricultural environment. Productivity is the major factor in agriculture system which is met using AIoT framework. But AI concept makes the system more expensive.

Cao et al [14] suggest a blockchain technology-based platform that includes internet of things to overcome the difficulties which exist in traditional supply chain. The system takes into account multi levels that are two-level supply chain featured for buyer and created formalized game models using and not using blockchain technique. Study shows that the engrossment of the blockchain-based plan can clue to amplified manufacture amount and entire leftover of the supply chain. It also stimulates added sustainability venture to harvest greener foods. Remarkably, we exhibit the cost of the blockchain-based policy diminutions in the reliability of the commercial situation in which the source sequence activates. Additionally, the consumer will continuously profit from the recognized blockchain-based policy; however, the supportive can profit in most cases but could be inferior off under definite circumstances. The acceptance and operative prices could compensate the profits produced by the accumulation of the blockchain-based policy.

Carolin et al. [15] excel that the digital technologies influence invention in all segments of the family, with outdated ones such as cultivation, the motorized industry, and marketing. Similar trends across sectors include that the Internet of Things and data are becoming key involvements for invention, innovation cycles are accelerating, services innovation is gaining importance, and collaborative innovation matters more. A sectoral method is desirable when scheming invention strategies in some provinces, particularly proposed data admission and digital technology embracing strategies. The present concentration of invention policies on enhancing R&D to chance R&D intensity targets also wants scrutiny. Anshari et al [16] suggest Cardinal bazaar with Fintech-empowered force convert agriculture's professional method into added sustainability in stretch of finance and spreading. FinTech propositions share croppers' opportune ways of receiving foundations of funding through crowdfunding and cardinal imbursement scheme. Thus, ordinal market can act as a policy for FinTech to assimilate the ground-breaking monetarist answer into wider agriculture's ecology. This study recommends a signifying digital market with FinTech permitted particularly crowdfunding and imbursement scheme in order to provision agriculture's sustainability. The classic attaches all performers (agriculturalists, property owners, stakeholders, and customers) into a policy that can endorse limpidity, authorization, inventiveness, and free assignation in agriculture. Andrea et al. [17] suggest that blockchain with Artificial Intelligence can enormously donate to refining the agri-food sequence: though they feature significant supremacy tests, which can prime to unwanted re-intermediation belongings (for blockchain); and damage of operator autonomy and activity, as well as confidentiality and honesty (for Artificial Intelligence). Lastly, if any answer that trusts on digital technologies resolves essential to be comprehensive, then the danger will be to broaden the digital gulf: more usually, FoodTech wants to grow in way that is well matched with all Sustainable Development Goals SDGs, not only those connected to sector of agri-food.

8.3   PROPOSED SYSTEM ARCHITECTURE

The suggested design includes five important actors:

a. Cloud agro-marketing and information module
b. Nodal center
c. Transport
d. Farmers
e. Customers

This representation is based on Perishable Agricultural Product (PAP) shop partakers.

The work, expected from this component, is as follows:

a. Cloud agro-marketing and information is a user interface module that is trained to reach the farmers in their native language.
b. Nodal center plays a major role and it performs the following actions:
   It collects and distributes products to the needy customer with the optimum market amount. It is a highly established organization that has the facility for cold storage and amenities to the farmers for selling purpose.
c. For supplying, the items produced to the respective nodal center for marketing with optimum cost required transportation services are available.

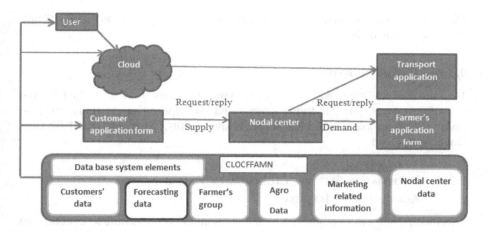

FIGURE 8.1 Proposed system architecture.

d. Farmers are serviced in their native language.
e. Customers are presented with products of optimum cost.
  Farmers facing current challenges are met with ICT [4, 5].

As shown in Figure 8.1, the information processing module forms the main source of agricultural information system which supports their stakeholders by providing messages related to cost-effectiveness by various procedures and actions through network mode. Instant messaging to farmers by providing voice response that tells the soil managing details and crop managing details, various procedures about protecting plant, details on weather prediction, current rates in market, details about the crop and people, possibilities for career, available welfare scheme from government etc. Emerging techniques help in updating the requirements of the farmers through voice messages based on the feedback from the customers. The union of farmers preserves the helpful schemes to meet the temporary credits of agriculturist for production of crop and its supportive activities.

8.3.1 FARMERS

The farmers can able to register their details (name, mobile number, account number, land type, land size, etc.). Cultivation can be made for product details such as type and variety, like the production type and variety, quantity, quality, price, and availability. Sales markets produce their product for money. They have to maintain agricultural information to solve the queries of customers.

8.3.2 CUSTOMERS

The customers can able to register their details (name, mobile number, account number) and are one who may be the Wholesaler *or Retailer*. For safekeeping, they have to pay the amount during registration and money back scheme at nodal center. They have made requirements of agricultural production to maintain agricultural report requirements on weekly basis.

8.3.3 TRANSPORT SYSTEM

This module includes all activities related to transportation. It includes the information of customers, possible transportation and the capacity of the transport, possibility of group loads, and time period of availability, expenses caused for each movement of load.

8.3.4 INFORMATION SYSTEM – CLOUD-BASED VIRTUAL AGRICULTURAL MARKETING

This module helps in satisfying customer needs and stores all available data that are related to the customer in the center location [6]. It links all the available nodal centers, which helps in sharing the data with all kind of people. Nodal center with the client application helps the users to reach the server. Concurrency lock is set to avoid updating of data by multiple users. It makes the required resources like I/O devices and memory devices available.

8.4 PROPOSED ARCHITECTURE DESCRIPTIONS

8.4.1 END-USER APPLICATION

The application of functions of trading agricultural products can be performed by using the **end-user applications**. These types of software applications are applied with the support of cloud-based technology that are operated by the transport domain [7], farmers, and wholesalers. Consumer presentation includes the modules of forecaster, advertisement, and demand details. Instant and dynamic presentations are effectively presented live based on predictions from orders and demand of the plants.

Farmer applications include module for prediction of production and its information with advertising details. The information on production tells the type of crop production, variety of crops, techniques of cultivation, images of production and product and content describing production. The advertising module has all templates of agricultural products, their details and thus exposing its details. These also include farmers needed details like prediction of quantity of production, quality, availability period and cost. It gives instant prediction and reporting of production details to each provider. The application of production forecast is same as application of customer forecast. A separate module for instant prediction for approximating the production of perishables of specific earner is offered.

Transport presentation consists of firm profiles and scheduling module of transport marketing product for different product loads and needs of effective scheduling **forecasts** for each **vendor's production**. The production prediction presentation is same as the customer prediction presentation. This presents a lively forecasting **element** for approximating the manufacture of **consumable goods from** each **vendor**. **The transportation application** consists of **company** profiles and **transportation** marketing product **planning modules** for different product loads and effective **planning needs**.

8.4.2 SUPPORTING FACILITIES

Supporting Facilities are based on advertising and information structure mechanisms for admission and facility control. It delivers agricultural knowledge components, marketing components, and data components, predicting component and agriculturalists association module.

8.4.2.1 Webpage for Production of Marketing Component:

The website allows farmers to enter personal and production data to reach customers. Customers can use their personal information to order the items they want. Farmer details and customer details calculate current demand for available products. If you have requirements, we will connect with other node centers to meet your product needs.

8.4.2.2 Weather Forecast

This is a presentation of science and technology to forecast the atmospheric circumstances of a specific setting. These methods are included in informal, quantitative methods using current data from test manufacturers.

8.4.2.3 Crop Insurance Management

This is an assurance preparation aimed at moderating farmers' economic damages from crop damage or destruction as a consequence of several manufacturing risks. Delivers crop insurance coverage and economic help to farmers due to any of their reported crop failures due to natural disasters, pests, or diseases. Crop advances are accessible to farmers who need advances for agricultural contributions such as diesel fuel for fertilizers, irrigation, and seeds.

8.4.2.3.1 Crop Income Tax

Farmers can make report income and expenses based on business.

Cultivation cost and production cost are to be calculated with crop growth based on the farmers' decisions due to weather information. Soil information and monitoring growth of crops at different regions is irregular.

8.4.2.3.2 Supply Chain Management Effect on Agricultural Product

Persons in the agriculture industry have also learned how crucial contemporary technologies can be in maximizing the integration of supply chain. Agricultural businesses are able to reduce inventory costs, increase product value, extend resources, shorten the time to market, and keep consumers thanks to today's information-driven, interconnected supply chains.

Additionally, a considerable amount of the cost incurred at one link in the chain is determined by the actions taken or not performed at one or more links in the chain. For the whole supply chain, including forecasting, production, purchase scheduling, product introduction, sales promotion, and more, appropriate coordination and planning are crucial.

However, the COVID-19 pandemic epidemic had a detrimental effect on the worldwide SCM market for agriculture. The implementation of the global lockdown led to a number of travel and transportation limitations, which ultimately interrupted the global agriculture supply chain. The market was also hindered on a global scale by a lack of aggregators, labor shortages, problems with the configuration of transport vehicles, price volatility, ineffective cold chain facilities, increase in the cost of fertilizers and pesticides, and other concerns. However, the major market players are presently concentrating on innovative approaches to deal with the loss, which is causing the worldwide agriculture SCM market to rapidly recover. Additionally, agricultural businesses are spending money on integrated SCM systems for better advancements.

Additionally, agricultural businesses are spending money on infrastructure and integrated SCM systems. A variety of models are emerging, including those where farmers or growers must adhere to specific guidelines, fruit and vegetable retail stores that directly purchase products from farmers through contractual agreements, and contemporary infrastructures that include cold storage, ripening rooms, and controlled atmosphere chambers. Contract farming for fruits and vegetables is one of these that is already used in a number of economies. The development of the worldwide agriculture SCM industry is being accelerated by these models one after another.

8.5 RESULTS AND DISCUSSION

Agricultural system is implemented in cloud environment. We use cloud sim toolkit for the implementation of system in java environment [9–13]. This system implementation includes agricultural website details such as user login, product details, purchase details, and payment details. Figures 8.2 to 8.11 show the results of these system implementation.

1. **Agricultural Front Page**

FIGURE 8.2 Agricultural website.

The previous figure shows the fertilizers details, equipment's, seeds, and disease control details. These details are entered through website of the system.

2. **Sign in page:**

Sign in to your account

Or Signup

Email address

Password

Forgot your password?

Sign in

FIGURE 8.3 Agricultural login page.

User can log-in into account. User has email address and password. Existing customers have login page details. User can log-in into account. User has email address and password. New customers have login page details.

Fertilizers Equipments Seeds Disease Control

Neem Plant

FIGURE 8.4 Agricultural products.

Agricultural products details are displayed. Here a number of agriproducts are given. User selected neem plant with color, size, and cost. The details are given in the following.

FIGURE 8.5   Neem plant.

Properties of neem plant are displayed, such as color, size, and cost.

FIGURE 8.6   Shopping cart.

The previous figure shows the shopping cart has neem plant and total cost of shopping can be displayed.

The previous figure shows the item details and their reviews and payment etc. It includes fertilizers details, review cart items, and pay.

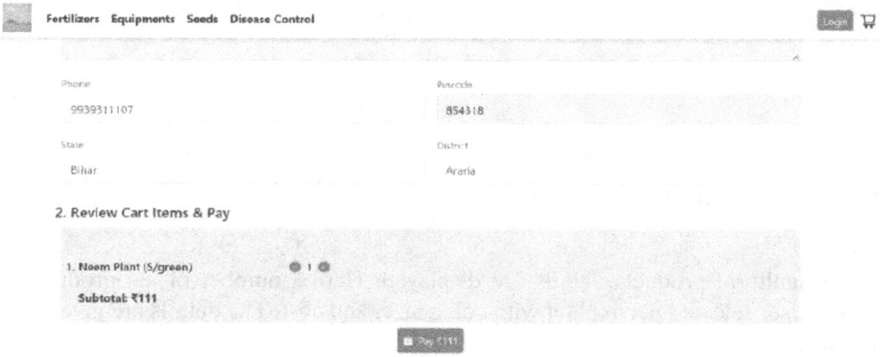

FIGURE 8.7   Cart items and payment.

FIGURE 8.8 Payment details.

The previous figure shows the payment details through UPI QR. It includes with pay with UPI QR code on your phone.

My Orders

#Order Id	Name	Amount	Details
#order_KfazWwJDmK03j4	hirsaguyathebuzs@gmail.com	₹1	Details

FIGURE 8.9 My order details.

The previous figure shows the order details. It incudes with ordered, name, amount, and details.

FIGURE 8.10 Order details.

The previous figure shows the order details and gives the overall the order cost details. It includes item description, quantity, and item total.

Update Your Account

1. Delivery Details

Name   Email (Cannot be Updated)

Manav Goyal   manavgoyalthebossi@gmail.com

Address

Phone   Pincode

Your 10-Digit Phone Number

Submit

FIGURE 8.11   Update your account.

The previous figure shows the update of your account with delivery details. It includes name, email, phone, and pin code.

8.6   CONCLUSION

Cloud computing techniques are used to store large amount of data and access the data at any time. Agricultural system can be used to sell their products with offer in the price and delivered the items to customers within the given time. In this chapter, we have given the process of virtual agricultural marketing and information system in cloud environment. We have to monitor crop growth, crop production according to weather conditions by using proposed agricultural system.

REFERENCES

1. Harmani, V.P., Himawan, B.M., Alhadi, M.A., Gunawan, A.A.S., Anderies, "Systematic Literature Review: Implementation of Artificial Intelligence in Precision Agriculture," 2022 5th International Conference on Information and Communications Technology (ICOIACT), Yogyakarta, Indonesia, 2022, pp. 479–484. doi: 10.1109/ICOIACT55506.2022.9971917
2. Keru Patil, R., Patil, S.S., "Cognitive Intelligence of a Cloud-Based Internet of Things in Precision Agriculture Applications," 2022 IEEE International Conference on Blockchain and Distributed Systems Security (ICBDS), Pune, India, 2022, pp. 1–6. doi: 10.1109/ICBDS53701.2022.9935964
3. Moutsinas, I. et al., "AgroNIT: Innovating Precision Agriculture," 2022 Global Information Infrastructure and Networking Symposium (GIIS), Argostoli, Greece, 2022, pp. 6–12. doi: 10.1109/GIIS56506.2022.9937000
4. Rahmouni, M., Hanifi, M., Savaglio, C., Fortino, G., Ghogho, M., "An AIoT Framework for Precision Agriculture," 2022 IEEE Intl Conf on Dependable, Autonomic and Secure Computing, 2022, pp. 1–6. doi: 10.1109/DASC/PiCom/CBDCom/Cy55231.2022.9927989
5. Sinha, G.R.: ICT Enabled Agriculture Transforming India. CSI Communication, 27–28 (October 2013)

6. Costopoulou, C.I., Lambrou, M.A.: An Architecture of Virtual Agricultural Market Systems: The Case of Trading Perishable Agricultural Products. Journal of Information Services and Use 20(1), 39–48 (2000)

7. Chaudhuri, S., Nath, B.: Application of Cloud Computing in Agricultural Sectors for Economic Development. Journal of Management and Social Science 1(2), 79–93 (2014)

8. https://cloudtweaks.com/cloud_computing_growth_infographic/

9. https://www.bsa.org/files/reports/BSA_2018_Global_Cloud_Scorecard.pdf (2012)

10. Alia, S.Z., Sidhub, R.S., Vatta, K.: Effectiveness of Minimum Support Price Policy for Paddy in India with a Case Study of Punjab. Agricultural Economics Research Review 25(2), 231–242 (2012)

11. Sujatha, D.C., Satheesh, A., Kumar, D., Manjula, S.: Smart Infrastructure at Home using Internet of Things. In: Satapathy, S.C., Avadahani, P.S., Udgata, S.K., Lakshminarayana, S. (eds.) ICT and Critical Infrastructure: Proceedings of the 48th Annual C Annual Convention of CSI – Volume II. AISC, vol. 249, pp. 627–634. Springer, Heidelberg (2014)

12. www.javatpoint.com

13. Dennis John Frailey, Stephen G. MacDonell, and Andrew Gray, Software Engineering Management, Guide to the Software Engineering Body of Knowledge (SWEBOK V3.0) Edition: 2004 Version Chapter: 8. IEEE Computer Society,

14. Cao, Y., et al.: An Analysis on the Role of Blockchain-Based Platforms in Agricultural Supply Chains. Transportation Research Part E: Logistics and Transportation Review 163, 102731 (2022)

15. Paunov, C., Planes-Satorra., S. "How are digital technologies changing innovation?: Evidence from agriculture, the automotive industry and retail." OECD Science, Technology and Industry Policy Papers 74, OECD Publishing (2019)

16. Anshari, M., et al.: Digital Marketplace and FinTech to Support Agriculture Sustainability. Energy Procedia 156, 234–238 (2019)

17. Renda, A.: The Age of Foodtech: Optimizing the Agri-Food Chain with Digital Technologies. Achieving the Sustainable Development Goals through Sustainable Food Systems 171–187 (2019)

9 Challenges and Prospects of Implementing Information and Communication Technology for Small-Scale Farmers

Karthikeyan Kaliyaperumal, V. Mahalakshmi,
P.M. Sithar Selvam, T. Priya, B. Lakshmi Narayana,
and T. Pradeep

9.1 INTRODUCTION

Even though up-to-date weather and climate data is crucial to the success of farmers' agricultural endeavors, farmers often struggle with climate-smart agriculture due to a deficiency of clear knowledge and clarifications of this data. The capacity of farmers to make a living is at risk when crops are damaged or yields are diminished as a result of high weather events or interannual changes in rainfall and temperature. Directly or indirectly, farmers may contribute to ecosystem degradation and habitat loss when they employ practices that reduce soil water retention and crop yield potential.

Farms having 2 ha below of cropland typically aim to produce staple crops for domestic use [1]. The lack of capital (a low asset base), skills, land, and labor is identified as one of the most critical issues facing small-scale farmers in the World Bank Rural Development Strategy [2]. Owing to urbanization and rapid industrialization, farm sizes across Asia have decreased significantly, especially in China (from 0.56 ha in 1980 to 0.4 ha in 1999), Pakistan (from 5.3 ha in 1973 to 3.1 ha in 2000), the Philippines (from 3.6 ha in 1971 to 2 ha in 1991), and India (from 2.2 ha in 1950 to 1.33 ha in 2001). According to recent estimates, 87% of the world's 500 million small-scale farmers live in Asia and the Pacific. One hundred and ninety-three million Chinese people are involved in agriculture, making them the world's largest population of small farmers (93 million). Many people in the populations of Indonesia (17 million), Vietnam (17 million), and Bangladesh (17 million) depend on farming as their primary source of income (10 million). The "Green Revolution" has helped several Asian countries thanks to the work of

DOI: 10.1201/9781003391302-9

individual farmers. In India, for instance, small-scale farmers account for half of agricultural GDP but only use 44% of the available land due to greater labor costs and a lower index of cropping intensity and variety.

Increases in temperature, shifts in rainfall patterns, and more intense and frequent flash floods and droughts are only some of the climate change effects that are predicted to impact the farming community [3, 4]. They threaten millions of people's ability to eat and survive [5]. To some extent, farmers can mitigate the effects of climate change on their livelihoods by becoming more attuned to seasonal patterns and adjusting their planting, watering, and harvesting practices accordingly [6, 7]. In most cases, either too much or too little water is used to irrigate the field, depending on whether the farmers are trying to combat dry weather or prepare for rain. Soil moisture, plant development, and available sunlight all play a role in determining when and how much water to apply [8]. Automatic irrigation, enabled by information and communication technology (ICT) advancements, can further facilitate this comprehensive use of watering systems. Farmers can improve their knowledge of when and how much to water their plants, as well as which crops and varieties to plant, by adopting this strategy. Expert systems, completely automated fertigation with the right sensors, and smart, optimized water irrigation are just a few of the methods for effective water management addressed in this chapter. There is a self-sufficient ecology contained within this framework.

9.2 CHALLENGES FOR SMALL-SCALE FARMERS

Numerous challenges stand in the way of small-scale farmers' efforts to reliably feed their community. They are especially susceptible to climate change effects because they lack the information and resources accessible to large-scale farmers [9].

9.2.1 WATER MANAGEMENT AND WATER SHORTAGE

Many Asian countries suffer from lower agricultural output during the dry season due to ineffective water management practices like flood irrigation [10, 11]. Due to the rise in demand for irrigation water from sources other than agriculture, water scarcity has become a significant obstacle to the industry's growth. As a result of excessive use and over-pumping, groundwater levels may drop. Due to the large suction head, small-scale farmers can only use more expensive pumps. Fertilizer and pesticide use that isn't strictly necessary can also pollute water and reduce crop yields [12].

9.2.2 HIGH-VALUE AGRICULTURAL PRODUCTS

Producing high-value agricultural goods can be difficult for small-scale farmers because of rules pertaining to food safety and quality that are both labor-intensive and demanding, as well as the significant volatility of commodity prices [13–15]. The semi-arid region's small farmers are particularly susceptible to the crop shocks brought on by natural calamities (e.g. Flash floods in Bangladesh, the Tsunami in Southeast Asia, and El Nino in the Philippines). Using ICT to predict natural disasters and implementing the appropriate preventative measures are two of the main challenges facing small-scale farmers today.

9.2.3 CLIMATE CHANGE EFFECTS

The effects of climate change are being felt keenly on the ground by farmers, especially those in developing nations. Due to their low heat tolerance, wheat, maize, and rice can be severely impacted by even a small change in temperature ($\cong 1°C$ for maize, wheat, and $\cong 2°C$ for rice) [16, 17]. However, small-scale farmers may struggle to figure out how to modify their greenhouse settings to meet the needs of plants and crops that thrive in mild warming because of limited resources and funding.

9.2.4 INNOVATIONS ON PRODUCTIVITY

New agriculture, dominated by value chains, can increase productivity on a small scale, which is beneficial to consumers and the farmers themselves. Promoting contract farming presents the greatest difficulty. High-value exports are made possible by both corporate and governmental sector actions along these supply chains [18].

9.2.5 AFFORDABILITY

The value farmers place on the technology and the cost at which it may be bought all play a role in the spectrum of preferences and levels of willingness to pay for smart agriculture practices among farmers [19, 20]. Technology adoption by farmers is influenced by many factors, including their demographics (age, gender, landholding size, income, agricultural system, geography, etc.), as well as the level and kind of government and semi-government financial incentives.

9.3 INFORMATION AND COMMUNICATION TECHNOLOGY (ICT)

Agricultural input and output prices, weather forecasts, and technological choices can all be disseminated to small-scale farmers with the help of ICT [21]. There are increasingly numerous cases where farmers on the small scale have benefited from the use of ICT. The "agribusiness" section of the Indian Tobacco Company (ITC) reached 38,000 villages and 4 million farmers in 9 different states of India by means of 6400 e-Choupals (Internet kiosks). Initiated in 2000 with an initial projected duration of five years, the initiative has since been extended twice. Due to its success, additional two years were added to its original duration. Free training and data on local and worldwide market pricing, as well as weather and best farming methods, are provided to the farmers in this initiative. With the e-Choupal platform, they've made purchases totaling about $400 million [22, 23]. As a result of the proliferation of "smart agriculture," which involves the use of cutting-edge ICTs to update conventional farming methods, significant gains have been made in agricultural production and sustainability. The adoption of ICT in farming has led to a reduction in negative effects on the natural environment [24]. As technology evolves, it becomes possible to set up a remote and constantly updated sensor network to keep tabs on the farm around the clock.

9.3.1 REMOTE MONITORING AND CONTROL

Sensing and acting on the environment are crucial components of smart farming. Costs for sensors continue to drop precipitously as semiconductor technology develops.

9.3.1.1 Sensors and Actuators

In a network of nodes, a sensor is one that can observe changes in its surroundings and report them to other nodes in the network, such as a local gateway. To put it simply, "a sensor node is comprised of four core modules: sensor/actuator module, communication module, processing module, and power source module" in a Wireless Sensor Network (WSN). While the sensing part of a WSN is in charge of gathering information about occurrences, the connecting part is in charge of communicating that information to other nodes. The power supply module keeps the sensor node functioning, while the processing module collects data, processes it, and formats notifications. Sensors for measuring temperature, humidity, water level, conductivity, salinity, and more are included in Table 9.1.

A machine's actuator is the part of the machine that actually does something when it gets a command, such as moving or controlling another part of the machine [25, 26]. Opening a window for ventilation and turning on an irrigation system's valve are also examples of tasks that could be handled by an actuator module. Actuators, like sensors, need a communication module to receive remote instructions and report on their current condition as necessary.

Sensor data collection and remote control of actuators deployed at a farm can both benefit greatly from the availability of wireless communication technologies [27, 28]. Today, most sensors have a tiny connection module that transmits detected data to a faraway location, thanks to the rapid development of technology. In order for a sensor communication module to talk to other nodes in a WSN, several different communication protocols are currently available. They include ZigBee, Bluetooth, Wibree, and WiFi. The capacities and ranges of these many forms of communication technology are extremely diverse.

TABLE 9.1
Variety of Sensors for Gathering Various Data

Sensors Used in Agriculture	Using the Appropriate Sensor, we can Obtain the Necessary Information
Soil	Estimation of water stress, rain/water flow, conductivity, temperature, water level, salinity, and dielectric permittivity
Plant	Conditions like as humidity, moisture, temperature, CO_2 concentration, hydrogen, and photosynthesis
Weather	Changes in factors like light, temperature, humidity, wind speed and direction, and atmospheric pressure

TABLE 9.2

Comparison of Communication Technologies

Variable	ZigBee (IEEE 802.15.4)	Wibree (Baby Bluetooth)	Bluetooth Low Energy (BLE)	WiFi (IEEE 802.11)	LoRaWAN	WiMAX (IEEE 802.16)
Frequency band range	868/915/ 2400 MHz	2.4 GHz	2400 MHz	2.4 GHz	EU: 868 MHz and 433 MHz USA:915 MHz and 433 MHz	2–66 GHz
Data rate	20/40/250 Kbps	1 Mbps	1024 Kbps	11–54 Mbps	250 bps–5.5 kbps	75 Mbps
Cover age range	1–100 m	5–10 m	30–300 ft	40 m (indoor) 140 m (outdoor)	Urban (3–6 km) Rural (15 km)	3 miles
Cost	Low	Low	Low	High	Very low	High

The range of a wireless network determines its classification, which can range from "Wide Area Network" (WAN) to "Local Area Network" (LAN) to "Personal Area Network" (PAN). In Table 9.2, authors have a comparison of several wireless communication methods. ZigBee is often regarded as the most cost-effective and energy-efficient communication network technology [29–31].

9.3.1.2 Technologies of Wireless Communication

Low data rate at ZigBee, low power consumption, and long battery life make it useful in areas as diverse as smart farming, smart home automation, and industrial automation [32, 33]. ZigBee's protocol stack is simple compared to that of other technologies (e.g. Bluetooth or Wireless). Approximately 65,000 devices can be connected to a network using ZigBee. Low and extremely low-duty cycles are supported by ZigBee nodes, extending battery life. ZigBee's ad hoc network architecture and support for multi-hop routing make it well suited for deployment in a dynamic setting [34, 35].

Bluetooth low energy is intended to deliver a high data rate over limited distance, in contrast to ZigBee. Low-cost options are available for devices that have limited battery life yet nevertheless need to be portable [36]. This allows for rapid data transfer between nearby Bluetooth devices, as well as the establishment of point-to-point and point-to-multipoint wireless connections. ZigBee and BLE were both developed to function in the unlicensed scientific, unrestricted industrial, and medical (ISM) spectrum, which enables communications over short distances. Low-data-rate short-range communication technologies include HomeRF, the Association of Infrared Data, and Z-Wave. The most popular wireless PAN protocols are IrDA, BLE, ZigBee, Z-Wave, and HomeRF [37].

WiFi, which stands for "wireless fidelity," is an IEEE 802.11-based wireless communication standard for LANs. IEEE 802.11 specifications come in a number of varieties, each with its own range and data-transfer-rate requirements (for example, 802.11a, 802.11n, and 802.11ah). IEEE 802.11 allows for both device-free (ad hoc) and infrastructure-based (standard) networks. Both infrastructural mode, where an access point controls communication between devices in the network via a WiFi interface, and client mode, where each device in the network must relay packets from the others, are possible for LAN connection [38]. Hundreds of clients can be supported by a single base station (BS) (access point). WiFi's capacity to distinguish between eight distinct quality-of-service (QoS) classes means it can accommodate a diverse set of user-endpoint applications. A wireless access point uses only 10–13 W of electricity, and devices use even less power when communicating, allowing for longer periods of time between charges.

With WiMAX (Worldwide Interoperability for Microwave Access), devices within range of a WiMAX BS can establish a point-to-multipoint connection. When using the 2–66 GHz spectrum for transmission, a BS' signal has the potential to travel 3 km while carrying 75 Mbps of data. WiMAX wireless networks can function in both licensed and unlicensed band (ISM) frequencies, with the latter being the more popular option. The data rate that each station in the BS' coverage area uses can be adjusted by the BS based on the quality of the signal it is receiving [39]. WiMAX also offers five QoS classes, which means the network can accommodate applications with varied QoS requirements, such as media content, web surfing, and streaming media [40]. WiMAX is categorized as a Wireless MAN (WMAN) because of its widespread use.

The LoRa Alliance has created a long-distance wireless system called Long Range WAN (LoRaWAN). Because of its extended range and single frequency, a single LoRa BS can link a large number of devices. In contrast to the 915 MHz used in the United States and the 433 MHz used in Asia, the 868 MHz used in Europe is for some reason considered the "European" standard. Although a LoRaWAN gateway can receive up a signal from an end-device up to 15 km distant in a rural setting, that distance shrinks to just 2–5 km in an urban setting. Distance and message duration are both factors in determining data transfer speeds. The data speeds of LoRaWAN, as stated by Lora Alliance, are between 0.3 and 50 kbps. The average data transfer rate in the United States is 0.9 kbps, while in Europe it ranges from 0.3 to 22 kbps. For long-distance communication, RuBee, like LoRaWAN, employs a very lower frequencies (131 kHz) carrier, which enables the transfer of 128-byte data packets. The RuBee interface has a minimal power need; therefore, the sensor's battery can persist for years without being changed (long-lasting battery life is possible for sensors with RuBee interfaces).

9.3.2 DATA AGGREGATION

As ICTs play an increasingly vital role in precision agriculture (PA), sensor platforms that can collect data from a wide variety of sensors, manage the actuators, make decisions based on the collected data, eliminate any unnecessary information (preprocess the data), and then send it on to the applications used by the end users are in high demand. A gateway, often situated close to the agricultural plant, is required for the sensor platform to begin collecting data from the sensors and issuing commands to the actuators. In addition, the time series sensor data can be saved by having this local gateway talk to the corresponding applications hosted in the cloud. Two potential results are shown in Figure 9.1. As shown in Figure 9.1a, the first possible setup has all sensors and actuators communicating with the gateway via a PAN network interface (such as Zigee), while the gateway then communicates with the BS

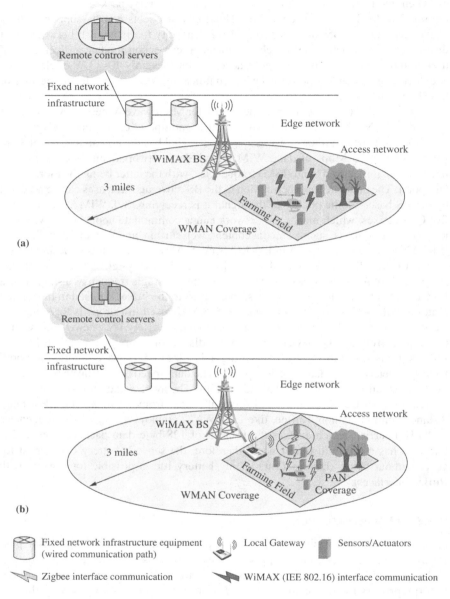

FIGURE 9.1 Smart farming makes use of wireless communication technologies such as: (a) sensors/actuators talking to the gateway via a wireless PAN; (b) sensors/actuators talking to each other over a WMAN interface.

via a WMAN connection (like WiMAX). The PAN transmits its coverage area data in an ad hoc fashion. The BS' job is to relay information to a distant cloud server once it has received it. The only difference between the two cases is how the data from sensors and actuators is transmitted. In this case, information is transmitted to the BS directly via the WMAN interface. Gateway capability for farming data collecting can be implemented without the need for a dedicated gateway device.

The gateways allow for regular data collection from the sensors. Several factors, such as the precision of the rate of change, the capacity of the gateway's storage and processing units, the availability of the network, and the sensors' batteries, might affect the intervals at which their data is polled (battery life for sensors might suffer if they were polled more frequently). In an alternative to regularly polling each sensor, data may be sent to the gateway only when a predetermined condition is met. The term "trap mechanism" is commonly used to describe this method. The amount of sensors and actuators on a farm can tax the capabilities of the local gateway. A local gateway would be necessary in this situation.

The increasing number of Internet of Things (IoT) devices has highlighted the need to boost processing power and data storage close to the network's periphery and entry points. Cisco came up with the term "Fog computing" to describe the small computing facilities embedded in edge and access network equipment (such as BSs, switches, and routers) that are used to accomplish this. Without sufficient processing power at the local gateway, data aggregation and preprocessing may be delegated to the edge and access routers and switches.

The capacity of networking equipment has been greatly leveraged by the unstoppable expansion of the semiconductor research sector. The network's data aggregation gateway may perform preparatory work before proceeding with the processing (e.g. storing or analyzing). As part of the preliminary processing, the data may be filtered dynamically (e.g. data cleaning, including elimination of duplicates, mistakes, and gaps). In this way, the gateway could lessen the burden on its resources required to process and store data. In addition, the gateway may serve as the nerve center for managing all of the actuators in a smart farm. If an indoor farm needs airflow, for instance, it can remotely operate the facility's windows or its irrigation system to provide it.

Both aerial and ground-based farms can benefit from data aggregation gateways' many applications (for tasks like weed detection and terrain leveling). If sensor data is not especially time-sensitive, it could be collected by a drone or other agricultural vehicle and used in smart farming.

A variety of sensor systems featuring a wide range of features are currently accessible. Smart farm net, sensor cloud, and IBM Bluemix are just a few examples of popular sensor platforms. In Table 9.3, we can get an overview of the existing sensor platform's gateway's functional capabilities.

9.3.3 CLOUD COMPUTING IN AGRICULTURE

As a result of cloud computing, users can access their services whenever and from whatever location they choose. This would provide farmers access to cutting-edge tools that analyze sensor data to draw conclusions about the state of their farms and help them make more informed decisions. Everywhere we go, the cloud is helping

TABLE 9.3

Capabilities That Function As a Gateway

Important Functionalities	Description
Monitor	Monitor sensors' reading.
Control	A farm's installed actuators can be controlled according to a set of rules.
Data processing	Data cleansing, data analysis (including supporting data visualization), data format modification, etc.
Data security	Safety and authenticity of sensor data. Data confidentiality is ensured by encrypted and decrypted transmissions.
Communicate with cloud and clients' devices (e.g. mobile phone, tab)	Cloud computing allows you to send raw or partially processed data and obtain feedback. Learn from rural dwellers.
Data and instruction storage	Information and instructions can be stored for later use.
Instant decision-making	Act quickly on the basis of the information you have gathered (e.g. ventilation achieved by opening a window).

to boost other businesses, as well as the entertainment industry and the healthcare sector. Similarly, cloud will help improve agricultural outputs with fewer negative effects on the environment, time, money, and risk. The following are some major niches that cloud can successfully exploit.

9.3.3.1 Farming Automation

Contextualizing data and integrating information from disparate sources are two of the many capabilities of cloud services (see Figure 9.2). That this can be done on the cloud is a crucial factor in the development of several automation systems (e.g. automation systems for the home and workplace). As the price of sensors continues to drop and the need to increase output in both quantity and quality increases, agriculture is poised to become increasingly dependent on data-driven and data-enabled decision-making in the near future. Information collected by sensors installed in a farm building and sent to the cloud will be used to make crucial agricultural decisions. Multiple programs can coexist in the cloud, and each one will make decisions based on the information it gets. Some examples of actuators that can be controlled by cloud at a farm site are aerial drones and autonomous tractors (a tractor that drives itself to the field).

9.3.3.2 Experience Sharing

In this case, farmers would upload data collected by their various sensors to the cloud. In addition, this can be used to record the farmers' vast knowledge. A single farmer or an entire community of farmers could receive instruction. The various available alternatives for connecting and exchanging data include text messaging service, interactive video conferencing service, and voice-based service.

9.3.3.3 Computational and Storage Support

Recent years have seen extensive research and modeling into agricultural output loss due to factors, including pests, plant diseases, and meteorological pattern. These studies

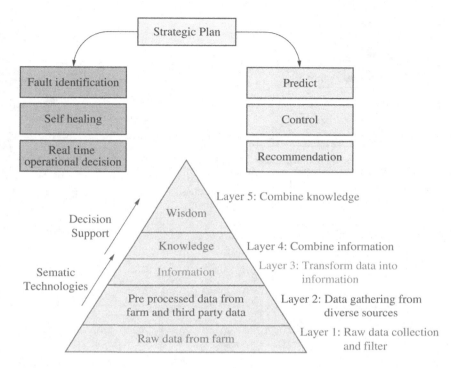

FIGURE 9.2   Using data to improve farming techniques.

demonstrate how farmers can reap the benefits of simulation software by improving their decision-making processes, leading to higher crop yields and less environmental damage. Furthermore, a significant amount of the dataset is required to comprehend biological systems and their relationships (the size of this dataset has ballooned during the previous five years). Large computation and storage facility are in high demand due to the growing need for data-intensive computation (such as computer simulations of farms and biological systems). The agriculture industry can gain from the utility model of compute and storage offered by cloud computing. Depending on the situation, cloud computing can provide its customers with highly scalable and available services. The agriculture industry may benefit greatly from this, as it may spur rapid expansion. Data from the farm and other sources is gathered by an application (a procedure) hosted in the cloud and processed there (such as pollution patterns, pest, disease-related information, and weather forecasts). From Figure 9.3, we can infer that such a procedure would take place. Intelligent farming is possible with the help of the semantic web and machine learning (data interpretation, knowledge acquisition, and appropriate action).

One of the smart agricultural sensor cloud systems that employs the principles of the semantic web is smart farm net, which is able to infer meaning from raw sensor data. In this short chapter, we'll discuss some of the ways in which the cloud could improve the state of modern agriculture.

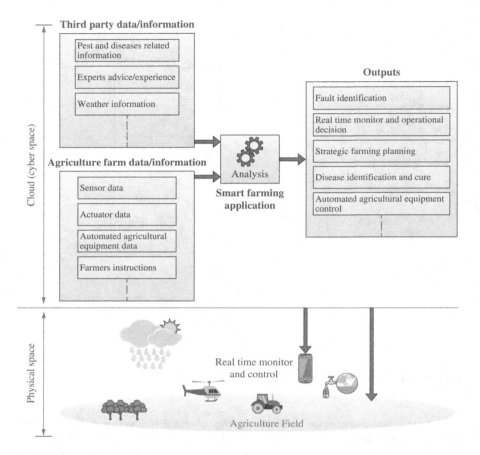

FIGURE 9.3   Cloud-assisted smart precision farming.

- Analyzing data: Predictive modeling and crop failure risk analysis models provide for the insightful interpretation of massive amounts of data.
- Pest and diseases modeling: Modeling pests and illnesses is becoming increasingly vital for farmers to make informed business decisions. Farmers need to fully understand the potential effects of environmental concerns including soil pH, climate change, pollution, and invasive species before making any major decisions about crop production. Analyzing data from a variety of sources (such weather forecasts and air pollution levels) is required to obtain such insights. The cloud may serve as a hub for cutting-edge data and expertise, allowing for more precise disease and pest forecasts to be made. In the event of a pest or disease outbreak, farmers will be able to minimize financial loss by following recommendations on when and how much fertilizer and insecticides to apply to their farm's soil. Based on the data it receives, the platform may be able to anticipate pest and disease attack patterns and offer preventative measures to farmers.

- Fault identification: Considering the vast computing resources available in the cloud, it stands to reason that pre- and post-processing of data will be much enhanced by using the cloud. It is expected that the cloud will be able to correlate sensor and actuator data during the preprocessing step, providing a better understanding of any inaccurate readings. All management mistakes on farms should be easily detected as well. With more time to make adjustments to the farm's operating plan after a catastrophic failure has been identified, the farm's output will improve.
- Intelligence accumulation: Cloud integrates data from multiple sources (see Figure 9.3). For instance, a cloud-hosted agricultural app may include the weather API in its calculations to figure out how much water has to be irrigated into a field in a given amount of time to reach a desired soil moisture level.
- Real-time monitor and operational decision: Because of the abundance of data storage and processing power, farmers will be able to monitor their operations in near real time. By way of illustration, the electrical surge caused by a lightning strike may fry expensive electronic equipment if it were left outside. For instance, in such a scenario, a cloud-based application used for monitoring and deciding on a farm might either take the appropriate action remotely or notify the farmers that they need to take such action.
- Crop harvesting period selection: Harvesting at the optimal moment, in terms of things like yield and revenue, may be a recommendation made by cloud-hosted software (yield market value). The software hosted on the cloud may recommend the best time to harvest the crops in order to maximize things like yield and revenue (yield market value).

9.4 ROLE OF ICT IN AUTOMATED AGRICULTURE

A wide range of farm duties can be handled by a robot specifically built for the agriculture industry. Now more than ever, machines are permeating every facet of society because to the rapid development of new technologies. In instance, industrial and agricultural productions have both experienced phenomenal expansions. Numerous nations are seeing an increase in their elderly population alongside a decrease in their birthrate. As a result, fewer people are entering the labor force in those nations. The number of people living on Earth is also rising quickly. These factors, and more, are driving rapid advancements in the study and implementation of automated agriculture. The term "automated equipment" is used to describe machinery in a farm that functions independently of human input. Robotic harvesters, autonomous tractors and sprayers, and unmanned aerial vehicles (UAVs) are just a few examples of the increasingly prevalent use of automation in agriculture. Images captured by drones might be analyzed using image recognition software to help diagnose plant illnesses, and an expert-based decision support system (DSS) could then offer guidance. Additionally, a pre-installed irrigation system can adjust its water delivery according to the prevailing conditions.

9.4.1 AUTOMATIC IRRIGATION

Decisions on when and how much water to apply during irrigation have to be made based on factors such as soil, crop, and weather conditions. Automatic irrigation has gained popularity as a means to reduce reliance on human judgment when making irrigation schedule decisions. Table 9.4 explains the differences between fixed-rate and variable-rate automatic irrigation systems. Computers and other forms of electronic communication help streamline the operation of farms. Connectivity interfaces link all the automated devices (sensors, actuators). It is possible to automate the management of a gateway or cloud-based intelligent application. The model for an irrigation-based DSS make use of information gathered via a wireless data collection network to make recommendations about when and how much water should be used. By using Bluetooth and GPS technology, we were able to remotely track the location of each sprinkler and keep tabs on the soil's hydration, temperature, and weather conditions. Based on data from field sensors and weather forecasts, created an IoT-based smart irrigation system that makes soil moisture predictions.

Real-time monitoring and decision-making of irrigation activities were both enhanced by the established smart irrigation system's usage of a site-specific irrigation controller and sensor output in the field. It is important to consider the energy requirements for autonomous operation during every phase of the sensor node development process (including design, development, communication, and deployment). Due to their inefficiency, batteries are rarely used in WSN nodes, which instead rely on solar power.

In the last decade, crop system models like DSSAT, APSIM, CropSyst, EPIC, STICS, DSSAT-GREET, and DSSAT-CSM have seen rapid growth as tools for simulating agricultural production systems. However, there has been a limited focus on enhancing the models themselves.

TABLE 9.4
Types of Automatic Irrigation System

Fixed Rate	Variable Rate
It's more cost-effective due to the consistent regulation of water usage. There is no relationship between water use and weather.	Optimal water usage based on weather conditions that minimizes costs.
Time and water pressure for irrigation are controlled permanently.	Variable control of irrigation time and water flow.
In order to operate, irrigation systems use ON/OFF switches. The controllers' performance degrades when the time delay or other system parameters change.	The use of an ANN in a sophisticated control system for irrigation efficiency.
Developed using an open-loop controller architecture. Its operations, such as when to begin and terminate watering and at what intervals, are programmed in advance. In this situation, it makes no difference whether or not the intended result or objective is accomplished.	Created using a feedback loop with no open points. Such a controller relies on sensors to determine the optimal watering schedule for plants.

9.4.2 AUTOMATIC FERTIGATION

Automatic fertigation eliminates the need for the time-consuming and labor-intensive process of applying fertilizers (including manual spreading, broadcasting, and spraying) to increase soil fertility. Both plant development and plant production are sensitive to a wide range of environmental factors, including the quantity of nutrients, the length of their delivery, the water flow, and many more. Fertilizer application to the root zone of a plant is an inefficient and error-prone human process, but sensors have made it fast and easy. Using GPS, real-time sensing, and Bluetooth technologies, created a decision support, input, and output module for an automated fertilizer applicator. A DSS regulates the fertilizer application rate by establishing the best possible dosage and pattern of application from real-time sensor data collected via Bluetooth connection modules. This data is mandatory and must be provided by the input module. Using sensors that evaluated PH value, humidity, soil moisture, air temperature, illumination, conductivity, CO_2 concentration, temperature, etc. in real time, he and his colleagues created and integrated a DSS for effective fertilization. An IEEE 802.11-based wireless sensor LAN and a GPS analysis server were employed in this setup (WiFi).

9.4.3 PRECISION AGRICULTURE (PA)

Target farming, prescription farming, and information-intensive agriculture are all names for PA. To maximize productivity, site-specific and efficiency of entire-farm production and profitability while minimizing harmful effects on wildlife and the environment, PA is an "integrated information and production-based farming system," as defined by Taylor and Whelan. The importance of production, economic, and ecological improvements in agriculture has PA on the cusp of becoming the next great agricultural revolution. With the use of GPS-guided grid sampling, inputs like fertilizer can be used more efficiently and applied at different rates across a field, which is great for combating plant diseases and enhancing the quality of the soil. Automation in mapping and data gathering, sensing technologies, computer-aided controls for variable rate application of agricultural inputs, and geospatial determination are the four key information technologies that make up PA technology (through GPS). When compared to the other four options, more farmers have opted to use GPS and GIS to increase their agricultural and livestock yields. On top of that, this method can be used to lessen the effects of leaching.

9.5 CHALLENGES IN ICT-BASED PRECISION FARMING

Before the full promise of ICT-based precision farming can be realized, a number of hurdles must be cleared. This chapter discusses several issues that warrant immediate attention and additional study.

- Sensor network security: The vast majority of farms' network sensors are exposed and therefore open to tampering. Since sensors have limited processing and power resources, it can be difficult to construct a reliable security mechanism management system. Since most WSN communication is broadcast, the network is susceptible to attack. Attacks on WSN typically take the form of eavesdropping, denial of service, or manipulation of data. In the case of automated agriculture facilities, for instance, if an attacker manipulates or injects misleading data into a WSN, the facility may make the wrong operational option. The potential dangers are facing an automated agricultural plant (some of them could be deliberate or accidental). Establishing potential safeguards against security threats is crucial.

- Reliable and available network infrastructure: As automated farms become more common, real-time monitoring and management are becoming increasingly important. Building a functional automated agriculture facility requires a robust communication network. Having a reliable connection between BS and the faraway cloud is essential. An automated farm could lose access to its central monitoring and control system in the event of a communication network failure. Critical data from sensors and actuators in agriculture systems must be protected (decision-makers should have the data within a reasonable amount of time). A breakdown in a communication network infrastructure could be caused by a number of different things, including a malfunctioning application, network device, network interface, or communication line. The farming operation requires a network design that ensures constant connectivity and minimal downtime. It's important to remember that increasing capital and operational expenditures is the main way we can get a highly stable and available network.

- Cost of sensors and actuators: At the moment, farmers in undeveloped and underdeveloped nations cannot afford the high cost of sensors and actuators.

- Power supply availability: Having a constant supply of electricity from the grid is essential for many pieces of machinery at a farm. The loss of electricity, whether from an accident or a natural calamity, would have a devastating effect on the farm as a whole. Hence, a storage and renewable power source must be built to ensure constant electricity to the farm.

- Educating farmers: The rate of technological development is breathtaking. Unfortunately, many farmers in third world and poor nations lack formal education. As a result, new technologies wouldn't be widely adopted.

  Farmers with less education would be less likely to accept ICT-based farming management. We need to improve farmers' ICT knowledge, awareness, and education in the field in the future.

- User-friendly applications: A number of farmers are technologically illiterate. As a result, they could be hesitant to adopt ICT for farm management. The farm management software should be simple enough for the farmers to use.

- Metadata, semantics, and ontology: Research in this area has progressed significantly, resulting in cutting-edge intelligent systems built on a foundation of existing data and knowledge. However, additional study is required to implement smart, automated farming.

- Fast fault identification: Future studies should investigate methods for more efficiently locating broken sensors/actuators, farm machinery, and communication network hardware.
- Analysis paralysis: Large volumes of data from sensors/actuators and other resources must be gathered for smart farming to be implemented, but this data is useless without a practical method to analyze it. Locating relevant information requires digging through data (and knowledge).

9.6 OPPORTUNITIES OF IMPLEMENTING ICT FOR SMALL-SCALE FARMERS

Implementing ICT can provide numerous opportunities for small-scale farmers, including:

- Access to information: ICT tools such as mobile apps and websites can provide small-scale farmers with real-time information on weather, market prices, pest and disease outbreaks, and other important agricultural data.
- Improved communication: ICT tools such as SMS messaging and social media can help small-scale farmers communicate with each other, extension workers, and buyers more effectively, facilitating the exchange of knowledge and market information.
- Increased efficiency: ICT tools such as precision farming technologies and farm management software can help small-scale farmers optimize their use of resources, improve crop yields, and reduce their costs.
- Improved market access: ICT tools such as e-commerce platforms and mobile payment systems can help small-scale farmers connect with buyers and sell their products more efficiently, reducing the need for intermediaries and improving their profit margins.
- Better risk management: ICT tools such as remote sensing and data analytics can help small-scale farmers identify and mitigate risks such as drought, flooding, and pest outbreaks, reducing the impact of these events on their crops and livelihoods.

Overall, the implementation of ICT can help small-scale farmers overcome many of the barriers they face, including limited access to information, finance, and markets. By providing small-scale farmers with the tools and information they need to improve their productivity and profitability, ICT can play a critical role in promoting sustainable agriculture and reducing poverty in rural communities.

9.7 CONCLUSION

Benefiting greatly from improved water management made possible by ICT and data management are small-scale farmers in both developed and developing nations. Greater crop yields and a boost to the economy could result from the widespread adoption of remote sensing and automation tools in agriculture. Cameras, UAVs, climate-based intelligent irrigation systems, insider information, and constant remote monitoring using smart handheld devices are all part of the toolkit. These advancements in practices and technology are providing a boost to small-scale farmers, and they are also providing consistent support to a wide variety of other interested parties, from gardeners to politicians. The potential exists for expanding ICT to all parts of the globe. Problems arise when trying to make these technologies accessible to small-scale farmers while keeping their price at a reasonable level and raising awareness about them through a variety of channels. Using these cutting-edge methods of agriculture not only boosts crop yields but also contributes to environmental sustainability.

REFERENCES

1. A. I. Sourav, A. W. R. Emanuel and D. B. Setyohadi, "Smart system architecture design in the field of precision agriculture based on IOT in Bangladesh," *ICIC Express Lett*, vol. 16, no. 10, pp. 1111–1118, 2022. doi: 10.24507/icicel.16.10.1111

2. A. Neef, K. Mizuno, I. Schad, P. M. Williams and F. Rwezimula, "Community-based microtrade in support of small-scale farmers in Thailand and Tanzania," *Law Dev Rev*, vol. 5, no. 1, pp. 80–100, 2012. doi: 10.1515/1943-3867.1148

3. F. Peprah, S. Gyamfi, M. Amo-Boateng, E. Buadi and M. Obeng, "Design and construction of smart solar powered egg incubator based on GSM/IoT," *Sci Afr*, vol. 17, 2022. doi: 10.1016/j.sciaf.2022.e01326

4. E. A. Abioye *et al.*, "Precision irrigation management using machine learning and digital farming solutions," *AgriEngineering*, vol. 4, no. 1, pp. 70–103, 2022. doi: 10.3390/agriengineering4010006

5. J. Lloret, S. Sendra, J. García-fernández, L. García and J. M. Jimenez, "A wifi-based sensor network for flood irrigation control in agriculture," *Electron*, vol. 10, no. 20, 2021. doi: 10.3390/electronics10202454

6. D. Vijendra Babu, K. V. Shijin, N. S. Sreejith, A. V. Sureshbabu and C. Karthikeyan, "Automatic irrigation systems for efficient usage of water using embedded control systems," *IOP Conf Ser: Mater Sci Eng*, vol. 993, no. 1, 2020. doi: 10.1088/1757-899X/993/1/012077

7. J.-J. Su, S.-T. Ding and H.-C. Chung, "Establishing a smart farm-scale piggery wastewater treatment system with the internet of things (IoT) applications," *Water (Switzerland)*, vol. 12, no. 6, 2020. doi: 10.3390/w12061654

8. B.-H. Kim and J.-R. Kim, "Implementation of smart agricultural water management system using IoT-based remote monitoring," *Int J Adv Sci Technol*, vol. 28, no. 5, pp. 44–52, 2019 [Online]. Available: https://www.scopus.com/inward/record.uri?eid=2-s2.0-85080089043&partnerID=40&md5=a0dad130b4ae22511a482d843657cefd

9. S. Abba, J. W. Namkusong, J.-A. Lee and M. L. Crespo, "Design and performance evaluation of a low-cost autonomous sensor interface for a smart IoT-based irrigation monitoring and control system," *Sensors (Switzerland)*, vol. 19, no. 17, 2019. doi: 10.3390/s19173643

10. Y. D. Chuah, J. V. Lee, S. S. Tan and C. K. Ng, "Implementation of smart monitoring system in vertical farming," *IOP Conf Ser: Earth Environ Sci*, vol. 268, no. 1, 2019. doi: 10.1088/1755-1315/268/1/012083

11. M. Ashwini, S. Gowrishankar and Siddaraju, "Internet of things based intelligent monitoring and reporting from agricultural fields," *Int J Control Theory Appl*, vol. 9, no. 10, pp. 4311–4320, 2016 [Online]. Available: https://www.scopus.com/inward/record.uri?eid=2-s2.0-84989271329&partnerID=40&md5=d906632e85f235be4d32e412809baffd

12. S.-O. Chung, S.-W. Kang, K.-S. Bae, M.-J. Ryu and Y.-J. Kim, "The potential of remote monitoring and control of protected crop production environment using mobile phone under 3G and Wi-Fi communication conditions," *Eng Agric Environ Food*, vol. 8, no. 4, pp. 251–256, 2015. doi: 10.1016/j.eaef.2015.04.007

13. B. J. P. Quezada and J. Fernández, 'Automation of agricultural irrigation system with open source', in *IFIP Advances in Information and Communication Technology*, vol. 427. pp. 232–233, 2014. doi: 10.1007/978-3-642-55128-4_36

14. K. M. Al-Aubidy, M. M. Ali, A. M. Derbas and A. W. Al-Mutairi, 'Real-time monitoring and intelligent control for greenhouses based on wireless sensor network', in *2014 IEEE 11th International Multi-Conference on Systems, Signals and Devices, SSD 2014*, 2014. doi: 10.1109/SSD.2014.6808765

15. D. Van Greunen and A. Fosu, 'ICT adoption challenges: Case of rural small-scale farmers in the Amathole District Municipality of South Africa', in *2022 IST-Africa Conference, IST-Africa 2022*, 2022. doi: 10.23919/IST-Africa56635.2022.9845556

16. X. Li, A. Sarkar, X. Xia and W. H. Memon, "Village environment, capital endowment, and farmers' participation in e-commerce sales behavior: A demand observable bivariate probit model approach," *Agriculture*, vol. 11, no. 9, 2021. doi: 10.3390/agriculture11090868

17. T. Gbangou, R. Sarku, E. Van Slobbe, F. Ludwig, G. Kranjac-Berisavljevic and S. Paparrizos, "Coproducing weather forecast information with and for smallholder farmers in Ghana: Evaluation and design principles," *Atmosphere (Basel)*, vol. 11, no. 9, 2020. doi: 10.3390/atmos11090902

18. A. Abid, S. Jie, W. Aslam, S. Batool and Y. Lili, "Application of structural equation modelling to develop a conceptual model for smallholder's credit access: The mediation of agility and innovativeness in organic food value chain finance," *PLoS One*, vol. 15, no. 8, 2020. doi: 10.1371/journal.pone.0235921

19. A. Oliveira Jr *et al.*, "IoT sensing platform as a driver for digital farming in rural Africa," *Sensors (Switzerland)*, vol. 20, no. 12, pp. 1–25, 2020. doi: 10.3390/s20123511

20. L. Karanja *et al.*, "Impacts and challenges of ICT based scale-up campaigns: Lessons learnt from the use of SMS to support maize farmers in the UPTAKE project, Tanzania," *Data Sci J*, vol. 19, no. 1, 2020. doi: 10.5334/dsj-2020-007

21. H. El Bilali, F. Bottalico, G. Ottomano Palmisano and R. Capone, 'Information and communication technologies for smart and sustainable agriculture', in *IFMBE Proceedings*, 2020, vol. 78, pp. 321–334. doi: 10.1007/978-3-030-40049-1_41

22. B. Matsenjwa, S. S. Grobbelaar and I. A. Meyer, "Pro-poor value chains for small scale farming innovation: Sustainability improvements through ICT," *South Afr J Ind Eng*, vol. 30, no. 4, pp. 156–171, 2019. doi: 10.7166/30-4-2176

23. A. Camacho and E. Conover, "The impact of receiving SMS price and weather information on small scale farmers in Colombia," *World Dev*, vol. 123, 2019. doi: 10.1016/j.worlddev.2019.06.020

24. D. P. Rubanga, K. Hatanaka and S. Shimada, "Development of a simplified smart agriculture system for small-scale greenhouse farming," *Sens Mater*, vol. 31, no. 3, pp. 831–843, 2019. doi: 10.18494/SAM.2019.2154

25. B. Vandana and S. S. Kumar, 'A smart phone based information sharing system in precision agriculture', in *AIP Conference Proceedings*, 2018, vol. 2039. doi: 10.1063/1.5078961

26. P. Gyeltshen and K. Osathanunkul, 'Linking small-scale farmers to market using ICT', in *3rd International Conference on Digital Arts, Media and Technology, ICDAMT 2018*, 2018, pp. 120–125. doi: 10.1109/ICDAMT.2018.8376507

27. M. Krone and P. Dannenberg, "Analysing the effects of information and communication technologies (ICTs) on the integration of East African farmers in a value chain context," *Z Wirtschgeogr*, vol. 62, no. 1, pp. 65–81, 2018. doi: 10.1515/zfw-2017-0029

28. U. Deichmann, A. Goyal and D. Mishra, "Will digital technologies transform agriculture in developing countries?" *Agric Econ (UK)*, vol. 47, pp. 21–33, 2016. doi: 10.1111/agec.12300

29. S. Hudson, N. Krogman and M. Beckie, "Social practices of knowledge mobilization for sustainable food production: Nutrition gardening and fish farming in the kolli hills of India," *Food Secur*, vol. 8, no. 3, pp. 523–533, 2016. doi: 10.1007/s12571-016-0580-z

30. E. T. Lwoga, P. Ngulube and C. Stilwell, "Managing indigenous knowledge for sustainable agricultural development in developing countries: Knowledge management approaches in the social context," *Int Inf Lib Rev*, vol. 42, no. 3, pp. 174–185, 2010. doi: 10.1080/10572317.2010.10762862

31. G. M. M. Alam, M. N. Khatun, M. N. I. Sarker, N. P. Joshi and H. Bhandari, "Promoting agri-food systems resilience through ICT in developing countries amid COVID-19," *Front Sustain Food Syst*, vol. 6, 2023. doi: 10.3389/fsufs.2022.972667

32. V. Okpukpara, B. C. Okpukpara, E. E. Omeje, I. C. Ukwuaba and M. Ogbuakanne, "Credit risk management in small-scale farming by formal financial institutions during the COVID-19 era: Nigerian perspective," *Agric Finance Rev*, 2023. doi: 10.1108/AFR-07-2022-0089

33. D. Moyer, M. Ostertag and J. Gershenson, 'Mitigation intermediary transactions within Kenya's agricultural supply chain', in *2022 IEEE Global Humanitarian Technology Conference, GHTC 2022*, 2022, pp. 250–256. doi: 10.1109/GHTC55712.2022.9910996

34. L. Selaledi, M. Maake and M. Mabelebele, "The acceptability of yellow mealworm as chicken feed: A case study of small-scale farmers in South Africa," *Agric Food Secur*, vol. 10, no. 1, 2021. doi: 10.1186/s40066-021-00288-8

35. C. Futemma, D. C. Monteiro Tourne, F. A. Vasconcelos Andrade, N. M. Dos Santos, G. S. S. Rosa Macedo and M. E. Pereira, "The Covid-19 pandemic and small-scale farmers: Surpassing or failing?" *Bol Mus Para Emílio Goeldi Cienc Hum*, vol. 16, no. 1, 2021. doi: 10.1590/2178-2547-BGOELDI-2020-0143

36. C. Spurk, P. Asule, R. Baah-Ofori, L. Chikopela, B. Diarra and C. Koch, "The status of perception, information exposure and knowledge of soil fertility among small-scale farmers in Ghana, Kenya, Mali and Zambia," *J Agric Educ Ext*, vol. 26, no. 2, pp. 141–161, 2020. doi: 10.1080/1389224X.2019.1656089

37. G. Mwanga, E. Mbega, Z. Yonah and M. G. G. Chagunda, "How information communication technology can enhance evidence-based decisions and farm-to-fork animal traceability for livestock farmers," *Sci World J*, vol. 2020, 2020. doi: 10.1155/2020/1279569

38. S. Shams, S. H. S. Newaz and R. R. Karri, "Information and communication technology for small-scale farmers: Challenges and opportunities," *Model Optim Sci Technol*, vol. 17, pp. 159–179, 2020. doi: 10.1007/978-3-030-37794-6_8

39. N. Odoi, "The information behaviour of Ugandan banana farmers in the context of participatory development communication," *Inf Res*, vol. 22, no. 3, p. 759, 2017 [Online]. Available: https://www.scopus.com/inward/record.uri?eid=2-s2.0-85029688587&partnerID=40&md5=798ce4a5af52e274836e5f7efee559d6

40. O. Akinbo, A. A. Adenle and D. Makinde, 'An effective regulatory regime supported by research and development is key to adoption of GM technology in west Africa: Burkina faso and nigeria as case studies', in *Genetically Modified Organisms in Developing Countries: Risk Analysis and Governance*, 2017, pp. 271–282. doi: 10.1017/9781316585269.024

10 Navigating Ethical and Legal Challenges in Smart Agriculture

Insights from Farmers

S. Mayakannan, M. Saravanan, R. Arunbharathi,
V. Prasanna Srinivasan, S Venkatesa Prabhu,
and Rakesh Kumar Maurya

10.1 INTRODUCTION ABOUT CHALLENGES FOR NEW DIGITAL TECHNOLOGIES TO THE FARMERS

Agricultural services, goods, inventions, decision-making, profits, and productivity have all benefited from the widespread adoption of digital technologies [1]. However, do minimum-holder farmers actually gain anything at all from data sharing? Is this information equally accessible and under the control of all agricultural stakeholders? How concerned are farmers about their data being secure, private, and under their control?

Every agricultural operator, but especially farmers, must deal with data obstacles such as a lack of transparency on these issues and the question of whether or not farm data can be labelled "personal". In addition, the current legal framework for data exchanges is based on contracts and license agreements with intricate terms and conditions [2–4]. It's clear that a lack of trust is at the heart of these partnerships, leaving smallholder farmers with very little leverage in negotiations [5–7].

Short-term, intervention-focused development options are unlikely to yield sustainable answers for farmers [8–10]. In deliberative democracies, where discussion and compromise are valued during decision-making, and where long-term, systemic aid is prioritized over short-term initiatives, farmers should be able to have a say in the development processes that affect them [11]. Farmers should be involved in consensus decision-making for climate-smart agriculture because farming is a locally specific problem that defies universal answers [12]. The developed world has an ethical obligation to help the small farmers in low-income countries who are particularly vulnerable to exploitation (not least because the wealth of developed countries is in part based on the import of food products from these very countries) [13, 14]. Promoting climate change adaptation agendas in the agricultural sector, notably through the concept and practice of climate-smart agriculture, is a crucial step in fulfilling this ethical duty [15–17].

In the process of implementing climate-smart agriculture, certain influential people may misuse their influence, leading to increased inequality and negatively

DOI: 10.1201/9781003391302-10

impacting farmers' rights and well-being [18, 19]. For instance, farmers may be compelled to sell their land to agribusinesses if climate-smart agriculture practices become mandatory [20, 21]. On the other hand, climate-smart agriculture development programs promise to work toward alleviating poverty, ensuring adequate nutrition, and fostering economic independence [22]. Because development has become a "business", it may be difficult to deliver on the promises made for these types of projects, which can have disastrous results [23]. Therefore, intervention-specific development choices are not likely to provide farmers with long-term, viable answers [24]. Instead of focusing aid on individual farmers or on specific projects, it is essential to offer structural support for all farmers [25–28]. Since farming is inherently a regionally specific problem, it can't be solved with a general method, and so farmers must actively participate in consensual decision-making for climate-smart agriculture [29].

Least developed country agricultural systems, in particular, confront new problems, such as increasing production to feed a growing population, especially in sub-Saharan Africa, adapting to climate transformation and its variability, and dropping the greenhouse gas emissions that agriculture causes (the three pillars of Climate Smart Agriculture) [30]. In light of these factors, it is essential that all systems of agriculture can demonstrate their diversity adjustment [31]. The goal of current R&D efforts is to improve the mobilization of ecological processes as one of the potential routes to such a change [32]. The primary motivation behind this is to help farmers raise more food and make more money by increasing productivity and making it more resilient to external factors [33, 34]. It's also important to improve agricultural systems' other performance metrics, such as their ability to make efficient use of resources and their effect on the environment [35].

This unequal distribution of wealth is largely attributable to the widespread misunderstanding of data rights and usage (especially among farmers) [36]. A widespread belief exists in the agricultural sector that the benefits and costs of data creation, collecting, distribution, and utilization are not shared fairly. Not all farmers have simple access to digital tools and the data they produce, revealing global power disparities [37–39]. The digital farming sector faces resource constraints, leading to a "digital divide" that separates developed and developing nations due to farmers' limited access to scientific data skills. [40, 41]. Since only large farms can afford the fee of getting the data-based information, small-scale farms in underdeveloped countries have less influence [42, 43]. Additionally, the demands of small farms are not always met by data-based recommendations [44, 45]. To add insult to injury, farmers have no leverage to alter the default terms of data licenses held by giant agribusinesses that regulate the agricultural technology sector [46–48]. The effects of these moral worries on society are undeniable. According to authors [49], "a lot is pre-supposed about the desirability of diverse implications of smart farming on society" when people talk about whether or not data should be shared and with whom, or whether or not different power (re)distributions are desirable [50].

To the general public, it may seem as though farmers have little say over how their personal data is collected, used, or shared [36]. Uncertain data supremacy and dangers of data misappropriation on the one hand, and the difficulty of obtaining critical data provided by others on the other, provide obstacles to their data sharing. Disparities in access to information underpin both forms of difficulty.

In this chapter, authors look first at barriers to digital technology adoption among farmers, with a focus on smallholder farmers. Though the benefits of digital agriculture are well known, why aren't farmers more involved in its planning, development, and oversight? In Section 13.2, authors go over how the Global Open Data for Agriculture and Nutrition (GODAN) inventiveness is trying to make it easier for farmers to use data-driven agriculture by defining who's responsible for what and finding a middle ground between the advantages of sharing data and the risks that come with it, as well as the rights of communities and businesses. Data governance (access, control, and permission) and practices will be discussed in detail.

GODAN/CTA/GFAR developed a toolbox on agricultural codes of conduct and other governance mechanisms that could allow for a more equitable distribution of benefits. The final section offers some final thoughts.

10.2 GODAN METHOD

A multinational coalition, the GODAN initiative 1, encourages the widespread dissemination of open data in agriculture with the goal of boosting global innovation and production in the field. Its current global network consists of approximately 1100 institutions (ranging from government and international organization to the private sector and educational institutions) spread across 118 countries.

To be more specific, GODAN backs international initiatives to make data with relevance to agriculture and nutrition freely accessible and usable everywhere in the globe. The primary objectives of this work are the open data in both the public and private sectors and to produce comprehensive policy. The major objective is to educate the public on ongoing efforts, recent innovations, and effective strategies. Authors should advise and help corporate and public sector organization on open data and open access policies, with an emphasis on fostering capacity development and diversity among open data users, in order to increase open data's accessibility, consumption, engagement, and awareness [51]. Finding a medium between the obvious advantages of accessible data and realistic concerns relating to privacy, security, community rights, and economic interests is essential if authors are to realize the full potential of this data revolution.

GODAN's vast international stakeholder network has improved communication and collaboration amongst influential groups, leading to an agreement on the legal, ethical, and societal implications of, for example, agricultural data ownership, data rights, privacy, and responsibilities. Such organization as the GODAN, the Global Forum on Agricultural Research (GFAR), the Technical Centre for Agricultural and Rural Cooperation ACP-EU (CTA), and the Kuratorium für Technik und Bauwesen in der Landwirtschaft (KTBL) convened in 2018 to discuss the moral, governmental, and legal ramifications of open data for smallholder farmers. Collective action was taken in the form of holding workshops and webinars, attending large conferences, advising on data policy at the national and international levels, and bolstering the capabilities of farmer groups and farmer associations. In general, this study addressed issues of food security and sustainability in poor nations by making farmers' data more easily accessible and shareable.

This chapter details some of the learnings GODAN gained via these interactions, focusing on issues and problems that are relevant to farmers' rights and the future of research that hopes to recycling data collected from farmers.

10.3   PROBLEMS ON THE MORAL SIGNIFICANCE

Concerns regarding the possible exploitation or misuse of data were generally relegated to the back burner until recently, when they were finally acknowledged at all. Yet, as smart farming's use of big data grows, it's more important than ever to consider the legal and moral implications of data governance (access, control, permission). Agribusiness can benefit from big data by increasing profits and output. However, there are a few obstacles to be aware of, including data ownership and rights, data governance, and the distribution of benefits. Questions, like "What opportunities do digital technology provide?", must be answered. To what extent does each participant in the value chain have access to the same data and analysis? How do large agribusinesses win the trust of individual farmers? It's common knowledge that whoever has access to the data also has the power to influence the conclusions drawn from it. The collection and use of data, how to bridge the digital divide, how to create transparency and build trust among stakeholders, and so on can all be illuminated if the right ethical questions are asked and if all stakeholders in the agricultural field (specifically farmers) are engaged in an open dialogue.

Due to its wide scope, agriculture encompasses a wide variety of farming practices and realities. Digital solutions should be developed keeping the needs of rural communities in mind if they are to fulfil their full potential. This is especially true in Africa, where the agricultural potential is still largely unrealized despite widespread illiteracy and a lack of familiarity with digital technologies. To ensure that investments pay off, smallholder farmers must face down obstacles and take calculated risks. The first obstacle is gaining access to the necessary information and services that are being offered by others; the second is ensuring that the information being shared will not be used against them.

Monopolies, knowledge gaps, and inequalities are all problems plaguing the agriculture industry. For smallholder farmers with minimal resources to reap the benefits of technology, they must first open up their most private farm data. Those with the expertise to turn raw data into actionable insights are notoriously tight-lipped about their back-end procedures and data storage plans. As a result, authors must consider whether or not the benefits to farmers outweigh the price of implementing this technology. Farmers should be able to provide input on data usage in a way that makes them feel like they are part of the decision-making process. Many people are interested in realizing the benefits of sharing their data and gaining access to useful information, but they want to feel secure in their right to privacy and control over their data at the same time. The openness and trustworthiness of their contacts with service providers; the importance they place on adaptability and individualization. So that they can spend as little time as possible dealing with bureaucratic formalities.

The aforementioned predicament has prompted serious concerns, including the following:

- When it comes to information, who owns it?
- Who gets to keep the data profits?
- What plans do authors have for using or sharing that information?
- Why isn't there more emphasis on secure storage of personal information? Why do authors care about farmers' access to information?
- What is the current status of national and international acknowledgment of these rights?
- So, what exactly does the General Data Protection Regulation (GDPR) do for farms?
- What laws, guidelines, and policies can be put in place to ensure that these rights are respected and upheld both domestically and internationally?
- How can farmers be made a part of data collection, analysis, transmission, and utilization?

Those working in agriculture have long faced these challenges. Yet, these issues must be properly and promptly addressed today if farmers' rights are to be protected. It is common knowledge that the concept of ownership is intricate, and farming records are not often considered the kind of property that can be owned. When applied to data, intellectual right property provides the same level of security as physical property. But none of these adequately protects individual data ownership. Data ownership can be established in a number of ways, including through the use of copyright; however, data is not always or even usually safeguarded by copyright. Statistics, mathematical formulas, geographical data, and news articles are all examples of facts that cannot be protected by intellectual property laws.

Because not all databases qualify as creative works under copyright law, the European Parliament's Database from 1996 creates sui generis, or new, rights in databases. Those responsible for creating databases can restrict access to their work by preventing the copying or redistribution of all or a significant portion of the data contained therein. The databases prove that sufficient effort was expended in acquiring, verifying, or presenting the data in order to qualify for this privilege. The 15-year duration of protection can be renewed if the database owner makes material changes to the database's contents. The freedom to exploit data connected to agricultural inventions is restricted by patents and plant breeders' rights, despite the fact that neither directly protects data.

In the case of agricultural data, defining who owns what can be quite a challenge. For instance, even in the context of copyright-protected data, copyright ownership might be shifted through contractual agreements. Instead of questioning who "owns" data, it would be more productive to inquire as to who controls and has access to information regarding farms. Farmers often own the data produced by their farms, but they have limited say in who else can access or utilize that data.

10.4   RESOLUTIONS FOR RULES OF ENGAGEMENT

A dearth of regulation concerning data collection, dissemination, and utilization of agricultural data, despite the increasing prevalence of rules and regulations protecting personal data (such as the European General Data Protection Regulation, GDPR3).

The latest EU Regulation on the free transit of non-personal data and its implications for digital agriculture, however, need to be debated. The European Union published a guideline on the handling of non-personal data a year after the General Data Protection Law entered into effect, and within it, a description of precise agricultural data as non-personal data is included. This underscores the necessity for further study on distinguishing between personal and non-personal agriculture data in order to help relieve future privacy concerns. By encouraging the development of industry-specific standards of behaviour that enable service providers to share data in an open, structured, and unobtrusive manner, the new law appropriately highlights the need of self-regulation within the data economy.

Transparent standards of behaviour for data sharing and self-regulation that are sensitive to the state and requirements of societies and strike a balance in the dissemination of advantage throughout locations in the agricultural chain are essential for steering a new paradigm in agricultural data governance. Since no laws have been passed to standardize data-sharing contracts, voluntary codes of behaviour have emerged to do so. In their contracts, those who have signed, subscribed, or joined commit to upholding the ideals outlined in these rules. Farming data is an example of the kind of sensitive data that circulates. Information collected on farms is shared with a wide range of third parties, including extension workers, consultants, agri-tech companies, farmer groups, banks, the government, and others, who then aggregate and combine the data and deliver it back to the farms as a service. The data that is made available as a result of these flows may be useful, but it must be protected by being anonymised or only shared under certain situations or with certain actors. However, smallholder farmers are in the worst position to convert their data privileges due to the fact that their agricultural data typically overlaps with home and personal data.

The European Union's Code of Conduct for Transparent and Equitable Sharing of Agricultural Data Through Contractual Agreement; The French Agricultural Data Use Charter (Charte sur utilization des données agricoles); and Australia's Farm Data Code, which will go into effect in 2020. Figure 10.1 depicts the important features of agricultural conduct codes. There are already codes of conduct in place that handle issues like terms, data ownership, data rights, privacy concerns, security, consent, disclosure, and openness. Compliance standards like this attempt to strike a compromise between farmers' wants and the benefits of Ag-data. These regulations are an example of industry and agribusinesses self-regulating, with the help of their own good intentions and sense of social responsibility; as such, they are not legally binding; though they do educate data providers, primarily farmers, on their legal protections, increase transparency in agricultural data flows, and change the way agribusinesses see data.

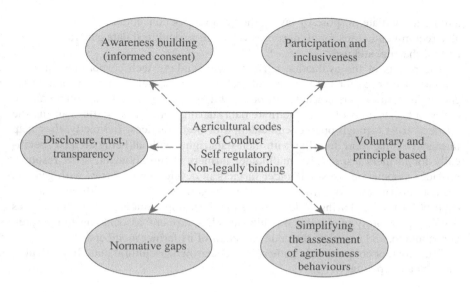

FIGURE 10.1 Important features of agricultural conduct codes.

10.5 GODAN/CTA/CFAR GUIDELINES

The GODAN, CTA, and GFAR held a meeting with legal and policy experts in July 2018 to address the moral, legal, and regulatory implications of information sharing among farmers. It was proposed that people work together to help farmers by sharing information more fairly.

Authors envision a world where smallholder farmers, who are particularly vulnerable to inequitable data flows, are not left behind as a result of larger scale efforts to improve the agri-food system as a whole.

Facilitating fair and ethical benefit distribution through transactions built on mutual interest and trust is a crucial component of such empowerment. GODAN, CTA, and GFAR have come together to improve data management by establishing and enforcing codes of behaviour, voluntary standards, and principles for the collection, use, and sharing of agricultural data. While there is currently no established legal structure for farming information sharing, it has been proposed that codes of conduct, voluntary standards, and principles be developed to address this gap. An online resource for agricultural rules of behaviour was released in May 2020 by GODAN, CTA, and GFAR. When developing this resource, authors first looked at other relevant codes of conduction, rules, and values for sharing farm data that had already been developed. During the course of the GODAN/CTA Sub-Group on Data Encryptions of Behaviour's deliberations, it was drafted for the purpose of public comment. The intended users of this resource are the farmers, agribusinesses, and associations that gather, manage, and share data. It also serves a more immediate purpose by laying the groundwork conceptually for broad, scalable recommendations for all parties involved in agricultural data generation, ownership, sharing, and use.

The results of the evaluation agribusinesses and Ag tech corporations are the primary audiences for current agricultural data codes; neither farmers nor farmers' organizations were consulted throughout their development. Companies can use codes of conduct as a tool to facilitate data sharing with farmers after earning the farmers' trust through open documentation of best practices. Indirectly, they help farmers become more familiar with their data rights without being created specifically for farmers (especially smallholder farmers at this moment). This resource provides associations of smallholder farmers in developing countries with generic, scalable instructions for utilizing, adjusting, negotiating, and establishing a farmer-centred farm data-sharing code. Among the most important aspects of these rules is the responsibility of credible organizations like farmers' associations to interpret, contribute to, and negotiate the code on behalf of its farmer members.

Protocols for cooperatively gathering and sharing agricultural data. In particular, they are anticipating:

- Raise consciousness about the importance of farm data collection, utilization, and sharing.
- Authors need more openness, honesty, and precision in how authors gather, use, and share data about farms.
- Support the equitable and fair gathering, utilization, and exchange of farm data for agricultural purposes.
- Create an environment where farmers feel safe and secure sharing their data in order to maximize its potential for agricultural benefit.
- Providers should be given leeway in determining how best to gather, use, and share data from farms; therefore, it is important to allow for this flexibility in implementation.

There are 17 different clauses available within the tool, and consumers should be able to find one that applies to their scenario before proceeding to the checkout page. Specifically, the clauses are as follows:

1. Definitions: Words and phrases with agricultural significance defined (For instance, who will be collecting the data, what kinds of data will be collected, and how they will be classified as either personal, agricultural, individual farm, raw, aggregated, etc.).
2. Farmers, and more specifically anyone who has created or gathered data about their farming operations, whether technically or manually, or commissioned data providers for this purpose, play an essential role in determining who has access to and uses data from their business, and who stands to gain from sharing that data with any partner that wishes to do so, due to their capacity for management and access. If providers want to provide farmers peace of mind, they should make sure they can still decide who gets access to data collected on their farms. However, it is in the farmer's best interest to

negotiate data use and sharing with any parties who have a monetary stake in the topic, such parties could include a tenant, landowner, cooperative, hardware owner of a precision agricultural system, and Ag Tech Provider.

3. Approval to collect, access, and exercise control: Only with the farmer's express permission may data about their farm be collected, accessed, or used in any way. The originator of agricultural data must give their informed consent for it to be collected, accessed, stored, and used in accordance with a legally binding contract. Consent needs to be voluntarily provided, specific, informed, and unambiguous. Consent must be freely granted and explicitly given by the individual giving it. The word "free" suggests that the farmer has a genuine say in the matter. When consent is given under improper circumstances, such as when there is undue pressure or impact that could change the result of the choice, it is not valid. To ensure that the farmer's consent is both informed and specific, it is necessary to include at least the following details regarding the provider, the data to be processed, the recipients of the data, and the intended use or disclosure of the data. The farmer also has the right to revoke approval at any moment, which should be made clear to them.

4. Purpose limitation: The collected, used, or shared data by providers shall be used exclusively for the purposes communicated to the farmer at the time of data collection. No data may be reused in ways inconsistent with the original agreement.

5. Notice: Farmers have the right to know if and how their personal information is being gathered.

6. Integrity and constancy: Farmers should be made more aware of the types of agricultural data being gathered by agribusinesses and ATPs, as well as the reasons for collecting, using, and sharing this data (e.g. algorithms). Farmers also need to know how to get in touch with the providers if they have any queries or complaints, such as via the ATPs, and what third parties have access to their data and the potential risks associated with sharing data with the providers.

The guiding principles and daily operations of all involved agribusinesses and Ag Tech Providers must be open and in line with the stipulations of the contracts. Unless both parties agree to a contract amendment, it will not go into effect.

1. Data creators' legal protections: The data provider (the farmer) should be entitled to the following protections under the terms of the agreement and the retention policy.
   • Right to portability: It is the responsibility of data providers to make farmer-specific information readily available.
   • Except for data that has been anonymised or aggregated and is no longer uniquely identifiable, a farmer must have access to his or her own farm data for the purposes of archiving or utilizing in other systems, in either its raw or processed (cleaned) form.
   • Data subjects have the right to have their data forgotten (erased), deleted, or returned to them.

2. Right to benefit: When providing their services, businesses should respect the rights of data creators to profit from or be compensated for the use of their work.

3. Limits on revelation, exploitation, and dissemination: No agricultural company or Ag Tech Provider will sell or disclose any farmer's personal information without first obtaining an enforceable agreement from that third party to be destined by the similar standards and regulations as the ATP's agreement with the farmer. If a sale of this kind is planned, farmers must be informed and given the chance to prevent it or have their information deleted. In accordance with the terms of their agreement with the farmer, an Ag Tech Supplier will not distribute or reveal any confidential information about the farm to any outside parties. It is the responsibility of the ATP to present the farmers with the third-party rule for acceptance or refusal if they differ from those of the ATP agreement.

4. Data retention and availability: When requested by the farmer or after a specified amount of time has passed, each agribusiness and Ag Tech Provider should delete or return the farmer's personal farm data. The ATP should stipulate that during the data retention term, the data held by the ATP must be made available to the farmers.

5. Contract termination: If it is clearly mentioned in the agreement and the data originator is made aware of the repercussions, then farmers should be given the option to opt out of the contract and cease the collection and use of their data. There ought to be a detailed outline of the steps required to cancel service in the contract.

6. Fraudulent or anti-competitive behaviour: Any illegal or anti-competitive use of data is unacceptable, such as when agribusinesses or Ag Tech Providers use agricultural data for commodity market speculation (e.g. discrimination in pricing).

7. Data protection safeguards: Data users/providers should be held accountable for their roles in protecting the privacy, security, and confidentiality of farmers' information in the contract. Safeguards should be in place to prevent farm records from being accidentally or maliciously deleted, corrupted, lost, or used without permission. Policies and procedures for breach notification should be put in place.

8. Protecting intellectual property and limiting liability: Liability terms need to be established. All parties' rights to prevent the further use or processing of sensitive information should be recognized in the contract. Protecting private information, financial information, trade secrets, and intellectual property from unauthorized changes is essential.

9. Simple and understandable contracts: Suppliers need to be accountable for drafting contracts that are not just comprehensible but also written in plain English for farmers to read. All ag data contracts should be written in clear and straightforward English. More specifically, contracts will define (1) key concepts and definitions; (2) the reason for data collection, sharing, and processing; (3) the rights and responsibilities of each party in regard to data; (4) the details of how ag data will be stored and used;

(5) methods by which the data's originator can ensure its accuracy; and (6) clear procedures for incorporating new applications.

10. Certification schemes: Transparency and confidence in data uses are bolstered by data certification program. In order to ensure that contracts adhere to codes or certification standards, a separate Supervisory Authority can be set up. It's important to provide incentives for following the rules of conduct. In accordance with these principles, all parties involved should have their agreements and guidelines reviewed by a third-party auditing team from a recognized, credible body. A certificate of compliance will be issued upon review.

11. Agreement with the national and international rule: When working on or creating a Code of Conduct, all parties involved must adhere to all applicable laws, both domestic and foreign.

Terminology, security, authorization, ownership, and authentication of data, as well as certification methods are only some of the major themes that these principles and recommendations cover in an effort to establish universal standards for data-sharing contracts. Clause 2 makes mention of accessing and controlling. It is explicitly detailed that farmers should retain ownership of their data. All data generated by a farmer's operations remains the farmer's property, and only that data will be used and shared if the farmer gives permission. Clause 3 should need farmers' permission before collecting, accessing, or using their personal data. To the extent that aggregated data is not relevant to farmer ownership, it should be made immediately and adequately available to farmers. Farmers must be compensated for their data and must be informed of the collection, use, and sharing of their data in a clear and unambiguous manner. Putting farmers in charge of their data and giving them options for how it's shared with others is one method to earn their trust in data sharing and reaping the benefits of big data. Third parties collecting information on farming should also have a contract in place with the farmer to protect the latter's right to have access to and management of his data.

Because of this, the farmer would have a larger voice in decision-making, and more say over who sees and how the data generated by his or her technological gadgets and machines is used. Throughout farming activities involving numerous stakeholders, it is essential that farmers be able to benefit from the sharing and utilization of data created on their farms. Agreements should be stated in simple, plain English and specify the data's permitted uses. This ensures that any changes or transfers of data can be traced back to their original source.

Codes of conduct also encourage the growth of certification programs, which is a really positive thing. With the use of certifications, farmers can choose tech companies whose data management methods meet the standards specified by an authoritative organization. Specifically, these norms address data storage and security, data processing and sharing, and data gathering.

The Ag-Data Transparency Assessor is one such tool. In 2016, a system was established to validate the contracts of Ag Tech Suppliers that met the 13 Privacy and Security Principles of the American Farm Bureau Federation ("Principles for Farm Data", 2014). The American Farm Bureau Federation developed this instrument with support from a coalition of organizations serving the agricultural sector, commodity exchanges, and ICT companies to evaluate ATPs' data contracts on a voluntary basis. The Evaluator provides ATPs with a tool to gauge their level of compliance with the Principles for Farm Data.

The law company, Janzen Agricultural Law LLC, functions as an independent administrator to assess the provided responses to these queries and the ATP's contracts and processes. After being analysed, the findings are published online so that farmers and other agricultural stakeholders can examine them. The "Ag-Data Transparent" seal can be used by ATPs if they have been granted permission to do so by Janzen Agricultural Law LLC. By displaying the seal, farmers will know that the ATP follows the Principles for Farm Data in its data management practices.

The "Ag Data Transparent" authorization and valuation method has been revised as of January 2020 to account for the rising prominence of personally protecting data rights. The agricultural banking industry is becoming a target for Ag Data Transparency assessments. The decision was made to expand the Seal's use to the agricultural financial sector in order to better protect farmers' personal information. Novel and restructured queries about data collection, use, sharing, and security for farmers have been added for technology providers seeking accreditation. Accurate information about the data's format or the identity of its primary user has been added in the revisions. The practice of firms selling data to third parties is considered, as is the query of who possesses the information and whether or not users have the option to "opt out".

These GFAR/GODAN/CTA/provisions are not meant to be exhaustive, and they cannot replace a solid institutional structure that can guide and operationalize decisions about privacy, ethics, and other sensitive topics. In sum, these recommendations lay forth a discretionary plan of action for exchanging agricultural data. Their purpose is to be used and consulted in accordance with national legislation. In addition to the already existing legally obligatory documents, this online resource will describe the duty of many different sectors. Standards of behaviour for more equitable and accountable data management are described, and the necessity for collaboration is acknowledged.

It's also a work in progress, with suggestions for how to make the tool even better at meeting farmers' requirements for ethical data sharing with the addition of a generic, scalable code of conduct template. Together, GODAN and Youths in Technology and Development Uganda (YITEDEV) will develop a toolkit on codes of behaviour to educate and inform smallholder farmers, particularly young people and women, of their rights in negotiations with other parties. A recommendation to use Uganda as a test case for the moral, permitted, and strategic consequences of data allotment distressing farmers was presented during the 2018 Bonn Expert Consultation. To better acquaint farmers with open data, privacy, and data rights, a virtual session will be held. In order to further refine the codes of conduct toolbox and hear the opinions of the farmers, a second workshop will be held.

10.6 CONCLUSION

The effectiveness and promise of today's agricultural technologies are beyond dispute. Efficiency, productivity, and profitability are all enhanced by the advent of digital innovations such as artificial intelligence (AI), the internet of things (IoT), blockchain, and autonomous systems. Technology is advancing at an ever-faster clip, and that trend shows no signs of abating. The complexity of the agri-food data value chain makes data challenges in agriculture more difficult to solve than in other industries. Many farmers, especially smallholders, feel helpless in today's digital age because they don't immediately gain from the ubiquitous data sharing and interchange. Some of the most fundamental challenges that farmers face in regard to digital agriculture include monopolies, data asymmetries, discrimination, a lack of transparency and trust, and a lack of legislation and regulation on data ownership, data rights, and privacy issues. Because they are uncertain of the worth of their data or worry about its security, many people are hesitant to volunteer it. This disinclination is compounded by the fact that they gain nothing from it.

Because they are excluded from the design and control of the processes involved in digital agriculture, smallholder farmers are unable to fully realize its benefits. Data governance is really about people, not just about tools and systems. While the aforementioned are undoubtedly important, they are not the exclusive determinants of a process's or an organization's projects' success.

Issues that farmers have had with the introduction of digital technologies into agriculture have been discussed in this chapter. Our research focused on governance models that pave the way for more equitable distribution of resources and transactions based on genuine concern and confidence among all parties involved. Creating standards for behaviour in farming is one such method. By providing a framework for more equitable and transparent data contracts in the agriculture sector, these principles and recommendations can help farmers strengthen their relationships with technology vendors and increase their comfort with the use of digital tools. The participation of stakeholders at all levels (including and especially farmers) in open dialogue to find solutions to their varied needs and concerns is essential to the success of any agricultural code of conduct, even if such codes are not mandated by law. Additionally, this method has the potential to increase confidence all across the data value chain.

REFERENCES

1. L. Galetto *et al.*, "Risks and opportunities associated with pollinators' conservation and management of pollination services in Latin America," *Ecol Austral*, vol. 32, no. 1, pp. 55–76, 2022. doi: 10.25260/EA.22.32.1.0.1790
2. N. Boltyanska, H. Podashevskaya, O. Skliar, R. Sklyar and O. Boltianskyi, "Problems of implementation of digital technologies in animal husbandry," *CEUR Workshop Proc*, vol. 3109, pp. 75–82, 2022.
3. K. Charvát *et al.*, "INSPIRE Hackathons and SmartAfriHub – Roadmap for addressing the agriculture data challenges in Africa," *Agris On-Line Pap Econ Inf*, vol. 13, no. 4, pp. 33–48, 2021. doi: 10.7160/AOL.2021.130404
4. M. S. Khan, N. Koizumi and J. L. Olds, "Biofixation of atmospheric nitrogen in the context of world staple crop production: Policy perspectives," *Sci Total Environ*, vol. 701, 2020. doi: 10.1016/j.scitotenv.2019.134945
5. P. Singh, 'Genetically modified crops in India: Politics, policies, and political economy', in *Policy Issues in Genetically Modified Crops: A Global Perspective*, 2020, pp. 75–96. doi: 10.1016/B978-0-12-820780-2.00004-2

6. H. El Bilali, F. Bottalico, G. Ottomano Palmisano and R. Capone, "Information and communication technologies for smart and sustainable agriculture," *IFMBE Proc*, vol. 78, pp. 321–334, 2020. doi: 10.1007/978-3-030-40049-1_41

7. F. K. van Evert, S. Fountas, D. Jakovetic, V. Crnojevic, I. Travlos and C. Kempenaar, "Big Data for weed control and crop protection," *Weed Res*, vol. 57, no. 4, pp. 218–233, 2017. doi: 10.1111/wre.12255

8. B. J. Shaw, 'Terre de Liens – Facilitating access to land for farmers into the long-term', in *The Science and Practice of Landscape Stewardship*, 2017, pp. 328–330. doi: 10.1017/9781316499016.032

9. M. N. Garcia-Casal *et al.*, "Staple crops biofortified with increased vitamins and minerals: Considerations for a public health strategy," *Ann N Y Acad Sci*, vol. 1390, no. 1, pp. 3–13, 2017. doi: 10.1111/nyas.13293

10. P. Rose, M. Bhat, K. Vidhani, N. Ajmeri, A. Gole and S. Ghaisas, 'Intelligent informatics platform for nano-agriculture', in *Proceedings of the IEEE Conference on Nanotechnology*, 2011, pp. 916–919. doi: 10.1109/NANO.2011.6144536

11. P. Benson, "Tobacco talk: Reflections on corporate power and the legal framing of consumption," *Med Anthropol Q*, vol. 24, no. 4, pp. 500–521, 2010. doi: 10.1111/j.1548-1387.2010.01120.x

12. H. Azadi and P. Ho, "Genetically modified and organic crops in developing countries: A review of options for food security," *Biotechnol Adv*, vol. 28, no. 1, pp. 160–168, 2010. doi: 10.1016/j.biotechadv.2009.11.003

13. R. Mrabet and R. Moussadek, 'Development of climate smart agriculture in Africa', in *Conservation Agriculture in Africa: Climate Smart Agricultural Development*, 2022, pp. 17–65. doi: 10.1079/9781789245745.0002

14. W.-M. Cheng *et al.*, 'A real and novel smart agriculture implementation with IoT technology', 2021. doi: 10.1109/ICOT54518.2021.9680638

15. A. Tendolkar and S. Ramya, 'CareBro (Personal Farm Assistant): An IoT based Smart Agriculture with Edge Computing', in *MPCIT 2020 – Proceedings: IEEE 3rd International Conference on 'Multimedia Processing, Communication and Information Technology'*, 2020, pp. 97–102. doi: 10.1109/MPCIT51588.2020.9350481

16. I. Bbudilman, "Climate-smart agriculture policy and (in)justice for smallholders in developing countries," *Futur Food J Food, Agric Soc*, vol. 7, no. 1, pp. 31–41, 2019. doi: 10.17170/kobra-2018122074

17. Y. Mohamed Hamada, 'Risk management in agriculture: Production and technical risk management', in *Risk and Contingency Management: Breakthroughs in Research and Practice*, 2017, pp. 300–335. doi: 10.4018/978-1-5225-3932-2.ch016

18. J. Anand, M. Dhanalakshmi and P. P. J. Raja, "Smart indication system for spinal cord stress detection," *Int J Recent Technol Eng*, vol. 8, no. 3, pp. 6164–6168, 2019.

19. H. Shilomboleni, 'Political economy challenges for climate smart agriculture in Africa', in *Social Innovation and Sustainability Transition*, Springer, 2022, pp. 261–272.

20. E. N. Sadjadi and R. Fernández, "Challenges and opportunities of agriculture digitalization in Spain," *Agronomy*, vol. 13, no. 1, 2023. doi: 10.3390/agronomy13010259

21. D. Duc Truong, T. Tho Dat and L. Huy Huan, "Factors affecting climate-smart agriculture practice adaptation of farming households in coastal central Vietnam: The case of Ninh Thuan Province," *Front Sustain Food Syst*, vol. 6, 2022. doi: 10.3389/fsufs.2022.790089

22. M. Uddin, A. Chowdhury and M. A. Kabir, "Legal and ethical aspects of deploying artificial intelligence in climate-smart agriculture," *AI Soc*, 2022. doi: 10.1007/s00146-022-01421-2

23. R. Kibugi, "Assessing Kenyan law and practice in the mainstreaming of a low carbon development pathway in Agriculture," *Carbon Clim Law Rev*, vol. 15, no. 1, pp. 60–79, 2021. doi: 10.21552/cclr/2021/1/8

24. M. A. Soharwardi, A. Firdous and A. R. Gill, "Are environment, informal sector and poverty interrelated?" *Int J Agric Ext*, vol. 9, no. 2, pp. 277–284, 2021. doi: 10.33687/ijae. 009.02.3579

25. J. Anand, A. Jones, T. K. Sandhya and K. Besna, 'Preserving national animal using wireless sensor network based hotspot algorithm', in *2013 International Conference on Green High Performance Computing (ICGHPC)*, 2013, pp. 1–6.

26. S. Jarial, "Internet of Things application in Indian agriculture, challenges and effect on the extension advisory services–a review," *J Agribus Dev Emerg Econ*, 2022, vol. 13, no. 4, 505–519.

27. H. F. Williamson and S. Leonelli, *Towards Responsible Plant Data Linkage: Data Challenges for Agricultural Research and Development*, Springer Nature, 2023.

28. M. Amiri-Zarandi, R. A. Dara, E. Duncan and E. D. G. Fraser, "Big data privacy in smart farming: A review," *Sustainability*, vol. 14, no. 15, p. 9120, 2022.

29. G. V. Fedotova, R. H. Ilyasov, N. E. Buletova, T. A. Yakushkina and T. K. Kurbanov, 'AI as a breakthrough technology of agriculture development', Advances in Intelligent Systems and Computing, vol. 1100, AISC, pp. 384–393, 2020. doi: 10.1007/978-3-030-39319-9_44

30. I. F. Gorlov, G. V. Fedotova, A. V. Glushchenko, M. I. Slozhenkina and N. I. Mosolova, "Digital technologies in the development of the agro-industrial complex," *Lect Notes Netw Syst*, vol. 87, pp. 220–229, 2020. doi: 10.1007/978-3-030-29586-8_26

31. R. Dhanalakshmi and J. Anand, 'Big data for personalized healthcare', in *Handb Intell Healthc Anal Knowl Eng with Big Data Anal*, Wiley, pp. 67–92, 2022. doi: 10.1002/ 9781119792550.ch4

32. L. Goparaju and F. Ahmad, "Analyzing the risk related to climate change attributes and their impact, a step towards climate-smart village (CSV): A geospatial approach to bring geoponics sustainability in India," *Spat Inf Res*, vol. 27, no. 6, pp. 613–625, 2019. doi: 10.1007/s41324-019-00258-0

33. J. Anand and K. Sivachandar, "Diverse sorting algorithm analysis for ACSFD in wireless sensor networks," *Int J Eng Adv Technol*, vol. 2, no. 3, pp. 57–59, 2013.

34. M. Jastrzębska, M. Kostrzewska and A. Saeid, 'Sustainable agriculture: A challenge for the future', in *Smart Agrochemicals for Sustainable Agriculture*, Elsevier, 2022, pp. 29–56.

35. B. K. Manik, "Revisit to policy formulation for climate-smart agriculture in India," *Int J Innov Technol Explor Eng*, vol. 8, no. 7C2, pp. 144–151, 2019.

36. R. Dhanalakshmi, J. Anand, K. Poonkavithai and V. Vijayakumar, 'Cloud-based glaucoma diagnosis in medical imaging using machine learning', in *Artificial Intelligence for Innovative Healthcare Informatics*, Springer, 2022, pp. 61–78.

37. F. A. Khan, A. Abubakar, M. Mahmoud, M. A. Al-Khasawneh and A. A. Alarood, "Cotton crop cultivation oriented semantic framework based on IoT smart farming application," *Int J Eng Adv Technol*, vol. 8, no. 3, pp. 480–484, 2019.

38. F Sarro, A Rainer, K Jan-Stol, D O'Connor, N Power 'ACM International Conference Proceeding Series', 50-100 2018 (200).

39. J. Verschuuren, "Towards an EU regulatory framework for climate-smart agriculture: The example of soil carbon sequestration," *Transnatl Environ Law*, vol. 7, no. 2, pp. 301–322, 2018. doi: 10.1017/S2047102517000395

40. R. Sharma, S. K. Chauhan and A. M. Tripathi, "Carbon sequestration potential in agroforestry system in India: An analysis for carbon project," *Agrofor Syst*, vol. 90, no. 4, pp. 631–644, 2016. doi: 10.1007/s10457-015-9840-8

41. C. Negra, S. Vermeulen, L. G. Barioni, T. Mamo, P. Melville and M. Tadesse, "Brazil, Ethiopia, and New Zealand lead the way on climate-smart agriculture," *Agric Food Secur*, vol. 3, no. 1, 2014. doi: 10.1186/s40066-014-0019-8

42. Y. Ren and S. Wang, "Reliability analysis of godan graphs," *Discret Appl Math*, vol. 307, pp. 180–190, 2022. doi: 10.1016/j.dam.2021.10.022

43. H. Zhang, S. Zhou and Q. Zhang, "Component connectivity of alternating group networks and godan graphs," *Int J Found Comput Sci*, 2022. doi: 10.1142/S0129054122500228

44. K. Kimbrough, 'Staging senseless violence: Early jōruri puppet theater and the culture of performance', in *The Tokugawa World*, 2021, pp. 578–593. doi: 10.4324/9781003198888-40

45. S. R. Luhar and D. Nimavat, "Destroying and recreating myths: A subversive response to caste ideology," *Contemp Voice Dalit*, 2021. doi: 10.1177/2455328X211050750

46. S. Siddiqi, "Spatial distribution analysis of unigrams and bigrams of Hindi literary document," *Int J Adv Comput Res*, vol. 8, no. 35, pp. 97–109, 2018. doi: 10.19101/IJACR. 2018.835003

47. R. Musker and B. Schaap, "Global open data in agriculture and nutrition (Godan) initiative partner network analysis [version 1; peer review: 2 approved with reservations]," *F1000Research*, vol. 7, 2018. doi: 10.12688/F1000RESEARCH.13044.1

48. R. Y. Pochekaev, ""King" Godan: Status of the ruling chinggisid in Mongolian and tibetan sources," *Zolotoordynskoe Obozr*, vol. 6, no. 1, pp. 6–17, 2018. doi: 10.22378/ 2313-6197.2018-6-1.6-17

49. S. Mulchand and M. Seema, "Formulation of polyherbomineral matrices for treatment of osteoporosis," *Asian J Pharm Clin Res*, vol. 11, no. 1, pp. 217–223, 2018. doi: 10.22159/ ajpcr.2018.v11i1.21777

50. A. Powell, "CABI's innovative use of technology, data, and knowledge transfer to reduce crop losses in the developing world," *Food Energy Secur*, vol. 6, no. 3, pp. 94–97, 2017. doi: 10.1002/fes3.113

51. A. Ponmalar, P. Saravanan, S. Deeba, B. R. Jyothi and J. Anand, 'IoT Enabled Inexhaustible E-vehicle using Transparent Solar Panel', in *2022 International Conference on Communication, Computing and Internet of Things (IC3IoT)*, 2022, pp. 1–5.

11 Decision Support System for Smart Agriculture in Predictive Analysis

Nestor Ulloa, R. Sharmila, E. Brindha,
R. Deepalakshmi, R. Arunbharathi,
and K. Divya Vani

11.1 INTRODUCTION

The effects of climatic change and its increased variability will be felt differently by the agricultural sectors of various nations [1]. Growers and farmers need to think about the environmental implications that could result from changes in management regimes, as well as the potential benefits and drawbacks to crop yields and financial stability posed by future weather patterns [2]. Extreme heat waves, protracted drought, and milder winters are all possible manifestations of these trends. Incorporating lessons from climate and environmental science into farm-scale management is difficult, notwithstanding breakthroughs in applying research and analyses over the previous half-century [3]. In many cases, crucial information and data are lacking, making it difficult to identify the repercussions of shifts in management techniques across multiple dimensions [4].

As precision farming, mobile devices, and data management software continue to gain popularity, there is a greater need than ever for a unified data platform to facilitate the communication of management decisions made at the farm level and resulting behaviour changes in response to location-certain bio-physical information and systematic tools [5–8]. With the help of technology, information gathered at the farm level may be combined with publicly available data on a regional scale to strengthen evidence-based policy and promote environmentally responsible management of agricultural areas [9].

This chapter's major objective is to show how tradeoffs brought on by climatic shifts at the size of individual farms can be mitigated through the use of decision support systems [10]. Authors also investigate how the farm-level tools might integrate with regional-level analysis to provide the data necessary for more effective evidence-based policymaking. We demonstrate how the aforementioned three factors can be considered with AgBiz LogicTM platform and decision-support framework designed to assist farmers in assessing the viability of existing and potential future management strategies in light of varying climate projections. These decision-making instruments are useful for assessing climate-smart choices since they consider the effects of climate change on the environment. Our example case mirrors the Pacific Northwest, a major producer of dryland Barley in India.

DOI: 10.1201/9781003391302-11

11.2   AgBiz LOGIC: SUPPORTING CLIMATE-AWARE AGRICULTURE DECISIONS

AgBiz Logic is a unified learning tool that stores and tracks financial information from growers and businesses [11]. Economic, financial, climate, and environmental modules can all benefit from the saved plans and scenarios. Farmers can learn more about the potential financial and economic impacts of climate change on their farms by using economic and financial calculators [12, 13]. This research delves deeper into the parts. The economic and financial calculators included in AgBiz Logic are as follows

AgBizProfit™ is a resource for assessing the viability of various investments over the long-, medium-, and short term. This section analyses the potential financial benefits of an investment using standard economic concepts like the total present range, yearly equivalent, and interior rate of yield.

Agricultural businesses can benefit from AgBizLease™ because it facilitates the creation of fair lease agreements for the use of agricultural assets such as crops, livestock, and other capital investments. This unit applies the principles of net present range analysis to the economics of a cash rent or crop-share lease between a tenant and landlord [14].

Financial liquidity, farm efficiency, profitability, and solvency or ranch's company are all factors considered by AgBiz Finance TM when advising agricultural producers on investment decisions [15]. Using the results of an AgBiz Finance analysis, farmers and ranchers can decide whether to make modifications to their agricultural and livestock systems or whether to invest in new technologies. Modifications to financial ratios and performance indicators are also computed [16–18].

AgBiz Logic has just added two new modules, AgBizClimate™ and AgBizEnvironment™, to its decision-support platform to better assist farmers [19].

Farmers and landowners can use AgBizClimate to revise their budgets in light of climate change's potential effects on crop yields. Using data unique to their enterprises, farmers may maximize net returns under a variety of climate change scenarios [20, 21]. While making decisions, AgBiz Environment considers a wide range of environmental impacts, including those related to soil erosion, soil loss, soil carbon sequestration, and greenhouse gas emissions, by employing environmental models and other forms of ecological accounting [22, 23].

AgBiz Logic allows you to deliver high-quality data faster and at a lesser price [24]. Eventually, a statistically representative "panel" of agricultural decision-makers might benefit from near real-time insights into management decisions thanks to linked farm management software with an encrypted database, as shown in Figure 11.1. AgBiz Logic's use of specific management data would give the granularity required for analysis with a technology like tradeoff analysis model for multi-dimensional impact assessment (TOA-MD) to be effectively implemented [25, 26]. Moreover, since users of AgBiz Logic would be basing their management decisions on the information they submit, they would have every reason to be as precise as possible. Finally, with AgBiz Logic, farmers have a simple, effective method of data entry, drastically cutting down on data-collecting expenses.

Farmers and researchers interested in how climate change and related policies are affecting international agricultural markets will find the AgBiz Logic platform

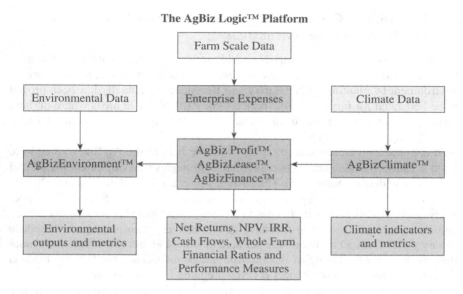

FIGURE 11.1   Logic system for AgBiz.

invaluable [27, 28]. The downscaled view of climate change affects projections of output and production inputs. The potential effects on yield encourage producers to make adjustments to input use, management, and technology use [29].

11.3   CONSIDERATION OF THE TRADEOFFS ASSOCIATED WITH CLIMATICALLY VARIED AT THE FARM SCALE

When it comes to analysing the effects of climatically varied and making investment decisions on a farm size, AgBiz Logic provides a uniform approach. AgBizClimate is a useful tool for agriculturalists, growers, and land owners to investigate average weather condition estimates (such as growth degree days and chilling days) that are pertinent to a commodity in their area [30]. Understanding how these predicted shifts will effect their output and risk allows users to make informed decisions about where to place their capital and how to allocate their yields and inputs for production [31]. When AgBizClimate is coupled with AgBiz Logic, customers are able to look ahead 20–30 years to see if their current businesses and operations will still be lucrative in that time, and if not, whether they need to make any long-term planning decisions now.

Researchers looked at how climate change might affect the profitability of both conventional and sustainable crop rotations [32–34]. Following an introduction to the AgBizClimate module for estimating the impacts of climate change on truck costs, crop yields, tractor, and other productivity inputs, we'll walk through the AgBizProfit module for determining whether or not a shift in crop rotation will increase profitability.

11.3.1 EFFECTS OF CLIMATE CHANGE AND INVESTMENTS IN NEW FARMING METHODS UNDER INVESTIGATION

We then consider how these variable yields influence overall earnings. The economic benefits of growing different crops are also studied. Adapting to the changing environment by planting winter Barley and Brassicaceae annually has been proved to be beneficial for farmers in this region [35]. Particularly in areas where dryland farming techniques are popular, Brassicaceae is being explored as a potential source of biodiesel fuel for aircraft.

It is possible to create what-if reports with the help of the Ag BizProfit add-on. Each scenario includes one to five alternative strategies that can be compared and contrasted with one another [36]. The current winter Barley fallow system in 2022 is compared to two alternative plans that improve Barley yields by 25 and 18%, respectively, and a fourth plan that changes to a rotation that includes both winter Barley and Brassicaceae. Lower soil moisture in the later cropping strategy will reduce Barley yields from 50 to 39 bushels per acre (about 14%), but this loss will be more than made up for by the higher income from the Brassicaceae crop [37–39]. For this scenario, a brand-new crop budget is being prepared for this program.

Changes in production, tractor, truck miles, and predicted years of life are just some of the impacts of switching to an annual cropping system with Brassicaceae shown in Table 11.1. Because of its high yield of 37 bushels (1,800 lbs/ac) and low trading rate, Brassicaceae can be cultivated in place of fallow during the winter Barley and Brassicaceae cycle [40]. The net returns from Barley are less than they would have been with contributions from net returns from Brassicaceae because of lower Barley yields and greater mechanical costs (Table 11.1). There will be an annual production of 38.71 barrels as a result.

Both the winter Barley and fallow cycles in 2045 account for the rising costs associated with weed, disease, and insect infestations as a result of warmer temperatures and greater precipitation. The price per acre of things to control pests and diseases and the price per treatment for an extra herbicide and pesticide application are all factored in. This means that in 2045, more hours will be spent operating tractors and sprayers on Barley and fallow fields to accommodate for these additional applications. Brassicaceae's inclusion in an annual cropping system eliminates the need for four different herbicides, cutting down on the time spent on the tractor and sprayer each year by a significant amount.

AgBiz Climate's Table 11.2 compares four cropping systems that involve both owned and leased land, including the net yield, total adjustable cash costs, and per-acre returns of each. Winter Barley and fallow cycles yielded mean net return of ₹483,570/ac on privately retained property in 2022, compared to ₹241,785/ac on rented land.

Low Barley yields (only 49.50 bu./ac) are a major factor in the dismal bottom line. Now consider the outcomes of climate change, which result in increased Barley harvests. In 2045, when yields are increased by 21.2% to 60.24 bushels, after-cost returns amount to ₹7,613 and ₹3,929/ac on owned property and rented land, respectively. We also provide our results for a case in which yield changes owing to climate change are less dramatic. Barley yields increased by only 18%

TABLE 11.1

Variations in Estimated Service Life and Annual Mileage for Tractors, Combines, Other Heavy Equipment, and Trucks

Yield (bu/ac)		Base: Barley and Fallow Rotation, 2022		Barley 21.2% and Fallow Revolution, 2045		Barley 18% and Fallow Revolution, 2045		Barley and Brassicaceae Revolution, 2045	
Brassicaceae yield								38	
Barley yield		55		65		59		41	
Yield increase				11		8		27	
Lifespan and Annual Usage of Machinery									
Machine	Size	Hours of Miles of Annual Use	Expected Life (Yrs)	Hours of Miles of Annual Use	Expected Life (Yrs)	Hours of Miles of Annual Use	Expected Life (Yrs)	Hours of Miles of Annual Use	Expected Life (Yrs)
Truck	2 1/2 ton. older	2,400	20.0	2,887	16.6	2,760	17.4	3,622	13.3
Rotary mower	27'	168	16.0	168	16.0	168	16.0	NA	NA
Additional Combine	32' Hillside	NA						163	6.7
Field sprayer	90'	183	15.0	275	10.0	275	10.0	46	59.8
Combine	30' Hillside	109	10.0	109	10.0	109	10.0	163	6.7
Air seeder	46'	98	16.0	98	16.0	98	16.0	195	8.5
Bank out wagon	860 bu. capicity	122	21.0	145	17.6	140	18.5	183	15.5
Tractor-rubber tracked	485 hp	568	16.0	685	13.6	678	13.6	589	15.4
Truck and trailer	Semi, used	3,000	21.0	3612	17.5	3462	18.5	4532	14.2

TABLE 11.2

Yields/ac, Total Returns and Total Variable Cash Expenses Were Calculated for Crops Grown-Up on Owned and Rented Land, as well as Annual Cropping Systems of Winter Barley and Brassicaceae and Cycles of Winter Barley and Fallow

	2022		2045		2045		2045	
	Winter Barley	Fallow	Winter Barley (21.2%)	Fallow	Winter Barley (18%)	Fallow	Winter Barley	Brassicaceae
Yield	₹27,342	₹0	₹32,008	₹0	₹30,780	₹0	₹21,120	₹22,594
Net returns	₹16,864	(₹5,239)	₹21,530	(₹5,976)	₹20,302	(₹5,976)	₹10,151	₹9,987
Average net returns	₹6,057		₹7,777		₹7,122		₹9,823	

Crops Yield on Rented Land

	2022		2045		2045		2045	
	Winter Barley	Fallow	Winter Barley (21.2%)	Fallow	Winter Barley (18%)	Fallow	Winter Barley	Brassicaceae
Yield	₹17,600	₹0	₹21,120	₹0	₹20,220	₹0	₹13,753	₹17,682
Net returns	₹9,905	(₹4,011)	₹12,525	(₹4,666)	₹11,542	(₹4,666)	₹4,666	₹6,631
Average net returns	₹2,947		₹3,929		₹34,38		₹5,812	

from the 2022 crop cycle, leading to a decline in net returns. A farmer who works his or her own land may expect to earn ₹85/ac in profit, while a landlord would bring in only ₹3,438/ac.

By assessing the prospective costs and advantages of climate change, we take into account the economic viability of modifying the agricultural system or adjusting management to account for unforeseen weather patterns.

Growing evidence suggests farmers in this region could reap the benefits of climate change by switching to an annual agricultural strategy centred around winter Barley and Brassicaceae [41]. One can make ₹10,069/ac on their own property and ₹5,812/ac on rented land, respectively (−₹327), by rotating winter Barley and Brassicaceae. The output from AgBiz Climate is seen in Figure 11.2 and Potential and Existing Effects of Climate Change on Annual Cropping Systems. Net returns' sensitivity to shifts in production and input costs is not addressed in this chapter; however, the authors are prepared to supply this information upon request.

This example demonstrates how ownership versus leasing might affect profits by comparing two cropping systems: fallow/winter Barley and Brassicaceae/ winter Barley. While it is possible to mimic a wide variety of alternative cropping systems, we only included the winter Barley/Brassicaceae combination because it is the one most farmers in this area employ [42, 43]. The impact of climate change on annual crop rotations of winter Barley and Brassicaceae increase net returns per acre regardless of whether the property is owned or leased, as is typically the case in this region.

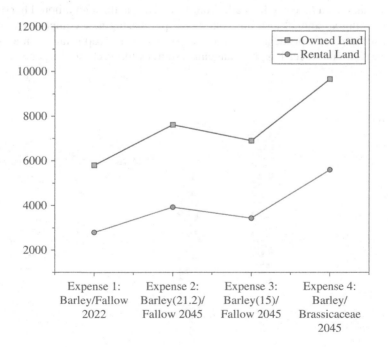

FIGURE 11.2   AgBiz climate output results.

11.3.2 Implementing Investment Strategies Profitably

The profitability of the winter Barley and Brassicaceae rotation for a single farmer has not been determined, despite our demonstration that it yields greater average net returns. The producer would have to buy a second combine and a vehicle if he wanted to move to an annual cropping method that contains Brassicaceae [44]. The timing of the cash flows is crucial to the success of this venture. Instead of investing in costly machinery, you may employ a specialized operator to gather your Brassicaceae crop, but this comes with its own set of risks, including the possibility that they won't be available when you need them [45]. The foundations of picking investments that will improve the company's financial performance are an economic profitability analysis and a financial feasibility study. If an option is economically viable, it will become apparent. However, an investment may not be viable if it cannot generate adequate cash flows to cover its ongoing principal and interest obligations. Additionally, adaption tactics may cause modifications to agricultural leases due to the increased inputs and expenditures required by the landowner or tenant. The per cent of the crop yield or annual cash leased paid to a tenant or landowner rises in proportion to the amount contributed by the tenant or landowner during the term of the lease.

An AgBizProfit analysis of the capital expenditures for the various adaption strategies is shown in Figure 11.3. With a discount rate of 5% and a research duration of eight years, the current Barley and fallow rotation yield an NPV of ₹382819/ac. Costing ₹3,358,247/ac, an extra combine and truck would increase the annual cropping system's net present value by a significant amount. Net income (NPI) of ₹28,652/harvested acre can be made from Brassicaceae through tailored harvesting. Implementing an annual farming system and purchasing new equipment would be the most financially prudent choice. However, a shift in crop rotations may not be possible if the producer has the financial resources to purchase the supplementary

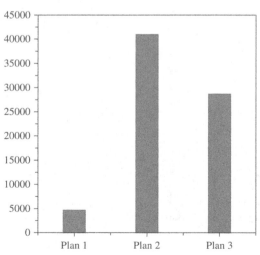

FIGURE 11.3   Results of *AgBizProfit* for owned land.

machinery essential to the new system. The switch to a Brassicaceae rotation's viability can be calculated with the help of the AgBizFinance module.

If you want to do an AgBizFinance study, you'll need a comprehensive financial statement, a description of all outstanding loans and leases, and a rundown of all cash flows for every aspect of your farm business. Unless you have access to extensive farm-specific data, it will be impossible to illustrate and understand the results of such an investigation. This chapter does not provide an AgBizFinance analysis or expand upon the topics raised within.

11.3.3 Analysing the Effect of Climatically Change on Agricultural Leases

Typically, contemporary farm leases are based on long-standing practices and norms. As profit margins shrink and climate change affects yields, production inputs, and crop rotations, it's possible that future leases will be based more on equitability, where the tenant and landowner are reimbursed more equally for their efforts into the lease. A part of AgBiz Logic called AgBiz Lease can help you decide if a lease is reasonable. Unfortunately, tenants of leased land often find that the net returns they receive do not adequately reward them for the financial risk they take by cultivating the land. Currently, crop leases are typically negotiated on the basis of the parties' respective contributions to overall costs, which results in fair arrangements for all parties involved. This resource would help tenants examine their land leases and make informed decisions about whether or not they are fair for the long run. For instance, if the need of pesticides and fungicides is increased in the future owing to climate change, the associated costs could be divided proportionally among farmers according to their harvest shares. These AgBiz Climate budgets could be used by AgBiz Lease to assess the fairness of present lease terms in light of fluctuating input costs and the impact on net returns.

For this winter Barley fallow rotation, the current crop-share lease is reasonable (see Figure 11.3), but it provides no financial benefits to either the renter or the landlord. Tenant and landowner will earn ₹8,677 and ₹3,438/ac, respectively, during the life of a ten-year lease. The production costs, including the tenant's share of fertiliser, herbicide, crop insurance, and the landowner's return on investment, exceed the yields and prices. A change from the crop-share lease to an annual cropping system of winter Barley and Brassicaceae with the same distribution of crop and production inputs would result in a net benefit of ₹13,835/ac for both the tenant and the landlord. In a fair crop-share lease, the tenant receives 73% of the harvest and the landowner receives 27%, as determined by AgBizLease's analysis. Based on their respective shares of the annual produce, the tenant would get ₹24,231/ac and the landowner would receive ₹7,285/ac (Figure 11.3) and probability of changing to an annual cropping system on owned land.

We demonstrate how a well-tuned integrated decision support tool can inform farmers and ranchers on how climate change will affect their businesses and the environment. Using AgBizClimate, we were able to show how climate change could reduce Barley production. To show how a firm may be adapted to the annual agricultural cycle, we used AgBizProfit. You can use AgBizFinance to prove that buying

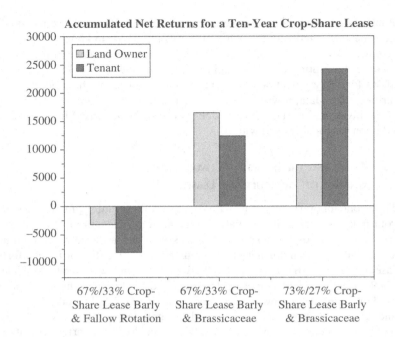

FIGURE 11.4 AgBizLease: The outcome of switching from a barley-and-fallow crop rotation to an annual farming scheme.

supplemental equipment for your yearly cropping system is a good financial move. While AgBiz Environment demonstrated how to achieve a compromise between economic growth and ecological sustainability, AgBizLease demonstrated how switching to an annual farming system affects harvest distribution as shown in Figure 11.4.

11.3.4 BASE SCENARIO AND PRELIMINARY SETUP

The 3800-ac farm receives between 12 and 18 in. of rain each year; thus, it is managed as a traditional dryland Barley farm. To preserve soil moisture, boost Barley yields, decrease erosion, and cut fuel costs, the farmer alternates winter Barley and fallow crops through direct sowing and chemical fallow. Glyphosate is used during the fallow year, and additional herbicides are used as needed throughout the crop year, to control weed growth. When necessary, pesticides are used. Planting with a direct-seed drill allows for the incorporation of any necessary fertiliser. On average, the farm harvests 49.5 bushels of winter Barley per acre. The farm owner leases out half of the land and owns the other half. The tenant is responsible for all of the expenditures involved with weed management, manure, and crop assurance, whereas the landowner keeps a third of the yield and is responsible for a third of the costs. These harvests correspond with those reported in the DA's Agricultural Census of 2007 for this area. If the crop and livestock enterprise budgets generated by AgBiz Logic, don't accurately reflect the grower's actual returns and expenses, the farmer can choose a more accurate one from a previous set of budgets. These predetermined spending plans provide a benchmark against which to measure future net returns after environmental factors are accounted for. Afterwards, the closest weather station is chosen using AgBizClimate for the agricultural or livestock businesses. This provides the producer with downscaled, location-specific weather forecast information that can be used to assess the potential effect of climatically change on their farm or business. Figure 11.5 shows the steps for selecting ABL predicted expense.

11.3.4.1 Logical Work of AgBiz

Later determination, which weather station is nearest to his or her farmland, the farmer can next priorities up to three meteorological factors that will have the greatest effect on Barley production. Here, we pick total number of frosty nights, the total number of rising degree days, and the total amount of seasonal precipitation.

Key climatic factors with the potential to significantly impact agricultural and livestock production yields and quality include:

- Accumulated growing degree days
- Accumulated seasonal precipitation
- Number of nights below freezing

Figures 11.6–11.8 depict the unique effects of several meteorological factors. Figures 11.7 and 11.8 show average values for the selected weather variables from 1972 to 1999, which serve as the model's baseline weather condition. For both the high and low emission scenarios, the average of the estimated future climatic variable is calculated for the years 2025–2059. The solid green and marron colour indicate the mean, with the shade representing the 5–95% limits of findings from 20 distinct climatically models.

By the 2045s, the low emissions future predicts an annual drop in the number of nights below freezing of 29 nights and the high emissions future predicts a decrease of 34 nights from the historical baseline (Figure 11.6). This data allows for the use of crop models or grower/expert assessments to project the effect of this weather variable on Barley yields in the future. The yields in this case study rise by 20% because of the reduction in the number of subfreezing nights; analysing the sensitivity of variations in yields can integrated into forthcoming assessments.

Figure 11.7 shows the changes in Fahrenheit degrees over the years. Under high emissions scenarios, the number of rising degree from March 1 to November 1 is projected to grow by 620° h by the 2030s, while under minimum emissions scenarios, same number is projected to climb by 525° h. Assuming a linear relationship, higher numbers of collected degree days above 50 increase Barley yields by 18%. Precipitation totals are shown monthly in Figure 11.8. The low emissions future and the high emissions future both predict an increase of 0.4 in. in accumulated water year precipitation relative to the historical baseline. An increase in precipitation, especially during the growing season, is predicted to boost Barley yields by 25%, according to the producer.

Table 11.3 illustrates that the visualization is contingent on crop models, the level of farmer engagement, and the estimates derived from various weather variables. We have estimated how average crop yields might change by the 2045s in this scenario. It will take "Your Changes" to yield into account. Growers can make a well-informed decision about the potential influence on Barley yields using data from

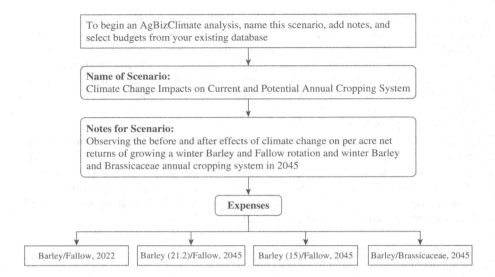

To begin an AgBizClimate analysis, name this scenario, add notes, and select budgets from your existing database

Name of Scenario:
Climate Change Impacts on Current and Potential Annual Cropping System

Notes for Scenario:
Observing the before and after effects of climate change on per acre net returns of growing a winter Barley and Fallow rotation and winter Barley and Brassicaceae annual cropping system in 2045

Expenses

| Barley/Fallow, 2022 | Barley (21.2)/Fallow, 2045 | Barley (15)/Fallow, 2045 | Barley/Brassicaceae, 2045 |

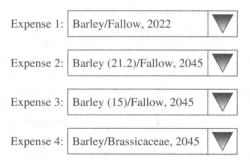

To begin an AgBizClimate analysis, name this scenario, add notes, and select budgets from your existing database

Name of Scenario:
Climate Change Impacts on Current and Potential Annual Cropping System

Notes for Scenario:
Observing the before and after effects of climate change on per acre net returns of growing a winter Barley and Fallow rotation and winter Barley and Brassicaceae annual cropping system in 2045

Expense 1: Barley/Fallow, 2022

Expense 2: Barley (21.2)/Fallow, 2045

Expense 3: Barley (15)/Fallow, 2045

Expense 4: Barley/Brassicaceae, 2045

FIGURE 11.5 Steps for selecting *ABL* predicted expense.

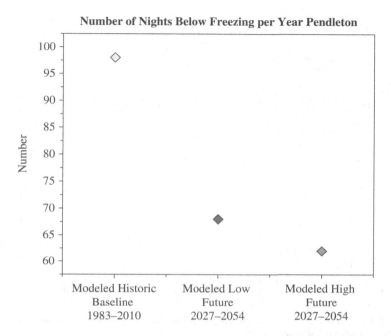

FIGURE 11.6 Potentially impacting crop and livestock companies are weather factors that can affect yields and product quality.

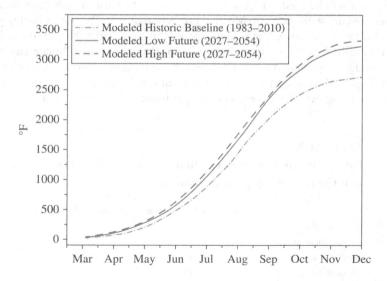

FIGURE 11.7 Predictive factors of the weather that could affect crop and livestock businesses' yields or product quality.

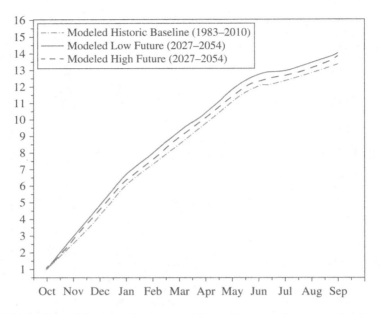

FIGURE 11.8   Potentially impacting crop and livestock companies are weather factors that can affect yields and product quality.

focus and the grower's own estimations indicated in Figures 11.6–11.8. Then, based on the most recent production forecast, a farmer revises their financial plan ("Your Changes"). It will be used to adjust the figures in all the various budgets considered. The user concurs with the Crop Models' prediction of a 21.2% rise in Barley yields in the illustrative scenario. The user compares this new Barley budget to the 15.0% figure established by the Grower Focus Group. Users of AgBizClimate can generate new budgets by changing certain inputs that have a one-to-one correlation with outputs (Figure 11.9). Examples of inputs that vary with output include custom hay or Barley harvesting, where payment is made per tonne of harvested product.

TABLE 11.3
Factors in the Environment that can Affect the Quantity and Quality of Crops and Animals

	Winter Barley Owned	Winter Barley Rented
Crop modelling	+21.2%	+21.2%
Grower focus groups	+16.0%	+16.0%
Weather Var. 1	+21.0%	+21.0%
Weather Var. 2	+16.0%	+16.0%
Weather Var. 3	+26.0%	+26.0%
Your changes	+21.2%	+21.2%

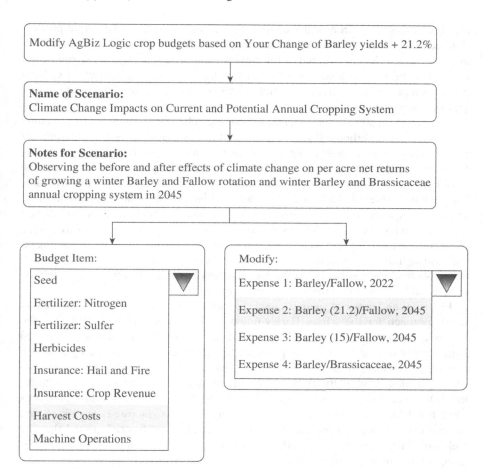

Modify AgBiz Logic crop budgets based on Your Change of Barley yields + 21.2%

Name of Scenario:
Climate Change Impacts on Current and Potential Annual Cropping System

Notes for Scenario:
Observing the before and after effects of climate change on per acre net returns
of growing a winter Barley and Fallow rotation and winter Barley and Brassicaceae
annual cropping system in 2045

Budget Item:

Seed

Fertilizer: Nitrogen

Fertilizer: Sulfer

Herbicides

Insurance: Hail and Fire

Insurance: Crop Revenue

Harvest Costs

Machine Operations

Modify:

Expense 1: Barley/Fallow, 2022

Expense 2: Barley (21.2)/Fallow, 2045

Expense 3: Barley (15)/Fallow, 2045

Expense 4: Barley/Brassicaceae, 2045

FIGURE 11.9 By adjusting 2015 harvest budgets obtain 2045 output.

11.3.5 ASSESSING ENVIRONMENTAL IMPACTS

Assuming farmers maximize net returns over time, AgBiz Logic modules track the difference between revenue and cash costs. This represents the static short-run net returns. Some examples of how a producer could classify their earnings are soil carbon, environmentally friendly production, environmental impact, and other sustainability and risk-management factors.

Whether environmental effect is considered an input or an output influences which of several approaches the AgBiz Environment module represents. Growers' bottom lines are influenced by "natural capital," which includes factors like environmental/land quality (such the quality of their soil). One of the byproducts of this industrial approach is improved ecological conditions. Way (2022) outlines three methods for maximising profits while considering environmental concerns at the corporate level. The first is the standard method, where adjustments to natural capital variables reflect changes in environmental quality; the second is the multiple output production method, where adjustments to environmental characteristics are best reflected; and the third is the constrained profit maximization method, where environmental regulations limit both choice and production volume. Environmental outcomes from production procedures and/or potential effects on producers' net returns are necessary for each of these strategies.

In order to measure environmental effects such changes in greenhouse gas emissions, soil erosion, carbon soil sequestration, and energy usage, the AgBiz Environment module may employ preexisting environmental models or calculators to do so. Extensive examples of such tools include the COMET-GHG farm inventory system, the Cool Farm Tool for estimating GHG emissions, and the Universal Soil Loss Equation. The outputs of these models and calculators can be used as either production inputs or (desired or undesirable) final products. Soil erosion, pesticide use, and soil carbon are all examples of inputs; while greenhouse gas emissions and soil carbon credits are more commonly thought of as outputs, soil carbon can also be an input depending on the context. Table 11.4 provides a brief summary of the several environmental modelling tools made accessible by AgBiz Environment and describes how they might be used to aid farmers in making well-informed decisions.

Financial and material savings connected with adopting a conservation management approach for the winter Barley-fallow cycle were calculated employing the AgBiz Environment module and its related environmental calculations. We used AgBiz Profit data to estimate the potential financial benefits of switching to no-till farming for farmers in the mid-Columbia (a more conservation-focused, water-conserving management method). No-till farming reduces labour and material requirements because it requires no tilling before or after harvest. No-till farming requires more herbicide use than conventional farming methods, as weeds are air-seeded rather than dug out and buried. A meta-analysis of scientific trials found that the yields of Barley grown using both systems were nearly the same in this microregion, coming in at around 63 bu./ac. Its yield is greater than the previous example's 49.5 bu./ac, which was calculated using data from the Ag Census in 2007. As the greater yields from the research trials are more typical of the conditions in this microregion, we chose to incorporate them into the AgBiz Environment (Table 11.4).

Cost differences between the two systems account for the difference in net returns in the baseline state, where yields and revenues are assumed to be similar. For this baseline scenario, conventional tillage's yield advantage would need to be around 6–7 bu./ac bigger than no-till for net returns to be equal, or no-net till's returns would

TABLE 11.4
The AgBiz Environment Toolkit Synopsis

Tool	Environmental Parameter
USLE	Soil Erosion
CFT	GAS emissions/Carbon Confiscation
EIQ value	Pesticides
COMET-farm	GAS emissions/Carbon Confiscation

be higher by roughly ₹2,374/ ac. If no-till farming is so beneficial, why isn't it being used by more farmers? It's possible that balancing danger with knowledge is the key. AgBizProfit does not currently include risk analysis in regard to managerial experience. Potential greenhouse gas emissions and soil erosion are further causing for worry.

Estimating shifts in soil erosion using the USLE. According to our preliminary findings, no-till increases soil carbon by 0.2 ton/year/ac compared to regular tillage. Since COMET-Farm does not account for variations in energy consumption, the results do not consider the resulting increases or decreases in carbon dioxide emissions. Based on climatic and soil models, COMET-Farm solely takes into consideration the levels of nitrous oxide and soil carbon activity. Normal tillage can cause an average of 5.19 tonnes of soil to be lost per acre per year, while no-till practices only lose about 1.04 tonnes of soil per acre per year due to erosion. Consequently, no-till is more eco-friendly than traditional tillage in these two regards.

This farm has Walla Walla silt loam soil, and its long-term mean soil loss with traditional tillage is 5.21 tons/ac/year, which is more than the 5.0-ton/ac/year criterion for maintaining productivity. That traditional tillage farms can maintain yields that are competitive with no-till farms, which is seriously called into question. The discrepancy between the two systems' yields is likely to expand over time if farmers adopt a multi-year net returns model instead of a no-till method.

This case study offers a methodology for assessing the relative merits of alternative management strategies, and it establishes the foundation for tracking shifts in soil carbon or other environmental results that can inform carbon accounting policies. Future studies should focus on integrating the economic and financial modules with AgBiz Climate and AgBiz Environment to create a fully integrated decision-support framework for producers, considering the effects of both on yield projections and environmental results.

11.4   LINKING TO THE TRADEOFF ANALYSIS MODEL FOR MULTI-DIMENSIONAL IMPACT ASSESSMENT (TOA-MD) PLATFORM FOR LANDSCAPE-SCALE TRADEOFF ANALYSIS

This section provides a brief overview of how the TOA-MD framework can be used to combine data from individual farms that have used software like AgBiz Logic to gather data with data from larger geographic areas in order to assist policy research at the regional level (tradeoff analysis model for multi-dimensional impact assessment – TOA-MD). This brief study provides an overview of the TOA-MD model and explores the information it requires, as well as the ways in which AgBiz Logic information could provide support. Authors read for a more in-depth explanation of how the TOA-MD model can be used to analyse climate-aware agriculture and for a specific case study.

To simulate how global warming and other environmental factors might affect a group of farms, the TOA-MD model was developed. The TOA-MD framework, which depends on the spreading of projected economical returns across the area agricultural population, can help farmers or growers decide whether to stick with the current production method (winter Barley fallow) or transition to a different system (annual cropping; winter Barley Brassicaceae).

TOA-MD is able to simulate a regional adoption rate because, unlike AgBiz Logic, it is not based on a single farm or a "representative" farm, but rather on a population of farms. TOA-MD uses data collected from the farming community to inform its recommendations. Statistics about the population, such as means, standard deviations, and correlation coefficients between the economic parameters in the models and the associated result changeable of interest, are among the most fundamental factors. These statistical characteristics can be estimated using a combination of observational data from a current production system and experimental, modelled, or expert data from a novel system that has not yet been deployed and is therefore not observable provided that sufficient biophysical and economic data is available.

Agricultural decision-makers must study the interplay between the consequences of adopting a new technology and the underlying biophysical and economic variables in order to assess the regional implications of adopting the technology. It is essential for the TOA-MD study that accurate projections of the impact of the new "technology" on agricultural production and profitability be made. There are several possible places to find such information, including formal crop and livestock simulation models, experimental or observational data, and expert assessment.

"Adoption-based tradeoffs" are a useful use of the TOA-MD model. When the pace at which a technology is adopted shifts in response to a financial incentive or some other element influencing adoption, we say that this shift is based on adoption. Take, for example, the scenario where farmers are offered a contract to absorb carbon from the atmosphere in order to reduce greenhouse gas emissions. A classic case of a compromise necessitated by widespread adoption. In this form of research, farmers' input and output costs are held constant, allowing us to isolate the effect of the incentive to shift management practices that boost soil carbon accumulation on their observed behaviour. Long-term climatic shifts can also spur adoption.

11.5 INFORMATION NEEDED FOR THE TOA-MD MODEL AND IT INTERACTS WITH AGRICULTURAL DECISION-MAKING SOFTWARE

The TOA-MD model takes as inputs the means, standard deviations, and correlations of outcomes of interest and economic returns from various production systems. Use a sizable sample of agriculture, and gather data over an extended enough time duration to statistically reason for seasonal volatility and further parameters that may have affected the reported findings. These categories serve as useful data subsets:

1. costs, yields, and production costs for all manufacturing processes;
2. factors such as farm size, family size, and revenue from sources other than agriculture;
3. in addition to any other social or environmental results.

The standard method of collecting statistics on agricultural output is through periodic government surveys. These forms of information have some restrictions. The first is that researchers typically have to wait a long time to access these data because they are only collected at irregular intervals (for example, in India, agricultural census is conducted every five years) and then released. The lack of granularity in these data is a significant drawback, especially when it comes to making managerial decisions about things like fertiliser and chemical application, gear use, and agricultural labour. The third drawback is the high cost of conducting such surveys, both for the people being surveyed (to complete lengthy, detailed questionnaires) and the entities interested in the results.

Integration of AgBiz Logic into the TOA-MD framework presents a number of challenges. The first stage in conducting a landscape size research is recruiting a representative sample of farms to use AgBiz Logic and contribute data for analysis. To do so, we'd need to choose a subset of farms using a method similar to that used in a census of agricultural output. The second step in estimating TOA-MD parameters without violating farmers' privacy would be to create software that facilitates communication and compiles data from individual farms into a database. Keep in mind that in most instances, data would need to be gathered over the course of numerous growing seasons, so that crop rotations and other variables in the farming system may be considered. Household characteristics of farmers could be gathered either as part of AgBiz Logic or with a different survey tool. It would be necessary to collect data on environmental and social outcomes in a way that is specific to the type of variable of interest. Samples of soil might be taken in the field and analysed in the lab to determine the amount of organic matter present; this could be done in conjunction with modelling or the application of specialized sensors.

Extrapolating from current biophysical and socio-economic variables allows for future forecasting. This is currently being done on a global scale using two novel scenario concepts: representative concentration pathways and shared socio-economic pathways. To translate these hypothetical future pathways into ones with the additional detail required for agricultural evaluations, "representative agricultural pathways" are now being built. These estimations, together with data gathered via technologies like AgBiz Logic, can now be used in regional integrated evaluations thanks to new approaches developed as part of the Agricultural Model Intercomparison and Improvement Project.

11.6 CONCLUSIONS

Farmers can benefit from using AgBiz Logic and other decision support systems to learn more about the relative effect of adjusting to a change, whether that change is in the form of future climatic circumstances, future policy, pricing, and cost shifts, or future lease terms. Researchers can use it to learn how producers' decisions on new programmes, management options, technology, and varieties affect their bottom lines and lead them to embrace either conventional or sustainable farming methods. These decision-making instruments are useful for assessing climate-smart solutions at the farm level because they consider the effects of climate change and the environment.

AgBiz Logic is one such solution that can help improve and update data on landscape-scale and regional technology evaluation. By linking farm management software to a trusted database, a data system can offer time series insights into management decisions to a statistically illustrative "panel" of agricultural decision-makers. Furthermore, the implementation of analyses employing a technology like TOA-MD necessitates a higher level of specificity than what AgBiz Logic's usage of precise management data would provide. Inputting accurate information into AgBiz

Logic is in everyone's best interest, as it will be used to inform future management decisions. Finally, with the help of programmes like AgBiz Logic, farmers have an easy way to enter data rapidly, saving them time and money.

REFERENCES

1. A. Ghahramani and A. D. Moore, "Impact of climate changes on existing crop-livestock farming systems," *Agric. Syst.*, vol. 146, pp. 142–155, 2016. doi: 10.1016/j.agsy.2016.05.011
2. A. Baig *et al.*, "Dietary habits of lesser bandicoot rat (Bandicota Bengalensis) in an agro-ecosystem, Pothwar Plateau, Pakistan," *Brazilian J. Biol.*, vol. 84, 2024. doi: 10.1590/1519-6984.251410
3. X. Xu and B. Mola-Yudego, "Where and when are plantations established? Land-use replacement patterns of fast-growing plantations on agricultural land," *Biomass Bioenergy*, vol. 144, 2021. doi: 10.1016/j.biombioe.2020.105921
4. P. Cottney, L. Black, E. White, and P. N. Williams, "The correct cover crop species integrated with slurry can increase biomass, quality and nitrogen cycling to positively affect yields in a subsequent spring barley rotation," *Agronomy*, vol. 10, no. 11, 2020. doi: 10.3390/agronomy10111760
5. S. Spatari *et al.*, "The role of biorefinery co-products, market proximity and feedstock environmental footprint in meeting biofuel policy goals for winter barley-to-ethanol," *Energies*, vol. 13, no. 9, 2020. doi: 10.3390/en13092236
6. D. Nilsson, H. Rosenqvist, and S. Bernesson, "Profitability of the production of energy grasses on marginal agricultural land in Sweden," *Biomass Bioenergy*, vol. 83, pp. 159–168, 2015. doi: 10.1016/j.biombioe.2015.09.007
7. A. Bomanowska, A. Rzetelska, and A. Rewicz, "Morphological variation of Bromus Hordeaceus subsp. Hordeaceus (Poaceae) in varied agricultural habitats," *Fragm. Florist. Geobot. Pol.*, vol. 20, no. 2, pp. 185–198, 2013, [Online]. Available: https://www.scopus.com/inward/record.uri?eid=2-s2.0-84893633067&partnerID=40&md5=b44a0932f56ea430185c6e7a976f5d20
8. J. J. Koritschoner, J. I. Whitworth Hulse, A. Cuchietti, and E. M. Arrieta, "Spatial patterns of nutrients balance of major crops in Argentina," *Sci. Total Environ.*, vol. 858, 2023. doi: 10.1016/j.scitotenv.2022.159863
9. A. Kosolapova, V. Yamaltdinova, E. Mitrofanova, D. Fomin, and I. Teterlev, "Biological activity of soil depending on fertilizer systems," *Bulg. J. Agric. Sci.*, vol. 22, no. 6, pp. 921–926, 2016, [Online]. Available: https://www.scopus.com/inward/record.uri?eid=2-s2.0-85006997566&partnerID=40&md5=fa8ae7eed1487eb6d47e73a4601d88b3
10. I.-K. Hong, H.-K. Yun, Y. Chae, S.-M. Lee, Y.-B. Jung, and M.-R. Lee, "A study on the utilization of urban garden design derived from the traditional farming method Gyeonjongbeop from the Joseon period: Focused on Imwongyeongjeji Bolliji," *J. People, Plants, Environ*, vol. 23, no. 4, pp. 423–432, 2020. doi: 10.11628/ksppe.2020.23.4.423
11. J. Liu, R. L. Desjardins, S. Wang, D. E. Worth, B. Qian, and J. Shang, "Climate impact from agricultural management practices in the Canadian Prairies: Carbon equivalence due to albedo change," *J. Environ. Manage.*, vol. 302, 2022. doi: 10.1016/j.jenvman.2021.113938
12. V. G. Ambrosini *et al.*, "Effect of diversified cropping systems on crop yield, legacy, and budget of potassium in a subtropical Oxisol," *F. Crop. Res.*, vol. 275, 2022. doi: 10.1016/j.fcr.2021.108342
13. H. H. Lee *et al.*, "Mitigation of global warming potential and greenhouse gas intensity in arable soil with green manure as source of nitrogen," *Environ. Pollut.*, vol. 288, 2021. doi: 10.1016/j.envpol.2021.117724
14. S. K. Motarjemi, A. E. Rosenbom, B. V. Iversen, and F. Plauborg, "Important factors when simulating the water and nitrogen balance in a tile-drained agricultural field under long-term monitoring," *Sci. Total Environ.*, vol. 787, 2021. doi: 10.1016/j.scitotenv.2021.147610

15. V. A. Lavrinova and T. S. Polunina, "Effect of combined treatments and chemicalization agents on soil mycobiota in spring barley crops," *E3S Web Conf.*, vol. 254, 2021. doi: 10.1051/e3sconf/202125405005

16. R. A. Wieme, J. P. Reganold, D. W. Crowder, K. M. Murphy, and L. A. Carpenter-Boggs, "Productivity and soil quality of organic forage, quinoa, and grain cropping systems in the dryland Pacific Northwest, USA," *Agric. Ecosyst. Environ.*, vol. 293, 2020. doi: 10.1016/j.agee.2020.106838

17. S. A. Salman, S. Shahid, H. A. Afan, M. S. Shiru, N. Al-Ansari, and Z. M. Yaseen, "Changes in climatic water availability and crop water demand for Iraq region," *Sustainability*, vol. 12, no. 8, 2020. doi: 10.3390/SU12083437

18. R. S. Abbood, "Production of wheat and barley crops in Maysan governorate for the period 2014–2018," *Int. J. Innov. Creat. Chang.*, vol. 12, no. 12, pp. 73–82, 2020, [Online]. Available: https://www.scopus.com/inward/record.uri?eid=2-s2.0-85084456985&partnerID=40&md5=2c42469fe590d34309cc4c64c280d09d

19. R. A. Wieme, L. A. Carpenter-Boggs, D. W. Crowder, K. M. Murphy, and J. P. Reganold, "Agronomic and economic performance of organic forage, quinoa, and grain crop rotations in the Palouse region of the Pacific Northwest, USA," *Agric. Syst.*, vol. 177, 2020. doi: 10.1016/j.agsy.2019.102709

20. M. Nouri and M. Bannayan, "On soil moisture deficit, low precipitation, and temperature extremes impacts on rainfed cereal productions in Iran," *Theor. Appl. Climatol.*, vol. 137, no. 3–4, pp. 2771–2783, 2019. doi: 10.1007/s00704-019-02766-3

21. U. M. Sainju, A. W. Lenssen, B. L. Allen, W. B. Stevens, and J. D. Jabro, "Nitrogen balance in dryland agroecosystem in response to tillage, crop rotation, and cultural practice," *Nutr. Cycl. Agroecosystems*, vol. 110, no. 3, pp. 467–483, 2018. doi: 10.1007/s10705-018-9909-7

22. A. Gobin, "Weather related risks in Belgian arable agriculture," *Agric. Syst.*, vol. 159, pp. 225–236, 2018. doi: 10.1016/j.agsy.2017.06.009

23. F. Kosmowski, J. Stevenson, J. Campbell, A. Ambel, and A. Haile Tsegay, "On the ground or in the air? A methodological experiment on crop residue cover measurement in Ethiopia," *Environ. Manage.*, vol. 60, no. 4, pp. 705–716, 2017. doi: 10.1007/s00267-017-0898-0

24. S. Oberholzer, V. Prasuhn, and A. Hund, "Crop water use under Swiss pedoclimatic conditions – Evaluation of lysimeter data covering a seven-year period," *F. Crop. Res.*, vol. 211, pp. 48–65, 2017. doi: 10.1016/j.fcr.2017.06.003

25. M. V. Arokiamary and J. Anand, "Analysis of dynamic interference constraints in cognitive radio cloud networks," *Int. J. Adv. Res. Sci. Commun. Technol.*, vol. 6, no. 1, pp. 815–823, 2021.

26. M. Geethalakshmi, J. A. Kanimozhiraman, R. Partheepan, and S. Santhosh, "Optimal routing path using trident form in wearable biomedical wireless sensor networks," *Turkish Online J. Qual. Inq.*, vol. 12, no. 7, pp. 5134–5143, 2021.

27. D. L. Liu, K. T. Zeleke, B. Wang, I. Macadam, F. Scott, and R. J. Martin, "Crop residue incorporation can mitigate negative climate change impacts on crop yield and improve water use efficiency in a semiarid environment," *Eur. J. Agron.*, vol. 85, pp. 51–68, 2017. doi: 10.1016/j.eja.2017.02.004

28. P. Thiebeau and E. S. Recous, "Crop residues decomposition dynamics in farms practising conservation agriculture in the Grand Est region, France," *Cah. Agric*, vol. 26, no. 6, 2017. doi: 10.1051/cagri/2017050

29. A. Marczuk, J. Caban, P. Savinykh, N. Turubanov, and D. Zyryanov, "Maintenance research of a horizontal ribbon mixer," *Eksploat. i Niezawodn.*, vol. 19, no. 1, pp. 121–125, 2017. doi: 10.17531/ein.2017.1.17

30. K. Jones *et al.*, "Evidence supports the potential for climate-smart agriculture in Tanzania," *Glob. Food Sec.*, vol. 36, 2023. doi: 10.1016/j.gfs.2022.100666

31. Y. Sun, E. Nurellari, W. Ding, L. Shu, and Z. Huo, "A partition-based mobile -crowdsensing-enabled task allocation for solar insecticidal lamp internet of things maintenance," *IEEE Internet Things J.*, vol. 9, no. 20, pp. 20547–20560, 2022. doi: 10.1109/JIOT.2022.3175732

32. J. Sun, D. Gong, K. Yao, B. Lu, C. Dai, and X. Wu, "Real-time semantic segmentation method for field grapes based on channel feature pyramid," *Nongye Gongcheng Xuebao/ Transactions Chinese Soc. Agric. Eng.*, vol. 38, no. 17, pp. 150–157, 2022. doi: 10.11975/ j.issn.1002-6819.2022.17.016

33. B. Wen, R. Cao, Q. Yang, J. Zhang, H. Zhu, and Z. Li, "Detecting leaf disease for Panax notoginseng using an improved YOLOv3 algorithm," *Nongye Gongcheng Xuebao/ Transactions Chinese Soc. Agric. Eng.*, vol. 38, no. 3, pp. 164–172, 2022. doi: 10.11975/ j.issn.1002-6819.2022.03.019

34. M. Devkota, Y. Singh, Y. A. Yigezu, I. Bashour, R. Mussadek, and R. Mrabet, "Conservation agriculture in the drylands of the middle East and North Africa (MENA) region: Past trend, current opportunities, challenges and future outlook," *Adv. Agron.*, vol. 172, pp. 253–305, 2022. doi: 0

35. P. N. Koundinya, N. T. Sanjukumar, and P. Rajalakshmi, "A comparative analysis of algorithms for pedestrian tracking using drone vision," in *2021 IEEE 4th International Conference on Computing, Power and Communication Technologies, GUCON 2021*, 2021. doi: 10.1109/GUCON50781.2021.9573995

36. S. Krug, S. Miethe, and T. Hutschenreuther, "Comparing BLE and NB-IoT as communication options for smart viticulture IoT applications," in *2021 IEEE Sensors Applications Symposium, SAS 2021 - Proceedings*, 2021. doi: 10.1109/SAS51076.2021.9530069

37. S. Niranjana, S. K. Hareshaa, I. Basker, and J. Anand, "Smart monitoring system for asthma patients," *Int. J. Electron. Commun. Eng.*, vol. 7, no. 5, pp. 5–9, 2020.

38. A. Ponmalar, P. Saravanan, S. Deeba, and B. R. Jyothi, "IoT enabled inexhaustible E-vehicle using transparent solar panel," in *2022 International Conference on Communication, Computing and Internet of Things (IC3IoT)*, 2022, pp. 1–5.

39. M. Geethalakshmi, J. Venkatesh, R. U. Mageswari, A. Mahalakshmi, J. Anand, and R. Partheepan, "Fuzzy based route optimization in wearable biomedical wireless sensor network," in *AIP Conference Proceedings*, 2023, vol. 2523, no. 1, p. 20156.

40. B. Chatterjee *et al.*, "Context-aware collaborative intelligence with spatio-temporal in-sensor-analytics for efficient communication in a large-area IoT testbed," *IEEE Internet Things J.*, vol. 8, no. 8, pp. 6800–6814, 2021. doi: 10.1109/JIOT.2020.3036087

41. R. J. O. Ogola and K. O. Ouko, "Expert's opinion on Irish potato farmers awareness and preferences towards climate smart agriculture practices attributes in Kenya; A conjoint analysis," *Cogent Food Agric.*, vol. 7, no. 1, 2021. doi: 10.1080/23311932.2021.1968163

42. B. Quete *et al.*, "Understanding the tradeoffs of LoRaWAN for IoT-based Smart Irrigation," in *2020 IEEE International Workshop on Metrology for Agriculture and Forestry, MetroAgriFor 2020 - Proceedings*, 2020, pp. 73–77. doi: 10.1109/ MetroAgriFor50201.2020.9277566

43. E. M. Kenny *et al.*, "Bayesian case-exclusion and personalized explanations for sustainable dairy farming (extended abstract)," in *IJCAI International Joint Conference on Artificial Intelligence*, 2020, vol. 2021-Janua, pp. 4740–4744. [Online]. Available: https:// www.scopus.com/inward/record.uri?eid=2-s2.0-85097344843&partnerID=40&md5= cf2f86fd145e98f25410d538f6aace38

44. J. Lewis and J. Rudnick, "The policy enabling environment for climate smart agriculture: A case study of California," *Front. Sustain. Food Syst.*, vol. 3, 2019. doi: 10.3389/fsufs. 2019.00031

45. E. M. Kenny *et al.*, "Predicting grass growth for sustainable dairy farming: A CBR system using bayesian case-exclusion and post-hoc, personalized explanation-by-example (XAI)", *Lecture Notes in Computer Science (Including Subseries Lecture Notes in Artificial Intelligence and Lecture Notes in Bioinformatics)*, vol. 11680 LNAI. pp. 172–187, 2019. doi: 10.1007/978-3-030-29249-2_12

12 Broad Framework of Digital Twins in Agricultural Domain

S. Muthukaruppasamy, G. Arun Sampaul Thomas,
J. Nandha Gopal, S. Ravindra, and K. Saravanan

12.1 INTRODUCTION

Agriculture performs a significant part in the growth of several nations and is crucial to reaching Endurable Progress Goal 2 of "Zero Hunger" [1]. The Food and Agriculture Organization (FAO) forecasts that agronomic yield should upsurge by 41% between 2011 and 2051 to meet the demands of a populace that is expected to reach 10 billion people by 2051 [2]. One tactic for increasing output is the inventive application of technologies, like drones, apps, and machines, along with utilitarian revolutions and public support. Agriculture uses 70% of the fresh water that people use worldwide [3]. This provides compelling evidence in favour of the advancement of technology like the internet of things (IoT) that would enable farms to produce more food while using less water. The bulk of garden-fresh water in marine terrain is used via irrigation structures, and 40% of the fresh water used in emerging states is lost owing to leaks and over-irrigation [4]. Since insufficient or excessive watering affects crop productivity, field sensors must control irrigation in agriculture effectively [5, 6]. By gathering data on the state of the plant and scaling it with elevated function and cost-effectiveness, maintaining vintage at regular standards, minimizing water waste, and finally improving the availability of filtered aquatic, artificial intelligence (AI) can enhance agrobusiness development in this environment [7]. To capitalize on this global issue, farms can use a digital twin (DT) prototype based on the IoT to effectively recognize their existing surroundings. This implies that a computer-generated illustration of a grange should be proficient enough to act in accordance with the analysis and decisions made by the system as well as acquire data from the farm. The main progress of a DT for smart agriculture that uses the IoT in an irrigation system depends on agriculturalist and/or AI decisions.

Digital farming techniques can stipulate agriculturalists with beneficial knowledge on a variety of topics, including (i) how to use irrigation administration policies, seeds, fertilizers, and chemicals; (ii) how to protect the environment; (iii) how to manage weather, crop scrutiny, and irritants; (iv) and how to meet consumer demands and deal with business conditions [8]. However, due to their complexity and dynamic nature, agricultural production systems require sophisticated management. It is projected that digitalization initiatives will improve decision-making support, monitoring, and data analysis and optimization capabilities. To improve the proficiency of these systems,

DOI: 10.1201/9781003391302-12

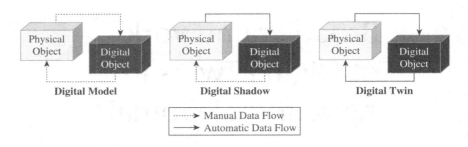

FIGURE 12.1 Depiction of Digital Twin Concept.

the "digital twin," a novel idea, consumes projected and applied in digital farming. NASA was the first organization to offer a simulated or digital depiction of corporeal organizations that replicates the behaviour of the original structure [9, 10]. As shown in Figure 12.1, the components of the DT can be seen by a network of linkages connecting both actual and virtual objects [11]. The physical coordination or physical planet in farming, which is a multifaceted and self-motivated environment, comprises essential information and characteristics of the object or tool, including its substantiality, living entities, shape, locality, and chiller [12]. A crucial component is the physical system; a DT without a physical world is only a prototypical, and a DT's system limits are established using the factual physical world [13].

The physical system might consist of a complete thing or only a single component that is dispersed over physical space. In agriculture, the physical world can include workers as well as people, robots, and agricultural equipment, including tractors, harvesters, and fertilizers. A crop with variable irrigation environments, weather, and mud or an animal with its unique structures, feeding schedules, and population of animals are other examples of such things [14]. A full entity (such as a finished machine), a component portion, or a single asset connected to other things can all be part of the physical universe. A component of the irrigation environments, weather, mud, or the figure of an animal might all be considered physical systems in an agricultural environment. To gather and obtain data from tangible things, the physical world requires sensors and measurement technology. A few instances of DTs in shrewd farming are the food supply chain, mud and climate radars for crops, Bayer sensors for ammonia water, moistness, and warmth, the GPS (Global Positioning System), and kinematic-global course-plotting protectorate for monitoring farming robots. The interaction between the real and virtual worlds is made possible by the DT that was created. This module enables data exchange amid computer-generated and corporeal structures. It analyses the information gleaned from the physical system, changes the state of the virtual system, and relays feedback from the virtual system to the physical system. According to the source, kind, and volume of the data, the rate and speed of data transfer, as well as the shortest practical delay between data collection and feedbacks, the connection components can be changed.

DTs of agricultural concepts have been linked between the real and virtual worlds using wireless and IoT technologies [15]. In a virtual system, models and data from the real world are exemplified. The virtual world also includes elements like

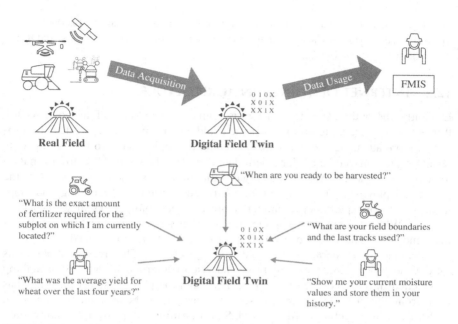

FIGURE 12.2   An illustrative picture of the agricultural digital twin system.

software, machine learning, data mining, AI models, and various modelling and processing techniques. To aid in management and give the physical structure feedback, several researchers have suggested employing AI techniques for data processing and analytics. The simulated twin may mimic and control the antedate matters, augment a progression, and provide actual structures that aren't yet obvious in the actual system. For instance, the presentation level of a DT stipulates that farmers have cloud dashboards for tracking weed growth, crop development, and expected yield in real time. A graphic of the DT notion in farming is exposed in Figure 12.2.

DT technologies can help farmers by continually monitoring the farming land and apprising them of the condition of the virtual world as the next stage of the digitization paradigm. Managers of agricultural farms have benefited from using digital technology by increasing productivity, production, and lowering losses. As the next stage of digitalization in the agricultural industry, there are various sorts of digital farming paradigms that can be applied to DT notions. The findings of this study demonstrate that research has not yet fully used DT principles in agricultural and food process mechanisms. Different levels of digital farming present different research opportunities and challenges. DT concepts can be effective in the agricultural area for soil and irrigation, plants, robotic systems, agricultural inputs, and food production. In this regard, the majority of reviews have concentrated on the creation of DTs by taking a few specific agricultural sectors into consideration. It might assist farmers in reducing the economic strain on the agricultural industry and labour concerns, and it might assist policymakers in their efforts to enhance the agricultural industry for the benefit of environmental and food security. Additionally, it makes it easier for academics to investigate ways to manage and monitor agricultural and post-harvest products, farm machinery, and crop yields, as well as ways to cut back on water, pesticides, and usage of energy in digital farming.

12.2   INTERNET OF THINGS IN AGRICULTURE

Evidently, the outbreak of IoT sensors is segment of making DT feasible. As IoT things are processed, digital-twin scheme could add minimal group of devices, providing more advantages to farmers. DTs could be implemented to forecast specific results depending on data. Along with data analytics, DTs amend an IoT formation to get good efficiency. Also, it aids organization to analyse the operation before the physical deployment. The majority of IoT-based agricultural technology developments consist of exploratory research that presents technologies in scaled-down pilot projects. When it comes to the application of IoT in agriculture, two kinds of equipment and devices have been developed that are used on farms to collect data about the climate, mud, yield characteristics, and other aspects [16]. The creation of platforms for data storage, organization, analysis, and visualization to aid in decision-making is included in the second category [17]. Although the phrase "smart farming" has been around for a while, a precise description that covers the technologies now used in the agriculture sector is still required. Smart farming comprises integrating intelligence and interaction technology into equipment, device, and radars to incorporate them into the cyber-physical farm administration cycle. [18]. Many technologies are seen to fall under this category, including (AI), Progression Executive, IoT, and big data. Information and Communication Technology (ICT) usage in agriculture is a booming industry with a lot of benefits, despite some remaining challenges.

12.3   SMART AGRICULTURAL-AIDED DIGITAL TWIN

Using technologies like AI, big data, IoT, and data analytics, a DT may connect the details of the farming land and freeholder. Then, it reacts to an autonomous choice created by the system. By giving the idea of smart farming, a DT for a smart farming is provided. A cyber-physical system is used to combine diverse services to figure out the information of a distinct system (i.e., an irrigation system and seeding system) and create a digital smart farm. It integrates several systems and gives agriculturalist a complete awareness condition of their crops. To adapt to environmental changes, the farm could be changed. Smart farming is built on the IoT, which has been used in several analyses of studies [19]. The fabrication progression of the malt firm is mimicked using AI algorithms and a range of malting processing parameters [20]. The prime situations and plans are therefore advised for the greatest consequences. The process culminates in the creation of malt, which contains the most alcohol. Additionally, the machine learning techniques are used to forecast the middling warmth of the jot heap using the environmental data. Analysis of this temperature, a key indication of the condition of the grain, is necessary for the functioning of grain storage.

The usage of cutting-edge resolutions in intricate links to industrial applications is also supported by evidence. AI, cloud computing, augmented reality, the IoT, interface technologies, ingrained technologies, large data processing techniques, data security, and other technologies are all included in DTs [21]. DT is a type of adaptive prototype living or non-living physical system that attempts to build, monitor, and improve the performance of its physical components and provide users with a pragmatic experience [22]. For instance, DT may at any moment be compared to the lifespan of a genuine machine. DT may be used in the product design to improve the physical model and carry out proactive conservation. However, the influence of DT technology on the fields of medication, farming, and health care is still in its infancy. DT expertise is vigorously involved in the development and commercialization of a variety of industrial and aeronautical processes [23]. Numerous factors, such as the mobility of resources (such as cattle), a lack of funding, an unstable environment, ongoing climate change (which affects soil quality), a lack of preparedness to share one's grange information, and a lack of methodological expertise among farmers, to name a few, may contribute to the slow growth of agriculture. The DT model and the IoT technology might be used to connect various resources to offer a more comprehensive perspective. Farmers will get an understanding of various criteria and factors that determine how a farm operates, the final yield that is produced, and the amount of resources that are used. So, farmers can make better decisions and have a smaller impact on the environment and natural resources.

12.3.1 SOILLESS VS. SOIL-BASED AGRICULTURE

Agricultural practices that increased production in ways that were previously unfeasible were made possible by industrial agriculture. The creation of settings that enable crops to thrive as effectively as possible is aided by biological developments. Due to faulty agricultural methods and overfarming in rural areas, more fertilizer must be used. Soilless agriculture is far superior to soil-based agriculture in many ways [24]. Soil-based agriculture and soilless agriculture differ significantly from one another. The differences are frequently found in the use of irrigation smooth, manure, and the capability to use unusable land, lower labour needs, and higher output. The pollution and environmental harm caused by soil-based agribusiness is another element influencing the emergence of diverse farming techniques, including conservatory or dimness net agrobusiness and vertical agriculture [25]. A land-saving method for farming that is suitable for greenhouses or tight spaces in cities is a vertical farm [26].

Vertical farming combines AI, big data analytics, robots, and the IoT. Erecting agricultural structures must amalgamate various hardware and data, make it easy to analyse data, and offer automated control of the system's installed components. Studies [27] show that vertical farming is not a viable solution for producing huge crops or low-value goods. Due to the installation of controlled-environment buildings, the preservation of current equipment, and other variables, erecting farms requires a significant investment. Researchers are combining various data sources, automating actuator reactions, and improving real-time data collection to create efficient vertical farming technologies. Due to the installation of controlled-environment buildings, the maintenance of existing equipment, and other reasons, vertical farming requires a significant investment [27]. Researchers are combining various data sources, automating actuator reactions, and improving real-time data collection to create efficient vertical farming technologies. A few of the vertical farming technologies that have lately experienced substantial breakthroughs are hydroponics, aeroponics, and aquaponics. Plant roots are immersed in a nutrient elucidation in hydroponics, a method of soilless growing [28]. In an aeroponic structure, the herbal extractions are continually misted with a nutrient solution to keep them alive. This makes it possible for the hanging roots to get enough oxygen through aquaponics and combines aquiculture. Using this mode, hydroponic plants are fed.

12.3.2 Hydroponics

One of the well-liked methods of soilless farming for growing plants indoors that uses less fertilizer and offers better protection from pests and bad weather is hydroponics [29]. High-value veggies can be grown hydroponically better than low-value field crops. When used in conjunction with a controlled environment, such as a greenhouse, hydroponic technology produces produce of the highest quality [30]. Different cool-season vegetables were tested using vegetative and yield metrics in open fields and naturally ventilated polyhouses at farming systems [23]. According to traditional agronomical methods, climatic variations, pests, and diseases have a significant impact on a crop's yield, which leads to low-quality yield. The availability, placement, and method of nutrient solution administration on plant roots are used to categorize the hydroponic approaches. The many hydroponic system types are clearly described in [31]. The resource needs of traditional agriculture and hydroponics have been contrasted by the paper's authors.

The operation of several hydroponic systems, including taper structures, and aquatic civilization is thoroughly detailed in [32]. Crops grown in hydroponic systems were found to produce more continuously throughout the year and require less growing time than crops grown in traditional systems. In hydroponics, the growing medium directs water and nutrients while allowing plenty of oxygen to reach the roots of the plant. Different growing media are effective in various hydroponic system types. The advantages and disadvantages of organic versus inorganic growing material are discussed for aquiculture in terms of managing marine and nutrients [33]. Different benefits of hydroponically cultivated crops over conventionally cultivated yields are examined [34]. While soilless growing methods, like hydroponic systems, are free of soil-borne vermin and syndromes, they can carry some dangers, such as those associated with waterborne infections. In hydroponic systems with recirculating systems, where viruses can accumulate over time, these hazards have more profound impacts. The difficulties with hydroponics also arise from the need for capital investments and knowledge on how to operate the control systems. The many hydroponic fertilizer usage reduction approaches that are described [35] prevent nutrient discharge into the environment.

12.4 DIGITAL TWIN IN CROP CULTIVATION

The adoption of digital devices in crop-making technologies, in particular, farming machines (tractors, fertilizers, and sprayers) plays an important role in enhancing performance by lowering the price of fuel, fertilizer, labour, and other factors that impinge on manufacturing performance and tenability [36]. Farming machinery applications and management regulations have been transformed by digitalization using obtained data and leading-edge data analysis techniques. It enables the function of contemporary manufacturing tools to be improved.

For instance, a digital farm machine can support and assist operation by posting and collecting data through sensing instruments and digital devices to set up the best and most efficient use of appliances, and the technology should enable the programmed function of the machines, according to the European Agricultural Machinery Association [36]. Due to the implementation of cutting-edge IoT technologies, agricultural technology has seen significant changes with the emergence of self-governing systems. The function of farming machines in the adoption of digitized agriculture was assessed in the information of data from sensors placed on self-governing agricultural machinery and uploaded through IoT channels [36, 37]. The data was then examined using data technologies to assist markets, customers, and farmers. In this scenario, farmers may be able to perform tasks more productively and improve the quality of their production by combining digital tools with robots and autonomous machinery [38]. New developments in digital technology enable the use of DT techniques to visualize the status of intelligent farm equipment in real time.

By extracting all data gathered from agriculture machinery, crops, robots, and automation models, IoT, satellite, and drone information, and reap climatic changing condition simulations in the virtual world, the DT of reap production may enable the identification of exotic and invisible issues before they manifest in the real world. Farming things, and crops in particular, require periodic data collection to aid report analysis and decision-making mechanisms [39], which can enhance tenable cultivating standards and lower crop production energy costs. Given this, more work should be done in the future to define and develop frameworks for DT paradigms that are more successful and useful. Even though digital sensors would not be able to capture and monitor every aspect of crop farming, collecting data from several sources can develop the digital depiction of the farm environment and operations [40]. Regular supervision of saplings in DT systems could aid in identifying anomaly from the proper healthiness of the saplings and predict the progress stages to decrease the problems of climatological and atmospheric effects. This is done by simulating dynamic farm conditions, taking into account how climatological and atmospheric conditions affect crop growth, and using data-accelerated models and sensor-interfacing techniques. Various DT concepts may be used in crop farming in the future to recreate the complex actual system in virtual space and use appropriate sensors, data collection systems, modelling, predicting, and simulation paths.

12.5 AGRIFOOD PRODUCTION SYSTEMS AND SUPPLY CHAIN DIGITAL TWINS

DTs modernize cultivation systems in agrifood production, controlling greenhouse gas (GHG), wastages of food, and undernutrition. Although the potentiality of cutting-edge virtual concepts needs to be envisaged, the agrifood manufacturing systems and supply networks are not yet on line to meet the objectives of tenable progress. They fall short of their most basic goal of giving safe and nutritional food to a growing global population, leaving 900 million people undernourished. They fail on numerous other fronts as well as being inefficient and toxic, breaking planetary boundaries. A common solution is transformation through improvements in digital technologies. Such recommendations strongly favour digital technologies, along with embedded systems, intelligent sensors, and AI. Despite its potency and expanding adoption across industrial domains, the potential of DT technology is examined for improving the sustainability of the agrifood sector, specifically through alleviating malnourishment and undernourishment, curtailing GHG exhalation, and averting loss of food.

12.5.1 Benefits of Virtualized Supply Chains and Agricultural Systems

DTs are digital simulations of real-world items. The accuracy and "liveness" of their digital counterparts are guaranteed by the employment of sensors that recognize living and good atmospheric aspects of items in livelihood state. In such cyber-physical designs, adjustments to the actual system alter its virtual duplicate concurrently and repeatedly. In present years, DTs are repurposed to focus on issues like bad climatological and atmospheric issues in challenging natural areas. DTs were first developed as experimental designs for satellites, spacecraft, societal infrastructures, and general civil engineering. By simulating the state of physical systems, advanced modelling approaches can be used to query DTs and identify the optimal behaviour. To recommend the most effective control strategies to the physical equivalent in DTs, reinforcement learning (RL), an area of AI that improvises self-ruling agents to decide solutions in critical systems, can be applied. The present state of a process is used as an input by real-time learning agents to forecast forthcoming action sequences that would optimize the process's performance. Self-governing agents can perform a range of control processes to determine which best coordinates with the control principles before directing the actual system.

12.5.2 Factors That Support and Restrict Virtualized Agrifood Value Chains

"Live" DTs grant extensive methods of computing the ecosystems for the simulation of saplings, plants, reaping machinery, store houses, and distribution of system. For trustworthy digital replication, sufficient scope of sensors and flawless contingency assessment are two prerequisites. To provide the optimum control strategies while using a DT, advanced decision-making systems must contain sensors that are sufficiently predicting the agent's aims. For instance, the DT of farming food storage depot can be used to forecast food wasting when it monitors pertinent factors like heat, food kind, and age of commodity. With significant scope of sensor, the DT could never be a precise representation of the physical system; hence, its state rendition and prospective projections are always speculative. In response, researchers suggest designing DTs by Bayesian methods; yet, it is still challenging to come up with trustworthy methods for managing DT uncertainty and decision-making.

To address these issues, it is crucial to implement DTs that accurately express uncertainty. A similar amount would need to be spent on data infrastructures, such as cloud computing and plant sensors, to create "actual" model of whole inventory chains that include distribution facilities like food store and kitchens in low-income neighbourhoods. It's likely, nevertheless, that firms at the forepart of DT research and advancement would reduce the motive to lay in cyber-physical systems that serve humanitarian and ecological changes, including agro-biodiversity. This might prevent DTs from being used to reform the agrifood sector, especially where it is most required. Second, the model is supported by temporally accurate, low-latency data streams in contemporary DT technologies. When sensors break down or fail to log data for extended periods of time, the design premise of the DT is violated in practice. If agents decide on control actions based on a model that incorporates false information from sensor, uncertain behaviour is likely to occur.

The requirement for technical innovation in the design of DTs that are resilient to periods when sensor is unavailable represents a substantial barrier to increased implementation. Third, modelling flaws can also be caused by mistakes in the design of the model, human coding errors, or a combination of error-free but inconsistent data or procedures. For instance, a minor notational mistake in the code of a computational structure for irrigation system forecasting maintenance could result in ill-cautioned decisions that cause failed crop yields and provide losses. Combining models that were created individually may be difficult due to the lack of general modelling criteria for DTs. For example, if a new item of cooling device is patched into present cold chain that normalize temperature in degrees Celsius but the designer intended it to supervise temperature in degrees Fahrenheit for eliminating obstructions, the food will start to degrade right away. DTs are currently not being widely and significantly deployed in the global food business due to numerous barriers.

12.6 MODERN POST-HARVEST TECHNOLOGY AND DIRECTIONS

In post-harvest activities, a "digital twin" is a computer state of harvested farming commodity based on data obtained from the products. The following components could be included in the DT study for food process mechanisms: (i) information gathered from an actual system (food processing mechanism) through sensors. It monitors the characteristics and variables of the commodities and atmospheric parameters; (ii) information provided by an IoT architecture for sensor contact, data repository, and big data analysis; and (iii) information used as input by a simulation platform for testing and optimization using data from the physical system. To support food process mechanisms by improvising DT architecture, it is essential to have exact information describing the product's production processes, such as labour and equipment, and to produce practical models with all of the current limitations and constraints [41].

12.6.1 DISCUSSION OF GRAIN ELEVATOR FUNCTION

The three main categories of fundamental operations are input, throughput, and output. Grain receipt, also known as input, is the process by which a cargo of grains arrives at the elevator, typically by truck or rail car. The load of the shipment is noted, and samples are obtained to be tested for factors, including humidity state and dockage. If the grain is approved, the truck returns to the weigh station to collect a receipt for the sale. It is also maintained for the elevator's inventory governance. Depending on the outcomes of the grain's laboratory examination, the cargo may require cleaning or drying, both of which elevators frequently perform. After that, the grain is moved about the plant using a variety of conveyance methods before being sent to the right storage bins. Sensors are frequently used in post-harvest storage to keep an eye on the grain's conditions (moisture and temperature) and identify the movement and real inventory inside the elevator. Blending decisions are frequently guided by worker experience or safe-storage requirements, which can assist to forecast the quality variation in the inventory. Before being sold, grain is blended to provide more specialized items for a customer by blending grains with different qualities (grade, protein content, etc.). The process of removing grains from the facilities that have specific, mutually agreed-upon characteristics is known as outcome (among buyer and seller, with principles and terminology given by government). The most common modes of transportation for grain are trucks, train carriages, and boats [42].

12.6.2 MANAGEMENT OF INVENTORIES AND THE SUPPLY CHAIN

The conventional techniques for keeping track of inventories include weight scale tickets and tracking entering/exiting weights. In addition, cables and some volume sensors are available to help elevators to estimate grain heights in bins, but typically, workers will tap the flank of the bin to make a sound to direct the level of grain. Also, they can use a tape to calculate from peak of the bin to the bottom of the grain. These practices are extremely labour-profound, put people in danger, and are also exceedingly inaccurate. Modern elevator inventory management relies mostly on guesswork and is hinged on scale and humidity readings. These measurements are the cornerstone of inventory tracking and it has major ramifications. First, the client will search for a precise grain variety with a definite quality while purchasing grain. Elevators must therefore avoid (i) offering higher quality grain at a lower rate and (ii) having the cargo trashed because the standard is below the established standard.

Grain dockage, or the production of a blend of high- and low-quality grains, is the cause of these problems. The quantity of each ingredient employed determines the features of mixture. While the proportions increased and the amount at which the components extract from each bin are off, the final commodity won't fulfil the proper standard requirements. To get the purity of grain being sold during the blending process, precise sensors will be used to check grain standard and flow rate. To track changes in grain, three types of sensor technologies (flow and identification sensors, bin level sensors) can be used. They can complement one another, each focusing on a different aspect of inventory management, to create a clearer picture of grain functions inside an elevator. They are also designed for bulk solids and liquids, such as grain elevators, which are the focus of most industry research and development. The most general type is bin-level sensors. Laser sensors, acoustic 3D imaging, and non-contact radar are a few examples of commercially available alternatives [43–45]. It has been investigated how well laser sensors can gauge the quantity of grain on surfaces with irregular shapes. It noted issues like field-of-view impediments (particularly while the grain's cone was higher than the eaves), dust in the bin's headspace interfering with operations, and long procedure times that could not be computed. In addition, industry research indicates that the grain silo environment poses difficulties for ultrasonography and remaining non-sensor systems. Mechanical things, like weights and cable devices, named "plumb-bob," could typically give straightforward measurements if the grain surface is even [45, 46]. Studies on the reliability of these cable systems for recording grain inventory have been conducted; reliability was found to be impacted by grain topology, bin diameter variation, and inaccurate bulk density determination. As stated before, bulk sensors compute the size of grain or volume; this should be emphasized. These estimations could not be changed to grain mass since the bulk solid's weight would cause a packing gradient inside the grain silo. Instead, it is necessary to use mathematical models to translate volume and bulk density to mass of grain [47–49].

12.6.3 SENSORS FOR SECURE STORAGE AFTER HARVEST

Grain bins are an intricate ecosystem that requires ongoing monitoring since they have many existent and non-existent elements that can interact to alter the situation so that grain is secured [50]. It is possible to monitor certain ecological traits to tell whether a grain bin is going to spoil. The majority of heat and relative humidity sensors can be found within grain bins, installed at consistently separate "nodes" in the cord that swing downward from the grain bin's apex. These sensors may provide information on the grain's temperature and moisture content [51, 52]. Another typical sensor that checks the heat and moisture of the air present in the aeration is a weather station, which can be used with cord for drying system automation [53, 54]. Grain breathes while being kept in a bin. Insect or mould damage may be indicated by fluctuations in CO_2 levels above normal respiration, according to several CO_2 sensors that have been created [55]. Bug traps are another device that could identify bugs by automated counting. The aforementioned detectors are still the ones that are most frequently used in industry, despite the fact that there are now marketable electromagnetic imaging devices [56, 57] that exhibit tremendous potential for inventory control and 3D moisture detection. The grain quality sensors under development consist of (i) fibre optic temperature and humidity sensors for spoilage detection and laser sensors to evaluate the risk of dust explosions [58–62]; (ii) hyperspectral imaging and machine vision to detect foreign objects, disease symptoms, or fungi; (iii) nano sensors to locate and determine the cause of the rotting; and (iv) PID controllers for dryer systems that are AI-optimized.

12.7 CONCLUSION

Digital technology aids agriculture by enhancing productivity, production, and reducing losses. There are numerous digital farming paradigms that might be used to digitally twin ideas as the next level of digitization in the agricultural sector. The outcome of this study depicts that DT ideas have not yet been fully applied in agricultural and food processing studies. Different facets of digital farming offer various problems and opportunities for research. DT paradigms are applicable to soil and irrigation, crop, robotics and agricultural machinery, and post-harvest food processing in the farming sector. In this regard, the majority of studies concentrate on the advancement of DTs by taking into account a few particular agricultural areas. Modern technology, including AI, complex statistical and optimization methods, big data analysis, and dimensional simulators, creates new ideas for the advancement of agriculture management. Using continuous and real-time data on agricultural resources, digital models can forecast and resolve unforeseen chaos on the farm land. It might help farmers lessen the financial burden on the agricultural sector and labour issues, and it might comfort policymakers to improve the agricultural sector for the sake of the environment and food security. It also makes it simpler for academics to research ways to control and keep track of farm equipment, crop yields, and agricultural and post-harvest products. It also enables them to look at ways to reduce the use of water, pesticides, and energy in digital farming. Advancement of DT systems is essential for monitoring, recording, and analysing the data to forecast and execute the pertinent solution for digital farming management.

REFERENCES

1. United Nations, "Goal 2: Zero Hunger," [Online] Available: https://www.un.org/sustainabledevelopment/hunger/
2. Food and Agriculture Organization of the United Nations, The State of Food and Agriculture: Leveraging Food Systems for Inclusive Rural Transformation, 2017, vol. 2, no. 7929. [Online]. Available: http://www.fao.org/
3. United Nations, "AQUASTAT," 2016. [Online]. Available: https://www.fao.org/aquastat/en/
4. J. Panchard, S. Rao, T.V. Prabhakar, J. Hubaux and H. Jamadagni, "Common sense net: A wireless sensor network for resource-poor agriculture in the semi-arid areas of developing countries," Inf. Technol. Int. Dev., vol. 4, pp. 51–67, 2007.
5. A.C. Charles, A.A. Namen and P.P.G.W. Rodrigues, "Comparison of data mining models applied to a surface meteorological station," Rbrh, vol. 22, pp. 1–9, 2017.
6. S. Mohammed, A. Elbeltagi, B. Bashir, K. Alsafadi, F. Alsilibe, A. Alsalman, M. Zeraatpisheh, A. Széles and E. Harsányi, "A comparative analysis of data mining techniques for agricultural and hydrological drought prediction in the eastern Mediterranean," April 2022, https://doi.org/10.1016/j.compag.2022.106925
7. F.A. Ward and M. Pulido-Velazquez, "Water conservation in irrigation can increase water use," Proc. Natl. Acad. Sci. U.S.A., vol. 105, no. 47, pp. 18215–18220, 2008.
8. N. Chergui, M.-T. Kechadi and M. McDonnell, "The Impact of Data Analytics in Digital Agriculture: A Review," In Proceedings of the 2020 International Multi-Conference on: Organization of Knowledge and Advanced Technologies (OCTA), Tunis, Tunisia, 6–8 February 2020, pp. 1–13.
9. M. Grieves and Vickers, "Mitigating unpredictable, undesirable emergent behaviour in complex systems," in Transdisciplinary Perspectives on Complex Systems, Springer, Cham, Switzerland, 2017, pp. 85–113.
10. E. Negri, L. Fumagalli and M. Macchi, "Review of the roles of digital twin in CPS-based production systems," Procedia Manuf., vol. 11, pp. 939–948, 2017.
11. Y. Liu, L. Zhang, Y. Yang, L. Zhou, L. Ren, F. Wang, R. Liu, Z. Pang, M.J. Deen, "A novel cloud-based framework for the elderly healthcare services using digital twin," IEEE Access, vol. 7, pp. 49088–49101, 2019.
12. M.G. Juarez, V.J. Botti and A.S. Giret, "Digital twins: Review and challenges," J. Comput. Inf. Sci. Eng., vol. 21, p. 030802, 2021.
13. J. Lu, X. Zheng, L. Schweiger and D. Kiritsis, "A cognitive approach to manage the complexity of digital twin systems," Springer, Cham, Switzerland, 2021.
14. S. Neethirajan and B. Kemp, "Digital twins in livestock farming," Animals, vol. 11, p. 1008, 2021.

15. S.K. Jo, D.H. Park and S.H. Kim, "Smart livestock farms using digital twin: Feasibility study," In Proceedings of the 2018 International Conference on Information and Communication Technology Convergence (ICTC), Jeju Island, Korea, 17–19 October 2018, pp. 1461–1463.
16. R.R. Agale, "Automated Irrigation and Crop Security System inAgriculture using Internet of Things," 2017 International Conference on Computing, Communication, Control and Automation (ICCUBEA), pp. 1–5, 2017.
17. S.V. Suakanto, J. Engel, M. Hutagalung and D. Angela, "Sensor Networks Data Acquisition and Task Management for Decision Support of Smart Farming," 2016 International Conference on Information Technology Systems and Innovation, ICITSI 2016 - Proceedings, 2017.
18. S. Wolfert, L. Ge, C. Verdouw and M.J. Bogaardt, "Big data in smart farming – A review," Agric. Syst., vol. 153, pp. 69–80, 2017.
19. M. Ayaz, M. Uddin, Z. Sharif, A. Mansour and E.M. Aggoune, "Internet-of-things (IoT)-based smart agriculture: Toward making the fields talk," in IEEE Access, vol. 7, pp. 129551–129583, 2019.
20. R Dolci, "IoT Solutions for Precision Farming and Food Manufacturing: Artificial Intelligence Applications in Digital Food," 2017 IEEE 41st COMPSAC, Turin, 2017, pp. 384–385.
21. Qi Qinglin, "Enabling technologies and tools for digital twin," J. Manuf. Syst., pp. 1–18, March 2021. 10.1016/j.jmsy.2019.10.001
22. B.R. Barricelli, E. Casiraghi, D. Fogli, "A survey on digital twin: Definitions, characteristics, applications, and design implications," in IEEE Access, vol. 7, pp. 167653–167671, 2019.
23. B. Sam and S. Regeena, "Comparative performance evaluation of cool season vegetables under poly house structure and in open field," IJERD, vol. 11, no. 12, pp. 13–18, December 2015.
24. AGRITECTURE. "Soilless Agriculture: An In-depth Overview," [Online] Available: https://www.agritecture.com/blog/2019/3/7/soilless-agriculture-an-in-depth-overview
25. G.M. Kumar and G. Sreedhar, "Vertical Farming Using Information and Communication," infosys.com, White Paper, 2019. [Online] Available: https://www.infosys.com/industries/agriculture/
26. K. Benke and B. Tomkins, "Future food-production systems: Vertical farming and controlled-environment agriculture," Sustain.: Sci. Pract. Policy, vol. 13, no. 1, pp. 13–26, 2017.
27. F. Kalantari, O.M. Tahir, A.M. Lahijani, S. Kalantari, "A review of vertical farming technology: A guide for implementation of building integrated agriculture in cities," Adv. Eng. Forum, vol. 24, pp. 76–91, 2017.
28. A. Kheir. "The vertical farm: A review of developments and implications for the vertical city," Buildings, vol. 8, no. 2, p. 24, 2018.
29. J. Jones, "Hydroponics: A Practical Guide for the Soilless Grower," CRC Press, 2016, pp. 1–30.
30. S. Nisha, A. Somen, K. Kaushal, S. Narendra and O. Chaurasia, "Hydroponics as an advanced technique for vegetable production: An overview," J. Soil Water Conserv., vol. 17, pp. 364–371, 2019.
31. "Hydroponics" Environment and Ecology. [Online] Available: https://environment.co/environmental-benefits-of-hydroponics/
32. "Basic Hydroponic Systems and How They Work." Simply Hydroponics LLC. [Online] Available: https://www.simplyhydro.com/system/n.
33. J.S. Rubio-Asensio, M. Parra and D.S. Intrigliolo, "Open field hydroponics in fruit crops: Developments and Challenges," in Fruit Crops, Elsevier, Netherlands, 2020, pp. 419–430.
34. P. Wootton-Beard, "Growing without soil: An overview of hydroponics", Farming Connect, September 2019.

35. M. Rufí-Salís, M.J. Calvo, A. Petit-Boix, G. Villalba and X. Gabarrell, "Exploring nutrient recovery from hydroponics in urban agriculture: An environmental assessment," Resources, Conservation and Recycling, vol. 155, p. 104683, 2020.

36. A.V.D. Reis, F.A. Medeiros, M.F. Ferreira, R.L.T. Machado, L.N. Romano, V.K. Marini and T.R. Francetto, "Technological trends in digital agriculture and their impact on agricultural machinery development practices," Revi. Ciência Agronômica, vol.51, pp. 1–12, 2021.

37. CEMA. European Agriculture Machinery Association, Digital Farming: What Does It Really Mean? 2017. [Online] Available: https://www.cema-agri.org/

38. S. Rotz, E. Gravely, I. Mosby, E. Duncan, E. Finnis, M. Horgan, J. LeBla, R. Martin, H.T. Neufeld, A. Nixon, L. Pant, V. Shalla and E. Fraser, "Automated pastures and the digital divide: How agricultural technologies are shaping labour and rural communities," J. Rural Stud., vol. 68, pp. 112–122, 2019.

39. V. Komasilovs, A. Zacepins, A. Kviesis, A. Nasirahmadi and B. Sturm, "Solution for remote real-time visual expertise of agricultural objects," Agron. Res., vol. 16, pp. 464–473, 2018.

40. M. Jans-Singh, K. Leeming, R. Choudhary and M. Girolami, "Digital twin of an urban-integrated hydroponic farm," Data-Cent. Eng., vol. 1, p. e20, 2020.

41. J.A. Hunt, "Level sensing of liquids and solids – A review of the technologies," Sens. Rev., vol. 27, no. 3, pp. 200–206, 2007.

42. J.A. Voigt, "Introduction to Grain Operations Webinar Series: GEAPS 500," [Online] Available: https://www.geaps.com/course/introduction-to-grain-operations/

43. Gholizadeh, Mohammad Haji, Assefa M. Melesse and Lakshmi Reddi, "A comprehensive review on water quality parameters estimation using remote sensing techniques." Sensors vol. 16, no. 8 p. 1298, 2016.

44. BinMaste, Sensors, software & systems to transform supply chain. Available https://www.binmaster.com/products/ (October 2021).

45. J.D. Lewis, "Technology review level measurement of bulk solids in bins, silos and hoppers," Monitoring Technologies, LLC, 2004.

46. J. Nie et al. "Artificial intelligence and digital twins in sustainable agriculture and forestry: a survey," Turk. J. Agric. For., vol. 46, no. 5, pp. 642–661, 2022.

47. ASABE, "Procedure for Establishing Volumetric Capacities of Cylindrical Grain Bins, ASABE EP 413, 2nd Edition, 2019.

48. R. Bhadra, M.E. Casada, A.P. Turner, M.D. Montross, S.A. Thompson, S.G. McNeill, R.G. Maghirang and J.M. Boac, "Stored grain pack factor measurements for soybeans, grain sorghum, oats, barley, and wheat," Trans. ASABE, vol. 61, no. 2, pp. 747–757, 2018.

49. S.A. Thompson, C.V. Schwab and I.J. Ross, "Calibration of a model for packing whole grains," Appl. Eng. Agric., vol. 7, no. 4, pp. 450–456, 1991.

50. F. Jian and D.S. Jayas, "The ecosystem approach to grain storage," Agric. Res., vol. 1, no. 2, pp. 148–156, 2012.

51. C. Gilmore, M. Asefi, J. Paliwal, J. LoVetri, "Industrial scale electromagnetic grain bin imaging," Comput. Electron. Agric., vol. 136, pp. 210–220, 2017.

52. G. Dyck et al. "Digital twins: A novel traceability concept for post-harvest handling," Smart Agric. Technol., p. 100079, 2022.

53. C.B. Singh and J.M. Fielke, "Recent developments in stored grain sensors, monitoring and management technology," IEEE Instrum. Meas. Mag., vol. 20, no. 3, pp. 32–36, 2017.

54. A. Tzachor, C.E. Richards and S. Jeen, "Transforming agrifood production systems and supply chains with digital twins." Sci. Food, vol. 6, no. 1, p. 47, 2022.

55. S. Neethirajan and D.S. Jayas, Sensors for grain storage, in: 2007 ASABE Annual International Meeting, Technical Papers, 2007, 076179.

56. M. Asefi, I. Jeffrey, J. LoVetri, C. Gilmore, P. Card and J. Paliwal, "Grain bin monitoring via electromagnetic imaging," Comput. Electron. Agric., vol. 119, pp. 133–141, 2015.

57. W. Purcell, T. Neubauer and K. Mallinger, "Digital twins in agriculture: challenges and opportunities for environmental sustainability," Curr. Opin. Environ. Sustain., vol. 61, pp. 101252, 2023.

58. L. Zhao, J. Wang, Z. Li, M. Hou, G. Dong, T. Liu, T. Sun and K.T.V. Grattan, "Quasi distributed fiber optic temperature and humidity sensor system for monitoring of grain storage in granaries," IEEE Sens. J., vol. 20, no. 16, pp. 9226–9233, 2020.
59. C. Pylianidis, S. Osinga and I.N. Athanasiadis, "Introducing digital twins to agriculture," Comput. Electron. Agric., vol. 184, p. 105942, 2021.
60. P. Angin, M. H. Anisi, F. Göksel, C. Gürsoy and A. Büyükgülcü, "A digital twin framework for smart agriculture," J. Wirel. Mob. Networks Ubiquitous Comput. Dependable Appl., vol. 11, no. 4, pp. 77–96, 2020.
61. W. Purcell and T. Neubauer, "Digital twins in agriculture: A state-of-the-art review," Smart Agric. Technol., vol. 3, p. 100094, 2022.
62. T.R. Sreedevi and M.B. Santosh Kumar, "Digital Twin in Smart Farming: A Categorical Literature Review and Exploring Possibilities in Hydroponics," 2020 Advanced Computing and Communication Technologies for High Performance Applications (ACCTHPA) (2020), pp. 120–124.

AUTHOR BIOGRAPHIES

Dr. S. Muthukaruppasamy (M.E., Ph.D., M.I.S.T.E.) received B.E degree in Electrical and Electronics Engineering from Manonmaniam Sundaranar University and M.E degree in power electronics and drives from Sathyabama University in 2000 and 2005, respectively. He completed Ph. D in Electrical Engineering from Anna University, Chennai, India. He has published many research papers in international journals.

Dr. G. Arun Sampaul Thomas (M.E., Ph.D., M.I.S.T.E. M.I.E.T.) received B.E. degree in Information Technology, and M.E. and Ph.D. degrees in Computer Science and Engineering from Anna University, Chennai, in 2006, 2010, and 2018, respectively. He is currently an Associate Professor and HOD in the department of Artificial Intelligence and Machine Learning, J.B. Institute of Engineering and Technology, Hyderabad, India. He has had an overall teaching experience of more than ten years. His research areas include computer networks, data science, big data analytics, and IoT. He presented papers at five international conferences and various national conferences. His papers were published in various international journals. He attended several seminars and workshops. He is an active life member of ISTE & IET.

Dr. J. Nandha Gopal (M.E., Ph.D.) received his B.E degree in Electronics and Communication Engineering from Odaiyappa College of Engineering and Technology, Theni, India in 2005 and M.E degree in Power Electronics and Drives from Anna University, Chennai, India in 2011. He received PhD degree from Anna University, Chennai, India in 2021. His current research area is Power Converters for renewable energy resources.

Dr. S. Ravindra (M.E., Ph.D.) received his M.E degree in Power Electronics and Drives from Sathyabama University. He completed Ph. D degree from JNTUK, Kakinada, India. His current research area is Power System, Security, Power system Stability, PMU placement.

Dr. K. Saravanan, (M.E., Ph.D) is working as an Associate Professor, Department of Computer Science & Engineering at College of Engineering, Guindy, Anna University, Chennai, Tamilnadu. His research interests include Cloud Computing, Software Engineering, Internet of Things, Smart cities. He has published papers in 20 international conferences and 35 international journals. He has also written 20 book chapters and edited 12 books with international publishers. He has done consultancy work for Municipal Corporations and Smart City schemes. He is an active researcher and academician. Also, he is reviewer for many reputed journals in Elsevier, IEEE etc. He is Fellow of IEI and member of ISTE, ISCA, ACM, etc.

13 Predictive Analytics of Climate Change
The Future of Global Warming Lies in Data Analytics

*G. Arun Sampaul Thomas, S. Muthukaruppasamy,
S. Sathish Kumar, K. Saravanan,
and Beulah J. Karthikeyan*

13.1 INTRODUCTION

We are the final generation that can take action to prevent the worst effects of climate change and the first one that can abolish poverty. If we don't live up to our moral and historical obligations, future generations will judge us harshly.

Ban Ki-moon, former UN Secretary General

Climate change is one of the most pressing global issues facing humanity today. Predictive analytics, a subfield of data analytics, is increasingly being used to help predict and mitigate the impacts of climate change. This approach involves analysing vast amounts of data from a variety of sources, such as satellite images, weather sensors, and climate models, to make predictions about future climate patterns and impacts. In recent years, there has been an emergent form of investigation exploring the potential of predictive analytics in the context of climate change.

The motivation behind exploring the potential of predictive analytics from the perspective of climate change lies in the urgent need to address the impacts of global warming on our planet. As climate change continues to have significant influences on humanoid civilization and the natural ecosystem, there is a growing recognition of the importance of developing accurate models that can predict future climate patterns and assess the potential influence of climate change on various sectors of society. Predictive analytics offers a powerful tool for achieving these goals, by harnessing the power of data to develop accurate and reliable models that can inform policy and decision-making related to climate change mitigation and adaptation.

Data scientists and analysts are no longer the only ones who use data [1]. Data is accessible to anyone. People are better able to make reasoned judgments when they have straightforward approach to comprehensible climate facts. Average folks can make up good quality, more informed conclusions about the world we live in when they have simple access to digestible weather facts. People can truly see all of the factors impacting their environment, how they interact and make their own decisions about how we should go about addressing the climate catastrophe when they need entry to instinctive climate assessment tools that offer helpful data visualizations.

Innovation is at the core of accessible data. Modern climate analysis indicator tools and technologies are capable of ingesting enormous earth observation and climate data sets to analyse and describe the dynamic relationship between society and nature quickly and ascertain whether actions addressing climate change are succeeding or failing to mitigate it. A single, collaborative, and interactive platform may be used to carry out all these tasks.

Do you know that during the past 20 years, approximately 70% of all extreme weather occurrences have been attributed to climate change [2]? "Global warming" describes a rise in the climate's median long-term temperature. The emergence of physical components like carbon dioxide (CO_2), CH_4, and N_2O has significantly changed the environment. Since 1990, increased greenhouse gas (GHG) emissions have caused a dramatic increase in earth's temperature [3, 4]. In the past 100 years, the standard temperature of the Globe has rocketed by 1 degree Celsius. Over the subsequent 200 years, the middling global temperature is projected to upsurge by around 6 degree Celsius, according to climatologists. For countries to effectively tackle global warming, they need an action plan. For this, they mostly use real-time data analytics. Predictive analytics has enormous potential for forecasting patterns related to global warming. There is a reason why climatologists are using ML and data analytics more frequently. Numerous studies have shown that these models are much more precise and more priced in the resulting states:

- Typical figures are not noteworthy adequate to prototypical structures, when there are immense expanses of data.
- While there are excellent prototypes, computing them using traditional production techniques is extremely expensive.

Data analytics has been used by climate scientists to distinguish pollution sources, organize crop cover, and standardize satellite sensors. Deep learning with neural networks, one of the most important branches of ML for data analysis, can pace up data analytics in the field by helping with pattern recognition, super-resolution, and global warming predictions. Innovative methods and technology are being developed by both governmental and private sector groups to combat global warming. The storage and real-time analysis of vast volumes of data relate to many factors, including temperature change, sea levels, carbon emissions, and forest cover. These technologies can find correlations between data, provide useful insights, and produce patterns and forecasts. In this method, prompt preventive measures or safeguards can be taken.

The equilibrium of energy entering and leaving the system of the planet controls its temperature [5]. Temperatures of the globe while solar energy is entering are captivated by the planet system. The globe does not warm when solar energy is bounced into space. The earth cools as engrossed energy is emanated back into space. There are several natural and human factors that can alter the planet's energy balance, including:

- Changes in the amount of energy from the sun that reaches earth as well as the planet's atmosphere and surface reflectivity.
- Modifications to the greenhouse effect, which alters how much heat is trapped by the atmosphere on earth.

Earth's microclimate is changing more quickly than it ever has throughout the record of modern-day evolution, and this change is mostly due to human activity [5]. The influences of climate change have already been felt in every part of the biosphere, and they are likely to worsen with time. These industries are crucial to contemporary society, and they encompass human health, food production, security, transportation, energy, ecosystems, and water supply.

13.1.1 CURBING EMISSIONS

Industry, energy, forestry, waste, agriculture, and land use all contribute to global GHG emissions. These sectors are significantly impacted by using energy in industrial and domestic buildings, deforestation, landfills, cattle and manure, road traffic, aircraft, and other issues. Remote sensors on satellites, aircraft, and drones are used to measure the emissions from these areas. Remote monitoring of emissions from any source on the earth is possible using this spaciotemporal data in conjunction with IoT and climate data analysis technologies. To hold companies and organizations accountable, it is necessary to be able to identify the sources and amounts of emissions. Consumers may choose which companies are turning green and which to support by having easy access to emissions data, which promotes openness.

13.1.2 TEMPERATURE TRENDS

Is the weather becoming warmer? What are the changes in value? What will their increase be? We employ trend analysis to provide answers to these queries. Simple linear regression is used to determine linear trends and statistical importance using historical and present temperature data obtained from sensors and satellites. The significance of a monotonic trend may also be determined using the Mann-Kendall test [6]. Although it may appear difficult, it is not necessary to manually analyse time series of climate data. These capabilities are integrated into modern visual analytics systems, which can rapidly and impeccably ingest and fuse temperature data into a single location where users can make use of data discovery tools to examine their data in collaborating representations that highlight trends and patterns. We can determine when and where there is a connection between specific behaviours and rising temperatures by combining this information with emissions data.

13.1.3   Rising Sea Levels

Rising sea levels and their effects on coastal towns are among the most worrisome elements of climate change [1]. We can record sea levels over time in large part thanks to GIS (geographic information systems) [7], satellite altimeters, radio waves, and distant tide gauges. Fleets of aquatic robots are used to assess water temperatures, and microwave remote sensing data may be extracted from GIS and used to monitor sea ice. Not only can this data be used to make forecasts using predictive models, but it can also be used to simulate floods using software. Why is this crucial? Perception. It probably won't make much of a difference if you simply inform folks that sea levels are increasing and provide them with a worksheet of statistics. The real ramifications, however, are probably more significant if you present them with predicted data in the form of flood simulations, and the typical person is more prone to take the certainty of the climate problem into account in real-life situations.

13.1.4   The Heavy AI Differences

We have access to a lot of data that can be used to fight climate change. However, the value of such information depends on our capacity to apply it to derive practical conclusions. Combining tried-and-true environmental effect measurement techniques with cutting-edge technology offers us the ability to unearth previously undiscovered insights and solutions. A tool that can cope with the diversity, amount, and velocity of ecological data that we are now dealing with is required for climate change data analysis technologies and approaches.

It takes a cutting-edge solution to help us connect the dots between the vast amount of climate data, map out many circumstances with climate situation assessment tools, and forecast events before they occur to develop an effective plan to deal with a catastrophe of this size. HEAVY.AI [7] supports all of this and more. Beyond the capabilities of common analytics tools, real-time data insights are discovered with HEAVY.AI. The large dimensions of data gathered by latter-day ecological scrutinizing IoT devices and sensors quickly overpower older GIS systems, whereas forecasters can cross-filter billions of position data chronicles, polygons, and other properties using HEAVY.AI's climate data analysis capabilities in milliseconds.

Because of the software, indigenous raster and earth surveillance and imaging data can now be quickly imported into HEAVY.AI 6.0. Our geospatial data platform, with the help of artificial intelligence (AI), can easily map and analyse your biggest geographical and time-series information in ways that were previously not conceivable. The complex interaction between the world and humanity is shown in a dynamic, engaging way through HEAVY.AI's interactive data visualizations.

Overall, these studies demonstrate the potential of predictive analytics in the context of climate change. By analysing vast amounts of data, researchers can develop models that help predict and mitigate the bearings of climate change on anthropological culture and the natural atmosphere. As such, predictive analytics is likely to play an increasingly important role in the combat in contradiction of climate change in the years to come.

13.2   IMPACT CLIMATE CHANGE POLICY WITHOUT
A TECHNOLOGY PREDICTION

Without big data and predictive analytics, it should go without saying that any policies or strategies to combat climate change would be extremely limited and one-dimensional. Without considering big data, the following hypothetical scenarios may be possible:

- The estimated amount of carbon emissions that must be reduced globally may be significantly off. Consider a situation where nations decide to reduce carbon emissions from all sources, such as automobiles, air conditioners, and industrial facilities, by 2% over the course of the following five years, even though, given the existing situation, a minimum reduction of 5% is required. Insufficient emission reduction results in increased global warming, sickness, and other issues.
- Sea levels are increasing because the glaciers melting more quickly than before. Coastal regions are particularly in danger because of this. Proactive measures, like home relocation, rehabilitation planning, and other activities, might be inadequate or delayed without reliable analytics and projections.
- A lot of environmental changes and ecological imbalances might go unreported across the planet. The proper viewpoint might not be developed if up-to-date, data-based perspectives are not given to the appropriate forum. Data comparison and tracking of environmental and ecological changes throughout time are crucial.

13.2.1   PREDICTIVE ANALYTICS-BASED IMPRESSION OF BIG DATA
AND CLIMATE TRANSFORMATION STRATEGIES

Predictive analytics-based big data had a considerable influence on plans and campaigns envisioned to address the global climate variation problem. Innovative tools and technologies are being developed by both public and private sector organizations to aid in the creation of cutting-edge climate change policies. Big data is used in the development of these applications and systems. Massive volumes of information are continuously acquired and assessed about a variety of elements, such as carbon emanations, temperature differences, sea level changes, and forest asylum. These tools may determine the relationships between various factors and offer useful information, forecasts, and trends based on which preventative or safety measures can be taken. The contributions of a few of the following tools and technologies can aid in a better understanding of how the fight against climate change is being impacted predictive analytics and big data.

13.2.1.1   Surging Seas

The interactive map and application were made by the independent non-profit group Climate Central. Surging Seas provides information on the escalating sea levels in the United States. As seen in Figures 13.1 and 13.2, the map may be used to see embedded widgets such as flood alarms, action plans, sea level trends, historical data, and precise sea levels at various locations. Big data analysis is the sole technique, in accordance with Richard Wiles, vice president for strategic communications and

FIGURE 13.1   Greatest Miami Beach will be underwater beneath estimated 5-ft sea level upsurge.

director of research at Climate Central, to inform people about their local climate in a way that they can understand.

13.2.2   A World without Data Analytics

Plans and programmes to combat global warming become one-dimensional without data analytics [2]. The following hypothetical scenarios are possible:

- The computations for lowering carbon emissions may remain impacted. Consider a system where firms consistently agree to implement a rule that demands industrial facilities, autos, and other sources to cut carbon emissions by 3% during the ensuing ten years.

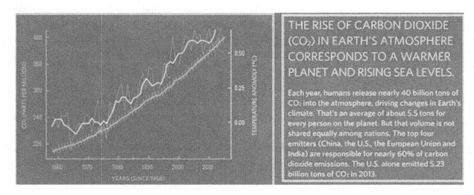

FIGURE 13.2 CO_2 surging sea levels.

- As a result of incorrect calculations, global warming will worsen because sea levels are rising faster than previously, and glaciers are melting swiftly, placing coastal areas at great risk. The actual need was a 6% reduction in carbon emissions. The appropriate authorities might not implement proactive housing relocation and rehabilitation planning measures if predictive analytics are not used.

13.3 TECHNOLOGY BEHIND CLIMATE CHANGE: A COMPARATIVE STUDY

The existence of programmes [8], like Worldwide Jungle Lookout [9], Microsoft Research's Maddingley Exemplary [10], and the Google Earth Engine [11], is evidence that significant effort has already been made on this front over the years. We must act quickly considering the speed of climate change. Predictive analytics and big data-based technologies have made it feasible for stakeholders to analyse enormous dimensions of information quickly and engender meaningful intuitions. Antennas remain gathering information on different factors, including rainfall, soil, and forest cover, and assisting in the establishment of connections across datasets. Big data and predictive analytics are two of the most critical tools that administrations will utilize as they search for ways to decrease the consequences of climate change.

13.3.1 Google Earth Engine

The Google Earth Engine relates environmental conditions across years or decades and pinpoints issues so that they can be rectified. Iran's Lake Urmia, a salt lake, serves as an illustration of how this operates. According to Google Earth, the lake had a turquoise tint in 1984 years or decades and pinpoints issues so that they can be rectified. After a while, the colour turned green. In 2012, everything is brown. Like this, Amazonian deforestation has been monitored. The engine gathers openly accessible satellite imagery to pinpoint environmental problems worldwide.

13.3.2 Climate by Data.Gov

http://www.data.gov/ has a massive compilation of more than 192,289 datasets on a range of subjects. Naturally, the weather is included in all these datasets. These databases offer reliable, current information on a variety of climate-related subjects. You could be prepared for live coverage of earthquakes occurring all around the world, time-lapse maps displaying how the Great Lakes' temperature varies throughout the year, and fertilizer awards, for example. A tiny project created in 2006 shows how helpful the input from this website could be. It dealt with a device that assessed how climate change affected crops. As a result, Monsanto bought the influence tool.

13.3.3 Worldwide Forest Power

It is a technique that aids footprint the world's reforest concealment. It provides a collaborative map with a plethora of evidence, such as the amount of forest cover, the amount of deforestation in a certain area, and forest fires. This programme, which is well liked, is used by several organizations, including Nestle, Unilever, and the Indonesian government.

13.3.4 Opower

A decrease in energy use is good for the environment. Every citizen must become involved in the effort to reduce energy use. The energy usage of neighbours frequently has an impact on residents. This behavioural pattern was employed by Opower, a business that specializes in energy analytics, to combat climate change. Citizens receive individualized data from Opower that compares their energy use to that of their neighbours and it is producing outcomes. Since its debut in 2007, Opower is capable to keep around 6 billion kilowatts of energy, which is adequate to power an urban of 1 million people for an entire year. Behavioral nudging, according to Opower's head of engineering, Rick McPhee, "helps minimize user consumption and is friendlier than mandatory blackouts."

Recent years have seen an emergent frame of study exploring the potential of predictive analytics in the context of climate change. In [12], Fu et al. developed a model using ML algorithms to accurately predict drought events several months in advance in the Yellow River basin of China. In [13], Tian et al. used predictive analytics to gauge the bearing of climate change on crop yields in China, developing a random forest model that predicted future crop yields under different climate scenarios. In [14], a study by Zhang et al. explored the use of deep learning algorithms to predict extreme heat events in urban areas of the United States, demonstrating the potential of these models to improve early warning systems for heat-related health impacts. These studies demonstrate the continued relevance of predictive analytics in the background of climate change, highlighting the potential of data-driven approaches to inform policy and decision-making related to climate change mitigation and adaptation.

13.4 DATA ANALYTICS CONTEST AGAINST CLIMATE CHANGE ON OUR BEHALF

On February 26, 2021, an iceberg with a surface area of 1,270 square kilometres detached from an Antarctic ice shelf which is greater than New York City [15]. For many people, this news may not be alarming when taken in isolation. Sadly, this is the result of a series of climate change-related incidents. One of the most hotly contested issues today is climate change. Scientists continue to call for action to stop climate change, while governments and regular people continue to dismiss the issue and ignore these warnings.

No matter what other people may think, climate change is a reality that could get worse if we do nothing to stop it. Scientists believe that human activity will have raised the universal warmth by 2.5 to 4 degree Celsius by the wind-up of the span, causing an uncontrollable restraint of occurrences that might render lifespan on earth for all incarnate things pretty much impossible. We must use every tool available to us to provide a harmless atmosphere for forthcoming compeers. Big Data analytics is a piece of technology that can aid in the fight against climate change and global warming.

An essential step in the healing process is examining the harm done by our previous errors. We've all made a lot of mistakes as people. The main ones include cutting down our forests, polluting the climate with fossil fuel pollution, and leaving plastic garbage in the ecosystem. But estimating the consequences of our errors is a difficult challenge. Scientists gather information on these impacts using sensors, satellite photos, and other instruments. The harm might then be assessed using this information, and future climate changes may be predicted. For instance, forest environmentalists have been analysing the magnitude of destruction to our forests, which are basically the globe's heart since they control atmospheric CO_2, using the data gathered from these endpoints. Environmental organizations operating in Antarctica were also able to foresee how warming temperatures would affect the pole's glaciers.

By identifying these implications of climate change, we can inform policymakers and the public and encourage them to act in the battle in contradiction of weather transformation. Additionally, the information gleaned from these analytics may be used to improve the strategies we undertake to safeguard the environment.

There remains time to make alternatives that will progress our efforts to mitigate global warming, even though some of the effects of our mistakes are long-lasting. By converting to cleaner, more natural energy sources to meet our needs, we can reduce emissions, a major cause of global warming. To provide us with energy, natural energy sources like wind and solar power require certain arrangements. We can choose the optimum locations for wind and solar farms so that they can supply us with the sustainable energy we need by using data analytics. Data analytics are being used by businesses all around the world to determine their carbon footprint. Businesses may use this information to establish best practices to reduce their environmental impact.

Climate variation is one of the most imminent extortions now confronting civilization. In the eras of reckless choices, behaviour have enhanced global warming, which might mark life for imminent generations tremendously difficult, if not impossible. Thankfully, there is still time for us to make restitution. Big Data analytics might be a very helpful tool in this process.

Using data analytics, the hazards of global warming may be mitigated [2]. One significant example is the research done by the private non-profit organization Climate Central. They created Surging Seas, an interactive map that displays data on United States' increasing sea levels. By exploring the map, one could see specific sea levels in different regions together with historical data, plans for response, and flood alerts. Miami Beach may soon be underwater, according to the application, because of rising sea levels. One of the main causes contributing to deforestation is illegal logging. Rainforest Connection (RFCx) uses data analytics and mobile devices to stop deforestation. To protect a rainforest region, they developed acoustic monitoring devices that gave them access to real-time alerts and improved their ability to react. RFCx analyses forest sounds in real-time using the TensorFlow ML framework to recognize noises that resemble logging trucks, chainsaws, and other sounds associated with illegal activities.

AI, data analytics, and ML were used to investigate Maria's impacts on Puerto Rico's El Yunque National Forest by Maria Uriarte, and Tian Zheng, a professor of statistics at the Data Science Society. The report's objective was to determine how tropical hurricanes impact both global warming and climate change as well as the spread of various tree species [16]. However, factors other than COP26 are also important for any climate policy's effectiveness, including local and regional politics, advances in science and technology, and, most importantly, solid, reliable data.

Whether it's to persuade decision-makers of the seriousness of the situation, counter the misinformation propagated by bad-faith players, or build solutions that may help us avoid worst case situations, data science and its surrounding fields have been essential to climate talks. Due to Hurricane Maria's tremendous destruction, searching through many high-resolution photographs was the only practical approach to identifying the impacted species. However, there remained a specific problem: How to tell one species from another when there was simply a green mass visible across a vast area?

They contrasted the high-resolution photos with a dataset that recognized and mapped each tree species in specific plots using AI and data analytics. They were able to analyse the aerial photos and ground data from fixed fields to identify how various species appeared from above.

The warming effects of CO_2 are one of several aspects of climate change that are hotly contested [17]. Contrary to popular belief, some argue that changes in temperature cause changes in atmospheric CO_2, rather than CO_2 causing a rise in global temperature. The study of historical climate change using ice core analysis revealed that CO_2 lags temperature. As a result, some argue that CO_2 lags the warming effects of CO_2. Since there is a positive feedback loop between CO_2 and global temperature, both sides of the debate are valid. In other words, when the temperature rises, CO_2 levels rise as well. This cycle of positive feedback worsens the impacts of global warming.

Global warming requires research into how the composition and distribution of forests are impacted by contemporary storms. When a cyclone destroys a forest, the plant is forced to degrade, which increases the quantity of CO_2 that is released into the sky. Trees retain less carbon when they regenerate after a storm because of their reduced size. As a result, as storms increase due to climate change, less carbon will be stored and more will be released, which will accelerate global warming.

The development of more habitable and environmentally friendly communities may greatly benefit from data analytics [3]. By analysing data gathered from IoT devices like smart meters, it can improve a city's energy efficiency. In this way, it can predict energy demand. Authorities may be enabled by clever solutions to model prospective zoning regulations, construct flood plains, and work on disaster preparedness and urban planning. To make cities more livable and effective, a sustainable city's administration can envision a cutting-edge analytics dashboard that displays real-time data on energy consumption, water availability, weather, and traffic.

The Green Horizon project (created by IBM) in China can track by forecasting air pollution and suggest alternative strategies [2]. To reduce pollution levels in a certain region, for example, it may be desirable to limit driving or close certain power plants. IBM is developing a new method to help communities forecast upcoming heat waves. It would explore a wide range of solutions to see how they reduce heat waves while simulating the environment on an urban scale. For instance, data analytics and ML algorithms might classify the optimum places to plant new trees to increase the number of trees in a region and lower the amount of heat generated by paving.

13.5 MACHINE LEARNING USE CASES FOR CLIMATE CHANGE

For instance, a study by Fu et al. [12] used predictive analytics to forecast drought events in the Yellow River basin of China. The biographers used a combination of meteorological data, satellite imagery, and machine learning (ML) algorithms to develop a model that accurately predicted droughts several months in advance. Another study by Tian et al. [13] used predictive analytics to evaluate the influence of climate change on crop yields in China. The authors used a combination of climate data and ML algorithms to predict future crop yields under different climate scenarios.

Predictive analytics has also been used to predict the blowout of contagious sicknesses in the context of climate change. For example, a study by Leclerc et al. [18] used ML algorithms to predict the spread of dengue fever in Brazil based on weather and climate data. The authors were able to accurately predict the number of dengue cases several weeks in advance. In addition, a study by Hosseini et al. [19] used predictive analytics to evaluate the influence of climate change on the spread of malaria in Iran. The authors used climate data and data analytics-based ML algorithms to predict the imminent spread of the disease under different climate scenarios.

Climate change is a significant global issue that has far-reaching repercussions, including rising sea levels, melting ice caps and glaciers, more frequent and intense storms and hurricanes, increased occurrences of droughts and wildfires, and altered precipitation patterns across different regions. To mitigate these risks, it is essential to reduce GHG emissions and adapt to the effects of climate change. In recent years, there has been growing attention towards using data science, advanced analytics, ML, and AI to address climate change, after decades of application in various industries such as finance and healthcare [20].

With respect to climate change, some cases of the key uses are as follows: [21]

- Predicting climate change impacts on crop yields;
- Identifying climate-vulnerable regions;
- Globally predicting wildfire risk;
- Predicting sea ice loss due to climate warming;
- Detecting climate change-induced drought;
- Predicting sea level rise.

13.5.1 PREDICTING EXTREME PRECIPITATION

Several 24-hour periods throughout which the quantity of rain or snowfall surpasses the normal for that place is considered an extreme precipitation event. The augmented vanishing of water from bushels and other bodies of water is partly to blame for the general rise in frequency and intensity of these catastrophes. Condensation occurs as water vapour ascends into the sky, creating clouds. These clouds may produce significant amounts of precipitation when they are driven over land by the wind. The increased frequency of severe precipitation events is believed to be related to climate change. Storm intensity increases when the atmosphere warms because it can store more water vapour. Flooding from excessive precipitation can result in both property damage and fatalities. It may also cause avalanches and mudslides, which can both block entire populations from necessary services. Extreme precipitation even has the potential to interfere with vital infrastructure like transportation.

ML methods and climate models can be used to anticipate extreme precipitation. The ability of climate models to forecast weather and climatic trends is improving. They still struggle to correctly predict severe precipitation, though. To anticipate future life-threatening rainfall occurrences, the climate exemplary incorporates climatological factors, such as humidity, surface pressure, and temperature, towards estimate how frequently a region would experience heavy rainfall or snowfall, the ML approach is fed historical data on daily weather patterns as well as climate change forecasts of GHG emissions.

We may attain several reasons (glitches or chances) and Key Performance Indicator (KPIs) connected to excessive rainfall while reasoning from fundamental principles, and we can traject them to arrive at suitable AI and ML resolutions. Some of the KPI values can be predicted using ML algorithms. Here are a few specifics:

- According to NOAA's Weather Prediction Center's Dr. David Novak, many instances of excessive rainfall share traits like high humidity and an air commotion (such as a winter storm, warm, or heavy cyclone). The more intense the rainfall you're likely to experience, the longer these circumstances last in the same location. Additionally, as it is well known that warmer air can contain more dampness, it makes sense that a warmer atmosphere might produce more intense rainfall. To determine the association among severe precipitation, air moisture, and warmer air, we will thus wish to develop and carry out hypothesis testing around these variables. To create prediction models for predicting severe precipitation, employ the associated characteristics.
- As was said in the preceding paragraph, warmer air can store moisture, which may eventually lead to significant rains. What then causes the air to get warmer? One of the causes is the existence of greenhouse vapours in the troposphere, which heat the atmosphere by absorbing infrared contamination from the superficial. The objective is to identify the causes of GHGs, develop and test hypotheses related to those causes, and then effectively use the knowledge to develop predictive or AI&ML models.

13.5.2 Demonstrating Carbon Confiscation

It is a technique for forecasting the amount of carbon that will be captured from the air and stored. The climate of the planet has fluctuated back and onward amid ice eternities and interglacial eras (warm epochs). This results from variations in earth's orbital path around the sun. Due to their extreme sensitivity to temperature fluctuations, climate models are unable to forecast what the climate will be like in 100 or 1000 years. ML algorithms are being used by researchers to simulate carbon sequestration and its long-term effects on climate change.

To develop predictive models for carbon sequestration, it would be necessary to comprehend some of the following while making assumptions based on fundamental principles:

- What may indicate whether carbon sequestration is successful? How can carbon sequestration technologies' effectiveness be modelled?
- What are all the types of carbon that can be treated using the carbon confiscation technique?
- How should the carbon forms be graded?
- What numerous kinds of carbon sequestration techniques are there, and what are the KPIs for each of them?

13.5.3 FORECASTING CO_2 EMISSIONS

When fuels are burned, the greenhouse vapours CO_2, CH_4, and N_2O are released. The bulk of GHG emissions from stationary combustion sources are made up of CO_2. The primary source of CO_2 emissions is the scorching of remnant oils. Researchers are estimating the maximum amount of CO_2 that may be emitted while still meeting a certain climatic target using climate models and ML algorithms (i.e., residing below 2 degree Celsius). The primary focus of carbon reporting is on this, with the following objectives:

- To prevent carbon emissions from going above a certain threshold that would cause an increase in the global temperature of about 1.5 degree celsius, what is the carbon budget globally at any given time?
- How much CO_2 is emitted by each nation, area, etc.? Different features of carbon accounting, such as those described earlier, can be predicted using AI and ML models. There are several ways to calculate GHG emissions at any given period, including the following:
    - Direct measurement: A continuous emissions monitoring system (CEMS) is used to detect CO_2 emissions directly.
    - Fuel input analysis: This method effectively uses a mass balance approach to calculate emissions by applying carbon content factors to the fuel input.
- In the fuel input analysis approach, relevant equations, such as the subsequent ones, may be cast off to compute emanations depending on the data available on the properties of the fuel being used. You may read the specifics in this chapter. The amount of CO_2, CH_4, or N_2O released is used to compute emissions.

13.5.4 FORECASTING GREENHOUSE VAPOUR ABSORPTIONS

Because GHGs prevent heat from escaping into space, the globe's weather remains warmhearted enough for life as we distinguish it. Future GHG concentrations are predicted by researchers using climate models. To make climate model forecasts more quickly and effectively, ML techniques are applied.

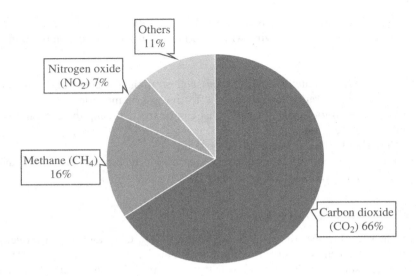

FIGURE 13.3   Green-house-gas-emissions-concentrations.

According to article [10], the next image depicted in Figure 13.3 illustrates the three main absorptions of GHG emanations, including CO_2, CH_4, and N_2O. Other main gases include sulphur hexafluoride, perfluorocarbon, and hydrofluorocarbon gases. The amount of heat that any GHG can trap in the atmosphere is determined by its global warming potential (GWP), which varies across all GHGs.

On occasion, it may be necessary to estimate or anticipate the concentrations depicted in the picture; in these situations, algebraic and ML approaches can be of great use.

13.5.5   FOREST DEPRIVATION

Many ways to addressing climate change and forest degradation depend heavily on forests. They provide oxygen, support plant and animal habitats, and aid in controlling the planet's temperature. However, the rate of forest deprivation is worrying. A significant issue that subsidizes climate variation is forest degradation. When forests are harmed or devastated, usually because of human activities, it happens. Forest degradation is mostly brought on by deforestation, forest fires, pests, and inadequate forest management. The local climate can be significantly impacted by the removal of trees and other plants. Trees and plants also serve to control warmth and precipitation intensities in addition to absorbing CO_2.

These crucial services are jeopardized by forest degradation, which contributes to climate change. As a result, the earth is getting warmer, and less CO_2 is being extracted from the atmosphere. Additionally, soil erosion brought on by forest degradation has been linked to desertification and a decline in biodiversity. To safeguard our ecosystem, it is crucial to discourse the issue of forest deprivation.

Stopping the loss of forests and establishing new ones must be the two halves of the answer to forest deprivation, which has a significant influence on climate change.

We requisite first lessen our reliance on wood products to stop forest damage. This may be accomplished by buying recycled paper goods, purchasing items with a forest certification, and investing in forest management methods. By establishing protected areas, encouraging forest conservation, and lowering deforestation-related emissions, we must also safeguard forests. Additionally, we must try to rebuild the damaged forest ecosystems and replace trees. Reforestation activities will assist in reducing climate change, providing habitat for species, and generating employment in the communities that rely on their forests. Here are some of the theories that, taken together, might lessen the destruction of forests.

- Reduced reliance on wood products;
- Early identification of forest degradation;
- Affinity of sites where shrubs can be regenerated.

Given the techniques for solving the problem, it is crucial for conservational researchers to be proficient in identifying forest deprivation as early and simply as conceivable so that some of the solutions can be used to lessen the effects of climate change. To automate this procedure, researchers use ML algorithms to create models using satellite data, such as high-pixeled photos from the Landsat series of satellites.

13.5.6 IDENTIFYING CLIMATE-VULNERABLE REGIONS

Regions that are susceptible to the impacts of climate change are referred to as climate vulnerable. These areas are often characterized as low-lying coastal regions, small island states, or tropical developing nations. Climate change manifests in various ways in these regions, including rising sea levels, intensified frequency of extreme weather events, changes in precipitation patterns, and decreased water availability. Identifying climate-vulnerable regions is a crucial initial step in addressing the issue of climate change. By pinpointing areas that are most at risk, resources and aid can be more effectively directed. Nevertheless, as climate change is a global issue, its impacts will ultimately affect all locations, exacerbating existing issues such as poverty, water scarcity, and food insecurity.

13.5.7 PREDICTING WILDFIRE RISK GLOBALLY

Wildfire danger has been connected to climate change. A wildfire is an untamed fire that began on poorly kept or unprepared property. They often happen when it's hot and dry, in late summer or early fall. Wildfire activity has recently increased all around the world, and experts think that climate change is a significant reason. Wildfires may have catastrophic effects, destroying natural areas and residential structures. Additionally, they contribute significantly to climate change by releasing massive volumes of CO_2 into the atmosphere.

We must act to stop wildfires from spreading and becoming more catastrophic because of climate change. Reducing the quantity of GHGs, we release into the environment is one approach to achieving this. Lessening the use of fossil fuels, growing more trees, and preserving natural places can all help with this. By establishing fire-resistant areas surrounding our homes and towns, as well as by putting an emergency plan in place, we may also be prepared for wildfires. By adopting these actions, we can reduce the danger of wildfires and safeguard our loved ones and property. Predicting wildfire risk is more important than ever as the wildfire season lengthens and gets worse. A potent technique for finding patterns and making predictions is ML. ML can assist in identifying at-risk locations and the variables that cause wildfires by examining data from previous wildfires. Predictive models may then be developed using this data to assist decision-makers in taking action to put out wildfires.

13.5.8 PREDICTING CLIMATE CHANGE IMPACTS ON CROP YIELDS

Making forecasts regarding upcoming crop production is known as agricultural yield forecasting. Making forecasts about future crop yields requires a rigorous examination of previous crop yields and weather patterns. With the continued warming of the planet's climate, farmers may use this approach to prepare for droughts, heat waves, and other extreme weather occurrences. Crop production prognostication is a difficult task that considers a variety of influences, including rainfall, soil humidity intensities, solar contamination, and weather. However, the reliability of the climate in a certain area might affect how accurate a forecast is. As an illustration, agricultural productions in the Sahel area of Africa vary greatly year after year because of the erratic nature of the rainfall. Forecasting agricultural production in this area is, therefore, very difficult. Nevertheless, predicting crop production is a useful contrivance that can assist farmers in adjusting to a varying environment.

13.5.9 FORECASTING SEA ICE LOSS DUE TO CLIMATE THAWING

There is broad systematic agreement that mortal actions like deforestation and the depletion of remnant gases are causing climate variation. Sea ice loss is the most obvious consequences of climate change. Sea ice is created when saltwater freezes, and it is crucial in controlling the temperature of the planet. The earth is kept cold by the reflection of sunlight by sea ice. Dark ocean water is revealed when sea ice melts, and this water absorbs more heat, warming the earth even more. In the upcoming years, sea ice is expected to continue to decrease, increasing climate change's effects and causing even more extreme weather patterns.

13.5.10 IMPROVING ESTIMATES OF CARBON EMISSIONS

A heat-trapping GHG called CO_2 is released into the atmosphere when people engage in activities like using motor vehicles, scorching coal or natural gas for vigour, and deforestation. To increase estimates of carbon emissions by 50% over current practices, scholars have built a climate-carbon cycle prototypical using AI&ML techniques.

13.5.11 DETECTING CLIMATE CHANGE-INDUCED DROUGHT

Drought brought on by climate change is a major source of worry. Climate change refugees may flee their homes due to drought, which can also affect agricultural output and cause famines. It is crucial to quickly identify droughts brought on by climate change so that proper action may be taken in regions that may experience these droughts soon. Drought brought on by climate change may be identified using a variety of deep learning approaches. Algorithms for image recognition can be used to find droughts brought on by climate change. For illustration, CNNs (Convolutional Neural Networks), which are renowned for their precision and enactment, might assist individuals in swiftly identifying regional changes brought on by climate change.

13.5.12 CLIMATE CHANGE ACTION PLAN

Plans to combat climate change may be included in national government plan or neighbourhood-level ingenuities like installing green ridges and reducing urban heat islands. Building data models on a variety of aspects, such as city infrastructure and vegetation, may be done using deep learning techniques.

13.6 PREDICTING CHANGES IN WEATHER TEMPERATURE USING MACHINE LEARNING MODELS

13.6.1 PROBLEM INTRODUCTION

We attempt to solve the challenge of estimating the middling temperature of globe's land and waters using more than a century of historical weather data [22]. We're going to pretend that there are no weather forecasts available to us. We have usage of historical world temperature averages for the past 100 years, including global maximum and minimum temperatures as well as ocean temperatures and global land. With everything said, we may conclude that the problem is one requiring regression techniques from ML. The goal makes this a regression job because it is continuous, and the fact that we have both the characteristics and the target that we want to forecast makes it supervised. Multiple regression models will get both the features and the targets in training phase, and they must figure a way to translate the data into a prediction. Additionally, because the target value is continuous, this is a regression problem (as opposed to discrete classes in classification). The backdrop we require is mostly complete, so let's begin! ML process, we need to clearly define our goals before getting started with the programming. Now that we are aware of our problem and model, the stages that form the backbone of my ML workflow are as follows:

1. State the query and choose the essential data (completed).
2. Get the data.
3. Recognize and fix any irregularities or missing data points.
4. Clean up and organize the data for the AI/ML/Data Science Model.
5. Create a reference model.
6. Use the training data to train the prototypical design.
7. Built on test data and make predictions.
8. Estimate enactment metrics and compare forecasts to the goals in the actual test set.

9. If performance is subpar, tweak the model, get new data, or attempt an alternative modelling approach.
10. Interpret the model and provide the numerical and visual findings.

13.6.2 DATA GATHERING

We need data to get started. We have received temperature information from Berkeley Earth Climate Change. To use a real-world example, see the Earth Surface Temperature Dataset on Kaggle.com. We assume the data in the dataset is correct as it was produced by one of the most renowned research universities in the world [23].

13.6.3 MAKING BETTER PREDICTIONS

Motivation for using data analytics builds on work done in the field of climate informatics, a topic created in 2011 that combines data analysis with climate research arch [2]. A wide range of topics are covered in this area, including improved flood prediction, paleoclimatology (reproducing historical climate conditions using data such as ice cores and climate shrinking), the use of large-scale models to make predictions at the hyperlocal scale, and the socioeconomic impacts of climate and weather. Data analytics can use a large amount of problematic climate and global warming simulations generated by climate models to uncover hidden and important information.

Among the earliest simulations of climate change, these models [10] of ice, cryosphere, land, oceans, and atmosphere were created at Princeton University in the 1960s. Claire Monteleone, a professor of computer science at the University of Colorado, Boulder, is unsatisfied with the correctness of these assumptions, even though fundamental scientific presumptions are generally accepted. This is especially true for long-term forecasts. "There is a lot of uncertainty," she continued. Even the future course of precipitation is up for debate. Monteleone has combined the projections of over 30 climate models [24] using data analytics to produce more accurate forecasts.

13.7 CONCLUSION

Every component of the industrial system requires a unique solution, but unfortunately, solutions are seldom straightforward and often come with significant difficulties and expenses. We recognize that individual efforts, even with the best intentions, are outweighed by the magnitude of necessary reforms in politics, economics, and technology. Effective policy is key to creating genuine change, and altering policy requires convincing elected officials that the public is concerned about the climate crisis and that their success depends on tackling it directly. The ability of big data analytics and ML models to process vast amounts of complex climate data, uncover hidden patterns, and provide real-time insights is critical. It has become an essential part of strategies and protocols aimed at mitigating and predicting trends in global warming. However, data analytics has limitations, and the decision to implement it for maximum benefit ultimately rests with the relevant authorities. Big data and analytics are redefining government policies around climate change. The use of big data in climate policies is becoming increasingly important, with its capacity to handle massive amounts of complex climate data, identify correlations as needed, and offer real-time insights. Although nearly all tools have been successful in providing real-time data, stakeholders must now determine specific measures to take while considering all available facts. It is undeniable that data analytics is transforming climate change policies.

REFERENCES

1. https://www.heavy.ai/blog/the-latest-on-climate-data-analysis-what-it-means-for-humankind
2. https://medium.com/swlh/the-future-of-global-warming-lies-in-data-analytics-63d255d6b62c
3. Arun Sampaul Thomas, G., & Harold Robinson, Y. (2020). IoT, big data, blockchain and machine learning besides its transmutation with modern technological applications. In Internet of Things and Big Data Applications. Springer Intelligent Systems Reference Library Book Series (ISRL) (Vol. 180, pp. 47–63). Springer, Cham. Print ISSN: 978-3-030-39118-8.
4. https://medium.com/analytics-vidhya/data-science-in-climate-change-7ba2dd948aa7
5. https://medium.com/mytake/understanding-climate-change-with-machine-learning-fb45a047dd2b
6. https://www.statisticshowto.com/mann-kendall-trend-test/
7. https://www.heavy.ai/technical-glossary/gis
8. https://www.kdnuggets.com/2015/12/big-data-predictive-analytics-climate-change.html
9. https://www.globalforestwatch.org/
10. https://www.princeton.edu/news/2018/01/19/syukuro-manabe-wins-crafoord-prize-fundamental-contributions-climate-change
11. https://earthengine.google.com/
12. Fu, Y., Li, C., Li, H., Li, L., Wang, Q., Zhang, Y., & Li, J. (2020). Forecasting drought using machine learning approaches: A case study in the yellow River basin, China. Journal of Hydrology, 590, 125450.
13. Tian, Y., Sun, H., Zhou, J., & Liu, X. (2021). Predicting crop yield under climate change scenarios with a random forest model. Journal of Cleaner Production, 281, 125148.
14. Zhang, J., Yang, Y., Li, H., Li, J., & Wang, Z. (2022). Predicting extreme heat events in urban areas using deep learning: A case study of the United States. Science of the Total Environment, 804, 150017.
15. https://seleritysas.com/blog/2021/04/15/how-data-analytics-can-support-our-fight-against-climate-change/
16. https://towardsdatascience.com/the-data-science-climate-change-curriculum-e93b2ba1b969
17. https://towardsdatascience.com/interpreting-climate-change-through-data-science-321de6161baf
18. Leclerc, Q.J., Fuller, N.M., & Knight, G.M. (2019). What datasets exist to support modeling of mosquito-borne disease transmission in urban environments? Journal of the Royal Society Interface, 16(159), 20190265.
19. Hosseini, S.M., Maleki, M., & Hajivand, M. (2020). The impact of climate change on malaria transmission in Iran: A data-driven modeling approach. Environmental Science and Pollution Research, 27(23), 29156–29166.
20. Arun Sampaul Thomas, G., & Harold Robinson, Y. (2020). Real-time health system (RTHS) centered Internet of Things (IoT) in healthcare industry: Benefits, use cases and advancements In. Multimedia Technologies in the Internet of Things Environment (Scopus Indexed). Springer, Singapore. ISSN: 978-981-15-7965-3.

21. https://vitalflux.com/machine-learning-use-cases-climate-change/#Predicting_extreme_precipitation
22. https://medium.com/swlh/predicting-weather-temperature-change-using-machine-learning-models-4f98c8983d08
23. https://www.kaggle.com/berkeleyearth/climate-change-earth-surface-temperature-data
24. https://unfoundation.org/blog/post/intergovernmental-panel-climate-change-30-years-informing-global-climate-action/

AUTHOR BIOGRAPHIES

Dr. G. Arun Sampaul Thomas (M.E., Ph.D, M.I.S.T.E., M.I.E.T.) received B.E. degree in Information Technology, and M.E. and Ph.D degrees in Computer Science and Engineering from Anna University, Chennai, in 2006, 2010, and 2018, respectively. He is currently an Associate Professor and HOD in the department of Artificial Intelligence and Machine Learning, J.B. Institute of Engineering and Technology, Hyderabad, India. He has overall teaching experience more than ten years. His research areas include Computer Networks, Data Science, Big Data Analytics, and IoT. He presented papers in five international conferences and various national conferences. His papers were published in various international journals. He attended several seminars and workshops. He is an active life member of ISTE and IET.

Dr. S. Muthukaruppasamy (M.E., Ph.D) received B.E. degree in Electrical and Electronics Engineering from Manonmaniam Sundaranar University and M.E. degree in Power Electronics and Drives from Sathyabama University in 2000 and 2005, respectively. He completed Ph.D. in Electrical Engineering from Anna University, Chennai, India. He has published 12 research papers in international journals.

Mr. S. Sathish Kumar (M.E., Ph.D) received B.E. degree in Computer Science and Engineering, and M.E. degree in Software Engineering from Anna University, Chennai, in 2010 and 2014, respectively. He is currently an Assistant Professor in the department of Artificial Intelligence and Machine Learning, J.B. Institute of Engineering and Technology, Hyderabad, India. He has overall teaching experience more than five years. His research areas include Machine Learning, Deep Learning, Computer Vision, Big Data Analytics, and IoT. He presented papers in four international conferences and various national conferences. His papers were published in various international journals. He attended several seminars and workshops.

Dr. K. Saravanan, (M.E., Ph.D) is working as an Associate Professor, Department of Computer Science & Engineering at College of Engineering, Guindy, Anna University, Chennai, Tamilnadu. His research interests include Cloud Computing, Software Engineering, Internet of Things, Smart cities. He has published papers in 20 international conferences and 35 international journals. He has also written 20 book chapters and edited 12 books with international publishers. He has done consultancy work for Municipal Corporations and Smart City schemes. He is an active researcher and academician. Also, he is reviewer for many reputed journals in Elsevier, IEEE etc. He is Fellow of IEI and member of ISTE, ISCA, ACM, etc.

Mrs. Beulah J Karthikeyan (M.E.) received B.E. degree in Computer Science and Engineering, and M.E. degree in Computer Science and Engineering from Anna University, Chennai, in 2017 and 2020, respectively. She is currently an Assistant Professor in the department of Artificial Intelligence and Machine Learning, J.B. Institute of Engineering and Technology, Hyderabad, India. Her research areas include Machine Learning, Deep Learning, Computer Vision, Big Data Analytics, and IoT. She attended several seminars and workshops.

14 Applications of Drones in Predictive Analytics

Dhiraj Kapila, Nestor Ulloa, S. Anita,
R. Siva Subramanian, Priti Kandewar, and P. Sujatha

14.1 OVERVIEW OF DRONES

Technology has come to play a crucial part in modern society, allowing people to pursue their endeavours with greater ease and efficiency. To improve productivity, humans are increasingly automating routine tasks so that they can devote their time and energy to more cerebral pursuits [1–3]. Drones and other unmanned aerial vehicles (UAVs) are rapidly expanding in significance as part of this automation toolset. This is due to the fact that drones offer numerous benefits, especially in challenging tasks, such as speed, efficiency, and lower danger. Drones are becoming increasingly useful, and it is for this reason that we wish to suggest a novel application in a novel setting, quantifying the associated benefits and hazards [4]. The agriculture industry is selected from the many possible settings. Agricultural tasks are becoming increasingly automated since they are physically demanding for people, hence it is preferable if machines perform these tasks instead. In addition, they are endeavours that need for ever-increasing efficiencies that can't be provided by mere human might [5].

Because of urbanization, the amount of land available for farming has decreased along with the global population, but the resulting increase in consumers' need for goods is a boon for the economy [6]. Consequently, intensive agriculture, as opposed to the conventional, extensive farming methods, must be used to maximize output while minimizing land use [7]. The obvious goal is to make this type of agriculture long-lasting while simultaneously protecting natural resources. One of the many facets of agriculture that we cover in this book is the effort to eradicate parasites. As a matter of fact, they can wipe out entire farms and render them unproductive [8]. Recently, this has become a major issue. Consider the entire olive groves that were wiped off in Puglia when the Xylella parasite struck, or the countless palm trees that were cut down when the "Red Punteruolo" pestilence swept through.

Types of drones, degrees of autonomy, drone sizes/weights, as well as types of power sources all help to categorize drones into distinct groups. Range, flight time, and payload capacity are all crucial characteristics of a drone [9].

Drones used to only be used for military, industrial, and meteorological purposes. Toy stores now sell mini UAVs for a few hundred dollars that can take live videos and photos [10].

A drone is a UAV that can be piloted from a distance and used to take still photographs or record video of a specific area, which can then be uploaded to a server. Drones are typically operated by a radio controller, smartphone, or tablet [11].

 DOI: 10.1201/9781003391302-14

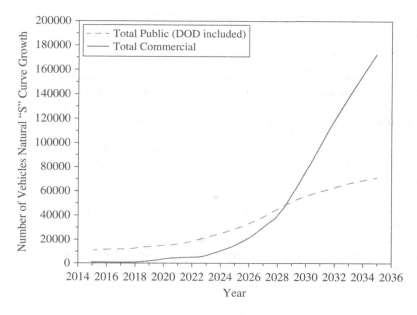

FIGURE 14.1 Estimates of the number of UAVs in service from 2015 to 2035.

What is possible and legally permissible in today's society is constrained by technology and legal issues [12]. In the United States, for instance, the Federal Aviation Administration (FAA) mandates that all drones be registered and must activate within visual line of sight of a pilot at all times [13]. Figure 14.1 depicts a likely future scenario for the application of drones in both public and private sectors.

Drones can be sorted in several ways according to their various qualities, including size, controls, wings, and more. On the basis of information acquired in, Tables 14.1 and 14.2 summarize these primary features.

Electronic components have become ever more affordable, smaller in size and less taxing on resources as a result of recent technical advancements [14]. Multi-rotor designs are replacing fixed-wing aircraft because of the increased specific energy made obtainable by lithium-ion batteries.

Aero-photogrammetry, thermal dispersal studies of the ground structures, and air quality analysis are only some of the remote sensing applications made possible by these aircraft [15]. The adoption of stabilization technologies and reliable flying helped make them a success, making it possible to use the aircraft safely even in bad weather. In addition, the multi-rotor aircraft's vertical flight capacity allows it to operate in confined locations while yet maintaining the same compact configuration as a conventional fixed-wing aircraft [16]. Finally, the capability for stable flying (hovering) enables more precise data from the sensor, and the potential of piloting remotely from ground position facilitates the completion of missions in hostile polluted places without placing the human operator in harm's way.

Several publications [17–19] propose using drones in the agricultural domain when it is required to keep an eye on crops or other items on the ground. Farmers

TABLE 14.1

Variation for Weight

UAS Specification	Mission Endurance (Hours)	Mission Speed (Miles per Hour)	Weight (Pounds)	Mission Altitude (Feet Above the Surface)	Mission Radius (Miles)	Overall Size (Feet)	Mission Endurance (Hours)
Nano	<1	<25	<1	<400	<1	<1	<1
Micro	1	10–25	1–4.5	<3,000	1–5	<3	1
Small UAS	1–4	75–150	4.5–5.5	<10,000	5–25	<10	1–4
Ultralight Aircraft	4–6	75–150	55–255	<15,000	25–75	<30	4–6
Light Sport Aircraft	6–12	75–150	255–1,320	<18,000	50–100	<45	6–12
Small Aircraft	24–36	100–200	1,320–12,500	<25,000	100–200	<60	24–36
Medium Aircraft	TBD	TBD	12,500–41,000	<1,00,000	TBD	TBD	TBD

are frequently confronted with a wide variety of challenges, including parasites and unexpected climatic changes, all of which may have devastating effects on the quality of agricultural products [10]. Drones with targeted sensors, cameras, and fertilizers can help farmers combat these risks and, in this case, eradicate parasites that pose a particular danger to crops in the field. Imagine we had a garden with a particular number of plants spaced out over the space. Some parasites may choose to colonize the area in order to feast on the local flora and spread their own kind. Timely and effective countermeasures may be warranted in this instance. Parasites can hide in the ground and travel and reproduce in a dispersed fashion, so their precise location is unknown [20]. A team of drones can be quite helpful in this scenario, as they can monitor the entire area and pinpoint the exact location of the attacked plants or the parasites as they move from plant to plant using the cameras. Unfortunately, drones in the real world are powered by batteries that have a finite lifespan and can quickly run out of juice, rendering them immobile. In addition, the insecticide is restricted due to the low weight limits of the drones.

TABLE 14.2

Variation for Control

Remote human pilot	Real-time control by remote pilot
Autonomous	Automated operation after human initiation
Swarm control	Cooperative mission accomplishment via control among the vehicles
Remote human operator	Human provides the flight parameters to invoke the built-in functions for vehicle control
Semi-autonomous	Human-controlled initiation and termination, autonomous mission execution

Due to these limitations, it is important to coordinate drones across the cultivated area so that they do not repeatedly fly over the same areas. Also, keeping track of how much pesticide was used and who was responsible for conducting monitoring can be a difficult coordination work [21, 22]. In order to provide drone coordination strategies for the precision agricultural area, this simulator needs parasites and drone movement modules. Additionally, standardized drone communication modules for sharing maps and topologies are necessary for reducing drone traffic, averting pesticide waste, and decreasing energy consumption. Given the newness of the field and the increasing interest from both industry and academics, we are unaware of any simulator that incorporates these modules at this time [23].

One of the earliest descriptions of a simulator accounts for the impact of parasites, plants, and drones in contemporary agricultural precision [24]. The possible applications of sensors and on-board cameras for agricultural drones are discussed, expanding upon prior studies. The simulator's issue statement has also been expanded to cover all relevant variables for assessing coordinating methods [25, 26].

14.2 AGRICULTURAL PRECISION

This paragraph serves as an introduction to some of the more fascinating uses of agricultural precision. Interest in "smart farming" and "precision agriculture" has been rising steadily in few years. As Internet of Things (IoT) promises to usher in a plethora of innovative products and services, businesses and academic institutions are investing more money into making it happen. As a result, product costs can be reduced while yields are raised and quality is improved.

In order to lessen the strain on already overworked human resources, modern advancements in communication technology have made it possible to offer unique solutions for the constant monitoring of agriculture, livestock, and the water system. As a result, the precision agricultural industry is adopting cutting-edge systems that use embedded technology and machine-to-machine (M2M) connections. In fact, it is crucial to keep a close eye on the weather in this industry. The communication protocols may allow for more efficient use of network resources by lowering the amount of data generated. These methods help to increase crop yields and ensure their traceability by enhancing environmental and agricultural sustainability [27–29].

Obviously, as the global population rises, so does the need for food. However, agricultural land is shrinking at an alarming rate. Consideration is given to potential solutions that could improve productivity and resource use in certain locations. Because of these concerns, farmers are always looking for ways to boost the productivity of their crops [30].

As a result, there are numerous areas of focus among researchers and businesses that can aid in agricultural process optimization. Resource management is a major focus in precision agriculture since more efficient use of available resources directly correlates to greater yields. The availability of water is one of the most significant resources. It's obvious that more resource-conserving practices need to be put in place. Typical methods of regulating irrigation are extremely wasteful. By coordinating amongst devices with different but equally important monitoring and actuation responsibilities, a smart irrigation control system may ensure that no water is wasted during the distribution process. Activation of the irrigation system is typically based on technician perceptions rather than weather forecasts, plant health, or environmental factors.

Full automation of a crop-field monitoring and irrigation system based on the IoT necessitates a deeper understanding of the surrounding ecosystem. By learning more about the surrounding environment, we may implement a more optimal strategy for the crops and their yields. These systems are made up of a network of interconnected smart devices that share data to improve each other's understanding of their surroundings and the quality of their collective decision-making. The system for global management and the adoption of global strategies, which may relate to the choice of the area to use and how these must be governed, can be completed by the addition of a software framework. The reliability of the communication networks in this broad, rural area remains an open subject.

With cellular networks increasing their coverage regions and introducing new technologies, users can take advantage of the improved quality of service that comes with the greater availability of features like low latency and high bandwidth, we may be able to let out a sigh of relief. machine-to-machine (M2M) communications provide for a wide variety of possible protocols. Message Queue Telemetry Transport (MQTT) and Constrained Application Protocol (CoAP) are heavily employed by these advantages. In specific, MQTT is used since it is accessible and efficient. An intermediary, or "broker," controls who can connect to which topics, and who can post new topics. Embedded-technology-based "smart" gadgets may aid in achieving better outcomes through the intelligent application of specialized approaches. It has been successful in lowering the need for additional labour, water, and fertiliser.

Figure 14.2 depicts an example of a smart device used to perform a task related to water management. In this case, sensors are used to track crop data via M2M protocols. Data is collected and stored by remote services. Environmental information, such as the current weather and the accessibility of water, is also gathered simultaneously. In the event of a water shortage, the flow of water is controlled by an algorithm.

14.2.1 Insights from Video Analysis Systems to Aid Precision Farming

One of the most critical issues in modern farming, whether it be crops or cattle, is that of tracking their health and development. Taking measurements based on images and employing intelligent data mining are necessary if we are to learn more about our environments and improve our understanding of them. UAV can be employed to capture aerial views of agricultural landscapes and livestock farms.

The Normalized Difference Vegetation Index (NDVI) is a common tool for gauging the flora's vitality and, by extension, the ecosystem's health. While this metric is helpful for assessment, it is insufficient for implementing a truly effective solution to raise output and product quality. Differencing zones allows for the application of effective policies. Using NDVI and classification algorithms, we may split crop fields into zones based on their similarities in a variety of ways. This can aid farmers in deciding what to do in each area [31]. Predicting the planting yield variation with NDVI data is an excellent way to go [32]. The analysis of collected images allows one to ascertain the health of plants. The NDVI index can be computed using

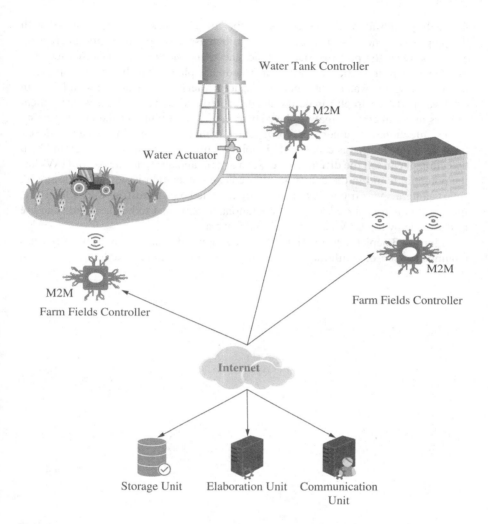

FIGURE 14.2   Network design based on machine-to-machine (M2M) interaction.

Equation 14.1 if the red channel is accessible, and using Equation 14.2 if only the blue spectra is available, as shown in the two recently published publications.

$$NDVI = \frac{NIR - Red}{NIR + Red} \tag{14.1}$$

$$NDVI = \frac{NIR - Blue}{NIR + Blue} \tag{14.2}$$

Video analysis has the potential to aid in the development of plantations in other vital domains, such as the identification of weeds in agriculture fields. The best way to identify this plant life is still up for debate. Herbicides are the go-to solution for dealing with a weed problem. A number of drawbacks have been noted with this approach. There is an urgent need to increase productivity while decreasing expenses. Over the past two decades, advancements in precision farming technology have been dramatic. In particular, weeds are plants that diminish crop yields by competing for water, nutrients, and space. Alternative, real-time solutions can be developed to help eliminate the need for herbicides. These devices use optical sensors and cameras to analyse their surroundings and pinpoint the exact location of any infection. By author [33], for instance, a machine visioning system is developed for a sprayer that is capable of pinpoint accuracy. Using a Gabor filter and blob detection, it can tell the difference between a plant and a weed. The use of UAVs has the potential to aid in the detection of weeds and plantation issues in this sector. A smart camera and infrared (IR) sensors are installed on a terrestrial UAV [34]. Here, information is transferred to the computational component to be classified. The use of herbicide by the UAV is permitted in the event of weeds.

Figure 14.3 depicts a terrestrial drone used for weed identification. This drone has a number of sensors built into it for taking readings on things like temperature and

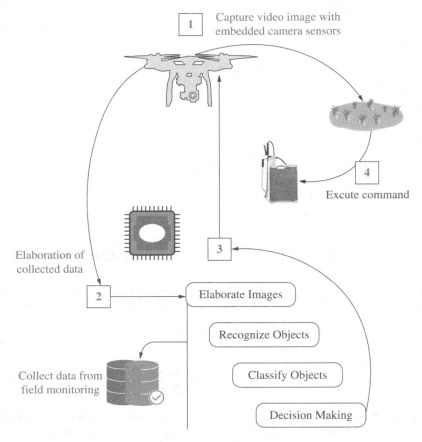

FIGURE 14.3　Terrain-based drone design used in precision farming.

humidity. In addition, it has a high-tech camera for capturing live views of the fields. The elaboration unit receives the images and does the video analysis, feature extraction, and object classification. The primary objective here is to locate weed plants and determine how numerous they are. Decision-making algorithms receive this information and use it to determine whether or not the drone should spray pesticides.

Precision livestock farming applications have proliferated in the recent decade. The encouraging findings that have been obtained explain the recent uptick in interest in this area.

Constant checks on animal development allow for better management of the farm's resources like food, water, and medical attention. For instance, the authors [35] offer an adaptive monitoring and analysis system for detecting objects and measuring pigs' development. During flight, a specialized 3-D camera captures photos to evaluate things by taking use of their depth. Once the depth photos are collected, an adjusted watershed algorithm is used to separate each animal into its own image. Pigs are hard to tell apart because of their similar appearance and their unpredictable lifestyle. Thus, state-of-the-art sensors like the time-of-flight camera are chosen because they provide the 3-D position data in the depth image rather than the RGB image [36].

14.2.2 Usage of Unmanned Aerial Vehicle in Agricultural Precision

UAVs have improved their contribution to large-scale agriculture by allowing for more precise crop-field surveillance in recent years [37]. By leveraging M2M and IoT technologies, we may gain a deeper understanding of the surrounding world, which will allow us to develop more nuanced algorithms for the various stages of decision-making [38, 39]. For example, pesticide pollution is still an issue today [40]. There are a number of changes that can be made to advance the mission. Long-term missions necessitate thoughtful solutions that support energy harvesting technology, such as calculating the energy needs of UAVs. Although UAV systems are designed to operate independently, several questions remain to be answered, containing some technical worries and questions about the normative laws of flying things [41]. UAVs are in high demand for agricultural insurance surveys, crop monitoring, and spraying. Using UAVs with high-resolution cameras is typical practice for area scanning [42, 43]. An aviation-based service is proposed by a number of products. Drones' missions often begin with them launching into flight and using GPS to navigate their surroundings. Flight control service has selected several waypoints across the map and set a predetermined route.

14.3 COORDINATION TECHNIQUES BASED ON ROUTING

Coordination methods are procedures used to maintain order within a collective. The term "coordination" is used in the drone industry to describe the process of leading a team of drones to achieve a single objective. As a result, packet exchange makes coordination possible. Drones are mobile nodes; therefore, communication with them is enabled using a wireless interface. The acronym "MANET" refers to "Mobile Ad Hoc Network," which describes this specific sort of network. This form of network is designed for ever-changing conditions. Drones' inherent mobility and finite energy resources present the primary challenge for MANET routing management. Routing updates in a dynamic network are provided by the periodic exchange of packets. When this occurs, routing algorithms need to do the following:

- Ensure routing tables are kept at a manageable size;
- Make the smartest decision for connecting to other nodes;
- Facilitate the upkeep of accurate routing tables;
- Get there quickly by transmitting few packets and at the ideal rate, the several routes and their associated expenses should be presented.

14.3.1 METHODS OF ROUTING

In general, we can divide routing protocols into subsequent categories:

- In proactive algorithms for MANETs, mobile nodes periodically send packets to each other. Because of this, routing may be done right away. In theory, every node's routing table would always reflect the most recent configuration. Characteristics of proactive protocols include as follows:
  - The transmission of packets occurs at regular intervals;
  - Applying Tables;
  - Refreshing Tables.

Some benefits of using proactive measures include as follows:

- Due to their periodic updates, routing tables include the actual network architecture and allow for instantaneous routing of informative packets.

The following are some of the drawbacks of using proactive protocols:

- Excess packet traffic.
- High signalling traffic.
- Reactive: Paths between nodes can be generated on demand via reactive protocols. Since MANET networks are always evolving, this is a plus. The following describe how a packet is transmitted using reactive protocols:
  - The process of determining the numerous routes between the origin and the destination nodes is known as route discovery.
  - The following are some benefits of reactive protocols that proactive protocols lack.
  - They only create new connections when necessary and remove heavy network traffic.
  - Currently, there are no databases that can be used to store routing information.
- Hybrid: The benefits of proactive protocols and those of reactive protocols are combined in hybrid protocols. Zone Routing Protocol (ZRP) and Location Aided Routing (LAR) [33] are two examples of algorithms that make use of hybrid approaches.
- Hierarchical: The packet overhead of proactive protocols is decreased by using hierarchical protocols. They categorize nodes and keep track of which

category each node's entry belongs to. Clusters are formed in the network, and a cluster with the most votes becomes the leader. This method creates a unified framework that is easier to expand. Proactive methods are used in each cluster to ensure that at least certain pathways are always reachable. We employ reactive methods of inter-cluster communication [44].

- Based on location: Based on the physical location of each node, these protocols are constantly revising the routing tables (GPS). The routing zone is where the routing protocol is intended to function, and it contains the expected zone, which is where the routing protocol supposes to evaluate the destination point [45].
- Aware of power – Conscious of power consumption: Each node in these approaches is conscious of the amount of energy it can consume. With this knowledge, the node may determine for itself, for example, whether to keep its power on or off, or which path will result in the lowest operating costs. The Power-Aware Routing Optimized (PARO) is one example of a power-aware approach [46].

14.3.2 ROUTING TYPE

The function of routing algorithms is to build and maintain up-to-date routing tables. There are two potential outcomes in the following:

- Statical routing: Static routing involves permanently storing a routing table on each node. Typically, the routing table's configuration is handled by an administrator. A manual update of the routing table is required if the network's topology is altered. This is why this method is used for mostly unchanging local area networks. Due to the elimination of unnecessary packet exchange caused by the modified routing table, this approach is actually quite efficient. Savings in bandwidth, processing power, and memory are only some of the benefits of static routing.
- Dynamic routing: A routing algorithm running on the node generates and updates the tables used in dynamic routing. Packets are exchanged between nodes, which increases the demand for network resources such as CPU and RAM. Algorithms of this kind are resilient to the ever-shifting nature of networks, allowing them to discover alternate routes to the same goal. Centralized and decentralized dynamic routing are two other categories that describe it.

14.3.3 SYNOPSIS OF THE COORDINATION ISSUES CONCERNING UAV

In the event of a parasite attack, our method uses a routing algorithm to coordinate the flights of drones, allowing for an accurate headcount to be collected.

14.3.4 DRONES

Each drone is fortified with its own little batteries, pesticide tank, and Wi-Fi module for coordinating with others in the region. Insecticide pumping and data transmission use up portion of the battery power, as does drone movement (Figure 14.4).

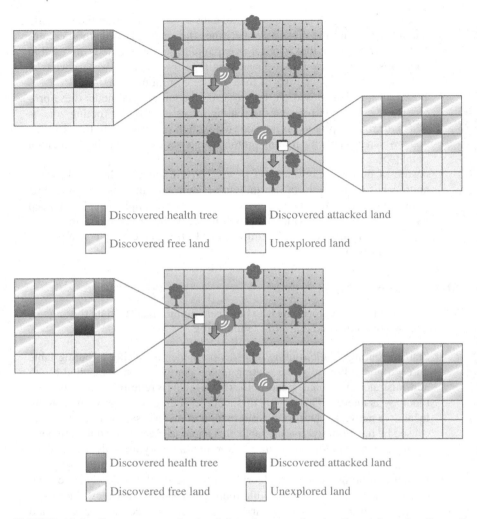

FIGURE 14.4 Common scenarios involving plants, explored cells, uncharted cells, and plant infections: (a) before the map swap; (b) after the map swap.

The primary states of drones are either constant motion or a pause while spraying insecticide on diseased plants. Depending on its task, the drone can move anywhere from very slowly to very quickly. The drone's current charge determines how quickly it can go to its destination after being recruited by another drone. More speed means more energy used by the UAV. When a drone's fuel tank or power supply is critically low, it automatically returns to base to be replenished. In the event of an emergency or if the drone has found parasites but the pesticide tank is empty or the battery is low, it might resort to the recruitment procedures. Drones are allowed to fly at any altitude between plant height and the maximum altitude. The height of each individual drone varies. To prevent accidental crashes, the drones are all flying at various heights.

To increase its visual range in the search for parasites, each drone is designed to position its camera in a slightly different way as it rises from the ground. The greater its height, the more inaccurate its parasite detection will be, leading to more garbage. Drones coordinate their efforts and share data wirelessly to accomplish their mission. Particular routing protocols are used to coordinate the flow of data. Several methods, including local floods and the link state, will be employed in this chapter. Thus, we aim to calculate the effect of different parameter settings on the two methods and draw comparisons where appropriate. There are two basic goals to this information sharing:

- Waste minimization by coordinated drone flight: Here, drones in close proximity to one another engage in a tidal wave of communication to help them decide what to do next; in this example, they decide to seek assistance from other drones.

The following are examples of how the drones' energy is lost:

- To stay airborne and move, drones waste energy. It has been found that the height of the drone has a direct proportional relationship to this loss.
- A greater altitude requires more power from the UAV because of the rarefied air; the drone uses more power to operate the pesticide pump.
- Drones use energy whenever they use the wireless module to send packets, and this usage was correlated with the amount of pesticide to be sprayed in millilitres.

The drones can conduct their parasite-hunting in two ways: at random or with the help of a distributed search algorithm (explained later).

Imagine a squadron of UAVs whose goal is to scout a region and wipe off any plant parasites they find. When an UAV spots a parasite, it uses the insecticide it carries to try to wipe off the infestation. Unfortunately, each drone only has so much insecticide on board. After a drone detects parasites in a specific location, it assumes leadership and must organize a coalition to combat the infestation using only the pesticides and energy at its disposal. The drone also shares some details about the parasites it has found with other drones. As a group, the drones will evaluate whether or not they have the equipment necessary to follow the pioneer.

It's important to keep in mind that the alliances created are only ephemeral in nature; once the parasites have been eliminated, the members of the coalition can go on to other endeavours.

Parasites are drawn to the dispersed plants in the field. It is considered that parasites do not coordinate their actions with one another but instead act according to the extent of their immediate environment. It faces just one direction and is restricted to the area immediately in front of it, which we will suppose to be three cells. The parasite, while in motion, can enter a neighbouring cell that it can see.

14.3.4.1 Parasites Mobility Model

Parasites are drawn to the dispersed plants in the field. It is considered that parasites do not coordinate their actions with one another but instead act according to the extent

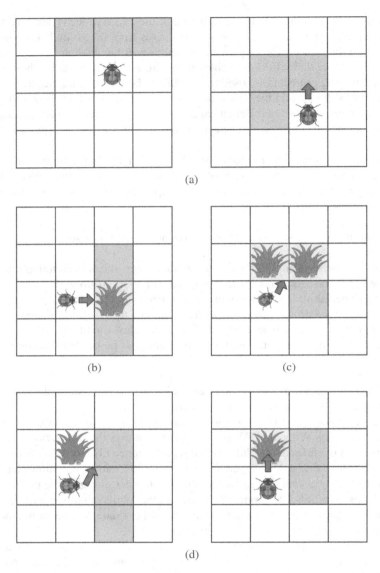

FIGURE 14.5 (a, b) Movement of the parasite; (b) the presence of a single plant; (c) the presence of a greater number of cells; (d) the absence of any cells.

of their immediate environment. The parasites in Figure 14.5 are believed to be unaffected by their surroundings, to be facing a specific direction, to be able to see up to three cells in front of them, and to be able to migrate into any of the visible and neighbouring cells. An illustration of parasite migration is shown in Figure 14.5(a). The parasite's orientation is to the north-west (NW); however, it has decided to relocate to the north (N), at which point it has already begun to shift its focus and new cells have begun to appear in its immediate vicinity. Cells with the ability to see are blue.

Potential migration routes for the parasite are as follows:

- Case 1: Like in Figure 14.5(b), the parasite only infects one of the visible cells, and it moves directly onto that cell.
- Case 2: More cells than depicted in Figure 14.5(c) contain plants, and the parasite randomly moves within one of these cells.
- Case 3: No readily apparent cells have a plant similar to that seen in Figure 14.5(d). The parasite takes a random path.
  - If the new position is different from the old one, the parasite will go in that direction, and if it encounters a plant while doing so, it will feed on it.
  - Unless something changes, it will keep moving in the previous direction.

14.4 PRECISION FARMING WITH SIMULATED UAV

14.4.1 UAVS SIMULATOR

In this scenario, we think of a fleet of UAVs/drones whose job is to keep an eye on a farm in order to wipe off any plant parasites they might find. When a UAV finds parasites, it sprays them with the insecticide it carries in an attempt to kill them. However, there is a finite supply of insecticide on board each drone. When a drone identifies parasites in a zone, it must organize a coalition depending on the available pesticides and energy sources, and it must also broadcast some information (such as its position, type, and no of capabilities) to the another Unmanned Aerial Network. The other drones are able to assess whether or not they have the means to contact the leader. It is important to note that the coalitions created are transient in nature; after the discovered parasites have been killed, the members of the coalition can conduct other responsibilities.

Drone navigation is simulated using an on-board topographic map. This map keeps track of the fields that have been explored so far, whether or not there are plants in the immediate area (cell), and whether or not any of those plants have been infected. All of this data is only available for as long as the simulator allows. The time it takes for an insect to reattach to a plant or for a new crop to be sown in the field is a reflection of the real world. Each square cell in the matrix represents a different section of the playing field, making up the map. A central location in the holding area has been hypothesized for the drone. What kind of plant is present, if any parasites are present, and, by extension, how susceptible the plant is to infection are all examples of information that could be stored in the cells of the plant. Additionally, the information in the cell can convey whether or not the plant is being cared for or whether or not the cell has been explored. After being moved, the drone's map is updated, wiping away any previous data and replacing it with fresh data. The drone can use this neighbourhood map to determine which field (cell) it needs to investigate next. When choosing a field, it picks a cell that hasn't been investigated yet.

Each of the blank cells is a potential winner. The probability of selection can be redistributed once certain cells have been visited. When the cell selection probability is set to 100%, all cells in the local map are unavailable. Maps can be shared between UAVs (drones within the drone's transmission range). It's possible that this will allow drones to quickly converge on the status of all cells in a given area without having to individually inspect each one. In addition, we consider the widespread presence of plants in the field that may serve as bait for the parasites. It is considered that parasites do not coordinate their actions with one another but instead act according to the extent of their immediate environment. It faces just one direction and is restricted to the area immediately in front of it, which we will supposed to be three cells. The parasite, while in motion, can enter a neighbouring cell that it can see.

14.4.2 SIMULATOR INDICATORS IN THE GUI

Each drone can fly and navigate its way around the area of interest thanks to its own batteries. It has a Wi-Fi module for coordinating with nearby drones and a pesticide tank for spraying the parasites. It is presumed that the communication range of each UAV is little. Yet, UAVs can communicate with one another through a chain of links. Millilitres (ml) are used to measure the fuel tank, while Watts (W) are used to measure battery power (W). In the front-end of the simulator, a graphical user interface (GUI) is used to set all these settings before evaluating the simulation. Drone movement, pesticide spraying, and communication all use up battery power in different ways (through radiation, signal processing, and other circuitry).

The user-friendly simulator interface assumes that a predetermined dose of pesticide is required to exterminate a given parasite. It is believed that drones can travel steadily from one cell to another, pausing only long enough to spray the poison on the tree where the parasites have attached themselves. The recommended simulator model would still work without this assumption, and the mobility model may be expanded even further. Using the simulator, you can also set a lower limit on how much pesticide to use (it is defined by GUI). In addition, the drone must return to its home base when the fuel tank drops below a certain threshold (set in the user interface). In the simulator, you can also determine how long it will take to fully charge the drone and refuel it. All drones have indicators that can change colour based on the quantity of remaining insecticide or the battery level, making for a user-friendly graphical interface.

Since Figure 14.6 is already available, we simply published it to facilitate comprehension of UAV levels. In addition, Figure 14.7(a) shows a coloured circle, representing the amount of pesticide left behind after each drone was flown, considering the definitions done for the colours. If you prefer visuals, Figure 14.7(b) shows the percentage of available charge for each drone in the i (P_i) series. Tree health indicators are also used to show the level of resistance to parasite assault (Figure 14.7(c)). When trees are infested with parasites, their health deteriorates proportionally to the amount of parasites present and the length of time they remain there. We denote the present health status of the ith tree as H_i, and the initial health status as H.

14.4.3 FRONT-END SIMULATOR

Using the simulator's primary user interface, users can specify spraying areas, the number of drones to be sent, the distribution of parasites, and the locations of the base stations from which the drones will take off and return to refuel and replenish their pesticide supplies. Furthermore, as demonstrated in [37], the expected lifespan

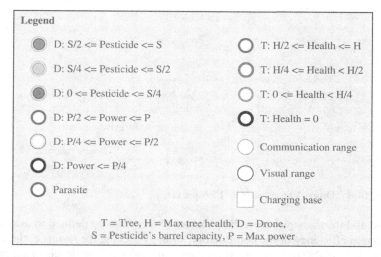

FIGURE 14.6   The UAV level examples.

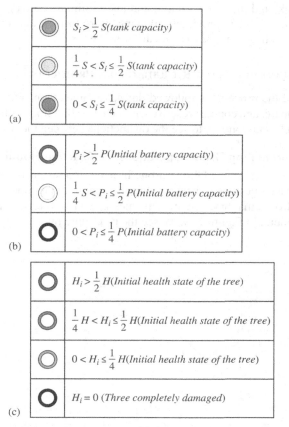

FIGURE 14.7   It's worth noting that the reference configuration provided. These include (a) a pesticide indicator, (b) a battery indicator, and (c) a tree health indicator.

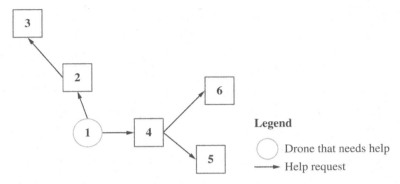

FIGURE 14.8   Drone 1 broadcasts an LSA packet.

of a tree and the damage caused by parasites to trees can be defined to evaluate the efficacy and efficiency of the coordination strategy among, for instance, the amount of pesticide available (ml), the maximum and minimum battery levels of a drone, the number of trees in the area under consideration, the tree's current health status after a parasite attack, and the drone's maximum and minimum battery level. A preview of the simulator's GUI is provided, allowing users to pick and create simulation parameters (including some described earlier in the text).

14.4.4   Methodologies for Recruiting New Protocols

Here, we detail the procedures followed during a comparison. We contrast reactive protocols, compare, and contrast reactive methods, like flooding, with proactive methods, such as link state routing, to see the distinctions between them.

14.4.4.1   Coordinating Drone Operations via Reactive Flooding

As demonstrated in Figure 14.8, the drone in need of assistance initiates a timeout and broadcasts a request for assistance. Once the maximum number of hops has been reached, any drones that have received the message will either save it or broadcast it to their neighbours. In Figure 14.9, we see the procedure by which the drone in need

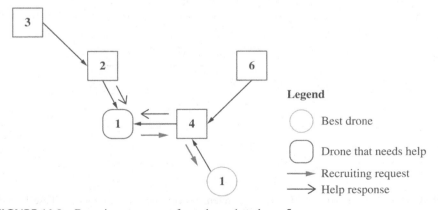

FIGURE 14.9   Recruitment request from drone 1 to drone 5.

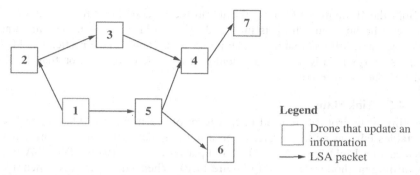

FIGURE 14.10 Drone 1 has sent a request for help.

of assistance reads the responses it has got and selects the drone that has the most pesticide. If two or more drones contain the same amount of pesticide, the one with the higher maximum battery life is picked. In a situation where two drones have the same amount of energy, the one that is closer to the controller will be selected. The drone with the quickest response time is the one it picks. Figure 14.10 shows the helping request for drone 1.The drone that needs assistance returns to its home base to refuel after sending a recruitment request to the drone it has determined to be the best candidate for the job. Upon receiving a request for assistance, any nearby drones will travel to the location specified by the request. In the event that the drone in need of assistance does not receive a response before the timeout expires (because no other drones are within range), it will save its current location so it can return after it has been recharged.

Recruitment packets employed in this protocol are as follows:

- Help packet: This datagram is transmitted in order to solicit assistance or to enlist the services of a specific drone out of the many that have responded to the call for assistance. This packet has a total of 28 bytes and is structured as follows:
- Destination IP Source IP Tagging, Tracking, and Location (TTL) X coordinate Y coordinate.

The "destination IP" column will provide the drone's final destination address. The inclusion of the network's broadcast address is mandatory when sending a request for assistance over a network. It is mandatory to mention the recruited drone's IP address in the recruitment request. The drone in need of assistance is revealed in the Source IP field. The "TTL" parameter shows the maximum hop count that can be achieved. The X and Y coordinate fields show locations of the parasites.

- Help response: The free drone has received an assistance packet with a broadcast address as the destination, prompting it to send this packet. It has a weight of 52 bytes and the following structure:
- Destination IP Source IP TTL Pesticide energy X coordinate Y coordinate Z coordinate.

Both the IP address of the recipient and the IP address of the sender must be entered. The hop count limit is indicated by the TTL parameter. The amount of pesticide (in millilitres) that the sender possesses is shown in the pesticide field. The sender's energy field is measured in joules. It is the sender's location that the X, Y, and Z variables represent (recruiter).

14.4.4.2 Link State

The link state protocol is used in this form of recruitment to keep nodes' routing tables current and accurate. Once a node detects a memory change, it will broadcast an Light sport Aircraft (LSA) packet to the network. The LSA packet forwarding method is depicted in Figure 14.10. When a drone moves, when it kills parasites, or when the state of a known network graph changes, an LSA packet is transmitted. Then, every drone is aware of the reachable network graph and the remaining pesticide stock for each node in that graph. Each drone keeps track of the IP addresses of the nodes it can access, the sequence numbers of the LSA packets it has received, and the pesticide stock remaining in its database. In times of crisis, this database will be used to select the most qualified drone recruits. The most generous pesticide-carrying drone wins. Dijkstra's algorithm is used to find the optimal route through the network graph to the drone of choice. As soon as a node receives a recruitment packet, it uses the Dijkstra algorithm to determine the next hop in the network and sends the packet to the correct destination. You can see this behaviour depicted in Figure 14.11, where the receiving node caches the packet and, if it's in range, heads to the area of the field where the drone in trouble is located.

Recruitment packets employed in this protocol are:

- LSA packet: This message will cause all nodes to revise their routing table. The anode will delete the original packet if it receives a copy. Leaving away the network diagram, this packet has the following components and a weight of 24 bytes:
  - Source IP Prop. IP TTL Sequence number Pesticide Graph.

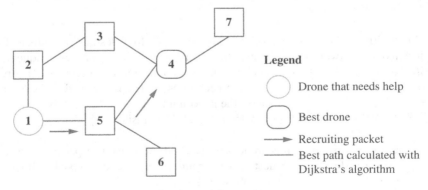

FIGURE 14.11   Drone 1 approaches drone 4 for employment.

Drone's original location is indicated in the "Source IP" section. In the LSA packet's "Propagator IP" field, the address of the drone that carried the message onwards is listed. The "TTL" field indicates the maximum number of hops allowed. The packet's sequence number is stored in the sequence number field. The amount of pesticide (in millilitres) that the sender possesses is shown in the pesticide field. Each node in the graph represents an IP address for a drone, and each edge indicates a direct connection between two of those nodes.

- The last of the aid packages: This datagram was sent by the drone that needed assistance. Only a neighbour found using the Dijkstra algorithm will disagree with you. Every node is capable of calculating the next hop. This data packet has a total of 24 bytes and is structured as follows:
  - Source IP Destination IP X coordinate Y coordinate.

An employed drone is indicated in the destination IP column. Drone's source IP address indicates which drone required assistance. In the X and Y fields, parasite locations are indicated.

14.4.5 ANALYSIS OF CAPABILITIES USING A VIRTUAL ENVIRONMENT

Parameters for the simulators are defined in Figure 14.12; we make use of an enhanced version of the simulator to generate novel findings in the context of interest. Following are some simulation results relating to energy used, parasites killed, and pesticides used. To evaluate how well the crew explored the region and salvaged the plants, we put the simulator's parameters and approach to the test.

Power consumption for both procedures is displayed in Figure 14.13(a). Reactive flooding outperforms the link state protocol in terms of performance. This is because reactive flooding makes use of shared maps, limiting the number of times a drone needs to move around an area being mapped. Figure 14.13(b) displays the temporal distribution of recruiting request counts. While the difference between the reactive flooding protocol and a protocol based on the link state paradigm is small, it is easy to see that the former yields a higher number.

A visual representation of the relative effectiveness of the two treatments under consideration is shown in Figure 14.13(c). This graph shows that the reactive flooding protocol outperforms the link state algorithm in terms of system performance, resulting in more parasite deaths. Lastly, Figure 14.13(d) demonstrates how the reactive flood technique permits a minimal quantity of communicated bytes in comparison to the link state-based protocol, which requires sending substantially extra packets to exchange data among drones.

14.5 CONCLUSIONS

Our research presents a novel simulator for precision agriculture, one that can assess the efficiency and cost of a fleet of drones outfitted with a wide range of

Drone's characteristics:

Weight of drone (g):	1500
Height of drone (m):	0.6
Max reached height (m):	50.0
Visual angle (°):	140
Min speed (m/s):	4
Max speed (m/s):	8
Recharging delay (ms):	15000
Spray delay (ms per mL):	600
Max loop cycle time (ms):	2400000

Consumption:

Spray consumption (j per ml):	10
Density of pesticide (g/cm^3)	1.5

Communication:

TTL (hop's number):	5
Bandwidth (bps):	11534336
Max range (m):	150.0
Propagation delay (m/s):	300000
Processing delay (ms):	4

Reactive Flooding:

Timeout to receive help response (ms):	2000

☑ Show communication/visual range
☑ Variable drone's speed

Parasite's characteristics:

Moving delay (ms per m):	2000
Parasites in a level of infestation:	1
Damage inflicted by parasite to tree (every s):	1
Needed pesticide to kill a parasite (ml per par.):	5

Tree's characteristics:

% trees in land:	50
Trees's health:	2500
Max trees's height (m):	3.0

Drone's barrels:

Pesticide (ml):	100
Max power (j):	400000
Min power (j):	1000

Other:

Number of charging bases:	8
Number of simulations:	1

Used protocol in help request:
○ Reactive Flooding   ○ Link-State

Distributed search drone's parameters:

Memory size to local map (Byte):	3025
DSM transmission period (ms):	1000
Deadline DSM (ms):	30000

FIGURE 14.12 Using the graphical user interface, the simulation's parameters can be changed, including the drone, parasites, plant, wireless network, energy levels, searching task, pesticides oil, protocol setup, and flooding range. From a User Interfaces (UI) perspective, the simulator setup process remains the same.

sensors and actuators. This study suggests cutting-edge methods for UAV teams to coordinate and control their operations. As a result, this work centres on the struggle against parasites, which are a serious threat because of their potential to wipe out an entire crop. The inspiration for the core idea comes from practical experience and need. After an attack by the Xylella a few years ago, several olive groves in Puglia were wiped out. Further, "Red Punteruolo" attacks cause the collapse of several palm fronds. We build a simulator to evaluate our method's efficacy by considering its financial and operational implications. This is a necessary step before using advanced technologies in the actual world. Results from multiple modelling programmes are discussed, including energy usage, parasite mortality, and pesticide use. Parameters and methods are analysed with the team's exploration capacity and resource conservation in mind. Results show that the proposed method is useful, and it performs well in terms of resource efficiency in networking during message exchange. In addition, we reduce emissions and extend the time that UAVs can spend in service. This expands the device's usefulness and increases its potential to eradicate parasites within the scope of its potential use.

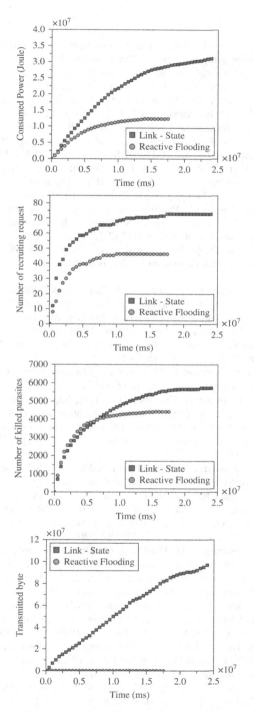

FIGURE 14.13 (a) No of killed parasites; (b) No of recruit requests; (c) Power consumption of transmitting bytes.; and (d) minimal quantity of transmitting bytes.

REFERENCES

1. G. Dolias, L. Benos and D. Bochtis, 'On the routing of unmanned aerial vehicles (UAVs) in precision farming sampling missions', in *Springer Optimization and Its Applications* (vol. 184), 2022, pp. 95–124. doi: 10.1007/978-3-030-84152-2_5
2. J. Anand, M. Dhanalakshmi and P. P. J. Raja, "Smart indication system for spinal cord stress Detection," *Int J Recent Technol Eng*, vol. 8, no. 3, pp. 6164–6168, 2019.
3. H. Ajay, A. R. Rao, M. Balavanan and R. Lalit, "A novel cardiac arrest alerting system using IoT," *Int J Sci Technol Eng*, vol. 3, no. 10, pp. 78–83, 2017.
4. M. Tropea and A. Serianni, 'Bio-inspired drones recruiting strategy for precision agriculture domain', 2020. doi: 10.1109/DS-RT50469.2020.9213516
5. F. De Rango, G. Potrino, M. Tropea, A. F. Santamaria and P. Fazio, "Scalable and ligthway bio-inspired coordination protocol for FANET in precision agriculture applications," *Comput Electr Eng*, vol. 74, pp. 305–318, 2019. doi: 10.1016/j.compeleceng.2019.01.018
6. G. Potrino, A. Serianni and N. Palmieri, 'Drones coordination protocols in the precision agriculture context', in *Proceedings of SPIE – The International Society for Optical Engineering*, 2019, vol. 11008. doi: 10.1117/12.2518973
7. A. Mukherjee, A. K. Panja, N. Dey and R. G. Crespo, "An intelligent edge enabled 6G-flying ad-hoc network ecosystem for precision agriculture," *Expert Syst*, 2022. doi: 10.1111/exsy.13090
8. N. Palmieri, A. F. Ganazhapa and L. M. S. Campoverde, 'UAVs support in a sensors' island for plants and crops monitoring', in *Proceedings of SPIE – The International Society for Optical Engineering*, 2021, vol. 11758. doi: 10.1117/12.2590036
9. U. R. Mogili and B. Deepak, 'An intelligent drone for agriculture applications with the aid of the MAVlink protocol', in *Lecture Notes in Mechanical Engineering*, 2020, pp. 195–205. doi: 10.1007/978-981-15-2696-1_19
10. J. Anand, R. P. Perinbam and D. Meganathan, "Q-learning-based optimized routing in biomedical wireless sensor networks," *IETE J Res*, vol. 63, no. 1, pp. 89–97, 2017.
11. R. C. Brito, J. F. Loureiro, A. Guedes and E. Todt, 'Optimization system for dynamic flight planning for groups of drones using cooperation with mobile recharge bases by means of multiagent system and recursive auctions', in *Proceedings – International Computer Software and Applications Conference*, 2019, vol. 2, pp. 537–542. doi: 10.1109/COMPSAC.2019.10262
12. R. Dhanalakshmi, J. Anand, A. K. Sivaraman and S. Rani, 'IoT-based water quality monitoring system using cloud for agriculture use', in *Cloud and Fog Computing Platforms for Internet of Things*, Chapman and Hall/CRC, 2022, pp. 183–196.
13. M. Tropea, A. F. Santamaria, G. Potrino and F. D. Rango, 'Bio-inspired recruiting protocol for FANET in precision agriculture domains: Pheromone parameters tuning', in *IFIP Wireless Days*, 2019. doi: 10.1109/WD.2019.8734209
14. M. Lowry, T. Pressburger, D. Dahl and M. Dalal, 'Towards autonomous piloting: Communicating with air traffic control', 2019. doi: 10.2514/6.2019-2207
15. R. Dhanalakshmi and J. Anand, 'Big data for personalized healthcare', in *Handb Intell Healthc Anal Knowl Eng with Big Data Anal,* wiley, 2022, pp. 67–92.
16. J. Anand, R. P. P. Jeevaratinam and M. Deivasigamani, "Performance of optimized routing in biomedical wireless sensor networks using evolutionary Algorithms," *Comptes rendus l'Académie Bulg des Sci*, vol. 68, no. 8, pp. 1049–1055, 2015.
17. C. Cambra, J. R. Díaz and J. Lloret, 'Deployment and performance study of an ad hoc network protocol for intelligent video sensing in precision agriculture', in *Lecture Notes in Computer Science (Including Subseries Lecture Notes in Artificial Intelligence and Lecture Notes in Bioinformatics)* (vol. 8629), 2015, pp. 165–175. doi: 10.1007/978-3-662-46338-3_14
18. R. Fu, X. Ren, Y. Li, Y. Wu, H. Sun and M. A. Al-Absi, "Machine learning-based UAV assisted agricultural information security architecture and intrusion detection," *IEEE Internet Things J*, p. 1, 2023. doi: 10.1109/JIOT.2023.3236322

19. P. Bhowmick, S. Bhadra and A. Panda, "A two-loop group formation tracking control scheme for networked tri-rotor UAVs using an ARE-based approach," *Asian J Control*, vol. 24, no. 6, pp. 2834–2849, 2022. doi: 10.1002/asjc.2722

20. M. D. Antunes and J. Panagopoulos, "Spatial distribution of kiwifruit quality and yield as affected by edaphoclimatic factors in northwest Portugal," *Acta Hortic*, vol. 1342, pp. 123–128, 2022. doi: 10.17660/ActaHortic.2022.1342.17

21. E. V. Vazquez-Carmona, J. I. Vasquez-Gomez, J. C. Herrera-Lozada and M. Antonio-Cruz, "Coverage path planning for spraying drones," *Comput Ind Eng*, vol. 168, 2022. doi: 10.1016/j.cie.2022.108125

22. H.-S. Lee, B.-S. Shin, J. A. Thomasson, T. Wang, Z. Zhang and X. Han, "Development of multiple UAV collaborative driving systems for improving field phenotyping," *Sensors*, vol. 22, no. 4, 2022. doi: 10.3390/s22041423

23. M. Mammarella *et al.*, "3D map reconstruction of an orchard using an angle-aware covering control strategy," *IFAC-PapersOnLine*, vol. 55, no. 32, pp. 271–276, 2022. doi: 10.1016/j.ifacol.2022.11.151

24. M. E. Minano, P. F. Pena, Z. He and D. M. Gomez, 'Self-awareness approach for complete coverage metrology using autonomous systems', in *2022 IEEE 9th International Workshop on Metrology for AeroSpace, MetroAeroSpace 2022 – Proceedings*, 2022, pp. 13–17. doi: 10.1109/MetroAeroSpace54187.2022.9856278

25. T. Elmokadem and A. V. Savkin, "Computationally-efficient distributed algorithms of navigation of teams of autonomous UAVs for 3d coverage and flocking," *Drones*, vol. 5, no. 4, 2021. doi: 10.3390/drones5040124

26. D. Avola, L. Cinque, A. Fagioli, G. L. Foresti, D. Pannone and C. Piciarelli, "Automatic estimation of optimal UAV flight parameters for real-time wide areas monitoring," *Multimed Tools Appl*, vol. 80, no. 16, pp. 25009–25031, 2021. doi: 10.1007/s11042-021-10859-3

27. A. G. Slongo, D. D. Moraes, L. Q. Mantovani and M. S. Venturini, "Handling qualities analysis of an unmanned aircraft vehicle for agricultural spraying," *J Aerosp Technol Manag*, vol. 12, no. SpecialEdition, pp. 38–51, 2020. doi: 10.5028/jatm.cab.1150

28. G. Castellanos, M. Deruyck, L. Martens and W. Joseph, "System assessment of WUSN using NB-IoT UAV-aided networks in potato crops," *IEEE Access*, vol. 8, pp. 56823–56836, 2020. doi: 10.1109/ACCESS.2020.2982086

29. U. R. Mogili and B. Deepak, 'Study of takeoff constraints for lifting an agriculture pesticide sprinkling multi-rotor system', in *Lecture Notes in Mechanical Engineering*, 2020, pp. 203–210. doi: 10.1007/978-981-15-1307-7_22

30. A. Akarsu and T. Girici, "Fairness aware multiple drone base station deployment," *IET Commun*, vol. 12, no. 4, pp. 425–431, 2018. doi: 10.1049/iet-com.2017.0978

31. H. Griffiths, H. Shen, N. Li, S. Rojas, N. Perkins and M. Liu, 'Vineyard management in virtual reality: Autonomous control of a transformable drone', in *Proceedings of SPIE – The International Society for Optical Engineering*, 2017, vol. 10218. doi: 10.1117/12.2267726

32. A. E. Morel *et al.*, 'Enhancing network-edge connectivity and computation security in drone video analytics', in *Proceedings – Applied Imagery Pattern Recognition Workshop*, October 2020-. doi: 10.1109/AIPR50011.2020.9425341

33. A. Refaai, V. S. Dattu, N. Gireesh, E. Dixit, C. H. Sandeep and D. Christopher, "Application of IoT-based drones in precision agriculture for pest Control," *Adv Mater Sci Eng*, vol. 2022, 2022. doi: 10.1155/2022/1160258

34. M. Ghamari, P. Rangel, M. Mehrubeoglu, G. S. Tewolde and R. Simon Sherratt, "Unmanned aerial vehicle communications for civil applications: A review," *IEEE Access*, vol. 10, pp. 102492–102531, 2022. doi: 10.1109/ACCESS.2022.3208571

35. C. Sastre, J. Wubben, C. T. Calafate, J. C. Cano and P. Manzoni, 'Collision-free swarm take-off based on trajectory analysis and UAV grouping', in *Proceedings – 2022 IEEE 23rd International Symposium on a World of Wireless, Mobile and Multimedia Networks, WoWMoM 2022*, 2022, pp. 477–482. doi: 10.1109/WoWMoM54355.2022.00074

36. F. Pasandideh, J. P. J. da Costa, R. Kunst, N. Islam, W. Hardjawana and E. Pignaton de Freitas, "A review of flying ad hoc networks: Key characteristics, applications, and wireless technologies," *Remote Sens*, vol. 14, no. 18, 2022. doi: 10.3390/rs14184459

37. D. Nath, A. Bandyopadhyay, A. Rana, T. Gaber and A. E. Hassanien, "A novel drone-station matching model in smart cities based on strict preferences," *Unmanned Syst*, vol. 11, no. 3, pp. 261–271, 2023. doi: 10.1142/S2301385023500115

38. C. P. L. de Jong, B. D. W. Remes, S. Hwang and C. De Wagter, "Never landing drone: Autonomous soaring of a unmanned aerial vehicle in front of a moving obstacle," *Int J Micro Air Veh*, vol. 13, 2021. doi: 10.1177/17568293211060500

39. W. Raza, A. Osman, F. Ferrini and F. De Natale, "Energy-efficient inference on the edge exploiting TinyML capabilities for UAVs," *Drones*, vol. 5, no. 4, 2021. doi: 10.3390/drones5040127

40. T. Yoo, S. Lee, K. Yoo and H. Kim, "Reinforcement learning based topology control for UAV networks," *Sensors*, vol. 23, no. 2, 2023. doi: 10.3390/s23020921

41. S. Singh and M. K. Sandhu, "Multi-level fuzzy inference system based handover decision model for unmanned vehicles," *Int J Electr Electron Eng Telecommun*, vol. 12, no. 1, pp. 35–45, 2023. doi: 10.18178/ijeetc.12.1.35-45

42. S. T. Muntaha, S. A. Hassan, H. Jung and M. Shamim Hossain, "Energy efficiency and hover time optimization in UAV-based HetNets," *IEEE Trans Intell Transp Syst*, vol. 22, no. 8, pp. 5103–5111, 2021. doi: 10.1109/TITS.2020.3015256

43. A. O. Lebedev and V. V. Vasil'ev, "UAV control algorithm in automatic mode using computer vision," *Optoelectron Instrum Data Process*, vol. 57, no. 4, pp. 406–411, 2021. doi: 10.3103/S8756699021040075

44. G. Raja, S. Anbalagan, A. Ganapathisubramaniyan, M. S. Selvakumar, A. K. Bashir and S. Mumtaz, "Efficient and secured swarm pattern multi-UAV Communication," *IEEE Trans Veh Technol*, vol. 70, no. 7, pp. 7050–7058, 2021. doi: 10.1109/TVT.2021.3082308

45. N. Kankanawadi, G. Karinagshetru, L. Patil, B. Ultheru, J. Baruch and T. Nallusamy, 'Conceptual design of a fixed wing vertical take-off and landing unmanned aerial vehicle', in *AIP Conference Proceedings*, 2021, vol. 2341. doi: 10.1063/5.0050366

46. P. Samarakkody, S. Guruge, D. Samaradeera, E. Jayatunga and P. Porambage, 'Enhance data collection process of a UAV-aided low power IOT wireless sensor network', 2021. doi: 10.1109/WCNCW49093.2021.9419977

15 Design of Autonomous Unmanned Ground Vehicles (UGVs) in Smart Agriculture

Yogesh Gangurde, Syam Narayanan S.,
Rajalakshmi P., and Naga Praveen Babu Mannam

15.1 INTRODUCTION

As the dawn rises over countryside hills and golden fields, a fleet of tiny robots awaken from their sleep and start their daily routine with a soft hum, rolling through the fields doing their job. These autonomous Unmanned Ground Vehicles (UGVs) are the most recent advancement in agricultural technology and are revolutionizing farming.

The era of manual labor and back-breaking work is over. Farmers may now rely on intelligent machines to execute a variety of activities thanks to the introduction of UGVs in agricultural applications (Figure 15.1). These robots can do everything from planting and harvesting to managing pests and weeds. They can detect and react to changes in soil characteristics, moisture levels, and more thanks to their advanced sensors and machine vision capabilities, ensuring that crops get the attention and care they require to thrive.

However, it goes beyond production and efficiency. The use of UGV in agriculture has the potential to increase sustainability and reduce adverse environmental effects of farming methods. These devices can support soil health and biodiversity by reducing the usage of chemical pesticides and fertilizers. Additionally, they can increase the safety and well-being of farm workers by lowering the demand for manual labor. Using UGVs for agricultural purposes heralds a new age in farming in which technology and nature coexist peacefully to make a sustainable self-sufficient world. We may anticipate a time when farming is more productive, profitable, and secure. Implementing UGVs in agriculture offers farmers the chance to broaden the scope of their operations and improve the effectiveness of their crop production as a result of the UGVs' capacity to work nonstop and with consistent precision. Because the machines can work around the clock, jobs that would have taken a long time to accomplish by hand can now be finished in a fraction of the time it would have taken previously. This may result in a considerable reduction in the expenditures associated with labor as well as an increase in overall productivity.

The ability of UGVs to collect and analyze enormous amounts of data is another advantage that they offer in the agricultural sector. These machines are able to acquire data about the growth patterns of crops, the moisture content of the soil, and other

FIGURE 15.1   Futuristic UGVs on farms (AI-generated image).

factors that influence crop yield because of the sophisticated sensors and machine learning algorithms that they are equipped with. This data can be used to improve and optimize farming techniques, which will ultimately result in increased crop yields and improved production quality. In addition to this, UGVs have the potential to assist in alleviating manpower shortages in the agriculture industry. The use of autonomous UGVs can provide a solution to the problem of decline in the number of young people entering the agricultural industry that is occurring in many countries. These UGVs can fill the gap left by the aging population and perform tasks that would otherwise require the use of manual labor.

The use of UGVs in agricultural applications is a fascinating technology that possesses the potential to completely revolutionize the farming industry. These machines can help farmers grow more crops with minimum resources by enhancing efficiency, productivity, and sustainability. Moreover, they can improve working conditions and promote environmental conservation. All of these benefits can be achieved simultaneously. We can anticipate seeing an increase in creative uses of UGVs in agriculture as technology advances, ultimately leading to a more profitable and eco-friendly future for the farming industry.

As interesting as the use of UGVs in agriculture may be, there are also some problems that need to be solved. One of the biggest challenges is the high cost of investment required to purchase and maintain these machines. As with any new technology, the upfront costs can be prohibitive for small- and medium-sized farms, which make up the majority of the agricultural sector. To ensure that UGVs are accessible to all farmers, it will be important to develop cost-effective models and financing options.

Another difficulty is ensuring that UGVs can work well in a variety of environments and weather conditions. Agriculture is a complicated business; crops grow in many different places and climates, which can be hard for machines to deal with. To solve this problem, UGVs need to have strong sensors and navigation systems that can adapt to different environments and terrains.

Concerns have also been raised about how the use of UGVs in agriculture will affect ethics and society. For example, more automation in farming could cause people to lose their jobs and make things even worse in rural areas. Concerns have also been raised about the privacy and security of data, since UGVs collect and send sensitive information about crops and farming methods. These worries must be taken care of by using and managing UGVs in a responsible and ethical way. Even with these problems, you can't ignore the potential benefits of UGVs in agriculture. With their ability to make farming more efficient, less harmful to the environment, and more productive, these machines show how farming could be more sustainable and productive in the future. By working with farmers, industry leaders, and policymakers, we can make sure that the use of UGVs in agriculture is guided by ethical, responsible, and sustainable principles. This will lead to a more prosperous and fair future for everyone.

15.2 SIGNIFICANCE AND EVOLUTION OF AGRICULTURE

Humans have been performing agriculture for approximately 12,000 years [1], i.e. since the Neolithic age, causing them to form permanent settlements on river banks having highly fertile soil and hence being highly arable, while changing their traditional hunter-gatherer lifestyle. The advent of agriculture in itself has been so significant that the revolution it caused has been termed Neolithic Revolution, referring to the era it occurred in [1]. The population has grown from about 5 million to nearly 7 billion in the last 10,000 years and still keeps growing. Currently, the global population is 7.6 billion people and is projected to reach about 9.8 billion people, an increase of 28.94% [2], by the year 2050 by the United Nations [2]. As the population increases, naturally the demand for food increases too. By 2050, the United Nations estimates that the global food demand will be doubled [2] in comparison to current food demand. According to the United Nations, urbanization is on rise too. It estimates that by 2050, 68% [2] of the world's population will be living in urban areas. This gives us an idea of some of the long-term problems posed by the progressing world in the area of agriculture. The availability of manual labor is on decline as it is, while as suggested by the United Nations, it will keep on decreasing in the future as well. Current agricultural practices in most parts of the world depend a lot on manual labor, except in developed countries like the USA, which have already deployed automated or semi-automatic machines and other technologies to reduce human labor. In traditional agriculture, pesticide spraying is done to keep pests like rodents and insects away from the farm crops to ensure maximum and healthy yield. The pesticide being sprayed is harmful for the humans who are operating the spraying machine, as well as for the environment due to excessive spraying [3, 4].

15.3 TECHNOLOGIES USEFUL FOR SOLVING THE PROBLEMS POSED BY THE CURRENT AGRICULTURAL PRACTICES

There are ways through which, by introducing the current technologies into the area of agriculture, much of the current problems can be solved, which in turn would also produce higher and safer yield, thereby also providing solutions to the previously discussed long-term problems. Technologies, like IoT (Internet of Things), use of various sensors like humidity sensors to detect the moisture content in the soil, use of robots for various operations like harvesting, spraying, and plowing, are the building blocks of smart agriculture [5]. UAVs (Unmanned Aerial Vehicles) and UGVs can be used for various purposes in agriculture. These technologies are useful in assisting farmers while requiring just a little involvement and effort from them [6–10].

15.4 USE OF ROBOTICS IN THE FIELD OF SMART AGRICULTURE

Robots are a key technology in smart agriculture that may assist in improving farming operations' productivity, efficiency, and sustainability (Figure 15.2). The advancement of robotics technology over the past several years has allowed for more accurate and productive agricultural methods, which has significantly improved agriculture [10, 11].

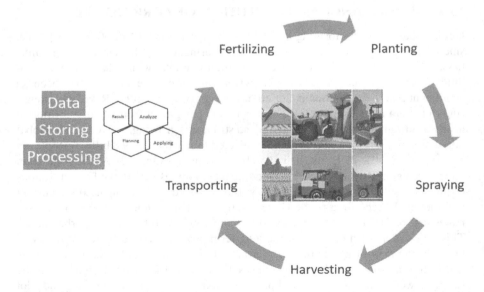

FIGURE 15.2 Smart agricultural processes.

The following are some applications of robots in smart agriculture:

Precision farming: Robotic technology can assist farmers in increasing the accuracy of their farming operations [12]. Robots with artificial intelligence (AI) and sensors can continuously monitor the health of the soil and crops, and they can also make exact modifications in reaction to shifting conditions. Using better resources like water, fertilizer, and pesticides, farmers may be able to increase yields while reducing expenses.

1. Autonomous farming: As autonomous robots may work without human supervision, farmers can automate time-consuming and monotonous operations. In contrast, drones can monitor agricultural health and spot pests and illnesses, while autonomous tractors can sow and collect crops. Productivity can rise, and labor expenses can be decreased as a result.

2. Soil and crop monitoring: Robotic technology may be used to keep an eye on soil conditions and crop development, giving farmers important information about the health of their crops. Drones can record high-resolution photographs of crops, enabling farmers to identify issues like nutrient deficits or disease outbreaks. Sensor-equipped robots can evaluate soil moisture, nutritional levels, and temperature [13, 14].

3. Weed and pest control: Weed and pest management may be handled by robots, which eliminates the need for dangerous chemicals that are bad for the environment and human health. Robotic weeders, for instance, can precisely detect and eliminate weeds, while robotic sprayers can administer pesticides just where they are required, minimizing waste and harm to the environment.

4. Harvesting: By automating the harvesting process, robotic technology can assist farmers in maximizing their crops. Robotic arms, for instance, can select produce precisely, lowering waste and raising yields. Moreover, automated harvesting lowers labor expenses and enables farmers to rapidly and effectively harvest crops.

5. Greenhouse and indoor farming: Robot technology is very helpful in indoor farming and greenhouse operations, where crop development is mostly dependent on climate management and illumination. While sensors and AI can assist in maintaining ideal growth conditions, robots can be used to automate chores like watering, fertilizing, and trimming.

Overall, robotics technology assists farmers greatly by providing more exact and effective agricultural methods that can boost yields, lower costs, and promote sustainability. As technology advances, we may anticipate seeing even more creative answers to the particular problems faced by smart agriculture [15].

15.5 HISTORY OF USE OF UGVs IN AGRICULTURE

Historically, farmers have plowed their fields and transported commodities with the help of animals like horses and oxen. Ground vehicles have been used in agriculture for ages. The invention of tools like tractors and combines during the Industrial Revolution transformed farming by boosting production and efficiency. These ground vehicles' potential for automation and autonomy was nonetheless constrained since they still needed a human operator. Precision agriculture's progress can be linked to the development of UGVs in agriculture [16]. With this method, soil and crop data are analyzed using technologies like Global Positioning System (GPS) and sensors, enabling the targeted and exact administration of inputs like fertilizers and insecticides. UGVs were invented as a result of the necessity for more accurate and efficient vehicles to apply these inputs brought on by the growth of precision agriculture.

Simple vehicles that could use GPS to follow a pre-programmed course were the first UGVs used in agriculture. These trucks were employed for activities, including field mapping, crop monitoring, and pesticide application. They still needed human operators to plan and manage their operations, though.

UGVs evolved with technology, becoming more capable of executing increasingly difficult jobs. They could identify and avoid obstacles, move across fields, and carry out duties like planting and harvesting crops thanks to their sensors and cameras. Robotic arms were added to certain UGVs, enabling them to carry out activities like fruit harvesting and trimming.

A variety of causes, including labor shortages, the need to boost production and efficiency, and the desire to reduce farming's environmental effect, have contributed to the development of UGVs in agriculture. UGVs have the ability to boost yields, decrease the demand for manual labor, and use less inputs like pesticides and fertilizers.

In conclusion, the necessity for more effective, accurate, and autonomous vehicles has spurred the progression of ground vehicles to UGVs in agriculture. We may anticipate seeing more advanced and capable UGVs produced and used in agriculture as technology develops, further transforming the sector.

15.6   AUTONOMOUS NAVIGATION FOR UGVs

The capacity of a robot or a vehicle to travel through an area without human assistance is known as autonomous navigation. UGVs can be guided by autonomous navigation to carry out operations, including planting, harvesting, spraying, and monitoring crops in the context of smart agriculture. These UGVs could be holonomic or nonholonomic systems [17] (Figure 15.3). Holonomic systems are the ones where the

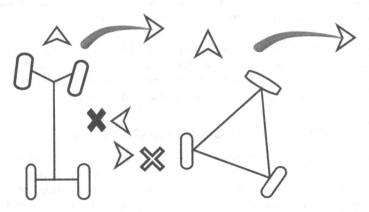

FIGURE 15.3   Non-holonomic and holonomic drive systems.

controllable DOF is equal to the DOF of the system, whereas a non-holonomic system is where the controllable DOF is not equal to the DOF of the system. Autonomous navigation has the potential to boost productivity, cut expenses, and boost crop yields in smart agriculture [18]. For UGVs used in smart agriculture, autonomous navigation involves a number of components. Perception, mapping, journey planning, and control are a few of them.

1. Perception: The UGV's capacity for perception is what allows it to perceive and comprehend its surroundings. Cameras, LiDAR (light detection and ranging), GPS, and IMU are a few examples of sensors that may be used to do this (inertial measurement unit). The location, orientation, and surroundings of the UGV are all made known by these sensors.
2. Mapping: A depiction of the area around the UGV is made by mapping. Techniques like simultaneous localization and mapping (SLAM) can be used for this. SLAM requires localizing the UGV inside the environment while also creating a map of the environment. This is accomplished by fusing movement data with sensor data from the UGV.
3. Path planning: Choosing the best route for the UGV to take is known as path planning. The UGV's present position, destination, and any potential roadblocks are taken into account in this process. The UGV's capabilities and limitations, like its top speed, turning radius, and capacity to go across various terrain types, are taken into account by path planning algorithms.
4. Control: Control is the UGV's capacity to carry out the intended course. Control algorithms that choose the UGV's speed and steering directives are used to achieve this. These algorithms consider the UGV's present condition, the planned route, and any sensor feedback. The UGV must stay on the intended path while avoiding hazards and keeping a safe distance from other objects. This is the responsibility of the control algorithms.

There are a number of difficulties that must be overcome for UGVs in smart agriculture to successfully navigate autonomously. They consist of the following:

1. Environmental variability: Agricultural ecosystems are very varied, with alterations in the landscape, the topography, and the weather. To be effective, autonomous navigation systems must be able to adjust to these changes.
2. Sensor reliability: Environmental variables like temperature, moisture, and dust all impact the sensor's accuracy and dependability. This may affect the UGV's capacity to correctly assess its surroundings.
3. Safety: Autonomous UGVs must function in a safe manner while around people and other things. They must be able to recognize impediments, avoid them, and operate within established safety parameters.
4. Scalability: To support huge agricultural fields and a large number of UGVs, autonomous navigation systems must be scalable.

Besides these difficulties, there have been a number of successful UGV implementations of autonomous navigation. For instance, John Deere has created a fleet of autonomous tractors that are capable of harvesting, spraying, and sowing seeds. These tractors can accurately traverse through fields and carry out chores thanks to a mix of GPS, LiDAR, and cameras. The TerraSentia robot created by the University of Illinois is another such example. The purpose of this robot is agricultural phenotyping, which entails assessing numerous plant characteristics, including height, leaf area, and biomass. The TerraSentia robot navigates around fields and gathers information on crops using a mix of LiDAR, cameras, and GPS.

15.7   ROBOT OPERATING SYSTEM (ROS)

Robot Operating System (ROS) is a free and open-source meta-operating system for robots. It offers all the features an operating system should have, such as hardware abstraction, low-level device control, common functionality implementation, message-passing between processes, and package management. Moreover, it offers resources and libraries for finding, creating, writing, and executing code across several machines. 'Robot frameworks', like Player, YARP, Orocos, CARMEN, Orca, MOOS, and Microsoft Robotics Studio, are comparable to ROS in various ways. The ROS runtime 'graph' is a loosely linked peer-to-peer network of processes using the ROS communication infrastructure that may be deployed across several computers. Asynchronous data streaming over topics, synchronous RPC-style communication through services, and data storage on a parameter server are just a few of the communication modes that ROS provides. Our Conceptual Overview goes into deeper information about them. Although it is feasible to connect ROS with real-time programming, ROS is not a real-time framework. The pr2 etherCAT system, used by the Willow Garage PR2 robot, carries ROS signals into and out of a real-time operation. The Orocos Real-time Toolkit and ROS are seamlessly integrated. Supporting code reuse in robotics research and development is the main objective of ROS. Executables may be independently written and freely connected at runtime thanks to ROS, a distributed architecture of processes (also known as Nodes). These operations may be organized into Stacks and Packages that are simple to share and distribute. Moreover, ROS provides a federated network of code repositories that permits distributed cooperation. This approach allows for autonomous decisions to be made about development and implementation at every level, from the file system to the community, yet it can all be combined via ROS infrastructure tools [19, 20].

The ROS file system is a critical component that enables effective communication and data sharing between robots and other devices. Although the ROS file system is comparable to the Unix file system, it has certain special features that make it more appropriate for robotics applications. Packages are collections of files comprising code, configuration files, data, and other resources required to operate a particular ROS node or application. These are how the ROS file system is structured. Each package has its own directory, which is home to a number of subdirectories that specify the functionality and organizational elements of the package [21]. One of the key benefits of the ROS file system is that it makes it simple to exchange and reuse packages among various robots and applications. The ROS package manager, which automates the process of obtaining, building, and installing packages from the ROS distribution, may be used to install and manage packages. Support for rosbag, a program that enables users to record and playback data from an active ROS system, is another essential component of the ROS file system. As it allows developers to record and examine sensor data, robot statuses, and other system events, this is very helpful for testing and debugging reasons.

15.8 SIGNIFICANCE OF ROS IN UNMANNED GROUND VEHICLES

1. The following are some crucial elements that make ROS significant for robotics in general: Standardization: The development, integration, and testing of UGV systems are made simpler by the standardized set of interfaces and tools provided by ROS. This lessens the difficulty and expense of creating and maintaining specialized robotic software.
2. Modularity: ROS is built to be modular, and its adaptable architecture enables developers to disassemble big robotic systems like UGVs into smaller, easier-to-manage parts. This makes it simpler to test and troubleshoot individual system components, as well as to replace or update them as necessary.
3. Reusability: ROS promotes the creation and exchange of reusable code and libraries since it is open-source and modular. By using pre-existing software components rather than beginning from scratch, developers can reduce the amount of time and resources needed for development.
4. Community: ROS has a sizable and vibrant group of users, academics, and developers who work together to build and advance the framework. This community offers assistance, information, and tools to new users so they can get started and fix issues.
5. Interoperability: ROS offers a common framework for communication that enables various components of a UGV system to talk to one another using a predetermined set of protocols. This facilitates the creation of more versatile and adaptive UGV systems by making it simpler to combine various hardware and software components from various manufacturers.

In general, ROS is important because it offers a strong and adaptable framework for creating, integrating, and managing complicated robotic systems like UGVs. It is a vital tool for robotics researchers, developers, and consumers because of its standardization, modularity, reusability, community support, and interoperability.

15.9 USABILITY OF ROS IN UNMANNED GROUND VEHICLES

Several robotics applications, including those involving autonomous cars, drones, industrial robots, and personal robots, heavily use ROS. The modular and adaptable design that ROS offers is one of its main features. This enables programmers to design complicated robot applications by combining many modules or packages, each with a distinct set of functionalities. Developers may use their favorite programming languages with ROS because it supports a wide range of them, including C++, Python, and Java. The capability of ROS to manage sophisticated robot hardware and sensors is another important benefit. Robots can communicate with a variety of sensors and devices thanks to the collection of drivers provided by ROS.

In contrast to the hardware interfaces, this enables developers to concentrate on the application logic and algorithms. A strong set of simulation and visualization capabilities are also included with ROS. Before putting their programs on actual robots, developers may test and debug them using these technologies in a virtual environment. This decreases the possibility of mistakes while saving time and money. In the development of autonomous cars, ROS has been crucial. Drones, autonomous vehicles, and self-driving automobiles are all controlled by ROS-based software. The navigation of autonomous vehicles requires a collection of tools for mapping, localization, and path planning, all of which are provided by ROS. Industrial robot development frequently makes use of ROS. Robot movement and communication with other equipment on the production floor are both managed by software built on the ROS platform. Moreover, ROS offers a selection of management and monitoring tools for industrial robots, assuring their dependability and safety.

Being a versatile and modular framework for creating complicated robot applications, ROS has emerged as a crucial tool in the robotics sector. Developers find it appealing because of its capacity for managing sophisticated hardware and sensors, support for several programming languages, and availability of robust simulation and visualization tools. In the creation of autonomous cars, drones, and industrial robots, ROS has been crucial, and its importance is only going to increase in the future [22].

15.10   USE OF ROS ENABLED AUTONOMOUS UGVs FOR SMART AGRICULTURE

As a potent tool for creating robotic systems capable of monitoring crops, planting, harvesting, and applying pesticides, ROS has become more popular in agriculture. Autonomous cars that can travel across fields and carry out activities with a high degree of precision and efficiency are being developed by using ROS-based technologies. The ability to integrate various sensors and hardware, such as cameras, LiDAR, and GPS, is one of the main benefits of using ROS in agriculture. These sensors give the robots vital information about their surroundings and allow them to carry out operations like mapping, localization, and obstacle recognition. For developers to build complicated agricultural robots, ROS offers a set of tools for combining various sensors and hardware. The path planning and navigation features that ROS offers are also crucial for agricultural robots [23]. These devices provide the robots the ability to move through fields, avoid hazards, and carry out duties effectively and accurately. In order to reduce the need for manual labor and the usage of pesticides, ROS-based systems may be used to build autonomous vehicles that can execute activities like agricultural spraying with extreme precision [2, 24, 25].

Moreover, ROS may be used to create robotic systems that can monitor crops and give farmers useful information. For instance, soil moisture, temperature, and other environmental variables may be tracked using ROS-based systems. By using this information to optimize irrigation and fertilizer application, crop output may be increased while wasting less water and fertilizer. By enabling the creation of complex robotic systems that are capable of carrying out activities with a high degree of accuracy and efficiency, the use of ROS in agriculture has the potential to completely transform the sector. With its capacity to manage sophisticated sensors and hardware, support different programming languages, and offer potent simulation and visualization tools, ROS offers a versatile and modular foundation for the creation of agricultural robots. We can anticipate seeing more advanced and functional ROS-based agricultural robots being created and used in the field as technology develops [26].

Since ROS offers a flexible and modular framework for creating and combining software components for UGV control and navigation [27, 28], it is especially well suited for UGVs. Following are some explanations for why ROS is particularly advantageous for UGVs:

1. Support for sensors and actuators: ROS offers a variety of drivers for sensors and actuators, including GPS, LiDAR, IMU, and cameras that are often used in UGVs. As a result, it is simpler to operate and interact with these devices in a standardized manner.

2. Navigation stack: ROS has a navigation stack that comprises algorithms for motion control, obstacle avoidance, and local and global path planning. These algorithms may be modified and refined to meet the unique requirements of a UGV, including the kind of terrain, the size and weight of the vehicle, and the mission requirements.

3. Testing and simulation: Before putting UGV software on a real robot, developers may test it in a simulation environment provided by ROS called Gazebo. By allowing developers to debug and improve software components in a secure and controlled environment, this can help save time and costs.

4. Flexibility and modularity: With a decentralized architecture that enables developers to split up UGV software into smaller, more manageable components, ROS is meant to be modular and adaptable. This makes it simpler to switch out or update components as needed, as well as to integrate and test various software modules.

5. Community support: ROS has a sizable and vibrant developer and user community that actively contributes to the growth and development of the framework. This community offers assistance, information, and tools to new users so they can get started and fix issues.

Overall, ROS is a strong and efficient platform for creating software for UGVs thanks to its support for sensors and actuators, navigation algorithms, simulation and testing tools, flexibility and modularity, and community support.

15.11 ROS NAVIGATION STACK AND ITS SIGNIFICANCE

Robots using the ROS can navigate thanks to the robust ROS Navigation Stack architecture. A collection of software packages called the navigation stack enables a robot to navigate from one place to another while avoiding risks and other obstacles. The parts that make up the ROS Navigation Stack are described in the following succinct manner:

1. Costmap: A 2D or 3D depiction of the robot's immediate surroundings is called a costmap. Each cell on the map is given a cost that represents how challenging it is for the robot to go through that space. Data from numerous

sensors, including cameras and laser scanners, are combined to create the costmap.

2. Localization: This process determines the robot's posture (position and orientation) in relation to its surroundings. It updates the robot's estimated posture using sensor data and keeps a precise map of the robot's position.

3. Path planning: Using the costmap and any impediments in the route, the path planning component creates a path from the robot's present location to its desired location. In order to choose the best path across the environment with the lowest cost of movement, it employs algorithms like A* or Dijkstra's algorithm.

4. Motion control: The motion control part instructs the robot's motors or controllers to move along the path that was produced. It keeps track of the robot's position and speed, adjusting the velocity orders as necessary to keep the intended trajectory.

5. Obstacle avoidance: The obstacle avoidance component keeps an eye out for any potential barriers or other dangers that the robot's sensors may pick up on. It plans a safe route that avoids obstacles while still getting to the destination using the costmap.

6. Global planner: The global planner creates a high-level plan to guide the robot from its starting point to its destination. Based on the robot's capabilities and any barriers in the area, it chooses the best route. The global planner employs a global path planning method, such as A* or Dijkstra's algorithm, to plan the path using the costmap.

7. Local planner: The local planner creates a low-level plan that is used to execute the global planner's high-level plan. It considers potential obstructions as well as the mechanics of the robot. A local path planning algorithm, such as Dynamic Window Approach (DWA) or Timed Elastic Band, is often used by the local planner (TEB).

8. Recovery behaviors: The robot can use recovery behaviors to get out of tricky situations like being trapped or losing localization. They act as a safety net to guarantee that the robot can navigate even in the event of unforeseen circumstances.

9. Map server: The navigation stack may store and retrieve maps using the map server. Maps can be read from a file or created instantly using sensor data.

The ROS Navigation Stack offers a thorough and adaptable foundation for robot navigation overall. It has been effectively applied to a variety of robotic systems, including ground robots, aerial robots, and underwater robots. It is widely used in robotics research and industry.

The ROS Navigation Stack has the following benefits and significance:

1. Modularity: The ROS Navigation Stack was created with a modular architecture, allowing for easy customization and adaptation to various robotic systems. The ability to replace or alter any portion of the stack, including the costmap, path planner, and obstacle avoidance, makes it simpler to create a navigation system that meets the special needs of a certain robot.

2. Flexibility: The ROS Navigation Stack is very adaptable, enabling developers to design navigation systems using a variety of sensors and hardware. It works with a range of robotic platforms, including terrestrial, aerial, and underwater robots, and supports a number of sensors, including laser scanners, cameras, and ultrasonic sensors.

3. Robustness: Even in demanding and dynamic contexts, the ROS Navigation Stack is built to be durable and dependable. It employs cutting-edge algorithms for path planning, localization, and obstacle avoidance to make sure that the robot can move around in complicated situations safely and effectively.

4. Open-source: The ROS Navigation Stack is an open-source project, making it accessible to the robotics community without charge. As a result, innovation and development in the field of robots are accelerated. Developers can now work together, share code, and build on previously completed projects.

5. Testing and simulation: Before implementing their navigation systems on a real robot, developers can test and validate them in a virtual environment thanks to the tools and packages provided by the ROS Navigation Stack. This makes it simpler to find mistakes, correct them, and improve performance prior to deploying a system in a real-world setting.

6. Community support: The ROS Navigation Stack has a sizable and vibrant developer and user community that actively supports the project by providing code, documentation, and assistance. Developers who are creating navigation systems can take advantage of the expertise and experience of other community members, which is a valuable resource.

15.12 SIMULTANEOUS LOCALIZATION AND MAPPING (SLAM) AND ITS USE FOR SMART AGRICULTURE

SLAM is a robotics technique that creates a map of an uncharted area while keeping track of the robot's location.

When a robot is placed in an environment that was not previously known to it and must explore and navigate through it in order to complete tasks like object recognition, path planning, and obstacle avoidance, the SLAM problem occurs. The robot must create a map of the environment and keep track of its own location inside it in order to accomplish this. In order to create a map of the surrounding area and determine the robot's position, SLAM algorithms often include a variety of sensors, including laser scanners, cameras, and odometry sensors. The sensors measure the robot's mobility and environment, which then use this data to estimate the robot's position and the locations of objects in the environment.

There are two main steps in the SLAM process:

1. Mapping: The robot uses its sensors to construct a map of its surroundings in this step. Techniques, like grid-based mapping, feature-based mapping, or occupancy grid mapping, can be used for this.

2. Localization: In this phase, the robot determines its location inside the environment using the map it created in the previous phase. Techniques, like probabilistic localization, feature-based localization, or Monte Carlo localization (MCL), can be used for this.

Robotics depends heavily on SLAM because it allows machines to function autonomously in unpredictable and changing settings. It has a wide range of applications in many industries, including construction, search and rescue, and agriculture, where robots must operate in difficult and unexpected settings.

With the development of autonomous robots, which are able to complete tasks without human assistance, SLAM has grown in significance. Drones, autonomous underwater vehicles, and self-driving automobiles all rely on SLAM to navigate and function in their particular surroundings. One of SLAM's main benefits is its real-time operation, which enables it to produce maps and estimate the robot's position as it moves through the environment. This is essential for applications like autonomous vehicles, which need real-time feedback to operate safely and efficiently. SLAM has a number of difficulties, including sensor noise, measurement error, and computing complexity. To overcome these difficulties and boost the precision and effectiveness of SLAM, researchers are constantly creating new algorithms and methodologies [29].

SLAM has a number of possible uses in smart agriculture, such as:

1. Crop monitoring and mapping: With the help of SLAM, agricultural robots or drones may map an entire field, assess the health of the crops, find signs of plant disease, and calculate the yield. Farmers can use this knowledge to better inform their decisions on the use of pesticides, fertilizer, and irrigation, which will result in a more effective use of resources and increased crop yields.
2. Precision farming: High-resolution maps of the agricultural field can be created using SLAM and used in precision farming. The application of fertilizers, herbicides, and other inputs can be precisely and accurately prescribed using these maps.
3. Autonomous navigation: Agricultural robots with SLAM capabilities can move across a field on their own while avoiding hazards and according to a predetermined route. This could decrease the demand for manual work and boost farming's effectiveness.
4. Harvesting: One of the most important uses of SLAM in smart agriculture is autonomous harvesting. Robots can move around a field, recognize and gather ripe crops, and protect the plants by employing SLAM. By doing so, the demand for physical labor may be lessened and the efficiency of the harvesting process may be improved.

By providing high-resolution maps of the field, enabling precision agriculture [30], enabling autonomous navigation, and increasing the effectiveness of the farming process, SLAM can be very helpful in smart agriculture.

15.13 ROS2 AND NAV2 VS. ROS1 NAVIGATION STACK

The new ROS (ROS2) was developed to overcome the shortcomings of the original ROS, including real-time performance, security, and scalability. An open-source framework called ROS2 is used to create robotic software applications. A more flexible architecture, compatibility for numerous operating systems, and improved networking are just a few of the enhancements it offers over ROS. ROS2 Nav2, also known as Navigation2, is a navigation stack for ROS2 that offers cutting-edge capabilities for mobile robots' autonomous navigation. It is based on the ROS2 framework and provides better performance, dependability, and adaptability than the ROS navigation stack, which it succeeded.

ROS2 Nav2 has a number of important properties, including:

1. Modular: The Nav2 stack is modular, enabling users to quickly add or remove components in accordance with their needs. This gives it a lot of flexibility and customization.
2. Improved path planning: Route planning has been improved, and Nav2's algorithms produce efficient and slick courses for the robot to follow.
3. Advanced localization: The MCL technique, which gives precise localization in dynamic situations, is one of the advanced localization algorithms that Nav2 offers.
4. Support for many robots: Nav2 supports multiple robot systems, enabling several robots to navigate independently of one another at the same time.
5. Improved scalability: Nav2 is made to be very scalable and is capable of handling huge, complicated landscapes with a variety of obstacles.

15.14 USE OF AUTONOMOUS MOBILE ROBOT (CLEARPATH HUSKY) FOR AGRICULTURAL SPRAYING APPLICATION

A spraying mechanism can be developed on top of Clearpath's Husky robot which is a good mobile platform that is capable of traversing on moderately rough terrain. It comes with the capability to perform autonomous navigation based on SICK LMS 151 LiDAR. The sensors that it generally uses include SwiftNav Real-Time Kinematics (RTK) GPS and SICK LMS1XX LiDARs. The top of the robot has a lot of area where multiple mountings can be made for carrying the mission payload which could vary from different sensors to different actuators, like robotic arms for harvesting, or a spraying mechanism for spraying (Figure 15.4).

The exact and targeted administration of insecticides, herbicides, or fertilizers to crops based on the real requirements of the plants is known as precision spraying. This method aims to maximize crop productivity, eliminate waste, and lessen the negative effects of agricultural activities on the environment.

Regardless of the real demands of the plants, the previous spraying technique required dispersing the same amount of chemicals across the entire area. As a result, some areas had excessive spraying, which may harm the crops, while other areas received little spraying, which may result in reduced yields. Also, it resulted in chemical runoff, which could pollute the land and water and harm the environment.

Contrarily, precision spraying entails analyzing the unique requirements of the crops, such as growth rate, nutrient levels, and pest infestations, using sensors and other technologies. The right amounts of chemicals are then applied to each plant based on this information, resulting in optimal crop development, increased yields, and little environmental effect. Many techniques, including aerial spraying, ground-based machinery, and even robotic systems, can be used for precision spraying. The unique application and the state of the technology determine the

FIGURE 15.4   Clear path Husky with smart spraying setup.

method to be used. In general, precision spraying is a very productive agricultural technique that can maximize crop yields while minimizing its negative environmental effects. It enables farmers to use chemicals more effectively and efficiently, leading to better crops, greater earnings, and an agricultural system that is more sustainable.

A more specialized and targeted approach to managing infestations can be offered to farmers using computer vision and AI, which can be used to identify pests in a range of crops. In order to detect symptoms of pest damage or infestations, machine learning algorithms are used to evaluate crop photos or videos.

Here are some of the steps involved in using computer vision and AI to detect pests:

1. Data gathering: The initial phase entails gathering a sizable dataset of pictures or videos of both healthy and pest-free crops. The machine learning algorithm is trained using this data to identify the telltale indications of pest damage.
2. Pre-processing: To improve the quality of the data and make it simpler for the algorithm to detect the pests, the photos or video recordings are first processed. Techniques, like filtering, cropping, or altering the contrast and brightness, may be used for this.
3. Training the algorithm: The machine learning algorithm is then trained to recognize the pests using the pre-processed data. In order to do this,

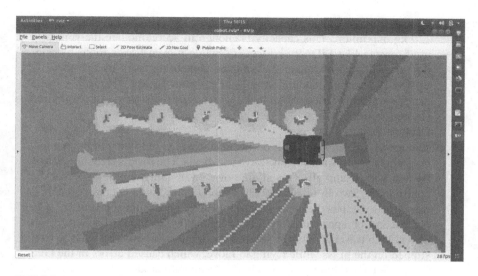

FIGURE 15.5 Path planning on Clearpath Husky using ROS navstack.

captioned photos or videos that show which areas are and are not affected by pests are sent into the algorithm.

4. Testing and validation: After the algorithm has been trained, it is put to the test and validated using a new dataset of photos or videos. This makes it easier to verify that the algorithm correctly recognizes the pests and does not produce false positives or false negatives.

5. Implementation: Using cameras or other sensors to take pictures or videos of the crops, the trained algorithm can then be put into practice in real time. The program analyzes the data in real time and spots any indications of infestations or damage from pests.

In the implementation part mentioned earlier, a pump can be switched on and off based on whether the crop needs to be sprayed or not, or how much spray it needs. This way the problem of excessive spraying gets solved. The robot can travel along the crop rows autonomously once the waypoints and goal locations are given, using the ROS navigation stack (Figure 15.5).

15.15 RAPID PROTOTYPING UGV FOR SMART AGRICULTURE (CASE STUDY)

15.15.1 DESIGN APPROACH

Following are the parameters that were considered while designing the autonomous UGV/rover:

1. Payload capacity:
   The size, shape, and design of the rover depend upon the required payload capacity for the specified mission of the rover. The autonomous rover being

discussed in this chapter is designed to carry a maximum payload of about 120 kg maximum. This capacity is enough to accommodate the generally used sensors like LiDAR and camera, while it even leaves room for adding an additional computer for complex computing tasks like performing SLAM and adding medium-sized manipulators as well. The robot has a plate on top with various holes that will act as a provision to install required payload/sensors.

2. Driving terrain:

The rover is designed to run on flat surfaces, i.e. on-road conditions, and does not have a suspension on any of its wheels. The rover's chassis is driven by four wheels and all of them are powered by individual motors that are controlled by two Robo Claw 2x30A motor controllers. On on-road conditions, the rover has the capability to reach the maximum speed of 1.977 m per second or approximately 7.1892 kilometer per hour. The rover was also able to traverse on short grass, although it was observed that the tires slipped on the grass while trying to move, which caused errors in the GPS waypoint navigation in auto mode, while manual mode did not face much issues, since the operator can adjust the speed accordingly to avoid slippage. The approach and departure angles are suitable for on-road application.

3. Mission requirements:

Autonomous rovers are required to perform missions as a UGV in dirty/ infeasible/dangerous environments. This rover was designed keeping in mind the ability to be able to go to such places. Its medium size lets it fit into these places with ease. The material of the robot was chosen to be stainless steel for enough rigidity while also being anti-rust.

15.15.2 HARDWARE USED

The electronic hardware and sensors used with the rover are as mentioned in Table 15.1.

TABLE 15.1
List of a Hardware Components in UGV

Sl. No.	Electronic Hardware and Sensors	Quantity
1.	Pixhawk4 controller	1
2.	RoboClaw 2x30A motor controllers	2
3.	Raspberry Pi companion computer	1
4.	Geared motors	4
5.	LiFePO4 Battery pack	1
6.	Power module	1
7.	Here3 GPS antenna	1
8.	Single-point LiDAR	1
9.	IP Camera	1
10.	4S LiPO Base station battery	1

15.15.3 HARDWARE DESCRIPTION AND FUNCTION

1. Pixhawk 4:

   Pixhawk is an open-source autopilot hardware, under BSD license, and is generally used with UAVs, i.e. drones, and less commonly with rover platforms. It has the capability to navigate the robot according to the provided inputs in manual as well as automatic mode, using computer teleoperation commands and GPS waypoints, respectively. It comes with different firmwares among which the Ardurover firmware was suitable for our application. The hardware is easy to use, has all the connections required (like GPS, PWM pins for motor control) on the same board, and can be operated using the open-source QGC (QGroundControl) software. Hence, this hardware was the preferred choice.

2. RoboClaw 2x30A:

   The robot chassis is driven around using four wheels that are powered by four geared motors. The amount of power supplied to the motor is controlled by two RoboClaw 30A motor controllers. The motor controller can supply a current of 30 A continuous and 60 A peak per channel.

3. Raspberry pi companion computer:

   A Raspberry pi board is being used to pass the communication between pixhawk and the remote base station that is being in turn passed to QGC on the remote computer/laptop. The data are sent over a Wi-Fi connection instead of radio, as the base station is equipped with a high gain antenna that increases operational range up to 1 km. This connection can be bypassed if operation via radio telemetry modules is required for a particular mission. The system was tested with a pair of 3DR 915MHz radio telemetry modules and it performed well, as expected.

4. Geared motors 300 W:

   The rover is an autonomous four-wheeled differential drive robot actuated using four geared electric motors, one for each wheel. The differential type drive was used for this robot as it makes it highly maneuverable and easy to control using the Ardupilot's rover firmware, with the downside being that the differential drive arrangement draws more current while turning in place due to high dynamic friction.

5. LiFePO4 battery:

   A Lithium Ferro-Phosphate battery was used with 54 Ah Capacity and an output voltage of 24 V. This battery provided the rover with a total runtime of approximately 4–4.5 hours and the charging time was close to 8 hours.

6. Power module:

   A power module is used for supplying power to all the electrical and electronic components on the rover.

7. Here3 GPS antenna:

   Here3 GPS is a GNSS (Global Navigation Satellite system) antenna which supports RTK getting location information from the GPS as well as the Russian GLONASS (Global'naya Navigatsionnaya Sputnikovaya Sistema) to get location information. If an RTK base station is included in the system, the GPS signals are expected to be accurate up to 2–3 cm; however, for this version of the UGV, RTK is not used and is a part of the future scope.

8. Single-point LiDAR:
   A single-point LiDAR has been installed on the front face of the robot, at its horizontal center. The maximum range of the LiDAR is about 6 m. And detected distance is directly shown on the QGC software once the option is enabled.

9. IP camera:
   An IP camera is mounted on the top of the rover, facing to the front side. The camera feed can be acquired on the remote PC using the Real-Time Streaming Protocol (RTSP), with a very low latency. The RTSP feed can be directly viewed in the QGC software upon entering the RTSP address and enabling the feed.

10. Lithium Polymer 4S battery for base station:
    A LiPo 4S battery is used to power the Wi-Fi base station. The capacity of the battery is 6200 mAh (milliampere-hour) and is observed to last for about 20 hours of continuous use.

15.15.4 SOFTWARE DESCRIPTION

The QGC software was used for sending and receiving data to and from the vehicle. This is an open-source software and has cross-platform support, including Windows, Ubuntu, and MacOS. It is a powerful ground control station and was used for deploying waypoints for GPS navigation.

15.15.5 EXPERIMENTAL ANALYSIS

Max average velocity test: This test was carried out to find out the maximum average velocity of the UGV. The UGV was manually operated and gave maximum thrust covering a stretch of 43 m available at our facility, in approximately 22 seconds. Hence, the maximum average velocity was found to be about 1.95 m/s or 7 km/h.

Payload test: The UGV was loaded with payloads that increased in weight gradually until the vehicle stopped performing locomotion nominally. This threshold was found out to be 110 kg.

Camera feed streaming: The IP camera installed on the UGV can be used for monitoring where the UGV is going while it is BVLOS (Beyond Visual Line Of Sight) so as to ensure proper control in order to avoid any physical damage to the hardware or living beings around the UGV. The IP camera's feed was obtained via RTSP on the QGC software.

Single-point LiDAR: The single-point LiDAR installed on the horizontal center of the front end of the robot was used to obtain data on the QGC software. The software displayed the distance in numbers. This is useful while operating the UGV BVLOS.

GPS navigation: The vehicle is fitted with a Here3 GPS antenna commonly used with DIY or hobby drones. The rover was made to traverse on plain roads as well as on grass (uneven terrain), and a significant difference was observed between the operation on the two terrains. The rover struggled to reach the goal once it was

FIGURE 15.6   Path traveled by UGV via GPS waypoints on regular terrain roads.

set into auto mode, while being operated on grass. The wheels kept slipping while turning, introducing errors in the navigation. Several waypoints were collected and physically marked with chalk on the ground on a plane road by manually driving the rover at locations and noting the waypoints. The rover was then made to travel to these waypoints autonomously using the QGC from the first waypoint, i.e. the takeoff/launch location. Figure 15.6 shows the route that was followed by the UGV via the waypoints given on a regular road. The path is traced on the QGC software display as the UGV travels along the waypoints it was given. The figure has orange lines that indicate the 'straight-line path' it was ideally supposed to take, while the red lines show the path that was actually taken by the UGV.

Figure 15.7 shows the path taken by the vehicle on uneven terrain. A grass patch was chosen to simulate uneven terrain for the experiment. The scheme here is the same as Figure 15.7, i.e. the 'straight-line path' that UGV was ideally supposed to take from one waypoint to another is shown with orange lines, while the path that was actually taken by the vehicle is tracked within the QGC software display with red lines. The differences between the red and the orange lines for both the scenarios, i.e. regular terrain (roads) and irregular terrain (grass patch), are discussed in detail in the observation section (refer Section 15.15.6).

In future, a planar LiDAR can be integrated into the UGV, and with higher computational power, the UGV can have the ability to perform SLAM as well.

15.15.6   Observations

The rover designed here uses Pixhawk4 to generate and follow a path to the given waypoints on a regular terrain – tar roads in this case. The rover's deviation from the intended straight-line path is less in the case of regular roads, while it is more in the case of irregular terrain like grass can be visually observed in Figures 15.6 and 15.7 each.

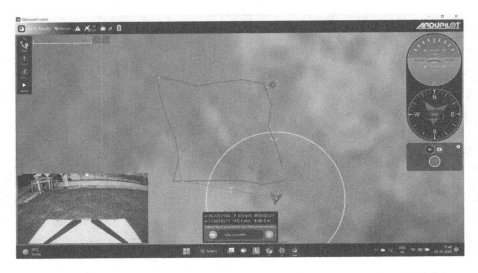

FIGURE 15.7   Path traveled by UGV via waypoints on irregular terrain (Grass patch).

In both cases, i.e. regular as well as irregular terrain, the UGV was observed to deviate from the ideal straight-line path between the individual waypoints; however, the deviation was observed to be a lot more on irregular surfaces as compared to the deviation of regular surface as can be seen while comparing both Figures 15.6 and 15.7. It was also observed that these deviations were small wherever the waypoints were placed far away from one another (~7–8 m), compared to the deviations when the waypoints were placed close to one another (~2–3 m). Placing an adequate number of waypoints at about 4–5 m appeared to be a good configuration for the best possible navigation.

The body and design of the rover are rugged enough to traverse through plain roads while carrying 100–110 kg of weight on top of the rover's body. While the robot goes BVLOS, i.e. Beyond Visual Line Of Sight, the robot can be properly driven using the RTSP, i.e. Real-Time Streaming Protocol – camera feed. Using the camera for correct guidance (manually), the rover can be operated from as far as 300 m with the help of the Wi-Fi base station and its long-range antenna. It can perform autonomous waypoint navigation using GPS waypoints provided using the QGC software. The rover follows a straight path to far away waypoints (>4 m) efficiently, yet faces difficulty navigating through close waypoints and turns.

15.16   CONCLUSION

Autonomous UGVs have the potential to change the agriculture industry by enhancing efficiency, decreasing costs, and raising productivity. Using advanced technologies such as GPS, sensors, and machine learning algorithms, these vehicles can conduct a variety of activities with precision and accuracy, including soil analysis, planting, and harvesting. This can assist farmers in optimizing agricultural yields, decreasing their dependency on human labor, and minimizing their environmental effect. In addition, autonomous UGVs may operate 24 hours a day, seven days a week, minimizing the amount of time required to accomplish jobs and accelerating output. Before the widespread use of autonomous UGVs in smart agriculture, several obstacles still need to be resolved. Concerns concerning the possible displacement of human workers must also be addressed. Despite various limitations, the benefits of employing autonomous UGVs in smart agriculture are substantial and cannot be overlooked. As technology continues to improve and more study is undertaken in this field, the agricultural industry may embrace more autonomous UGVs, resulting in higher efficiency, productivity, and sustainability.

ACKNOWLEDGMENT

The authors would like to express their gratitude to the National Mission – Interdisciplinary Cyber-Physical Systems (NM-ICPS), TIHAN, Indian Institute of Technology (IIT) Hyderabad for providing facilities for the conduct of this research.

REFERENCES

1. Tauger, Mark B. Agriculture in World History. Routledge, 2020.
2. United Nations. "World urbanization prospects: The 2018 revision." Economic and Social Affairs 1 (2018): 1–2. Working Paper No. ESA/P/WP.252).
3. Damalas, Christos A., and Ilias G. Eleftherohorinos. "Pesticide exposure, safety issues, and risk assessment indicators." International Journal of Environmental Research and Public Health 8.5 (2011): 1402–1419.
4. Dhanalakshmi, R., Jose Anand, Arun Kumar Sivaraman, Sita Rani, and Alex Khang. "IoT-Based Water Quality Monitoring System Using Cloud for Agriculture Use", in: Pankaj Bhambri, Sita Rani, Gaurav Gupta, Cloud and Fog Computing Platforms for Internet of Things, 1st Edition, Routledge Taylor & Francis Group, May 2022.
5. Vikram, P.R.K.R. "Agricultural Robot – A pesticide spraying device." International Journal of Future Generation Communication and Networking 13.1 (2020): 150–160.
6. Bak, T., and H. Jakobsen. "Agricultural robotic platform with four wheel steering for weed detection." Biosystems Engineering 87.2 (2004): 125–136.
7. Blackmore, B.S., H. Have, and S.A. Fountas. "Specification of Behavioural Requirements for an Autonomous Tractor", in: Proceedings of the 6th International Symposium on Fruit, Nut and Vegetable Production Engineering conference, Germany, Institute für Agrartechnik Bornim e.V.
8. Bogue, R. "Robots poised to revolutionise agriculture." Industrial Robot International Journal 43.5 (2016): 450–456.
9. CEMA–European Agricultural Machinery: Mechanization: a game-changer for sustainable agrifood systems. https://www.cema-agri.org/publications/31-press-releases-publications/927-mechanization-a-game-changer-for-sustainable-agrifood-systems
10. Goel, Raj Kumar, et al. "Smart agriculture–Urgent need of the day in developing countries." Sustainable Computing: Informatics and Systems 30 (2021): 100512.
11. Ramya, E., Jose Anand, R. Renugha Devi, K. RoshniPrasenth, and Neethu Anna Issac. "Solar Grass Cutter with Water Spraying Vehicle", in: Proceedings of IEEE International Conference on Advancements in Electrical, Electronics, Communication, Computing and Automation (ICAECA)), p. 6, 8–9 Oct 2021.
12. Ruckelshausen, A., P. Biber, M. Dorna, H. Gremmes, R. Klose, and A. Linz, et al. An autonomous field robot platform for individual plant phenotyping. Precision Agriculture 9 (2009): 841–847.

13. World Health Organization. WHO Coronavirus Disease (COVID-19) Dashboard. 2023. Available online: https://covid19.who.int/ (accessed on 17 February 2023).
14. Zhang, Xin, and Eric A. Davidson. "Improving nitrogen and water management in crop production on a national scale." AGU Fall Meeting Abstracts 2018 (2018). B22B-01. https://ui.adsabs.harvard.edu/abs/2018AGUFM.B22B..01Z
15. Oliveira, Luiz F.P., António P. Moreira, and Manuel F. Silva. "Advances in agriculture robotics: A state-of-the-art review and challenges ahead." Robotics 10.2 (2021): 52.
16. Perez-Ruiz, M., P. Gonzalez-de-Santos, A. Ribeiro, C. Fernandez-Quintanilla, A. Peruzzi, and M. Vieri, et al. Highlights and preliminary results for autonomous crop protection. Computers and Electronics in Agriculture 110 (2015): 150–161.
17. Lakkad, S. Modeling and simulation of steering systems for autonomous vehicles. master thesis. The Florida State University, US; 2004 Gonzalez-de-Santos P., Ribeiro A., Fernandez-Quintanilla C., Lopez-Granados F., Brandstoetter M., Tomic S., et al. (2017) Fleets of robots for environmentally-safe Pest control in agriculture. Precision Agric 18, 574–614.
18. O'Connor, M., T. Bell, G. Elkaim, and B. Parkinson. "Automatic steering of farm vehicles using GPS", in: Proceedings of the 3rd International Conference on Precision Agriculture, Minneapolis, USA, pp. 767–777, 1996.
19. Chitta, Sachin, et al. "Ros_Control: A generic and simple control framework for ROS." The Journal of Open Source Software 2.20 (2017): 456–456.
20. Nicolopoulou-Stamati, Polyxeni, et al. "Chemical pesticides and human health: The urgent need for a new concept in agriculture." Frontiers in Public Health 4 (2016): 148.
21. Quigley, Morgan, et al. "ROS: An open-source robot operating system." ICRA Workshop on Open Source Software 3.3.2 (2009).
22. Jose Anand, C. Aasish, S. Syam Narayanan, and R. Asad Ahmed, "Drones for Disaster Response and Management", in: Saravanan Krishnan, M. Murugappan, Internet of Drones, 1st Edition, CRC Press, pp. 173–196, 15 May 2023.
23. Pak, Jeonghyeon, et al. "Field evaluation of path-planning algorithms for autonomous mobile robot in smart farms." IEEE Access 10 (2022): 60253–60266.
24. Gonzalez-de-Santos, Pablo, Roemi Fernandez, Delia Sepúlveda, Eduardo Navas, and Manuel Armada. (2020). Unmanned Ground Vehicles for Smart Farms. 10.5772/ intechopen.90683.
25. Vetter, A.A. "Quantitative evaluation of DGPS guidance for ground based agricultural applications." Applied Engineering in Agriculture 11.3 (1995): 459–464.
26. Mahmud, Mohd Saiful Azimi, et al. "Robotics and automation in agriculture: present present and future applications." Applications of Modelling and Simulation 4 (2020): 130–140.
27. Wang, Huijuan, Yuan Yu, and Quanbo Yuan. "Application of Dijkstra Algorithm in Robot Path-Planning", in: 2011 second international conference on mechanic automation and control engineering, IEEE, 2011.
28. Wonnacott, Dereck, et al. "Autonomous Navigation Planning with ROS." Michigan Technological University, pp. 2–12, 2012.
29. Grisetti, Giorgio, Cyrill Stachniss, and Wolfram Burgard. "Improved techniques for grid mapping with rao-blackwellized particle filters." IEEE Transactions on Robotics 23.1 (2007): 34–46.
30. Sundari, M.S., A. Jose Anand, and T.S. Nagarajan. "Smart Aerial Imaging Solution in Precision Agriculture", in: 2022 International Conference on Data Science, Agents' Artificial Intelligence (ICDSAAI), Chennai, India, pp. 1–3, 2022.

Index

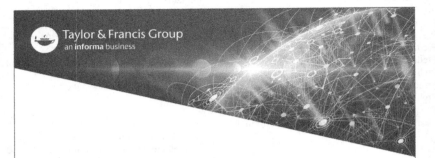

Printed in the United States
by Baker & Taylor Publisher Services